# CHURCH UNITY
# WITHOUT UNIFORMITY

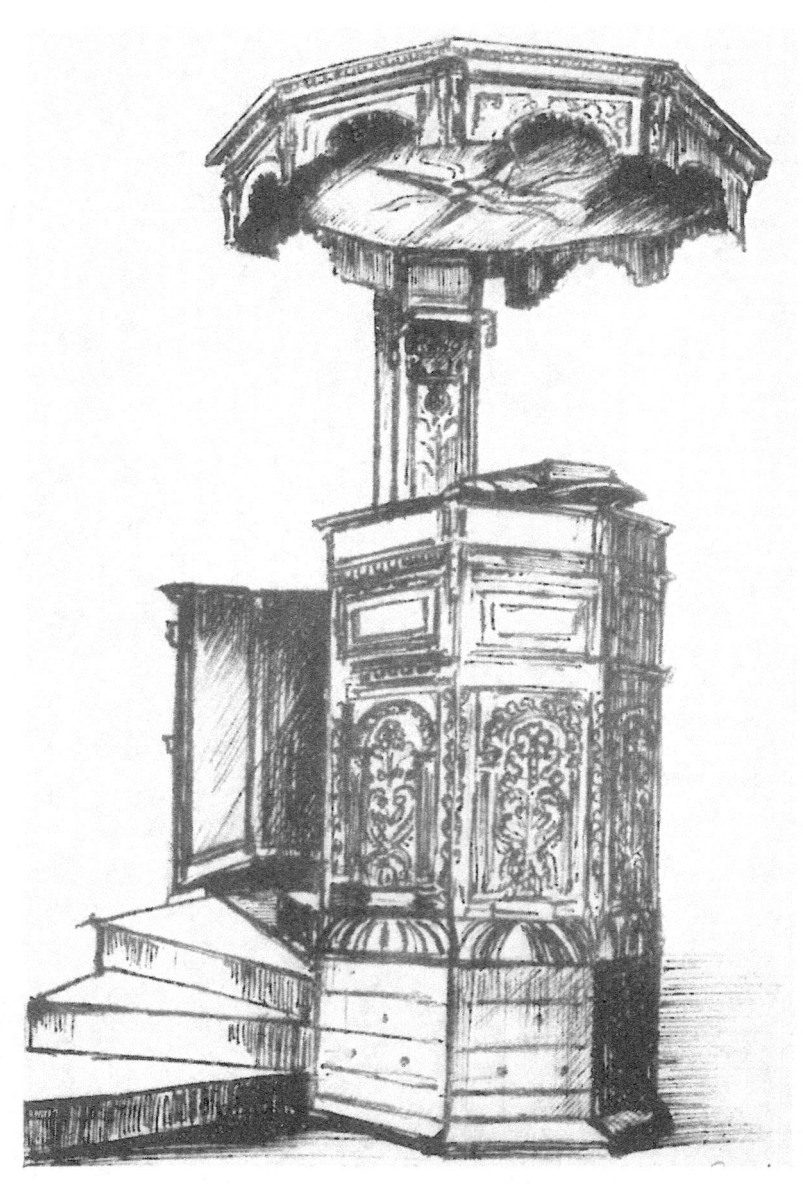

RICHARD BAXTER'S PULPIT AT KIDDERMINSTER

# CHURCH UNITY
# WITHOUT UNIFORMITY

*A Study of Seventeenth-century English Church Movements and of Richard Baxter's Proposals for a Comprehensive Church*

A 1662 TERCENTENARY VOLUME

*by*
A. HAROLD WOOD

*With a foreword by*
E. GORDON RUPP

WIPF & STOCK · Eugene, Oregon

To
MY WIFE


Wipf and Stock Publishers
199 W 8th Ave, Suite 3
Eugene, OR 97401

Church Unity Without Uniformity
A Study of Seventeenth-century English Church Movements and of Richard Baxter's Proposal for a Comprehensive Church
By Wood, A. Harold and Rupp, Gordon
Copyright©1963 Methodist Publishing - Epworth Press
ISBN 13: 978-1-4982-8054-9
Publication date 2/2/2016
Previously published by Epworth Press, 1963

Every effort has been made to trace the current copyright owner of this publication but without success. If you have any information or interest in the copyright, please contact the publishers.

CONTENTS

Foreword by the Rev. Professor E. Gordon Rupp    9

Author's Note    11

Introduction    13

I. *Baxter's Ecclesiastical Principles*    17
    1. Every Minister a 'Bishop of the Flock'    20
    2. Reformation through Discipline    22
    3. 'The Primitive Episcopacy' or Parochial Episcopacy    27
    4. The Association of Pastors    32
    5. Episcopal Ordination not Essential, and no Re-ordination    34
    6. Freedom in Forms of Worship    39
    7. A National Comprehensive Church: 'The Confederate Parish Churches of England'    43
    8. Unity without Uniformity    48

II. *Early Protests against Uniformity*    54
    1. In Elizabeth's Reign    54
    2. Under James I    57

III. *Laudian Uniformity Attempted*    63
    1. 'Romanizing' Ritual    63
    2. A New Theory of the Church and Episcopacy    65
    3. The Beginning of the Bishops' Wars    69
    4. The Long Parliament's Policy towards the Laudian Church    71
    5. Uprooting Episcopacy 'Root and Branch' the Next Step?    72
    6. Moderate Episcopal Concessions in 1641 resembling Puritan Demands in 1661    77

IV. *Presbyterian Uniformity Attempted*   81
    1. The Westminster Assembly and the Solemn League and Covenant   83
    2. 'A lame Erastian Presbytery'   86
    3. Presbyterian versus Independent   89
    4. The Failure of Parliamentary Presbyterianism   93

V. *Experiments in Unity without Uniformity (1649–60)*   97
    1. The Federated Puritan State Churches   97
    2. Baxter's Voluntary County Associations   101
    3. Archbishop Usher's Discussions with Baxter   105
    4. Negotiations for Presbyterian and Independent Unity   108
    5. Efforts to unite Episcopal Parties in the Church of England   114

VI. *Charles II's Negotiations with Ecclesiastical Parties (1660)*   118
    1. The Return of the King and the Bishops to England   118
    2. 'The First Address and Proposals of the Ministers'   127
    3. Archbishop Usher's 'Reduction of Episcopacy unto the Form of Synodical Government received in the Ancient Church'   130
    4. 'The Bishops' Answer to the First Proposals of the London Ministers'   135
    5. Baxter's 'Defence of the Ministers' Proposals'   137

VII. *The King's Declaration (25th October 1660) and High Hopes of Unity*   142
    1. Baxter's 'Petition to the King upon our sight of the First Draft of the Declaration'   144
    2. The Ministers' Audience with the King on 22nd October   148
    3. The Draft Declaration, the Ministers' Suggested Alterations, and the Actual Amendments   151
    4. Was Re-union without Re-ordination proposed?   158
    5. Failure—at the Nearest Approach to Unity   161

CONTENTS 7

VIII. *Baxter and the Bishops at the Savoy Conference (1661)*   170
   1. The King's Warrant   171
   2. Sketch of the 'Presbyterian' Ministers at the Savoy Conference   175
   3. Baxter's 'Reformed Liturgy' presented to the Savoy Conference   178
   4. Baxter's 'Exceptions to the Prayer Book'   184
   5. The 'Exceptions to the Prayer Book' presented by the Ministers   186
   6. Baxter's 'Petition for Peace and Concord presented to the Bishops with the proposed Reformation of the Liturgy'   191
   7. 'Answer of the Bishops'   195
   8. 'Rejoinder of the Ministers'   198
   9. The Complete Failure of the Conference—and the Reasons   204
   10. A Summing up of Baxter's Proposals for Church Unity   214
   11. A Sketch of Proposals for Reform : 1603, 1641, 1660, 1661   217

IX. *The Destruction of Unity by the Act of Uniformity (1662)*   225
   1. The Bill before Parliament   225
   2. The Requirements of the Act of Uniformity   228
   3. The Expulsion of the Nonconformists   230
   4. Indulgence refused and Harsher Laws passed (1663–70)   233

X. *Baxter's Continued Efforts for Unity after 1662*   241
   1. The Nonconformist Baxter a Communicant in Parish Churches   241
   2. Baxter's Negotiations with Bridgman and Bishop Wilkins, 1668—and the Hindrance of Re-ordination   246
   3. The King's Declaration of Indulgence, 1672   252
   4. The Distribution of Dissent in 1672   254

8    CHURCH UNITY WITHOUT UNIFORMITY

  5. Baxter's Proposals to the Earl of Orrery and
   Bishop Morley, 1673    257
  6. Negotiations with Tillotson and others, 1675–80   259

XI. *Toleration without Unity (1689)*    263
  1. The Church and Dissent brought closer by
   James II's Rule and the Revolution of 1688   263
  2. The Bill for Comprehension   267
  3. Tillotson's Plan for Re-union (Jerusalem
   Chamber Commission, 1689)   268
  4. Convocation and the Hardening against Dissent   271
  5. Toleration for Protestant Dissenters granted
   by Parliament   275
  6. Attempts to unite Presbyterians and
   Congregationalists, 1691   276
  7. Renewed Hatred of Dissent   280

XII. *Some of the Effects of Disunity in the
  Eighteenth Century*   284
  1. The Disabilities of Dissent and of the
   Establishment   284
  2. The Ravages of Heresy and Inertia   287
  3. The Decline of the Presbyterians   290

XIII. *Can there be Unity without Uniformity Today?*   293
  1. A United Evangelical Church for a Divided
   World   293
  2. A Constitutional Episcopacy   294
  3. Baxter's Association of Pastors   295
  4. Extension of Orders (Supplemental Ordination)
   —but no Re-ordination   297
  5. Diversity of Worship   304
  6. A National Comprehensive Church   306
  7. Uniformity no longer contemplated   308
  8. Is there a WILL to Unity?   310

 *Bibliography*   314
 *Index*   321

# FOREWORD

THE tercentenary commemorations of the 1662 Prayer Book and of the Great Ejectment have brought back into the living memory of the English Churches a debate about uniformity and unity, comprehension and toleration that is timely and pertinent to the ecumenical conversation. For this reason Dr Wood's lucid account of the negotiations between Puritans and the leaders of the restored Church of England is greatly to be welcomed. He is to be congratulated on the persistence with which he has contrived to do the research and reading, beginning with a busy missionary life and during a full life of ministering and teaching in Australia, which have produced this worthy contribution to an important and not yet concluded debate. One of the many merits of this volume is that it concentrates on documents in which Richard Baxter is the central figure, and gives an extended series of quotations from his works which are many of them of surprising contemporary relevance. No satisfactory life of Baxter has yet been written, but something of his sombre, earnest dignity emerges through these pages. Though Dr Wood can speak of him as 'Presbyterian' in inverted commas, it is evident that 'moderate episcopalian' is equally apt, while in Dr Wood's concluding summary he is shown affirming important stresses in the Congregationalist position. The truth is, and it is the measure of his greatness that it is impossible to label him, that he is indeed 'mere' Nonconformist, 'mere' Catholic. Like that other great ecumaniac before the ecumenical movement, Martin Bucer, he was an awkward figure, with the same temperamental defects, the same fatal long-windedness, the same earnest tactlessness, leaving friend and foe alike dazed and wounded with the violence with which he launched innumerable olive branches from his rigid catapult. In some things he is more like John Calvin than any other English Reformer, and his Puritanism retains traits of the first age of Calvinism, before it became systematized in the age of William Perkins. But the spirit of Calvin's 'Institutes' (Predestination is not its central theme) in the concern for the Church, for godly discipline, and above all for the office of the pastor and his cure of souls is at the heart of all Baxter's concerns and intransigencies. For whatever be the significance of 1662, these documents abundantly illustrate that this was no lay anti-clerical movement, but a crisis of the pastoral office, a crisis of what Wordsworth profoundly discerned as 'clerical integrity'. So that despite his stubbornness, which verged on fanaticism, there is about Baxter a shining integrity which makes his opponents, and not only Charles II and Judge Jeffreys, but the good and worthy bishops, appear a little shabby in comparison. There are several issues on which Baxter's observations, however, look forward rather than backwards. If this tragic series of colloquies can only really be understood by the historian as the climax of a hundred years of controversy about the third dimension of the Church, 'the discipline of Christ'—the theologian will find plenty to discuss in the arguments about re-ordination and about uniformity and comprehension. It is plain that any major re-unions in this country will involve elements of liberty and consent such as the seventeenth century had only partially glimpsed (though some of the most luminous intuitions are here in Richard Baxter); it is clear also that there are questions of faith and integrities of conscience such as were exemplified by both sides in this tragic division. Christians, who have grown up in this broken ecclesiastical home, should have an eye and a heart to detect amid the discord and uncharity, the things which belong to the true, the coming peace of Zion's city. They will find much to ponder in these pages.

E. GORDON RUPP

*University of Manchester*         *All Saints' Day*, 1962

## AUTHOR'S NOTE

MOST of this book was written during my missionary service in Tonga (1924–37), when I studied from books sent from London to those islands in the South Pacific. Upon returning to Australia, church and school duties prevented me from completing the thesis and submitting it to the Melbourne College of Divinity for a Doctorate in Divinity until 1948. Since then, I have not been able to reduce and revise it for publication until this Tercentenary Year, 1962, when perhaps the commemoration of the expulsion of Richard Baxter and 2000 other Nonconformists gives some significance to its appearance. I am aware that many books about Baxter have been written in recent years, but there are certain features of this study that may warrant another. My interest in the Puritan period was given specific direction by the suggestion of the late Dr F. J. Powicke, Baxter's biographer, who wrote to me in Tonga over thirty years ago:

'I have often thought that it would be a piece of work well worth doing, just to concentrate on the Savoy Conference (April–July 1661) in the light of all the papers collected by Baxter in the *Reliquiae Baxterianae* and submit them to careful analysis so as to get at the "Presbyterian" point of view throughout, the proposals arising therefrom, and their precise significance for the "Church" had they been adopted. All the materials for such a study are suggested by Baxter, and they link up naturally with a study of the High Church position as represented by the bishops, the history of this party from Laud downwards, and the intrinsic cleavage between it and Baxter's position (which he perceived clearly enough but hoped to bridge over), and the extrinsic influences at work which rendered compromise impossible. All this might be summed up by way of introduction to the main theme—a clear and full exposition of the "Presbyterian" programme of reform, with due insistence on what Baxter distinguishes as essential demands and desirables.

'Then the way would be open to deal briefly with the later

attempts, all by Baxter more or less against his will, to recover lost ground down to 1689. It should be noted, too, that the comprehension aimed at never really included the Independents. It would have widened the Church without effect on the stream of Nonconformity, except by adding to the depth and strength of its current. But what it might have done towards mollifying the temper of the Establishment and lowering its sacerdotal claims is another question worth considering. Its possible effect, also, on "Presbyterianism" is a matter deserving at least speculative inquiry. Would there have been the Presbyterian drift into Arianism and Unitarianism?

'This points to a small yet fruitful field which a candidate for the D.D. would find quite enough for his purpose and important.'

I have endeavoured to fulfil most of the task suggested by Dr Powicke. This book is offered not only in commemoration of the Nonconformists of 1662, but as an encouragement to all, Episcopal and Nonconformist, who desire 'Unity without Uniformity' in 1962.

I am greatly honoured by the kindness of the Rev. Professor Gordon Rupp, who examined my thesis in 1948, in writing his Foreword. I also thank the Rev. S. J. Hooper, Minister of Baxter Congregational Church, Kidderminster, for kindly supplying a drawing of Baxter's pulpit. My daughter Elizabeth has given me very valuable assistance by reading the proofs.

A. H. W.

*Kew,*
*Victoria,*
*Australia.*
*February 1962.*

# INTRODUCTION

THE CHRISTIAN CHURCH in the modern world may regard as impracticable some of the terms that Richard Baxter proposed for unity in the Church of England after the Restoration of 1660. Yet, even though the situation now is different, all who pray for the re-union of Christendom may find inspiration in the work of a Puritan divine who dedicated his life to reconciliation.

The expression of Church unity without uniformity in what Baxter called 'The Confederate Parish Churches of England' deserves more than passing consideration. Some may still believe that the type of uniformity enforced in the Church of England after the failure of the Savoy Conference in 1661 is essential for the stability of that Church. Others may feel that the present battle for the nation's soul requires from Christians not only spiritual unity, but a system such as Baxter desired, so as to permit people of varying ecclesiastical positions to worship and witness together.

Baxter was a pioneer in proposing that various elements of Church polity should be brought into a united Church. Few today realize that a seventeenth-century Puritan declared for that ideal in these terms:

> 'I have truly told the world near forty years that I am past doubt that neither the Episcopal, Presbyterian, nor Independent way alone, may well settle the Church; but that each of the three parties (and those called Erastians) have somewhat of the truth in particular and somewhat of faultiness, and if ever the Church be well settled it must be by taking the best and leaving out the worst of every party, and till that can be done, we must bear with what we cannot amend.' [1]

With that statement we may well compare the hope envisaged in *A Sketch of a United Church*, drawn up in England in 1935 by the first conference of representatives of the Church of England and the Federal Council of the Evangelical Free Churches, that England might have a Church 'in which the Episcopal, Presbyterian, and Congregational systems all find harmonious expression'.

Thus Richard Baxter was an apostle of Christian unity before his time. It was also his misfortune to advocate unity when the political hatred engendered by the Civil War drew Christian men apart and caused divisions that have persisted in the English-speaking world to this day.

These conclusions are revealed by a study of Baxter's proposals and the negotiations in which he took a leading part.

(1) The cause of Christian unity in 1660–62 was ruined by the political passions and the religious persecutions and recriminations of the Civil War and the Interregnum which followed.

(2) There was a similarity between Baxter's proposals and the demands for reform made by Puritans for a century before the Restoration. Furthermore, Baxter's plan for modified episcopacy had the approval of Archbishop Usher and a few other bishops during the Civil War period.

(3) The uniformity of the Presbyterian system, temporarily introduced into England after 1645, was no more acceptable to the majority of Englishmen than repressive Laudian uniformity had been.

(4) Unity might have been preserved in the Church of England if the bishops in 1660–62 had not been determined upon expelling the Puritan elements. They were resolved to maintain control of the Church by enforcing uniformity in ritual and worship and by requiring oaths of canonical obedience from all the clergy they ordained and instituted.

(5) Unity would have been possible if the spiritual authority of the parish clergy had been granted. The chief aim of the Puritans always was the maintenance of *discipline* through the exercise of the pastoral office. This was the first of Baxter's principles. His hopes for unity were raised by the promise in the King's Declaration of 25th October 1660 that the powers of pastors over their congregations would be recognized.

(6) The number and influence of 'moderate episcopal' clergy like Baxter have not been generally admitted. These 'Church' Puritans wished to remain within the Church of England but desired the rights of discipline for parish clergy, stricter religious supervision of communicants, more preaching and catechizing, less ritual and more freedom in forms of worship, and more attention to the promotion of godliness through the work of faithful and capable ministers.

(7) Baxter and most of those called Presbyterians in 1660 had

little in common with the Scottish Church. They were moderate episcopal clergy seeking a reduction in the powers of the bishops to those believed to have been found in primitive episcopacy. They could have been retained within the Church of England by the adoption of Archbishop Usher's 'Reduction of Episcopacy unto the Form of Synodical Government received in the Ancient Church'.

(8) When it was evident that the bishops would not accept the Puritan proposals in 1661, the moderate episcopal and Presbyterian ministers should have made common cause with the Independents. In fact, the failure of these parties to unite just before the Restoration, during the negotiations of 1658, was an unrelieved tragedy for the future of religion in England. It was unfortunate that the other parties had an antipathy towards the Independents, not only because of their congregational and democratic principles, but also because they were republican and anti-Royalist. Here again, political considerations spoilt the chances for Church unity. The Independents and smaller sects were not included in the negotiations between Baxter's friends and the bishops in 1660–61. When the opportunity for a moderate-episcopal–Presbyterian–Independent agreement had been lost before the Act of Uniformity came into force, all these parties suffered alike and remained divided.

(9) The King's Declaration of 25th October 1660 promised the possibility of receiving non-episcopally ordained ministers in the Church of England without re-ordination. Had this expectation been realized, the Church would have absorbed many ministers ordained by presbyteries or by county associations during the Interregnum. The Church could have followed the precedents to be found in the 1571 Act and in the recognition without re-ordination of ministers ordained by presbyteries on the Continent and in Scotland. Any such expectation was destroyed by the bishops in 1661.

(10) If the negotiations at the Restoration had been successful, most of the English ministers and people could have been united in the national Church. The Church of England would have consisted not only of Laudian clergy, but also of Baxter's moderate episcopal friends (a very large section of the Church, even if Baxter was not correct in thinking they were the majority), together with many, if not all, of the orthodox English Presbyterians. Theoretically, this was possible. Unhappily, the Restoration bishops had no

desire for reconciliation with Puritans of any kind, and it was because of their attitude that the Church was divided by the Act of Uniformity. Since 1662 this division has been permanent. If those in the Church of England today who follow the Laudian clergy's policy of 1662 would abate their conditions, the spiritual descendants of Richard Baxter would welcome re-union in our time.

NOTE TO INTRODUCTION

1. *Reliquiae Baxterianae*, App. IV, p. 69.

CHAPTER I

# BAXTER'S ECCLESIASTICAL PRINCIPLES

RICHARD BAXTER was regarded as the most influential Puritan of his time, and the estimate of his genius and devotion has grown with the passing of the years. Benjamin Jowett said of him that he was 'one of the greatest Englishmen not only of his own time but of any time'.[1] Bishop Wilkins said in Baxter's lifetime that if he had lived in the days of the primitive Church, he would have been one of the Fathers of the Church.[2] Sir James Stephen referred to him as 'the most voluminous theological writer in the English language'.[3] Beyond that, the quality of his books induced Samuel Johnson, critic of the Dissenters, to recommend them to Boswell with the words, 'Read any of them, for they are all good.'[4] A modern reviewer has well said: 'Baxter was a prophet of moderation, seeking to hold the balance between the Prelatist on the one hand and the Separatist on the other, and clinging to the hope of a united Protestant England, of one English Church broad-based on simple Christianity.'[5]

Opinions such as these are the more noteworthy when they concern one who held only one pastorate for any considerable time, who had no ecclesiastical distinction (although he refused a bishopric), and who suffered indignities and imprisonment in his later years. Yet, as his statue still stands in Kidderminster to remind us of the unsurpassed preaching and pastoral standards he created in that town, so Baxter's figure commands general respect as an invincible idealist who strove for the peace and unity of the Church.

Born in 1615, Baxter was ordained deacon in 1638 and sought no higher status. In 1641 he became reader and lecturer, though not the official incumbent, at Kidderminster. Here until 1660 (except for a period of chaplaincy with the Parliamentary forces) he pursued a ministry that Anglicans and Nonconformists alike have taken as a pattern. Its character can be seen in the classic, *The Reformed Pastor,* in which Baxter emphasized visitation and catechizing, as well as the preaching for which Puritans were renowned. At Kidderminster he showed what was always his main concern, the spiritual reformation of the nation through parish pastoral work. In association with pastors of like mind, he gave a model that many counties in England were beginning to follow when the Restoration took place.

After the return of Charles II, there was the period of negotiations that will be examined in detail in the main section of this book. With the failure of Baxter's efforts and the expulsion of Nonconformist ministers under the Act of Uniformity of 1662, Baxter's ministry continued 'Under the Cross', as his modern biographer, Dr F. J. Powicke, has said. The persistent controversialist continued his campaigns for the purity and unity of the Church, although in his own heart he knew that the struggle was hopeless. His crusades ceased only with his death in 1691, and *Reliquiae Baxterianae*, the narrative of his life and times, was his bequest to all who shared his consuming desire for reconciliation.

It must be admitted that Baxter was often unfortunate in his disputatious methods, despite his self-applied designation of 'Reconciler'. It has been said that he was always 'trying to make peace by fighting' [6] and that 'he waged war to make peace'.[7] He never entirely escaped from the 'itch' of disputing. In his minor conflicts with Anabaptists and Quakers, he lost a sense of proportion. 'The most practised logician in England',[8] he poured forth streams of closely reasoned arguments, some sharp and even bitter. Not only in his writings, but also in oral debates which he continued at great length, he often proved against himself the truth of his maxim, 'Overdoing is undoing.'

At the Savoy Conference (April–July 1661) he was the most prominent figure, but did the least successful work of his career, though that conference was foredoomed to failure in any case. However, he enunciated then certain principles to show what a truly comprehensive Church the Church of England might have become. He had the vision of a national Church, purified and united. Whatever the opinions of his controversial methods may have been, his greatest critics could not gainsay his zeal. Matthew Sylvester's funeral sermon contained this unexaggerated sentence: 'When Baxter spoke of weighty soul concerns you might find his very spirit drenched therein.' His spirit was truly drenched when he spoke of the reformation and the unity of the Church.

Baxter's ecclesiastical position has not been easily understood. He called himself: 'A Catholic Christian, for love, concern and peace of all true Christians and obedience to all lawful commands of rulers, but made, called and used as a Nonconformist.' [9]

When seeking a licence to preach under the Declaration of Indulgence of 1672, he styled himself a 'mere Nonconformist', purposely avoiding any denominational name. As he firmly believed in the necessity for a national Church, built upon properly disciplined parish churches, he had no sympathy with Independency or any system of 'gathered' churches. At no time did he advance proposals for the Presbyterian system. He may best be called moderate episcopal, adhering to this position both before and after his expulsion in 1662.

In spite of all discouragements, Baxter became still more tolerant and catholic in later years. He would have found place for elements from various systems, and might have included all but extreme sectaries in the national Church of his dreams. With characteristic acuteness he exposed the root of our mistrust of other denominations in these words:

'The Devil saith to the Presbyterian, O take heed of the Independents! and to the Independents, Take heed of these Presbyterians. To the Anabaptist he suggesteth, Avoid these Protestants; Take heed of them, for they baptize infants; And to the Protestant he saith, Take heed of these Anabaptists, for they are against baptizing any till they come to full age. To one he saith, Away from that Church, or think not those persons to be religious; for they pray by the book; and to the other he saith, Take heed of these people, as whimsical and proud, and brain-sick heretics, for they pray without book by the Spirit. To one sort he saith, Take heed of these people, for they wear a surplice, or kneel at the Sacrament, or answer the priests in the responses of the Common Prayer. To the other he saith, Take heed of these disobedient, stubborn, self-conceited people that will sit at the Sacrament, and will not conform to the orders of the Church. I am not now minding whose opinion is right or wrong, among all these parties, or any like them. But how charitable to your souls the Devil is when he would destroy your charity and your souls; and how piously and kindly he would have you to take heed when he would lead you to perdition; and how great a Reformer he will be, if he may but do it by DIVIDING.'[10]

### 1. Every Minister a 'Bishop of the Flock'

Every pastor should have the 'Power of the Keys'[11] in his own congregation; he must be an *'episcopus gregis'*.[12] Baxter asserted that Scripture did not know a pastor without the power to govern.[13] A pastor would be false to his trust if he gave the Sacrament to an unworthy person, or absolved without assurance of repentance, or read in a burial service that God had taken the soul of anyone whom the pastor knew to be a sinner. The pastor must decide what persons might be baptized, and refuse to baptize the children of infidels or notorious evildoers. A stern and uncompromising attitude indeed, but this was essential Puritanism.

A diocesan bishop should not attempt to do in a thousand parishes what each pastor should do in his own. It was as farcical to expect one doctor to have charge of the health of a thousand parishes, leaving assistants to read out his prescriptions, as to make a prelate responsible for the souls of all in his diocese and entrust a parish clergyman only with the reading of the Prayer Book.[14] Baxter also used the analogy of a schoolmaster who might say that he was educating the children in hundreds of schools where there were only 'curate ushers who only teach the boys as far as they are willing to learn, and for all their untractableness, disobedience, absence and faults, present their names to a chancellor's court, set up by the sole schoolmaster'.[15]

The very word 'pastor' was stressed because it indicated the rights of a minister who was not a bishop's curate but a governor in his own congregation. Baxter therefore objected to the alteration in the Prayer Book in 1662 from 'Bishops, pastors and ministers' to 'Bishops, priests and deacons', 'lest the priests be supposed to be pastors'.[16]

Just as Baxter contended for the rights of the pastoral office against diocesan bishops and lay chancellors, so he required that every person in the parish must submit himself to the pastor's discipline. There were two parts in every church, the *pars gubernans* and the *pars gubernata*. 'I will be a pastor to none that will not be under DISCIPLINE; that were to be A HALF-PASTOR.'[17]

He deplored that Protestant ministers, recoiling from Roman Catholic practices such as auricular confession, had gone too far in the opposite direction and had neglected the personal oversight of the flock—as grave an omission as giving up preaching to their people. The pastoral office must be exercised solemnly and assiduously; there could be no recreation for a minister, Baxter said, except one hour's walk or less before dinner, when thousands of souls were dying. That may be criticized now as too intense, but it is an evidence of a typical Puritan pastor's devotion to duty.

Baxter drew a distinction between secular and spiritual coercion.

'There is a magistrate's discipline, and a pastoral discipline. Discipline by the sword is the magistrate's work; discipline by the WORD is the pastor's work. And there is a coercive excommunication, and a pastoral excommunication. To command upon pain of corporal punishment, that a heretic or impenitent, wicked man shall forbear the sacred ordinances and privileges, a magistrate may do; but to command it only upon divine and spiritual penalties, belongeth to the pastors of the church.'[18]

Thus a pastor could not fine or imprison, but only appeal to men's consciences. On the other hand, though a magistrate might force people to hear God's Word preached and to pay tithes, he could not force them to receive the Communion.

The reason for forming the Worcestershire Association during the Commonwealth period was the restoration of discipline in adjacent parishes on the lines Baxter was following with such success at Kidderminster. After the removal of episcopal government at the close of the Civil War and as a result of the unpopularity of the Parliamentary Presbyterian system, chaos reigned in many parishes; and it was during this confused period that some became sectaries rather than be connected with a system that lacked discipline. Under these circumstances, Baxter sought to establish associations of pastors who would decide those who were to be debarred from the sacraments.

That Baxter placed supreme importance upon the pastor's powers over his own congregation can be seen from his willingness, in the final analysis, to accept diocesan episcopacy or any other system, if only the pastor had the right to exercise discipline in his parish. Baxter's indictment of the bishops was summed up in the crushing sentence: 'Your Prelacy is NOT OF GOD because it is DESTRUCTIVE OF DISCIPLINE.'[19]

## 2. Reformation through Discipline

Puritans classified the duties of the ministry as leadership in (1) worship, (2) preaching, (3) catechizing, (4) discipline. Ritualists emphasized uniformity in forms of worship; Puritans repudiated the advisability of uniformity and esteemed other duties as even more important than worship. Preaching was regarded by all Puritans as the supreme means for effecting reformation; and Baxter believed that equally indispensable with preaching were catechizing (the regular visiting and questioning of families to enforce the teaching given from the pulpit) and discipline (guarding the Communion Table).

It has not always been understood that Puritans like Baxter esteemed catechizing and discipline as far more important than questions of the liturgy and ceremonies to which historians have given most prominence in the controversies of the period. Baxter's words make clear that his chief aim was spiritual reformation.

> 'I can well remember the time when I was earnest for the reformation of matters of ceremony. . . . Alas, can we think that the reformation is wrought when we cast out a few ceremonies and change some vestures and gestures and forms! O no, sirs! It is the CONVERTING AND SAVING OF SOULS that is our business.'[20]

Baxter even gave spiritual reformation as the real objective in the Civil War. When he thought of the time-serving clergy, overlooked by the Laudian bishops, who instead gave their energies to persecuting Puritans, Baxter declared that the war was waged to secure 'A faithful ministry and exercise of DISCIPLINE in the Church.'—'It was hopes of a reformation that we fought and suffered for.'[21]

The reformation of England necessitated the restoration of discipline, 'the exercise of Christ's Kingly Office in the Church',[22] as Baxter passionately termed it.

> 'The main reason that turneth my heart against the English Prelacy is because it did destroy Church DISCIPLINE and almost destroy the Church through want of it.'[23]

So vital was parish-reform to Baxter that he was prepared to forfeit other benefits from the King's Declaration of 25th October 1660, and even to discard Usher's form of modified episcopacy, if only the exercise of discipline could be secured in the parishes. He also believed that his success at Kidderminster could convince Independents that when there was effective discipline the parish system was superior to the 'gathered' churches. There were no sects at Kidderminster, where Baxter was a pastor to everyone in the parish who would accept his discipline.

The unwieldly diocesan system in Baxter's day made the spiritual reformation of England impossible. There were only twenty-five diocesan bishops and two archbishops. There were 9725 parish churches. The parishes also were large, some in London embracing more than 50,000 souls. In most towns there were between 2000 and 5000, and in the villages up to 2000. Baxter's reiterated complaint was that diocesan bishops could not care for the souls of so many in their dioceses, nor did they attempt to do so.[24]

The Laudian bishops regarded their duties as, mainly, ordaining clergy, consecrating churches, and confirming children; other duties were civil, or were concerned with ecclesiastical courts, and they gave much attention to attendance at the House of Lords. In their triennial visitations they summoned clergy and churchwardens to a town and received from them the records of delinquents, chiefly those ministers who had not observed the ceremonies and prescribed forms of worship. Baxter exposed this as a fantastic departure from the work of bishops in the primitive Church, and as entirely unrelated to the task of spiritual reformation in England.

Baxter declared that all bishops in the ancient Church had only ONE CONGREGATION. They had to teach, catechize, rebuke, confirm after individual examination, visit the sick, admit to Communion those who were worthy, absolve those who were truly penitent, and carry out all other pastoral duties. These duties involved knowing individuals in the congregation personally. It was dishonouring the office and trifling with a sacred trust to deny these rights to the parish ministers in England, and to perform one duty, confirmation, perfunctorily, and on irregular visits.

In the twenty-five years before 1659, Baxter declared that he could not point from his own knowledge to even one instance where a sinner had been repelled from Communion.[25] Of what value, then, was the rubric which the bishops at the Savoy Conference claimed was sufficient?

'If any of these be a notorious evil liver, the curate, having knowledge thereof, shall call him and advertise him in any wise not to presume to the Lord's Table.'

That rubric was ignored in practice, and it was hypocritical to urge it as a proper substitute for the course that Baxter and his associates desired.

Nothing was resented more than allowing a parish clergyman merely to accuse a person to a Laudian bishop's court where the lay chancellor decided the matter, the minister then being permitted only to read to his congregation the decision the lay chancellor had made in the court. This Baxter denounced as 'The English disease or corruption of Episcopacy—Lay Chancellors.'[26]

At Kidderminster, on the other hand, Baxter's ministry gave a pattern for England.[27] He required an open confession of faith before a communicant was received, with a promise to abide by the discipline Baxter would use. Two days a week were devoted to visiting the families of the parish, each home receiving a visit of about one hour. By visiting fifteen or sixteen families weekly, he was able to deal with about 800 families every year. He had three other ministers assisting him, with three or four deacons, and about twenty 'godly men'; these were not lay elders of the Presbyterian system, of which he disapproved, but men who 'met as trustees of the whole church and were chosen annually for that purpose'.

In carrying out this work, Baxter insisted that every family had Bibles and catechisms. He distributed these where needed, and he ascertained on subsequent visits whether they had been used or not. Catechizing applied the preaching of the previous sabbath, and to this was added family prayer, a characteristic Puritan exercise. Many of Baxter's people became so accustomed to praying before others that he declared 'very few ministers did match them'.

Baxter's chosen lay helpers gave him advice about cases that called for discipline. At the parochial monthly meeting three justices of the peace were present as members of the Church. Persons brought before the meeting were admonished and called upon to repent. Those still recalcitrant were brought before the monthly meeting of the Worcestershire Association (when it had been formed in 1653). If this effort also failed, the offender was admonished three times publicly in the parish church and finally excommunicated.

Those who find fault with the rigidity of this system should not, at least, overlook the earnestness of Baxter. His *Call to the Unconverted* and many other writings reveal his conviction that God indeed was appealing to sinners through him.

'What is reformation but the instructing and importunate persuading of sinners to entertain my Christ and grace as offered them, and the governing my Church according to my word?'[28]

This reformation of England depended upon ministers being godly, scholarly, and industrious. The Puritan ministers were genuinely shocked that the Laudian bishops thought so little of the sacred office that they did not insist upon these qualities in all clergymen. It amazed them that Laud evidently preferred that thousands of people should be without a godly minister rather than such a minister should officiate, for instance, without a surplice.[29] While sinners were not being repelled from Communion, a distant bishop would send his order to silence zealous Puritan pastors altogether, and to replace them with conforming but 'scandalous' ministers. Laud concentrated on enforcing ritual and ceremonies, but Puritan ministers deplored above all the widespread evils of the day—drunkenness, profanity, immorality, and the utter neglect of the ordinances of God by a large section of the nation. It did not need the further moral decline in the Restoration period to prove that the Puritans' reproof of the nation's laxity and their desire for spiritual reformation were justified.

The Communion Table must be guarded, and it was the pastor's sacred right to guard it—Baxter never faltered in insisting upon this. The appeals he and other pastors made in parish meetings and county associations were to the conscience; they were made within the Church, not through a civil court inflicting civil penalties. Baxter was in the Calvinist tradition in demanding that a divinely instituted Church should exercise its own discipline. He and his associates were 'Genevan High Churchmen', and it was for their Churchmanship that they were forced to leave a State-dominated Church in 1662.

It may not be sufficiently recognized that the guarding of the Communion Table touched the heart of the Puritan position. The practice of Roman Catholics had been to allow men to receive the Sacrament to their own damnation if they did so unworthily. In safeguarding Communion, Calvinists made excommunication an 'engine against immorality',[30] so that not only would the Table be preserved from defilement, but ungodliness would be investigated and reproved.

The Injunctions of Elizabeth, 1559, s.XXI, had included the power given to curates to repel from Communion those 'which be openly known to live in sin notorious without repentance'; but this specific instruction had been withdrawn.[31] The Puritans were striving for the restoration of this power of discipline. Hence the Millenary Petition in 1603 had specially asked James I:

> 'that examination may go before the Communion . . . that the discipline and excommunication may be administered according to Christ's own institution, or, at the least, that enormities may be redressed, as namely, that excommunication come not forth under the name of lay persons, chancellors, officials &c . . . that none be excommunicated WITHOUT CONSENT OF HIS PASTOR'.

In 1661, therefore, Baxter was repeating a demand that Puritans had made since 1559. In the words of the Millenary Petition of 1603, he asked for 'not a disorderly innovation, but a due and godly reformation'.

It cannot be denied that, even if a pastor like Baxter might be free from harshness in administration, the powers of excommunication the Puritans desired could cause deep resentment. The ostracism that followed excommunication gave great offence then; it would be inconceivable in our tolerant age. Church people were commanded to 'avoid' the excommunicated person; avoiding meant 'no familiarity with him, not only in God's worship, but in common conversation, further than nature and civil relationships bind us'.[32] In Kidderminster itself, only 600 out of 1800 were willing to accept Baxter's discipline. The fact was that England would not submit to the system. In Scotland, where the Reformation had been effected by powerful preaching that had transformed the nation, and where Church courts had been set up in which the people, through their lay elders, had constitutional

## BAXTER'S ECCLESIASTICAL PRINCIPLES

representation, the position was quite different. The Scots allowed the enforcement of the decisions of the Presbyterian Church by the magistrates. Englishmen had a stronger love of liberty. Proof could be seen in the objections to the Presbyterian system of discipline set up by the Long Parliament, even with the safeguards of appeal to Parliament (which Baillie stigmatized as a 'lame Erastian Presbytery'), and in the fact that Presbyterian Church courts were established in only a few places in England after Parliament gave approval in 1647.

Baxter, however, was consistent throughout; there must be reformation through the pastors' discipline. His 'Reformed Liturgy', presented to the bishops at the Savoy Conference, made this clear.

'Let none be admitted by the minister to the Sacrament of the Lord's Supper till they have at years of discretion understood the meaning of their baptismal covenant, and with their own mouths, and their own consent openly before the church, ratified and confirmed, and also promised, that by the grace of God, they will evermore endeavour themselves faithfully to observe and keep such things as by their mouth and confession they have assented to; and so being instructed in the Christian religion, do openly make a credible profession of their own faith, and promise to be obedient to the will of God.'

A large part of Baxter's 'Liturgy' (see pp. 178–84) is concerned with forms of admonition to the impenitent, forms of confession to be made publicly before the congregation, and forms of prayer for a sinner still impenitent after public admonition. These forms, which Baxter considered vitally necessary for reformation through discipline, he conscientiously offered to the Laudian bishops; but he could hardly have expected them to accept them.

### 3. *'The Primitive Episcopacy' or Parochial Episcopacy*

'My judgment of Church-government is for that form of Episcopacy which is described in Ignatius and Cyprian and was the usage then of the Christian churches.'[33]

Such was Baxter's statement when applying for a licence under the Declaration of Indulgence of 1672. He persisted always that the majority of the ministers ejected with him in 1662 agreed in upholding the primitive episcopacy, not Presbyterianism. 'Why and with what front do you call us all Presbyterians who offered Bishop Usher's Model to the King and you in 1660?'[34]

He regarded Ignatius of Antioch as his greatest authority: 'There is to every church one altar, and ONE BISHOP with the presbytery and the deacons my fellow-servants.'[35] And thus: 'Every Church had but one altar, and one Bishop with his fellow-elders and deacons as the note of its unity.'[36] Baxter added, 'Thus it continued also in the days of Justin, Tertullian and Cyprian, no Bishop having more than one Church or Altar, without any other formed self-communicating Church under him, but only oratories in city or country.'[37]

It is unnecessary to discuss matters that have filled almost countless volumes on the subject of episcopacy, but the convictions Baxter held after incessant research can be briefly stated. He declared that for 200 years the principle of *one church* and *one bishop* was maintained, except in a few large cities such as Rome and Alexandria where one bishop had the oversight of several churches. Justin Martyr and Tertullian narrated how they received the Sacrament from the 'bishop' every Lord's Day, this proving that there was always a bishop in the congregation.[38] Justin was quoted also to show that, whether the countrymen and the citizens had several churches or met in one city church together, they formed but a single congregation because every church had a present bishop.[39]

'None of us calleth himself or taketh himself to be Episcopus Episcoporum.'[40] (Cyprian in Concil. Carthagin.) To this Baxter referred as more evidence that every bishop in those days was *episcopus gregis*.[41] Baxter thus summed up the position in the primitive Church:

> 'It is evident that then a church was a congregation met for holy worship and not many hundred congregations making one church. ... That this church had ordinarily a Bishop present (not present in one congregation and many hundred without). That the Bishop baptized, and took the confessions of the baptized, and performed the ordinary worship, and administered the Lord's Supper. That discipline was exercised in these church assemblies, and therefore the Bishop was present. They took the Sacrament from none but the Bishop's hand which proveth that the Bishop was present whenever the Sacrament

was administered. They had these assemblies every Lord's Day. All which set together plainly sheweth that THEN EVERY CHURCH HAD A PRESENT BISHOP AND WAS NO MORE THAN ONE CONGREGATION.'[42]

Baxter referred more than once to Gregory Thaumaturgus who, although he had only seventeen Christians in his church at Neocaesarea, was a bishop, and when a new church was formed near by he made Alexander the Collier its independent bishop.[43] He pointed out that in St Patrick's time there were 365 bishops in Ireland, as against twenty-three in Baxter's time.[44] He deplored that now the 'Bishop of the Flock' had become a 'Bishop of Bishops', the original personal pastoral office of a bishop had grown 'to a pompous domination mostly secular', and 'the Bishops of single churches . . . to be the Bishops of multitudes of churches turned into one Diocesan Church of another species'.[45]

Clearly the difference between the opinions of Baxter and his opponents arose chiefly from the meaning given to 'a Church'. Baxter relied on the New Testament references: 'Ordain elders in every Church' (Acts xiv.23); 'Bishops in every city' (Titus i.5). In this matter Baxter declared:

'I am not deterred from any truth by names. I have formerly said that it is my opinion that the truth about church-government is parcelled out into the hands of each party, Episcopal, Presbyterian, Independent, and Erastian, and in this point in question THE INDEPENDENTS ARE MOST RIGHT.'[46]

Baxter asserted that the change from primitive practice came gradually. First, aratories or chapels were set up outside cities, the country people who lived there still going to the city church for Communion. Later, 'communicating congregations were gathered in the country villages' with resident presbyters (hitherto the presbyters had lived with the bishop). Then these 'Country Bishops' or *chorepiscopi* became regarded as bishops of the 'same order' as city bishops. With the acceptance of Christianity by Roman emperors in the fourth century, more honours were given to city bishops and gradually the *chorepiscopi* were suppressed and bishops were restricted to important towns and their number declined in inverse ratio to their prestige.

Baxter quoted the vehement passage from Chrysostom who

denounced the bishops of the inflated dioceses and threatened worse than hell-fire for those whose dioceses were too large to govern.[47] Baxter declared : 'O what would this man have said had he lived now in England !'

Furthermore, the diocesan system in England had become a secular system in the enforcement of its authority. The silencing of Puritan ministers or the punishment of churchwardens was dealt with as in a civil court, with the bishop's lay chancellor acting as judge and other laymen as proctors. 'Did a Chancellor ever convert a sinner?' Baxter asked. Under Laudian episcopacy, the ministers' part in Church government was limited to such matters as informing bishops about persons not kneeling for Communion; and even these reports were sent by churchwardens to the lay chancellor. As Baxter bitterly said, the Laudian bishops wanted ministers who were only readers and informers—the bishops' puppets. The bishops' knowledge of their parishes was practically confined to infrequent visits when many folk were confirmed without any personal knowledge of their beliefs and covenants. (This can be compared with Gladstone's description of confirmations by Archbishop Vernon-Harcourt in York in the early nineteenth century, when the Archbishop's hands were extended and the words of confirmation said once for a crowd of hundreds.)[48]

Great reliance was always placed by Baxter upon Archbishop Usher's opinions. For instance, he declared that Usher :

'told me his judgment that Bishops and Presbyters differ not as two orders but in degree, and that he that hath the order hath intrinsical power to ordain though he is regularly to do it under the Bishop's oversight and therefore it is not invalid and null but only irregular or schismatical when it is done disobediently against the Bishop. And he took presbyters to be governors of the flocks, and the Synods of Bishops to be but for CONCORD and not to have a proper governing power over the PARTICULAR BISHOPS' [meaning the parochial bishops].[49]

Usher approved an association of pastors meeting in every market town, with a president for life who must not have the pastoral care of more than his own congregation and not interfere with other pastors in theirs. This was Baxter's own method as practised in the Worcestershire Association. Amplifying Usher's

BAXTER'S ECCLESIASTICAL PRINCIPLES 31

plan, Baxter believed that (provided always that the pastors governed their own flocks) there might be a graded system of presidents, on this pattern:

(a) A pastor or 'Bishop of the Flock' in a particular church.
(b) A president of such pastors in any large parish, a 'Parish Bishop'.
(c) A fixed (permanent) president of a classis or synod (or association) of many pastors from various parishes, without a negative voice in the consultations.
(d) A president of a province containing many classes or synods, again without a negative voice.
(e) 'Unfixed' (temporary) general pastors, itinerant, without a particular church but having the care of all the churches, as the successors of the apostles.

Needless to say, such a complicated system would not commend itself to Laudian bishops. With its restrictions, and in avoiding such terms as 'archbishop' and 'bishop' in favour of a new term, 'president', Baxter's suggestion exposed the fastidious working of his mind.

In other writings, Baxter advocated: firstly, the *episcopus gregis*, as *de jure divino*, in every church or parish; secondly, the *episcopus presbytorum*, when there were many presbyters in one church, with at least lawful ecclesiastical status; and, thirdly, archbishops as *de jure divino* successors of the apostles—but no diocesan bishops! [50]

Baxter relied on Hooker for support in arguing that presbyters had inherent rights of ordaining and excommunicating (in conjunction with bishops, Hooker made clear). He brought this forward when Usher's scheme was proposed in the negotiations after the Restoration. He also used the admission of Dr Hammond (with whom he argued in 1659) that in New Testament times a presbyter did govern his flock. A presbyter who might only preach and administer sacraments without powers of discipline was only 'a subject presbyter,' a 'bishop's curate', 'a new sort of half-sub-presbyter'.[51] Why should they be given no discretion whatever about the lessons to be read, the prayers to be said, the subjects for Baptism or Communion, and no discretion also in burials (except for the unbaptized, the suicides, and those excommunicated by a lay chancellor!)? As Christ was a Prophet, Priest, and King,

Baxter contended, the pastors must follow Him first in their teaching, second in leading worship, third in the *kingly* act of governing. In this argument Baxter's case appeared at its strongest.

Baxter allowed that *de facto* there should be no ordination without the president whom, however, he denied a *de jure* negative voice.

Fortunately, by agreeing to support Usher's simple plan of modified episcopacy, the Puritan ministers in 1660-61 escaped the misunderstandings that would have accompanied Baxter's complicated schemes, and yet they were able to advocate together with Baxter a 'true, ancient and primitive episcopacy'.

### 4. *The Association of Pastors*

An essential part of Baxter's system was the associating of neighbouring pastors, each of whom governed his own parish. Ungodliness increased during the Civil War and post-War periods, and there was ecclesiastical confusion because of the abolition of episcopacy and the unpopularity of its substitute, Parliamentary Presbyterianism. The association of pastors was the answer to the need. The general adoption of this practice would have led to the realization of what Baxter called 'The Confederate Parish Churches of England'. The purposes of the associations were consultation and debate. Debates on theological points were useful, but undoubtedly the chief objective was the co-ordination of efforts to secure disciplinary control over communicants.

In Baxter's county, the Worcestershire Association met monthly in five towns. The ministers engaged in a public lecture followed by discussion, a conference to receive doubts about discipline and worship, the consideration of complaints against any minister who was a member of the association, and consultations about persons who had been excommunicated or, as impenitent, might be worthy of excommunication. A quarterly meeting of the five sections was held at the county town of Worcester.

Some county associations also ordained candidates after examination. The Worcestershire Association evidently generally abstained from this. Two other features Baxter was willing to include:

(*a*) Appointing laymen, not with the powers of ordained Presbyterian elders, but to assist pastors in admonition, instruction, and spiritual oversight. They might be called assisting elders.

## BAXTER'S ECCLESIASTICAL PRINCIPLES

(b) Allowing magistrates to be present to learn who were the offenders reported from the parishes and even to correct the association if it became heretical. Once again Baxter was complicating his system with this impracticable and dangerous feature.

As the associations actually functioned, they were advisory councils, with no direct jurisdiction over any congregation and with a working basis that could include churches of various parties. The system peculiarly suited the varied pattern of church life springing up in the Interregnum. Prelatical clergy abstained from membership. Baxter made it clear that there was nothing to debar orthodox Presbyterian and Independent ministers in Worcestershire joining. The fact was that, except for one possibly classified as an Independent, all the ministers in Baxter's Association were moderate episcopal clergy, 'mere Catholics', 'Protestant Episcopal divines', not partisans in politics but faithful parish ministers.

In 1691 Baxter wrote, in reference to his experiment:

'But few of the rigid Presbyterians or Independents joined with us; and, indeed, Worcestershire and the adjoining counties had but few of either sort. But the main body of our Association were men that thought the Episcopal, Presbyterian and Independent had each of them some good in which they excelled the other two parties, and each of them some mistakes; and that to select out of all three the best part, and leave the worst, was the most desirable (and ancient) form of government.'[52]

And again his opinion was definitely given:

'The greatest advantage which I found for concord and pacification was among a great number of ministers and people who had addicted themselves to NO SECT OR PARTY at all, though the vulgar called them by the name of Presbyterians. And the truth is, as far as I could discover, this was the case of the greatest number of the godly ministers and people throughout England. For though Presbytery generally took in Scotland, yet it was but a stranger here.'[53]

It is significant that Baxter could speak well of some bishops during the Commonwealth, when it brought him no advantage to say this, and when they had no authority at the time. Of such bishops as Usher, Hall, and Morton, he said: 'I heartily reverence

## 34  CHURCH UNITY WITHOUT UNIFORMITY

and desire their union.' With them, and with all faithful ministers, Baxter believed that full co-operation was possible, on the broad grounds outlined in his *Christian Concord* (The Agreement of the Associated Pastors and Churches of Worcestershire). If the Restoration had not taken place it is possible that Baxter's type of voluntary county associations might have been adopted by the moderate clergy in all parts of England.

### 5. *Episcopal Ordination not Essential, and no Re-ordination*

In 1638 Baxter was ordained deacon at Worcester by Bishop Thornborough. Evidently he did not wish to take priest's orders when this would have been possible. When he was offered a bishopric in 1660, no demur seems to have been raised because his ordination had been only to the diaconate.

Nearly all Baxter's colleagues at the Savoy Conference in 1661, though called Presbyterians, had been episcopally ordained (see details in list on pp. 175-7). Yet a large number of the ministers ejected from the Church in 1662 had been ordained only by presbyteries or classes or by voluntary county associations. Baxter contended for the validity of these ordinations although he had not himself taken part in them: 'I never practised any myself.' [54]

There was a strong case for the validity of ordination by presbyteries or associations during the Commonwealth and Protectorate, on the ground of expediency. Should ministers be required (Baxter asked) to go to bishops who were imprisoned or were living in retirement in order to continue a true Church in England? Should they go to bishops like Wren who had silenced fifty ministers in his diocese of Norwich in two years for not reading the book permitting sports on the Lord's Day, or like Pierce, who had said that preaching was unnecessary and who had silenced all 'lecturers' in his diocese?

Beyond the question of expediency there was the fact that presbyterial ordinations had actually been recognized in England. These cases were of two kinds: foreign ordinations and non-episcopal ordinations in Britain.

'What need I tell an Englishman that these objectors are not sons of the Church of England, whatever they pretend, when the world knows that the CHURCH OF ENGLAND TOOK HIM TO BE A TRUE MINISTER THAT WAS ORDAINED in France, Holland,

Scotland, Geneva, Heidelberg &c, BY MERE PRESBYTERS WITHOUT A BISHOP. The world knows that we did not ordain those again that were so ordained; no more than we baptized those again that were there baptized. The world knows that we gave them the right hand of fellowship as true Churches of Christ, when we set light by ROME.' [55]

Baxter had the following cases in mind : [56]

(a) William Whittingham (who married Calvin's sister and wrote the preface to Knox's *Liturgy* as well as much of the translation of the Geneva Bible and hymns still in use), who was ordained by elders in Geneva in 1555, and who became Dean of Durham in 1563, the bishops not requiring episcopal ordination.

(b) Walter Travers, who succeeded on appeal to the Privy Council in securing recognition of his ordination by the Presbytery of Antwerp, and who stated in the course of his appeal that there were many ministers holding benefices in England who had been ordained in Scotland and on the Continent. Travers had deliberately gone to the Continent to be ordained by a presbytery because he refused episcopal ordination.

(c) John Morison, ordained by the Synod of Lothian, and not re-ordained when given the Archbishop of Canterbury's licence in 1582, Archbishop Grindal declaring that Morison :

'had been called to the ministry by the imposition of hands according to the laudable form and rite of the Reformed Church of Scotland. And since the Congregation of the County of Lothian is conformable to the orthodox faith and sincere religion now received in the realm of England, we therefore, approving and ratifying the form of your ordination and preferment, grant you a licence and faculty in such orders by your token, you may and have power to celebrate the Divine offices, to minister the Sacraments....' [57]

(d) Robert Wright, ordained by presbyters at Antwerp, afterwards chaplain to Lord Rich.

(e) Dr de Laune, ordained by the Presbytery at Leyden, afterwards admitted to a benefice without re-ordination. The future Bishop Cosin was then secretary to Bishop Overall, who did not require re-ordination but said, 'Re-ordination we must not admit, no more than re-baptism.'

The 1571 Act had not required re-ordination for those who subscribed to the Thirty-nine Articles. Bishop Cosin, one of the stoutest opponents Baxter met at the Savoy Conference in 1661, has recorded that the object of the 1571 Act was to accept Protestant ministers ordained on the Continent. This opinion, given in 1650 while Cosin was an exile in France, stated:

'If at any time a minister so ordained in these French Churches came to incorporate himself in ours, and to receive a public charge or cure of souls among us in the Church of England (as I have known some of them to have done so of late, and can instance in many other before my time), our Bishops did not re-ordain him before they admitted to his charge, as they would have done if his former ordination in France had been void. Nor did our laws require more of him, than to declare his public consent to the religion received among us, and to subscribe the Articles established.'[58]

Other Caroline bishops (Andrewes and Hall) were equally explicit in supporting the principle of not re-ordaining those ordained in the Reformed Churches.

It is true that there was another reason for this provision in the 1571 Act, namely, that Romish priests who had received orders during the reigns of Henry VIII and Mary could receive charges under Elizabeth without re-ordination, provided that they signified assent to the Thirty-nine Articles.[59] Evidently, the 1571 Act was intended to include both these priests and also ministers ordained abroad. Strype declared that it was meant 'undoubtedly to comprehend Papists, and likewise such as received their orders in some of the foreign Reformed Churches when they were in exile under Queen Mary'.[60]

Keble, in his preface to Hooker's works, puts the matter beyond doubt:

'Nearly up to the time when Hooker wrote (1594) numbers had been admitted to the ministry of the Church of England with no better than presbyterian ordination; and it appears by Travers' Supplication to the Council [see above] that such was the construction not uncommonly put upon the Statute of the 13th of Elizabeth (1571), permitting those who had received orders in any other form than that of the English Service Book, on giving certain securities, to exercise their calling in England.'[61]

Archbishop Bancroft directed that Scottish ministers, presbyterially ordained, were not to be re-ordained because it would reflect upon the Reformed Churches.[62] Baxter, in referring to his action, could point to Bancroft as 'the violentest of all the enemies of them called Puritans in those times'.[63]

The precedent of the 1571 Act is of great importance because it was included in the King's Declaration of 25th October 1660, when the benefits of that Act were offered to non-episcopally ordained ministers. Had that offer been endorsed, re-ordination would not have been required in the Restoration Settlement of the Church of England. When the Act of Uniformity of 1662 destroyed all such expectations, and specifically required episcopal ordination for all ministers, Clarendon significantly commented:

'This was NEW; for there had been many, and at present there were some, who possessed benefices with cure of souls, and other ecclesiastical promotions, who had never received orders but in France or in Holland, and these men must now receive new ordination, which had been always held unlawful in the church.'[64]

There can be no doubt, however, that a distinction was generally made between those ordained without bishops abroad and those who spurned episcopal ordination in England when it was available. Bishop Hall ('Episcopacy by Divine Right') expressed this difference between the two classes when he said: 'We can at once tenderly respect them and justly censure you.'

Nevertheless Baxter (in *Christian Concord*) relied on fourteen Anglican authorities whom he quoted in opposing the *necessity* of episcopal ordination. These included Bishop Jewel, Bishop Prideaux, Bishop Downame, and Field, Dean of Gloucester. Field had declared that, as presbyters might confirm and absolve in necessity, so might they ordain under similar circumstances, referring also to the Roman practice of allowing ordination by *chorepiscopi* or 'Country Bishops'. Bishop Downame, allowing non-episcopal ordination in cases of necessity, stated that if a Pope's licence conferred the right on a presbyter to ordain others, how much stronger the right of 'a company of presbyters to whom in the want of a bishop the charge of the Church is devolved'.[65]

Baxter also referred to Hooker, Whitgift, and Andrewes in allowing non-episcopal ordination in cases of necessity. Could not the suppression of episcopacy for fifteen years before the Restoration cover the validity of non-episcopal ordinations in that period? Evidently the King and those of his advisers who offered a settlement in 1660 were prepared to admit this for the sake of the unity of the Church of England, as the King's Declaration of 25th December 1660 indicated.

When dealing with the theory of succession Baxter drew attention to the arguments the English bishops had advanced against the Papists to prove an uninterrupted succession at the time of the Elizabethan Settlement and the falsity of the fable of the Nag's Head ordination in Cheapside. He added:

'Though we should grant the necessity of such succession, yet we need not grant the nullity of our calling. . . . It is known to be but the later declining generation of Bishops, such as Montague, Laud, and their confederates, most in King Charles the First's days, very few in King James's, and scarce any at all in Queen Elizabeth's, that do join with the Papists in pleading the necessity of succession.'[66]

Further, Baxter insisted that, if a layman might baptize in case of necessity, surely a presbytery might ordain, particularly when episcopacy was not functioning in England. He alluded to the practice also in the days of Ignatius when ordinations were performed by the city pastors and not by diocesan bishops.

Archbishop Usher (Baxter reminded his readers) had tried to convince Charles I of the validity of presbyterial ordination by these arguments: first, that because like confers like, therefore presbyters may ordain presbyters; second, if cardinals elect a pope and bishops consecrate an archbishop, how much more reason is there for believing that those of the same order may ordain presbyters.[67]

It followed from all this that re-ordination was unthinkable, and the attitude of his friend John Howe had Baxter's complete endorsement. Howe had received only presbyterial ordination. It was suggested to him by the Bishop of Exeter (Seth Ward, whom Howe had defended before Cromwell under different cir-

## BAXTER'S ECCLESIASTICAL PRINCIPLES 39

cumstances) that he should be re-ordained by bishops. Ward pressed the point, 'What hurt is there in being twice ordained?' To this Howe made the noble reply, 'Hurt, my Lord! It hurts my understanding; the thought is shocking; it is an absurdity; nothing can have two beginnings. I am sure I am a minister of Christ, and am ready to debate that matter with your Lordship, if you please; and I can't begin to be a minister again.'

Baxter would not have objected to re-ordination, provided always that there was no repudiation of the previous ordination, and this would have been made clear by using the words, 'IF THOU ART NOT ALREADY ORDAINED.' Such a form was proposed by Tillotson in the suggestions for comprehension in 1689. Another form, which avoided any slur upon previous ordinations and provided an adequate commission for a minister in a re-united Church in any age, was offered by Bishop Wilkins in negotiations with Baxter in 1668: 'Take thou authority to preach the Word of God and to administer the Sacraments in any congregation of the Church of England WHERE THOU SHALT BE LAWFULLY ADMITTED THEREUNTO.'

In recent years these forms have been quoted approvingly by Church of England representatives.[68]

Baxter's main concern was to recognize the rights of those who had exercised their ministry in Christ's Church in England, having had the choice or approval of their congregations, having shown their conformity to the apostolic faith, their godliness and ministerial ability, and having received the imposition of hands by 'true bishops' or *episcopi gregis*, that is, by synods of presbyters, either with or without a diocesan bishop—especially during the Interregnum.

### 6. *Freedom in Forms of Worship*

Baxter at his ordination had subscribed to the Prayer Book. He said later that he did this without very much thought, but it is apparent that he had no scruples about its use. He was always convinced of the lawfulness of a liturgy, and at Kidderminster he used the Prayer Book until it was suppressed by order of Parliament, claiming always the right to omit a few features or to abridge the service.

Baxter's willingness to use the Prayer Book has been obscured by the incidents at the Savoy Conference, when he and his associates offered a list of objections, and he presented a monumental alternative liturgy, which he had composed in a fortnight. Where he was opposed to the bishops was in the requirement to swear to use every part and to use nothing else when he believed the Prayer Book contained some defects and redundancies. He also stoutly maintained that extempore prayer should be permitted. It was unfortunate that he was linked in popular opinion with those who objected to the Prayer Book in its entirety. At his last trial, for instance, Judge Jeffreys scorned any other suggestion : 'He hates the Liturgy, he would have nothing but long-winded cant without the Book.' Actually, even after expulsion from his pulpit in 1662, Baxter used parts of the Prayer Book when he could conduct worship at all.

The real opponents to the Prayer Book were the orthodox Presbyterians and the Independents, not Baxter and the moderate episcopal clergy. It was Milton who called the Prayer Book 'this Romish liturgy'. It was Baillie, the Scottish Commissioner at the Westminster Assembly, who described it as 'the great idol of England'. The Cromwellian soldiery who broke up the service Evelyn attended on Christmas Day 1657 called the service of Holy Communion in the Prayer Book 'the mass in English'. With all such intolerance Baxter had no sympathy.

Baxter's contention was that liturgical freedom should be given as it had been for at least three centuries in the early Church. Expelling godly ministers through insisting upon uniformity in every detail also outraged Baxter's principles of pastoral rights. The position was made worse when the bishops replaced them with ministers of 'scandalous' character who readily complied with liturgical requirements.

With regard to the ceremonies, which seem to some historians to be the centre of the whole dispute between Puritans and bishops, Baxter was distinctly moderate. Even where his judgement was not satisfied, he was prepared to use a disputed ceremony for the sake of peace. 'It is not Liturgies nor Ceremonies that essentiate the Church of England.' [69] His attitude on the various controversial points below is seen to be liberal and practical:

THE SURPLICE : 'I have no censure for those that wear the surplice, though I never wore it.' [70]

THE CROSS IN BAPTISM : 'Of all our ceremonies, there is none that I have more suspected to be simply unlawful than the Cross in Baptism. . . . Yet dare I not peremptorily say that it is unlawful, nor will I condemn either ancients or moderns that use it. . . . Only my own practice I was forced to suspend, and must do if it were again imposed on me, till I were better satisfied.'[71]

'But that man may adjoin such a human sacrament as the Cross in Baptism to God's Sacrament, I am not satisfied in, and cannot assent or consent to it, that such a solemn dedicating sign, should be stated in God's public worship by man. . . . And if God would have had such Sacraments used, He could as well have instituted them as He did the rest.'[72]

THE RING IN MARRIAGE: Baxter had no objection if no superstitious meaning was attached to it. 'For the ring in marriage, I see no reason to scruple the lawfulness of it.'

KNEELING AT COMMUNION: Baxter opposed this in principle, and also the practice of putting the elements into individual hands because the words of institution were in the plural.

> 'Kneeling at the Sacrament is a novelty introduced many hundred years after Christ, and contrary to such canons and customs of the Church to which for antiquity and universality you owe much more respect than to the canons of the late Bishops in England.'[73]

> 'That none should kneel in public worship on the Lord's Day, no, not in prayer, much less in receiving the Eucharist, was a custom so ancient and universal in the Church, that it was everywhere observed before General Councils were made use of; and in the first General Council of Nicaea, it was made the last Canon; and other General Councils after renewed it; so that I know not how any ceremony can possibly pretend to greater ecclesiastical authority than this had.'[74]

At the same time Baxter could declare that he had not refused Communion to those who desired to receive kneeling, provided that they did not ask for a separate observance from the rest of the congregation.

> 'I never did hitherto, to my remembrance, refuse to give the Sacrament to anyone, merely because they would not take it sitting or standing; nor did ever forbid or repel any on that account; nor ever mean to do.'[75]

In his reply to the Kidderminster squire, Sir Ralph Clare, Baxter made it clear that his qualified permission to give the Sacrament to him kneeling applied only to anyone who would submit himself to his discipline as pastor. He agreed to give the elements to those who knelt while others received sitting and only declined Sir Ralph Clare's request for a separate time.

'If any of my pastoral charge . . . will profess that they think it a sin against God for them to receive the Sacrament unless it be put into their hands kneeling, and *ergo* that they dare not in conscience take it otherwise, I do purpose to condescend to their weakness and so to give it them. . . . And I shall expect that at the first receiving they will openly profess that they take not the bread for the substantial body of Christ, nor worship the bread.' [76]

THE TERM 'ALTAR' : This word Baxter adopted in a metaphorical sense only as his own 'Reformed Liturgy' showed.

THE USE OF ORGANS AND CHOIRS : He accepted the use of organs. 'It is not a human invention; as the last Psalm and many others show, which call us to praise the Lord with instruments of music.' [77]

He opposed giving singing entirely to choirs and excluding the congregation. 'I am not willing to join in such a church where I shall be shut out of this noble work of praise.' [78]

HOLY DAYS : Baxter would accept these for the sake of peace.

'It is not long since many were cast out of the ministerial service or suspended, for not reading a book authorizing dancing and other recreations on the Lord's Day. In a word, to reproach them as Precisians and Puritans, for the strictness of their lives, and yet at the same time to persuade men that they are ungodly for not keeping holy days . . . draws too near the manners of the pagans.' [79]

SET PRAYERS : Baxter did not object to these but he was emphatic in demanding provision for extemporaneous prayer also.

RESPONSES : He preferred no responses to prayers, and his own 'Reformed Liturgy' made no provision for any.

Baxter exalted the preaching office. The bishops stressed the uniform use of the Prayer Book. Baxter declared that men were saved by the preaching of the Word, rather than by the Sacraments or any ceremonies. In his *Answer to Dodwell* (p. 85) he said:

'You deprecate preaching; you say that a true minister of Christ hath no necessary work but to administer Sacraments; and you ask how can we prove that preaching is at all any essential part of the ministerial office? Well, what of Christ's own practice and His command to those whom He called and sent; and their practice; and the Holy Ghost's determination by them.... On the other hand, where do you find that ever anyone in the New Testament was ordained a mass Priest, or Sacrament Priest, and not a Teacher?'

Yet, with all his emphasis upon preaching, Baxter did not use an unadorned service or neglect praise and prayer. Not only did his own suggested 'Reformed Liturgy' amply illustrate this, but his practice at Kidderminster showed that he included five prayers and five Psalms in each service, with much attention to congregational singing.

In his 'Reformed Liturgy' (see pp. 178-84) he submitted an alternative for the Common Prayer, not a substitute as some critics have imagined. Not only its massive and exalted style, but its formidable list of Scriptural references, used for every line of the Liturgy in the margin, shows the central Puritan position—faithfulness to the Word of God, the supreme standard in teaching, in praise, and in prayer. With the Word of God as his guide, Baxter contended that there should be both liberty of 'prophesying' and liberty in forms of worship.

### 7. *A National Comprehensive Church:*
### *'The Confederate Parish Churches of England'*

'The Church of England is nothing but a Christian Kingdom, consisting of a Christian supreme Power, and combined Christians and Churches governed by that Power.'[80] No one paid more respect than Baxter to the ideal of kingship and to the support of religion by the civil power, the 'Christian sovereign-magistrate'. He held the 'Elizabethan Church' view that the king was head of the Church as well as the State, and he agreed with Hooker that 'one and the self-same people are the Church and the commonwealth' (*i.e.,* the nation).

Baxter's ideal Church depended on the character of the ministry. There were enough warnings, both before and after the Restoration, of the dire results for religion and morality when there were unworthy men in the ministry: 'The great cause of the ruin of a national church is the ignorance, viciousness, pride, malignity, covetousness, and persecuting cruelty, of a degenerate, carnal, worldly clergy.'[81]

A favourite phrase, 'The Confederate Parish Churches of England',[82] aptly expressed what Baxter believed the national Church should be. If those called 'Orthodox Protestant Nonconformists' had been retained in the Church of England, and if there had been a godly ministry with disciplined congregations everywhere, the number of actual dissenters would have been negligible. It was because of Baxter's adherence to this ideal of comprehension that the question of toleration hardly concerned him.

The use of force in a national Church he repudiated. It was for this reason that before 1640 he denounced so often the bishops' courts with their lay chancellors. Similarly, he disapproved the Presbyterian system of handing over excommunicated persons to the magistrates. At the same time he believed that the civil power should preserve order and orthodoxy in the national Church; this should be exercised only by the general powers of the State in upholding virtue and order in the community and in preventing dire heresy infecting the Church. In his system, godly magistrates were introduced as church members into church-meetings where the impenitent were called upon to confess their faults.

Baxter also differed from orthodox Presbyterians in not conceding the rights of presbyteries to control individual pastors and their congregations. This he regarded as a step towards the prelatical system which he ceaselessly denounced. In one case, ten or twelve congregations might be affected; in the other, there would be hundreds of parishes; but in both a number of churches was treated as 'one governed church' and the pastor's rights over his own congregation were removed or reduced.

He strongly upheld the parish system against the 'gathered churches' of Independency. He opposed the Independents conscientiously but with criticisms that seem to us today most unworthy of his spirit; he said, for instance, that Independents were 'members of a singular society as if they were loth to have too much company in Heaven'.[83] He disagreed not only with their separation from a national Church but with their giving a congregation the 'Power of the Keys'. Later chapters in this book will show Baxter's failure to press for unity with Independents in 1658 and to secure any toleration for them in the negotiations with the King in 1660. He gave as his reasons, the Independents'

> 'separation, or their gathering other churches out of parish-churches that had had faithful ministers. If they would have taken parish-churches on independent principles, WITHOUT SEPARATION, neither I nor my acquaintance did oppose them, no, nor their endeavours to reform such churches. . . . We never denied the Independents the liberty of preaching lectures as often as they would; nor yet the liberty of taking parish-churches. [This was during the Interregnum.] They commonly had presentations, and the public maintenance; and no subscription, declaration, liturgy, or ceremony, was imposed on them.'[84]

It was in this connexion that Baxter called upon the bishops in 1661 to give to the moderate episcopal party he represented the same liberty of remaining within the national Church as the so-called 'Presbyterians' had given the Independents in the 'Federated Puritan State Churches' of the Cromwellian period.

Baxter would not countenance separation from the Church just because some individuals within it were unworthy, 'taking a very few that can talk more than the rest, and making them the Church'.[85] The nation as a whole could never be saved by such methods. There would be no co-ordination of effort in Independency, without synods or associations. On the other hand, the events that followed expulsion in 1662 proved that under persecution the Independents could preserve their identity more easily than a highly organized body of the orthodox Presbyterian type or Baxter's loosely defined moderate episcopal party.

*Comprehension*, to include all godly parish ministers who desired unity within the one Church, would secure a truly *national* Church. A policy of uniformity failed to do this before 1662, and the policy enforced by the Act of Uniformity made the Church of England an established *sect* and not the Church of the whole nation. 'Under Laud, the church was too much the church of the Court. Under the Long Parliament and the Commonwealth, it was too much the church of the Westminster Assembly and of the army. . . . The Church in 1660 was to become the Church of the Bishops and of the squirearchy. The same sin was committed, and the same penalty has followed. The Church would NOT BE NATIONAL, and half the nation has left it.'[86]

Was Baxter, however, sufficiently tolerant? Jeremy Taylor has been naturally regarded as the finest example of a tolerant spirit among episcopal divines; suffering from sequestration in 1644, and thenceforward without a parish for sixteen years, he supported toleration in his *The Liberty of Prophesying*. Beside him, Baxter sometimes seems uncharitable. Judged on some statements, his views were even fierce : 'Unlimited toleration was to be abhorred.' And again, 'Toleration! dainty word for soul-murder! God grant that my eye may never see such a toleration!' True it is that he believed that the basis of Church unity should be so broad that no one would have reasonable excuse for remaining outside the national Church. His refusal to consider toleration in 1660–61 cost his cause very dear; it mattered little that his consent to toleration might have had no effect upon the final issue. When they pinned their faith to comprehension without toleration, Baxter and his friends lost all.

Nevertheless, Baxter was one of the few wise men in his generation. He knew that only a national comprehensive Church could withstand the inroads of Popery. The history of Christianity in the last 300 years well supports what he said in his last trial, before Judge Jeffreys :

'These things will surely be understood one day, what tools one sort of Protestants are made to persecute and vex the other.'

Baxter shared with his generation an abhorrence of Popery and a fear of its revival in England which many today would regard as exaggerated. He even believed he could see Popery raising its head in some of the smaller sects (Usher and others shared that belief). Yet it was through the work of the prelatists especially that he feared Rome's work was being advanced, and the lapsing of some Anglicans to Romanism convinced him he was right. Notwithstanding all this, he refused to join in hounding down all Papists, and he rejected outright the prevalent interpretation of the Pope as Antichrist or 'the Beast' in the Book of Revelation.

At the 1655 Committee before Cromwell, Baxter startled other

Puritans with his moderation. He proposed toleration for all who accepted the Creed, the Lord's Prayer, the Decalogue, the Scriptures, and the two sacraments; and when asked about whether this might not allow toleration even for Papists he was not dismayed. At that time the divines whom Cromwell consulted were considering the fundamentals of religion for official recognition. In 1661 Baxter's attitude was different, no doubt because of the fears that Romanist influence was already returning surreptitiously with the King's connivance.

Although Baxter ardently hoped for the widest re-union of Christians, and ultimately union with a purified and penitent Papacy, he had no illusions about the harm Rome was doing in his day to the cause of religion; but still he retained a sense of proportion and could say:

'Christianity is our religion. Protesting against Popery is our negation.... Protestancy as such is but our wiping off the dirt .... We still profess before men and angels that we own no religion but the Christian religion, nor any church but the Christian Church, nor dream of any Catholic Church but one, containing all the true Christians in the world, united in Jesus Christ as the Head.'[87]

Baxter wished to restore what he believed to be the breadth and comprehensiveness of the primitive Church, and not the exclusiveness of the mediaeval Church or of the Anglican diocesan system which had followed the mediaeval pattern. In this he may be said to have anticipated the spirit which is prompting movements for Christian unity in the twentieth century.

Lamentably, the failure to unite the Church of England on Baxter's comprehensive terms resulted in the multiplying of sects as well as the encouraging of Roman Catholicism.

'Thousands have been drawn into Popery, and confirmed in it already, by this argument, and I am persuaded that all the ... books that ever were written, have not done so much to make Papists in England, as the multitude of sects among us. Yea, some professors of religious strictness, of great esteem for godliness, have turned Papists themselves when they were giddy and weary with turnings, and when they had run from sect to sect and found no consistency in any.'[88]

No argument advanced by Baxter impresses us more than his declaration that the essential unity of the Church should be *unity in holiness*.

'Talk no more childishly about our petty differences in ceremonies and forms of worship, about Bishops and Common Prayer Books, and holy-days, and such like, as long as you refuse agreement in the main. There is a difference between you that is a hundred times greater than these. . . . All your pretended desires of unity and concord are base hypocrisy, as long as you refuse to unite with us in the way and state of HOLINESS.'[89]

'If once we were united in the Spirit, and in holiness, we should manage all our differences in a holy manner, and be awakened and disposed to seek after healing in a healing way. It would put us upon inquiring after peace, and studying the meetest terms of peace, till we had found out the way in which we should accord.'[90]

How, then, could such unity be achieved? Not by uniformity, as the event clearly demonstrated. Baxter's oft-repeated view was this: 'It is the will of God that the unity of the Church should not be laid upon indifferent, small and doubtful points.'[91]

He looked forward to an ideal union 'when our Unity is not laid upon our uniformity in these unnecessary things', for example, ceremonies and oaths of canonical obedience. 'We are certain that leaving these unnecessary things at liberty, to be used only by those that will, is the way to unity.'[92]

## 8. *Unity without Uniformity*

What has just been considered illustrates Baxter's ideal and also shows the difference between him and Laud, who said: 'Unity cannot long continue in the Church where Uniformity is kept out at the church door.' England's experience under Laud showed how unity was frustrated by insisting upon uniformity in every detail of the Liturgy. Whereas Peter and Paul went to Heaven without the disputed ceremonies, Baxter often said, no Christian pastor in seventeenth-century England was given liberty to use, or dispense with, any forms in the Prayer Book according to his discretion. Baxter insisted that only things *necessary* should be required, and what those things were emerged in the negotiations with the bishops in 1660–61. The general principle Baxter upheld

# BAXTER'S ECCLESIASTICAL PRINCIPLES 49

was found in his oft-quoted maxim : 'In things necessary, unity; in things indifferent, liberty; in all things, charity.'

The things necessary were set forth as 'The True and Easy Terms of Unity and Concord',[93] from which they may be summarized :

1. Assent to the Sacramental Covenant, the Creed, the Lord's Prayer, the Decalogue, and the infallible truth of Scripture.

2. Faithful pastors, acceptable to ordainers and the flock, in every church.

3. Force to reside only in magistrates, pastors and flock being subject to them.

4. Pastors to satisfy preliminary tests of scholarship, orthodoxy, and piety.

5. Opposition to civil or spiritual government to be reproved and prevented.

6. No obligation to use forms, liturgies, or homilies.

7. Pastors to choose subjects of preaching and to arrange worship.

8. Each pastor to baptize, preach, administer the Lord's Supper, and exercise discipline at his discretion.

9. Neighbouring churches to keep in contact with each other so that anyone rejected by one church would not be admitted to others without consultation of pastors.

10. Synods to be used only for the sake of unity and for helping junior ministers.

11. If the State set up higher authorities in the Church, such as diocesan bishops or moderators, no minister to be forced to swear to obey such authorities but actually to obey. Even so the prelate was not to exercise his spiritual power except through a COUNCIL OF PASTORS. No lay chancellors or other laymen to have any control of pastors.

12. All pastors and people to swear obedience to the King.

It was the insistence upon uniformity even in details that Baxter most strenuously opposed.

'Nothing hath more divided the Church than the proud impositions of men that think so highly of their own words and forms and ceremonious devices that no man shall have communion with Christ and the Church in any other way. NEVER WILL THE CHURCH UNITE ON SUCH TERMS. . . . Experience might tell these men that they are building but a Babel and dividing the Church.'[94]

No one should have objected to the general principle he frequently enunciated: 'Lay the unity of the Church upon nothing but what is ESSENTIAL TO THE CHURCH.' 'Stick close to this one Bible, and let nothing come into your faith or religion but what comes thence; and when controversies arise, try them by this.'[95]

There was a modern note in the statement of Baxter's passionate assertion that Christians should unite BECAUSE THEY ARE ACTUALLY ONE IN GOD, the opening words of the Lord's Prayer being given in support. He declared: 'God will own no church which is so independent as not to be a member of the universal Church; nor any person who is so independent as not to come to Him as in communion with all Christians in the world.'[96]

Differences of intellect, temperament, and strength of faith were to be expected; but the essentials of faith accepted by all Christians and included in the BAPTISMAL COVENANT should make them one. Again there is a modern ring in this: 'It is not as Romanists, Greeks . . . Lutherans, Calvinists, Arminians &c, that men are saved but as CATHOLIC CHRISTIANS, aspiring to the highest perfection.'[97]

Baxter's affinity of spirit with modern ecumenical Christians can be detected in the high place he gave to Christian missions in foreign countries. He also believed that foreign missions would do much to unite Christians, and he dilated upon the need for world evangelization as a motive for effecting unity among the Churches in Europe.

This stern Puritan was more modern or, at least, more catholic in spirit than some Churchmen today. To the end of his days he advocated unity on the widest terms, and he gave evidence of it in his ministry. Richard Kirk, a Scot who visited London in 1690, shortly before Baxter's death, remarked upon the comprehensiveness and charity of his pulpit prayers—for the King and royal family and Parliament, for the Churches of the East, for Convocation (which was then considering the Comprehension Bill that was to prove abortive), and for Christian unity throughout the world, with the reconciling of Protestants so that 'party nor sect be never heard any more among them'.

At the Bicentenary of the Ejection in 1862, Dr Alexander

McLaren used words which could have come from Baxter's lips and which are illuminating to the advocates of Christian unity in 1962 :

'In opposition to all impossible dreams of uniformity, let them [i.e., the Nonconformists] proclaim the higher truth of a DIVERSE UNITY. . . . In opposition to schismatical terms of communion, let them proclaim that nothing is necessary to Christian communion but what is necessary to being a Christian . . . . The future of England will be to that Church which shall know how to reconcile most perfectly the rights of the individual and the power of the society; the claims of free thought and the claims of definite dogmatic truth. An established Church, be-articled, and be-liturgied, and be-bishoped, will not do it. Narrow Dissenterisms will not do it. But Churches which take the Bible for their creed, and Christ for their sole Master, and all their members for brethren, ought to do it.' [98]

In the World Council of Churches, Christians may realize the fruition of Baxter's pathetic hope, which he uttered in the hour of bitter persecution and disunity (before Judge Jeffreys in 1685): 'These things will surely be understood one day.'

## NOTES TO CHAPTER I

1. Hastings, *Dictionary of Religion and Ethics*, 'Baxter', p. 440.
2. Orme, *Life and Times of Richard Baxter*, vol. 2, p. 447.
3. Stephen, *Essays in Ecclesiastical Biography*, p. 337.
4. Hastings, *Dictionary of Religion and Ethics*, 'Baxter', p. 439.
5. *Expository Times*, vol. 38, p. 394.
6. *Bicentenary Lectures*, p. 197.
7. Hastings, *Dictionary of Religion and Ethics*, 'Baxter', p. 440.
8. Barclay, *Inner Life of the Religious Societies of the Commonwealth*, p. 330.
9. *A Treatise on Episcopacy*, 1681, title page.
10. *Cure of Church Divisions*, 1670, pp. 71–2.
11. *Reliquiae Baxterianae*, II, p. 401; III, p. 112.
12. *Christian Concord*, 1653, p. 78.
13. *Five Disputations*, 1659, II, p. 6; 'Answer to Dodwell' in Powicke, *Richard Baxter*, vol. 2, p. 218.
14. *The Reformed Pastor*, pp. 10, 52.
15. *A Treatise on Episcopacy*, II, p. 152.
16. *Ibid.*, p. 126.
17. *Reliquiae Baxterianae*, II, p. 161.
18. *Practical Works*, vol 1, 'Christian Politics', p. 754.

19. *Five Disputations*, p. 21.
20. *The Reformed Pastor*, p. 387.
21. *Ibid.*, pp. 378, 380.
22. *Ibid.*, p. 397.
23. *Five Disputations*, preface to Second Disputation.
24. *Reliquiae Baxterianae*, II, p. 396; *Five Disputations*, II, p. 33; *A Treatise on Episcopacy*, I, p. 5.
25. *Five Disputations*, I, p. 16; *A Treatise on Episcopacy*, II, pp. 184–6.
26. *Reliquiae Baxterianae*, III, p. 169.
27. Powicke, *Richard Baxter*, vol. 1, pp. 98–105; Brown, *Puritan Preaching in England*, pp. 171, 190.
28. *The Reformed Pastor*, p. 380.
29. *Ibid.*, p. 152.
30. Shaw, *History of the English Church, 1640–1660*, vol. 1, 208.
31. Gee and Hardy, *Documents Illustrative of English Church History*, p. 428.
32. *Christian Concord*, X.
33. Powicke, *Richard Baxter*, vol. 2, p. 72.
34. *A Treatise on Episcopacy*, II, p. 88.
35. *Ibid.*, II, p. 21.
36. *Ibid.*, I, p. 17.
37. *Ibid.*, I, p. 17; *Reliquiae Baxterianae*, App. I, p. 10 and App. II, p. 24.
38. *Five Disputations*, III, p. 92.
39. *A Treatise on Episcopacy*, II, p. 29.
40. *Five Disputations*, III, p. 183.
41. *Ibid.*, III, p. 67; *Christian Concord*, p. 80.
42. *A Treatise on Episcopacy*, II, pp. 29–30.
43. *Ibid.*, II, p. 48; *Five Disputations*, III, pp. 93, 181.
44. *A Treatise on Episcopacy*, II, p. 47; *Five Disputations*, III, p. 87.
45. *A Treatise on Episcopacy*, I, p. 27.
46. *Five Disputations*, p. 65.
47. *A Treatise on Episcopacy*, II, pp. 100–1.
48. Hunkin, *Episcopal Ordination and Confirmation*, p. 105.
49. *A Treatise on Episcopacy*, I, p. 69.
50. *Five Disputations*, III, pp. 12–21, 31.
51. *A Treatise on Episcopacy*, II, p. 135.
52. *Preface to Church Concord*, 1691.
53. *Reliquiae Baxterianae*, I, p. 146.
54. *Ibid.*, III, p. 38.
55. *Christian Concord*, p. 52.
56. Hunkin, *Episcopal Ordination and Confirmation*, p. 17 et seq.; Carter, *The Anglican via Media*, pp. 96, 188; *A Call for Christian Unity*, pp. 199, 204.
57. Strype, *Grindal*, quoted by Drysdale, *History of the Presbyterians in England*, p. 133.
58. *A Call for Christian Unity*, p. 205; Slosser, *Christian Unity*, p. 89.
59. Slosser, *Christian Unity*, p. 90.
60. Strype, *Annals*, II, p. 71, quoted in Hunkin, *Episcopal Ordination and Confirmation*, p. 16, and Carter, *The Reformation and Re-union*, p. 86.
61. Quoted in Slosser, *Christian Unity*, p. 84.
62. Burnet, *Vindication*, pp. 84–5, quoted in Carter, *The Reformation and Re-union*, p. 180.
63. *Five Disputations*, p. 179.

64. Clarendon, *Continuation of his Life*, p. 1077.
65. *Christian Concord*, p. 58.
66. *Reliquiae Baxterianae*, App. II, p. 23.
67. *A Treatise on Episcopacy*, II, p. 232.
68. 'Second Memorandum on the Status of the Existing Free Church Ministry, 19th June 1925'; Bell, *Documents on Christian Unity*, vol. 2, p. 83.
69. *Reliquiae Baxterianae*, App. IV, p. 69.
70. *Ibid.*, II, p. 426.
71. *Five Disputations*, p. 418.
72. *Reliquiae Baxterianae*, II, p. 428.
73. *Ibid.*, II, p. 157.
74. *Five Disputations*, p. 410.
75. *Reliquiae Baxterianae*, II, p. 159.
76. *Ibid.*, II, p. 160; *Practical Works*, vol. 1, 'Christian Directory', p. 687.
77. *Works*, vol. 1, p. 705.
78. *Ibid.*, vol. 1, p. 705.
79. *Five Disputations*, p. 416.
80. *Reliquiae Baxterianae*, App. IV, p. 69.
81. *Ibid.*, II, p. 231, 'Against the Revolt to a Foreign Jurisdiction' (1691).
82. *Ibid.*, App. IV, p. 69.
83. *The Reformed Pastor*, p. 298.
84. *Reliquiae Baxterianae*, III, p. 131.
85. *Ibid.*, III, p. 67.
86. Vaughan, *English Nonconformity*, 1862, p. 218.
87. 'Key for Catholicks' (1659), preface, p. 6.
88. 'A Defence of the Principles of Love' (1671), p. 52, quoted in Powicke, *Richard Baxter*, vol. 1, p. 257.
89. *Works*, vol. 4, 'Catholic Unity', pp. 668–9.
90. *Ibid.*, p. 681.
91. *Ibid.*, p. 687.
92. *Reliquiae Baxterianae*, II, p. 211.
93. Morgan, *The Nonconformity of Richard Baxter*, pp. 207–9.
94. *Works*, vol. 4, 'True Catholic, and Catholic Church Described', p. 747. See also 'Catholic Unity', pp. 649–51, 668–71, 677.
95. *Ibid.*, 'True Catholic, and Catholic Church Described', pp. 757, 745.
96. *Ibid.*, 'True and Only Way of Christian Concord, p. 705.
97. *Ibid.*, 'True Catholic, and Catholic Church Described', p. 758.
98. *Ejection of 1662 and the Free Churches*, p. 34.

CHAPTER II

# EARLY PROTESTS AGAINST UNIFORMITY

1. *In Elizabeth's Reign*

BY THE ELIZABETHAN SETTLEMENT, the attempt was made to include all parties in the Church of England, all except obdurate Romanists or those Protestants who were determined upon a reformation on the complete Genevan pattern. The Queen herself decided this policy of preserving a balance between the parties.

When the Act of Uniformity of 1559 was passed in the House of Lords, all the bishops present dissented. The total number then deprived of their livings, and representing the Romanist clergy, was 192, including 14 bishops, 13 deans, 14 archdeacons, 15 heads of colleges, 80 rectors of churches. There were 9400 ecclesiastics in England at that time.[1]

Political considerations were the deciding factor in the Elizabethan Settlement, just as in the Restoration Settlement a hundred years later. It was essential in Elizabeth's reign that the nation should be united against any foreign aggressor, and to Elizabeth unity involved uniformity; not only must all men worship in the one Church but their forms of worship must be identical. A secondary motive was the preservation of orderliness in worship. 'Upon this fatal rock of uniformity in things merely indifferent, in the opinion of the imposers, was the peace of the Church of England split.... The rigorous pressing of this Act was the occasion of all the mischiefs that befell the Church for above eighty years.'[2]

The year 1562 marks the beginning of opposition in the Church to the Queen and the Court party. A proposal in the Lower House of Convocation to abolish compulsion in the use of the surplice, kneeling at Communion, the cross in Baptism, and the ring in marriage, was lost by only one vote. This significant meeting took place in the chapter house of St Paul's. Of those present, 43 favoured the proposal for abolition of compulsion and 35 opposed, but with the counting of proxies the motion was lost by 58 votes to 59. Such was the strength of reforming feeling even when it was known that the Queen was opposed to any freedom in these matters.

Fervent reformers objected to the vestments and ceremonies which had been used in the Roman Church as evidences of continued Popish practices. These reformers were evidently a considerable body of the English bishops and clergy; and they represented the beliefs and usages of the Protestants of Scotland, Geneva, and Calvinistic Churches elsewhere.

Many clergy were deprived of their livings after 1562; one was Miles Coverdale, once Bishop of Exeter and translator of the Scriptures. These Churchmen had a programme of reform resembling the desire of those ejected in 1662. They contended that bishops should not have the sole exercise of discipline, and they complained that bishops and lay chancellors were using powers given by the Canon Law of the Pope, not by Scripture. They advocated the guarding of the Lord's Table against unworthy communicants. Freedom should be allowed in the use of the liturgy, and responses to the prayers made optional. There should be more preaching. Objection was made to lessons from the Apocrypha, fasting in Lent, saints' days, trading on the sabbath, the use of godparents, bowing at the name of Jesus, early confirmation, enforcing kneeling at Communion, the surplice, the ring in marriage, and the cross in Baptism. All these proposals emanated from clergy as anxious to remain within the Church of England and to accept modified episcopacy as Baxter and his party were a hundred years later.

In 1571 the Subscription (Thirty-nine Articles) Act—for the Reformation of Disorders in the Ministers of the Church (13 Elizabeth cap. 12)—was passed.[3] This recognized the validity of the orders of those who had not been instituted or consecrated according to the Edwardian Act of Uniformity. Although this was intended for the benefit of Roman priests whose orders existed before the Act of Edward VI, it was evidently designed also to enable, and actually did enable, ministers ordained abroad while exiled during the reign of Mary to receive appointment under Elizabeth without reordination. The only requirement was that ministers subscribed to the Articles and gave their assent before Christmas 1571. This Act was passed against the wishes of the Queen. Here, surely, was ground for the expectation that episcopal ordination would not be absolutely required in England.

In 1570 Thomas Cartwright had to vacate his chair as Lady Margaret Professor of Divinity at Cambridge because of his advocacy of innovations in Church government. The clergy at Northampton in 1571 set up lectures—'prophesyings'—which Cartwright's friends and all Puritans favoured. This was done with the approval of Bishop Scambler of Peterborough. As the practice began to spread the Queen insisted upon the suppression of this 'nursery of Puritanism'.

The first 'presbytery' was not established until 1572 at Wandsworth. Even then it was not a synod or presbytery in the full Presbyterian system, but a 'parochial eldership' of eleven elders desiring the promotion of godliness in the parish by guarding the Lord's Table against the unworthy.

'An Admonition to Parliament' (1572) requested permission to practise Church discipline. It was known that many members of this Parliament were in sympathy with Puritan ideals. The only result of this approach, however, was the prompt imprisonment in Newgate of two ministers concerned in the petition. The Queen's Edict against Prophesying followed in 1577. Elizabeth had stated that 'she would suppress the Papistical religion that it should not grow, and she would root out Puritanism and the favourers thereof'.

Archbishop Grindal, who had succeeded Parker in 1575, refused to carry out the Queen's policy against preaching. Although he said that ten bishops in his province supported him in disobeying the Queen, he was suspended until he died, six years later, in 1583. Whitgift, always the stern foe of the Puritans, became Archbishop and received the Queen's charge 'to restore the discipline of the Church and the uniformity established by law which through the connivance of some prelates and the obstinacy of the Puritans is run out of square'. As many as sixty-four ministers were suspended in one county (Norfolk) by the High Commission Court, Whitgift's instrument for repression. His 'Articles' insisted upon the use of the whole of the Prayer Book and the acceptance of the sections of the Thirty-nine Articles relating to Church government. Burleigh and other councillors, as well as Puritan sympathizers in Parliament, opposed Whitgift's policy with no avail.

In 1584 a Bill was introduced into Parliament requiring only the doctrinal Articles for subscription according to the Act of 1571, and not those concerning Church government, and disallowing suspensions of ministers except for doctrinal heresy or misconduct. When many petitions were sent to Parliament supporting this Bill, the Queen ordered Parliament not to meddle in matters which (she declared) related to her spiritual supremacy. In the same way, when a Bill was introduced in 1586 for permitting variations in the Prayer Book, the Queen forbade discussion, sent Peter Wentworth and other members to the Tower, and told the Speaker to inform Parliament 'that she was already settled in her religion and would not begin again, that changes in religion were dangerous, and that it was not reasonable for them to call in question the established religion'.

The national peril from Spain, plots against the Queen's life, and the foolishness of some of the reformers themselves brought support to the Queen's side. The Martin Marprelate Tracts (1588–89) injured the cause of reform by their violence against the bishops.

A servile Parliament passed the Act of 1593 inflicting penalties even to death for denying the Queen's complete powers in ecclesiastical affairs. Two Brownists, extreme Independents, were executed for denying the royal supremacy. In 1589 Bancroft, future Archbishop of Canterbury (1604–10), began to claim divine right for episcopacy and the necessity for the subjection of presbyters to bishops. The policy of uniformity was supported by influential Erastians who upheld the domination of the Church by the State. It seemed that uniformity was triumphant, but protests were not entirely silenced.

## 2. *Under James I*

Everyone in England had known what Elizabeth's ecclesiastical policy had been, but at the outset there was much doubt about what the first Stuart King would do. Some expected the son of Mary Queen of Scots to be indulgent towards Papists; no one was to know that he would have reasons of State—the appeasement of Spain—for relaxing penal laws against them. English Puritans hoped that a king from Presbyterian Scotland would be approachable and, maybe, responsive to their appeals for reform; but little did they know the real nature of James.

In Scotland he may have been dissembling when he said that

Scotland had 'the purest Kirk in the world', and when he called the English Prayer Book 'an evil-said Mass', the English bishops 'papistical bishops', and their copes and ceremonies 'badges of Popery'. In actual fact, he could hardly conceal his growing dislike of the Presbyterian system with its dogmatic claims. Andrew Melville had presumed to pluck his sleeve and call him 'God's silly vassal!' He was not likely to forget Melville's burning words:

'Sir, I must tell you, there are two kings and two kingdoms in Scotland; there is King James, the head of this commonwealth, and there is Christ Jesus, the King of the Church, whose subject James the Sixth is, and of whose kingdom he is not a king nor a lord, nor a head, but a member.... You are not the head of the church; you cannot give us that eternal life which we seek for even in this world, and you cannot deprive us of it. Permit us then freely to meet in the name of Christ, and to attend to the interests of that church of which you are the chief member.'[4]

In an atmosphere not so tense there had been a well-remembered conversation with another Scots minister, David Ferguson:

'David, why may I not have bishops in Scotland as well as they have in England?'

'Yea, sir, ye may have bishops here; but remember ye must make us all bishops, else ye will never content us.... We are Paul's bishops, sir, Christ's bishops.'

'Ye would all be alike,' the King replied. 'Ye cannot abide any to be above you.'

When he became King of England he was surrounded by bishops who were echoing Bancroft's pronouncement upon the 'divine right of bishops'. This accorded well with his own favourite theory of the divine right of kings. His bishops could support his claims to control Church and State, and in both spheres they could be his willing lieutenants. But would the mass of Englishmen be as ready to submit to him, a conceited and unprepossessing foreigner, as to Elizabeth? Where Elizabeth had been disarmingly hungry for popularity and prepared to yield if necessary to retain it, James expected submission from his new subjects as of divine right without doing anything to deserve it.

Almost as soon as James entered his new kingdom he received the first protest against uniformity. The Millenary Petition was not signed by 1000 ministers, not indeed signed at all, but it was presented by no less than 825 ministers. None of them was a Presbyterian, all of them were willing to use the Prayer Book, but they asked for these modifications—the optional wearing of the surplice, no obligation to use the cross in Baptism, the ring in marriage, or a lesson from the Apocrypha. They requested that the terms 'priest' and 'absolution' be corrected, that confirmation be taken away as superfluous, that sabbath-keeping be enforced, that there be 'examination before Communion' (the vital Puritan policy), 'that none be excommunicated without consent of the pastor'. These petitioners expressly declared themselves to be 'neither as factious men affecting a popular party in the Church, nor as schismatics aiming at the dissolution of the state ecclesiastical . . . not desiring a disorderly innovation, but a due and GODLY REFORMATION'.[5]

James was in no mood to receive the Puritans' requests. It was in vain that Bacon, no lover of Puritanism, sagely counselled the King to allow the surplice, the cross, and the ring to be optional, and to permit freedom to omit parts of the Prayer Book. All that James would concede was the calling of the Hampton Court Conference of 1604. To this he summoned nine bishops, seven deans, and three other non-Puritans, together with four Puritan divines. Of these, Dr John Rainoldes was leader, a moderate episcopalian of the type Baxter and Usher represented later, one who himself had declined a bishopric; Sparke had debated with Archbishop Whitgift in 1584; Chadderton and Knewstubs had signed the Presbyterian 'Book of Discipline' (1583), although only Knewstubs had acted upon it. These four divines fairly represented the moderate episcopal party.

For three days James held private conferences with the nineteen prelatists, and only on the fourth and last day were the four Puritan divines called. James took full opportunity to display his theological learning, and chose to regard the requests as though they were novelties and designed to change Church government to the Presbyterian pattern. It was not a Presbyterian demand that pastors should be allowed to examine their people before Communion, but James took it to be anti-episcopal and said the request 'smelt whereunto that tended to make everyone in his cure to be bishop which he liked not of'. The Puritans asked that the clergy should hold meetings every three weeks and that matters not settled in these meetings be referred to the episcopal synod where the bishops and clergy together would decide the issues. It was when Rainoldes mentioned the desirability of the bishop consulting a synod that James interrupted with this outburst :

'If you aim at a Scottish Presbytery, it agreeth as well with monarchy as God and the devil. . . . If once you [the bishops] were out, and they in place, I know what would become of my supremacy. No Bishop, no King. . . . If this be all your party hath to say, I will make them conform themselves, or else will harry them out of the land or else I will do worse.'

The historian Gardiner has commented in grim but amply justified terms : 'In two minutes James had sealed his own fate and that of England for ever.'

Indeed, if these requests had been granted in 1604, the history of the century would have been changed. The Puritans would have remained within the Church; Independency would have become quite insignificant if it had survived at all; Presbyterianism would have been unknown in England; the Church would have had constitutional episcopacy, and there would have been unity without uniformity.

As it was, James was true to his word. Ten ministers who had presented the Millenary Petition were imprisoned. Hundreds were deprived of their livings; the ejections of the century had begun. It was at this time that Archbishop Bancroft visited Andrew Melville in prison in Scotland but found the dauntless Presbyterian leader the accuser as he plucked Bancroft's lawn sleeves, calling them 'Romish rags', and adding : 'I regard you as the capital enemy of all the Reformed Churches in Europe, and as such I will profess myself an enemy to you and your proceedings to the effusion of the last drop of my blood.'

It was Bancroft whose divine right of episcopacy James had enthusiastically endorsed at the Hampton Court Conference—Bancroft who had eulogized that endorsement by kneeling before the King and protesting 'that his heart melted within him with joy' and he 'made haste to acknowledge to Almighty God His singular mercy in giving us such a King as since Christ's time the like he thought had not been seen'.

Without the slightest proof that the Puritans wanted non-episcopal government, James could be satisfied only by the canons of 1604 which declared that anyone affirming episcopacy to be re-

## EARLY PROTESTS AGAINST UNIFORMITY 61

pugnant to the Word should be excommunicated, together with anyone refusing to subscribe to the established forms of worship. The Prayer Book, reviewed and sanctioned by the Convocation of 1604 which drew up those canons, did nothing to meet Puritan objections, except by omitting two lessons from the Apocrypha, adding a few prayers, and giving explanations to the titles 'absolution' and 'confirmation'. The temper of the King was evident in his proclamation issued for the use of the 1604 Prayer Book: 'We do admonish all men that hereafter they shall not expect nor attempt any further alteration in the common and public form of God's service from this which is now established.'[6]

There was a profound fear of Popery reviving in England during the reigns of James I and Charles I. The memories of the Smithfield fires, the great Spanish assault upon England's liberties, and the Gunpowder Plot in 1605, were very vivid. It was believed that the Jesuits were planning rebellion and foreign conquest throughout Europe. No Protestant failed to realize what Roman Catholic ascendancy would involve, and it was believed that, if restored, Roman Catholic bishops would claim the right to approve or disapprove elections to the House of Commons. Fears were intensified when James sought a match for his son with a Spanish princess and when he could hardly be persuaded by the Commons to give any support to his own daughter and son-in-law in Bohemia lest offence be given to Spain. James had told the Spanish Ambassador of his support for Philip's plans 'to reunite Christendom by admitting the Pope as spiritual head of the Church' and his own desire to go 'as near the Roman form as can lawfully be done, for it hath ever been my way to go with the Church of Rome *usque ad aras*'.

The Puritans accused the bishops of lukewarmness towards Continental Protestants during the Thirty Years War (1618-48) as well as for their countenance of opinions and practices in the Church of England regarded as tending Romewards and not Genevawards. They could see the bishops steadily extending their control over the clergy. In 1622 James published 'Directions to Preachers', prohibiting any sermons on the controversial doctrines of election and predestination and any references to 'the power, prerogative and jurisdiction, authority or duty, of sovereign princes'. Obviously, these directions sought to silence Puritan preachers who had been attacking both the new Arminian doctrines popular with the new bishops and the royal policy itself. The wit Selden remarked, twenty years later, with reference to this attitude : 'The Arminians [led by the bishops] who held that we have free will, yet say, when we come to the King, there must be no liberty.'

When Charles succeeded in 1625, he began, in league with Laud, to enforce uniformity more sternly than ever throughout the Church.

## NOTES TO CHAPTER II

1. Luckock, *Studies in the History of the Prayer Book*, pp. 126–36.
2. Neal, *History of the Puritans*, vol. 1, p. 120.
3. Gee and Hardy, *Documents Illustrative of English Church History*, p. 478.
4. McCrie, *Life of Andrew Melville*, p. 181.
5. Luckock, *Studies in the History of the Prayer Book*, pp. 218–19; Gee and Hardy, *Documents Illustrative of English Church History*, p. 511.
6. Gee and Hardy, *Documents Illustrative of English Church History*, p. 515.

CHAPTER III

# LAUDIAN UNIFORMITY ATTEMPTED

## 1. *'Romanizing' Ritual*

IN THE YEAR of Charles I's accession, Pym stated that, under the name of Puritans, Laud 'collecteth the greatest part of His Majesty's true subjects'. Laud was assailing liberty, and, as Pym declared: 'The greatest liberty in the Kingdom is religion.' Another member of the Commons, Hollis, averred with pride, 'Religion is the heart of England, and England is the heart of the Protestant religion in all the other parts of Christendom.'

Laud roused resentment, not just because of his insistence upon every detail of ritual and his inquisitorial control of the parishes, but because he was regarded as a secret agent of Rome. His refusal of a cardinal's hat did not remove suspicion. Charitable views of his motives were not easy when Puritans were being punished for not accepting his 'Romanizing' ritual at the very time that the authority of Rome was reviving in Europe.

Laud deferred to the Pope as the *Principium Unitatis*. He believed the Reformed Churches on the Continent were defective through lack of episcopal ordination. And yet he considered that re-union with Rome would have to wait 'until Rome were other than it is'. Schism he regarded as worse than defective doctrine, and he disagreed with the reformers at many points. Undoubtedly he desired eventual re-union with Rome though he believed he was acting honourably and in loyalty to his position in the Church of England; and he was preparing for this by restoring Roman Catholic usages which went beyond even the disputed forms of the Prayer Book.

Not only Laudian sympathizers today, but those who trace their spiritual ancestry to the Puritans, applaud his work in promoting reverence and seemliness in Church worship. His motives were the purest when he prevented sacred buildings being used for secular meetings and the Holy Table being used for purposes other than the administration of Holy Communion

Laud believed firmly that 'Ceremonies are the hedges that fence the substance of religion from all the indignities which profaneness and sacrilege too commonly put upon it.' Another Caroline divine said that the Church of England was between 'the meretricious gaudiness of the Church of Rome and the squalid sluttery of fanatic conventicles'! Certainly Laud's full wrath fell upon 'the squalid sluttery'! He remarked: 'This is the misery, 'tis a superstition now-a-days for any man to come with more reverence into a church than a tinker and his bitch come into an ale-house. . . . All that I laboured for in this particular was that the external worship of God in this Church might be kept up in UNIFORMITY AND DECENCY AND SOME BEAUTY OF HOLINESS.'

The new 'Romanizing' ritual Laud introduced included the following (as found by the Committee of the Long Parliament in 1641): the use of candlesticks, crucifixes, and images; bowing to the east; penance; prayers for the dead; private confession; preaching that a sacrifice was offered upon the altar.

The effect of Laud's policy was that the Puritans became defenders of the authorized customs of the Church against Laud's 'innovations'. Unfortunately, their defence was made through the scurrilous attacks of pamphleteers as well as the protests of preachers; the first type suffered physical mutilation by Laud's orders, the second were suspended from their livings. Laud's usual question to clergymen brought before him for not using his ritual was, 'Are you conformable?' To the reply, 'Yes, as far as it is established by law', he would make the rejoinder, 'Are you conformable to the NEW CONFORMITY?'

The 'new conformity' was regarded by the Puritans as 'Romanizing'. Laud's policy was connected in men's minds with the results of Charles's marriage to Henrietta Maria. Her actions in bringing priests from France and setting up her own chapel in the Palace were resented.

When Parliament carried its final resolutions against the King's rule, before its sittings ceased for eleven years in 1629, one member gave his views during the last debate: 'I desire we may look into the belly and bowels of this Trojan horse, to see if there be not even in it ready to open the gates to Romish tyranny, for an Arminian is the spawn of a Papist.' In addition to denouncing Arminianism, a sub-committee of the Parliament a few days before the dissolution of 1629 had given details of the introduction of ceremonies specially prohibited in the Injunctions in Elizabeth's reign, the increase in avowed Roman Catholics, and the appointment of bishops with Romanist sympathies. Some Churchmen like Bishop Mainwaring had actually gone over to Rome; and re-union with Rome was being advocated by Bishop Montague and Secretary Windebank.

Falkland, friend of the future Earl of Clarendon, declared that the Laudian bishops' aim was 'to try how much of a Papist might be brought in without Popery, and to destroy as much as they could of the Gospel without bringing themselves into danger of being destroyed by the law'. In the debate on the Grand Remonstrance in 1641, Falkland said that the Laudian bishops were 'so absolutely, directly, and cordially Papists that it is all that £1500 a year can do to keep them from confessing it'. Evelyn, always an opponent of Puritans and the most loyal of Churchmen throughout the Interregnum, wrote of the 'general design which the Jesuited party of the Papists ever had and still have to ruin the Church of England'.[1] The Puritan Colonel Hutchinson referred with alarm to the appointment of Roman Catholics to positions in the State: 'The foolish Protestants were meditating reconciliation with the Church of Rome. . . . Nothing but the mercy of God prevented the utter subversion of Protestantism in the three Kingdoms.'[2]

The Scot, Samuel Rutherford, may have sounded extreme to some when he said, 'The prelate is both the egg and the nest to cleck [hatch] and bring forth Popery.'[3] Even those who did not suspect Laudianism as tending towards Rome resented the interference of the bishops with liberty.

## 2. *A New Theory of the Church and Episcopacy*

In the Laudian system the diocesan bishop was the 'only governor' and the parish clergy were merely his curates. This was diametrically opposed to the principles Baxter enunciated. Baxter declared that Laud's theory, which maintained that the parish church was not a Church but only part of the Church, was supported by only four or five bishops before 1660.

The Laudian bishops denied Baxter's first principle, the rights of the pastor over his flock. The bishops' courts, with punishments ordered by lay chancellors, as well as episcopal visitations of parishes, supplanted the pastor in ruling the congregations. Preaching was discouraged by the bishops. Uniformity in ritual was enforced. Pastoral discipline was forbidden. With the decline in preaching and the disuse of pastoral authority, ungodliness went on unchecked, the Puritans alleged. One of the evils which troubled Puritans most was the prevalence of sabbath-breaking, and Laud had no sympathy with their feelings in this regard.

From the time that Laud was rebuked at Oxford for stating in his B.D. thesis that episcopacy was the *esse* of the Church and for asserting that the Continental non-episcopal Churches were not true Churches, he had emphasized the position of the bishop as the guarantor of orthodoxy and the symbol of unity. Far from the bishop being the symbol of unity, a modern writer (Dr Vincent Taylor) has said that the shadow of a bishop falls across every wound in the Body of Christ.

Laud's theories of the Church and episcopacy were regarded as dangerous innovations, not held by most of the early Elizabethan bishops. Hooker had contended for episcopacy only as of the *bene esse* of the Church. The canons of 1604 had included the non-episcopal Church of Scotland as equally a part of the Holy Catholic Church with the Church of England. Laud, on the other hand, appointed bishops who supported the divine right of episcopacy and who regarded Rome as a true Church because it was episcopal and the Reformed Churches as not true Churches if they were not episcopal.

The extent to which Laud had departed from the friendly attitude English Protestants had cultivated with Continental Reformed Churches for nearly a century could be seen in his forbidding Englishmen from attending Calvinistic and non-episcopal churches on the Continent. He even endeavoured to deprive the Huguenots and Flemings in England of the rights of worship granted them when they had sought asylum in England, unless they accepted his new conformity in worship.

Laud's full opportunity to demonstrate his policy came with his appointment as Archbishop of Canterbury in 1633. Had James been alive he would have curbed Laud's zeal. He had spoken of Laud as one who 'loves to toss and change, and to bring things to a pitch of reformation floating in his own brain, which may endanger the steadfastness of that which is in a good pass'. Charles supported Laud, marking 'Orthodox' or 'Puritan' against the names of clergy on Laud's lists to indicate the promotion or disgrace they merited.

The rift between the Laudian clergy and the Parliamentary party was widening. This party was quick to see that Laudian bishops who preached in favour of the King's arbitrary claims to levy taxation were equally determined to exercise their own arbitrary control over parish ministers.

It was apparent that the key to Laud's policy was the AUTHORITY OF EPISCOPACY. This also, to many, seemed an innovation. Archbishop Whitgift had denied that any form of Church government was commanded in the New Testament. Even when opposing Cartwright's claim for the divine right of Presbyterianism Whitgift had relied only on expediency ('I deny that Scripture has set down any one certain form of Church-government to be perpetual. . . . The government of the Church must be according to the form of government in the commonwealth.'). That most learned layman, Bacon, had argued for episcopacy only because it was 'as much more convenient for kingdoms than parity of ministers and government by synods'. Laud went far beyond them all. A modern writer, John Morley, has seen that in this theory of episcopacy lay the secret of Laudianism :

> 'Vestments and ceremonial . . . all these and similar things were matter of passionate discussion, veiling grave differences of faith under what look like mere triflings about indifferent form. But the power and station of the bishop, his temporal prerogative, his coercive jurisdiction, his usurping arrogance, his subservience to the Crown, were what made men's hearts hot within them.'[4]

Baxter shrewdly perceived that Laud was driving a wedge between the episcopal party and the Puritans and also between the English Church and the foreign Reformed Churches, and doing this by two requirements : uniformity in worship and submission to episcopal authority. In point of fact, Laudianism triumphed in 1662 by the enforcement of these two principles. Baxter correctly represented the Laudian position in these words :

> 'To make up one member of any . . . Church . . . he must subscribe, and conform, not only in point of judgment to their Confession of Faith, but in point of practice also to all their rules, orders, and usages, in preaching, praying, administration of the Sacraments, and all external rites and ceremonies pre-

scribed by public authority ... which if any man ... refuse to do, he cannot be of such and such a national church. ... You must make me mad, or unacquainted with mankind, before you make me believe that a whole kingdom will ever be so perfect in judgment, or so much of the same temper &c. as to be all of ONE MIND IN EVERY WORD, CIRCUMSTANCE, CEREMONY AND MODE OF WORSHIP, AND DISCIPLINE.'[5]

Laudian prelacy itself would not have been disapproved so widely by Puritans if it had not become the instrument for enforcing rigid uniformity. The High Commission became the chief means for carrying out this policy. Particular objection was taken to the *ex officio* oath by which an accused person was compelled to give evidence and be liable to conviction on his own testimony. The detestation in which the High Commission was held was reflected in the words of the Grand Remonstrance in Parliament (1641, cl. 52): 'The High Commission grew to such excess of sharpness and severity as was not much less than the Romish Inquisition.'

In the episcopal visitations penalties were inflicted for all deviations from Laud's policy. The Table was not allowed to remain in the nave but was removed to the east and placed behind a rail. 'Lectures' were suppressed, even if these had been endowed by companies or by local gentry. Churchwardens were punished, clergy were suspended. The father of John Howe was suspended from his curacy for praying 'that the young prince might not be brought up in Popery'[6] (a reference to the future Charles II and his mother, Henrietta Maria). One of Laud's bishops, Wren, deprived sixty clergy of their livings in his diocese of Norwich in two years.

The fact that these persecutions by bishops and the High Commission and Star Chamber courts occurred during the eleven years of absolute government (1629–40) rankled in the minds of Parliamentarians. It is not surprising that when the King was forced to call Parliament at last, Laud's work was summarily ended.

During those eleven years 20,000 Englishmen had emigrated to America, 'sober, peaceable and truly conscientious sons of the Church of England', not Separatists like the Puritan Fathers who had cried, 'Farewell, Babylon; farewell, Rome' when they left England. These 20,000 Puritans were men anxious to remain within the Church of England who cried, when they sailed, 'Farewell, dear England; farewell, Church of God in England, and all Christian friends there. We do not go to New England as Separatists from the Church of England though we cannot but separate from CORRUPTIONS in it.'

One of the remarkable results of the Laudian policy was the opposition it had aroused among laymen. The Puritan practices of constant preaching, catechizing, Bible-reading and family worship developed a laity well versed in Scriptural doctrines and zealous for the soundness of the Church. It was among Puritan laymen in Parliament that opposition to Laud became most pronounced.

Laud had used secular penalties inflicted by lay chancellors. Bishops had been given secular positions and were powerful at Court. This added to their unpopularity with the gentry smarting under the royal despotism. Perhaps the climax to the growth of episcopal presumption was the granting by Convocation of subsidies to Charles to wage war against the Scots when the Short Parliament of 1640 had refused to help him. It was not without reason that the Scottish Wars were called the Bishops' Wars.

### 3. *The Beginning of the Bishops' Wars*

When visiting Scotland in 1617 Laud had declared that there was 'no religion at all that I could see'—because of the absence of the ritual that was the essence of religion in his opinion. He had desired James at once to force the Scots into conformity with the rites of the English Church, but the King had shrewdly observed, 'He knows not the stomach of that people. . . . On my soul, he will repent it.' [7]

It is true that James had always desired 'to make that stubborn Kirk stoop more to the English pattern', but he had acted cautiously. Scotland had been obliged to accept a nominal episcopacy in 1610, but the bishops did little more than preside at synods. Lay members were no longer allowed to sit in the presbyteries. The Articles of Perth in 1618 permitted kneeling at Communion and other forms abhorred by the Scots but these 'ceremonies' were observed by very few. James would not go beyond these efforts.

Pinning his faith as ever to uniformity in ritual, Laud determined to enforce this and also to establish complete episcopal control of the Scottish Church. In 1637 the blow fell. The new Book of Canons and Service Book, though issued by the Scottish bishops, was actually the work of Laud and his bishops and had the approval of Charles. The King could not have more deeply affronted national sentiment than by introducing this book without any reference to the General Assembly or the Scottish Parliament. This was followed by a riotous refusal to accept the book and the drawing up of the National Covenant. Practically the whole Scottish nation believed, in the words of the National Covenant, 'that the innovations have no warrant of the Word of God and do sensibly tend to the re-establishing of the Popish religion and tyranny'; and they were resolved not to 'countenance the surplice, the attire of the mass priest' or to 'hear the reading of the new fatherless Service Book filled with Popish errors'.[8]

The Covenant in Scotland was the first organized protest against Laudianism and the tyranny of Charles. The General Assembly met, deposed the Scottish bishops, annulled the Acts of Assembly since 1618, denounced Laud and all his works, and triumphantly re-established complete Presbyterianism.

The inevitable result was war between Charles and Scotland, the Bishops' Wars, as it was popularly styled. The English soldiery were half-hearted, readier to kill any officers suspected of Popery than to meet the Scots. Charles, realizing the futility of the enterprise, called the Short Parliament in April 1640 to provide him with financial assistance for the war. Parliament refused. It was now that the English bishops thought to support the King's cause that was so clearly their own. Not only did Convocation vote six subsidies, taxing the English clergy 'for the supply of His Majesty', but ordered a prayer in which the Scots were called 'rebels' to be read in all English churches. The sitting of Convocation itself was illegal as Parliament had been dissolved in less than one month and Convocation had no authority to sit after the dissolution.

Convocation also drew up the ill-famed canons of 1640 in which it was stated to be an offence to bear arms against the King; this was stigmatized as resistance to the powers ordained of God. The most notorious of the canons was the sixth containing the *Et Cetera* Oath by which clergy were ordered to swear 'never to give consent to alter the government of this Church by Archbishops, Bishops, Deans and Archdeacons, ET CETERA'. This dragnet clause was held by Puritans to include the acceptance of lay chancellors and the whole repressive administration of Laudian episcopacy. The Long Parliament eventually declared this Book of Canons null and void, but not before the majority of the clergy had refused outright to take the *Et Cetera* Oath.

The significance of the canons of 1640 is that the bishops' requirements were made in similar terms at the Restoration; all clergy had to take an oath asseverating the unlawfulness of bearing arms against the King and vowing not to attempt the alteration of anything in the government of the Church of England by diocesan bishops. Thus the doctrines of passive obedience and diocesan episcopacy finally succeeded after 1660.

4. *The Long Parliament's Policy towards the Laudian Church*

As matters of Church policy were to divide the Long Parliament in little more than a year it is important to notice the distribution of parties in the Church of England in 1640:

(1) The High Church party (those more or less sympathetic towards Laud), which has been estimated by Masson to number 4000 out of 9000 clergy with only a very small section of the laity.

(2) A large body of opinion advocating various forms of modified episcopacy, perhaps 4000 clergy, and very many laymen. This estimate supports Baxter's contention concerning the strength of the moderate episcopal party. The laymen included many of those members of Parliament who afterwards rallied to the King's side in the War but were in favour of drastic limitations being placed upon the bishops' powers.

(3) Various sections entirely antagonistic to episcopal government, totalling about 1000 of the clergy, with a powerful section of the laity, especially in London and the eastern counties. Some of these were already resolved to advocate Presbyterianism, influenced by the example of Scotland, and they were dubbed by their opponents 'the Scotizing English'. A few others were gradually associating themselves with Independency. Most of them, however, were like Cromwell who said, 'I can tell you what I would NOT have; though I cannot, what I would.'

The few Roman Catholics were mostly in the north and west. Queen Henrietta Maria had not helped the King's cause by issuing a proclamation in her own name in April 1640 calling upon Roman Catholics in the north of England to provide funds for war against the Scots.

The King was desperately in need of funds. As soon as the Long Parliament was called in November 1640 it began discussing the state of the Church. There was almost complete unanimity in removing the worst features of Laudianism. The victims of the High Commission were released. The High Commission and Star Chamber Court were abolished. The Convocation of 1640 was declared illegal, its canons were annulled, and action was taken against thirteen bishops who were held responsible. Commissioners were appointed to direct the removal of altars and images. A committee was set up to deal with 'scandalous' ministers and those guilty of Laudian innovations. And Laud was imprisoned.

We may think today that the Puritan fear of a Romish revival was exaggerated, but Pym and the leaders of the Long Parliament opposed Laud's innovations because they regarded them as a bridge to Popery. 'Laud had revived anti-episcopalianism in England, not now as an ecclesiastical ideal, but as a political and religious necessity. In 1640 it required an effort of memory or imagination to picture a Bench of truly Protestant Bishops. . . . Episcopacy had defenders in the Long Parliament, but the Bishops themselves had none.' [9]

At the outset the Long Parliament did not think of doing more than curtailing the bishops' powers. If the Laudian clergy had acquiesced in Parliament's orders against ritualism, and if the bishops had agreed to surrender their secular powers including their seats in the House of Lords, episcopacy itself would not have been assailed. Clarendon states that at first there was NOT ONE PRESBYTERIAN in the Long Parliament. It was feared that the King would dissolve the Parliament, annul its ecclesiastical reforms, and resume his arbitrary rule at the first opportunity; and he would have the ready assistance of the Laudian bishops in doing this.

5. *Uprooting Episcopacy 'Root and Branch' the Next Step?*

Skirmishes against episcopacy were beginning in various quarters. The Scottish Treaty Commissioners were in London, with their army on English soil reinforcing their influence. Alexander Henderson and his colleagues were using their pulpit oratory in London churches to extol the glories of a Scriptural Presbyterian system. Five London clergymen united their initials to form the *nom de plume* 'Smectymnuus' in publishing an address to the Parliament in favour of establishing Presbyterianism as the State Church of England. Some of these five were famous in the Westminster Assembly and in the Savoy Conference in 1661—Stephen Marshall, Edmund Calamy, Thomas Young, Matthew Newcomen, William Spurstow. John Milton, whose old tutor (Thomas Young) was one of the five, was busy using his 'left hand' in vigorous prose supporting the new movement. In his pamphlets he described a bishop as a 'belly-god, proud and covetous', Lucifer as 'the first prelate angel', and the Prayer Book as 'the skeleton of a mass-book'. Such vituperation was bound to defeat itself.

An indication of the antipathy towards the bishops could be seen in petitions for the abolition of episcopacy, the most noteworthy being the 'Root and Branch' Petition from London, with 15,000 signatures (11th December 1640), which declared:

'The offices and jurisdictions of Archbishops, Bishops . . . being the same way of Church-government which is in the Roman Church, and which was in England in the time of Popery, little change thereof being made . . . and other Reformed Churches having upon their rejection of the Pope cast the prelates out also as members of the beast. . . .'

The petitioners complained also that the bishops and their party believed 'that the Church of Rome is a true Church and in the worst times never erred in fundamentals'.

Parliament at this time was unwilling to accede to such a sweeping request for the abolition of episcopacy. The best defence of bishops that Lord Digby, an upholder of episcopacy, could make was thus expressed:

'Let us not destroy Bishops, but make them such as they were in PRIMITIVE TIMES. . . . Do their Courts and subordinations offend? Let them be brought to govern as in the primitive times, by ASSEMBLIES OF THEIR CLERGY. Doth their intermeddling in SECULAR [affairs?] EXCLUDE them from the capacity.'[10]

This shows the general support for modifying episcopacy in the manner that Baxter always advocated.

However, it is also significant that Lord Digby saw a danger in what might follow the abolition of episcopacy itself. 'If we hearken to those who would quite extirpate Episcopacy I am confident that instead of every Bishop we should put down in a Diocese, we should ERECT A POPE IN EACH PARISH.'[11]

John Pym, the mighty leader of the Commons, was not opposed to episcopacy entirely at this stage. In the debate on the 'Root and Branch' Petition on 8th February 1641 he said:

> 'He thought it was not the intention of the House to abolish either Episcopacy or the Book of Common Prayer, but to REFORM both wherein offence was given to the people; and that if that could be effected . . . they should do a work such as had not been done since the Reformation.'[12]

A better indication of the general Puritan feeling than 'Smectymnuus' or the 'Root and Branch' Petition was the Ministers' Petition and Remonstrance, a document signed by moderate Puritan clergymen, numbering between 700 and 800. This gave practical as well as moderate proposals for reforming episcopacy and shows a striking parallel to Baxter's writings. Baxter was then a very young clergyman and not concerned with these movements. It is well to note carefully the resemblances between these statements in the Ministers' Petition and Remonstrance in 1641 and Baxter's pronouncements in 1660–61, namely that bishops should not have the SOLE power of ordination and jurisdiction; the bishops' dioceses were too large; bishops should not be the sole pastors of their dioceses leaving pastors to be merely their curates; bishops should not have the sole power of confirming; and there should not be any imposition of an oath of canonical obedience nor the requirement of acceptance of every detail of the Prayer Book. These requests came, not from Presbyterians or Separatists, but from a large body of loyal Churchmen of the moderate episcopal party.

The first reform proposed in Parliament was the removal of bishops from the House of Lords. The Bishops' Exclusion Bill was passed by the Commons on 10th March 1641, but the House of Lords delayed and obstructed the measure. In the meantime anti-episcopal feeling was rising, particularly in the politically powerful City of London. The bishops had only themselves to blame for this.

Three days after the House of Lords, at last, had rejected the Bishops' Exclusion Bill on 27th May 1641, Sir Edward Dering introduced the 'Root and Branch' Bill in the House of Commons. Pym and Hampden, with their friends, were now turning against the bishops because of what had occurred in the House of Lords. In consequence the Abolition of Episcopacy Bill was carried on the second reading in the Commons by 139 votes to 108. In the debate Vane denounced the episcopal system in these words: 'The whole fabric of the building is so rotten and corrupt from the very foundation of it to the top, that if we pull it not down now it will fall about the ears of all those that endeavour it within a very few years.'

Falkland's conclusion was that 'those who hated the Bishops hated them worse than the devil, and those who loved them did not love them as well as their dinner'. The defence of episcopacy was made in a lukewarm spirit. It is true that many of those who voted to abolish episcopacy did so through pique because the bishops had influenced the House of Lords to refuse to remove them from their seats. Nevertheless, in this debate can be seen the line of demarcation between the two parties; those who defended bishops then became the Royalist party in the Civil War. However, the 'Root and Branch' Bill did not receive the royal assent.

It was also Vane who brought forward striking proposals to substitute virtually lay control of the Church for episcopal government. His 'Puritan State Church' would have been controlled by lay Parliamentary commissioners. This thoroughly Erastian scheme bore no resemblance, of course, to Presbyterianism.

Although Vane's scheme remained only an academic suggestion, it merits mention because of some similarities to Baxter's plan. Every shire was to be a diocese. A presbytery of twelve divines was to assist the president (bishop) in each diocese. Ordination, suspension, and excommunication would necessitate the action of the president and seven of the divines. The president was to be chosen by the King from three names presented by the clergy. A diocesan synod was to be held annually, and a national synod every three years, this consisting of all the presidents and certain elected presbyters.

In the religious excitement and confusion that prevailed, the Parliamentary Puritans began to make tactical errors. Detailed legislation was enacted by the Commons in August and September 1641 directing the removal of rails, pictures, and images—and this without the consent of the House of Lords. Disputes took place in many parishes. Then the Prayer Book itself was brought in question; Clarendon believed it was about to be suppressed. When, long after the Civil War had broken out, Parliament banned the Prayer Book it made its worst blunder, and one that was inconsistent with the pleas for religious freedom. Thousands were willing to bleed for the Prayer Book although they would not lift a finger to defend the bishops.

Soon there was news that threw the Parliament into greater dismay. The Irish Rebellion and the inflated lists of the massacres of Protestants convinced even the most moderate that there was a widespread Popish conspiracy. It was believed that the Queen, if not Charles also, had been privy to the Rebellion. The Irish rebels indeed called themselves the Queen's Army.

Faced with mounting difficulties, Pym determined upon the Grand Remonstrance (22nd November 1641) that would inform the nation of Parliament's position. In this document Parliament disclaimed any intention of 'letting loose the golden reins of discipline and government in the Church' or giving a general toleration of sects. A system of Church government conformable to Scripture should be considered by a special synod of divines; and that system would then become the established Church. 'Root and Branch' supporters were once more found on the opposite side to the defenders of episcopacy in the debate. The Grand Remonstrance passed by 159 to 148 after one of the most heated scenes in the long history of the Commons.

When replying to the Grand Remonstrance, and on other occasions, Charles refuted the charges that he favoured Popery. He also defended episcopacy, which he was prepared 'to maintain not only against all innovations of Popery, but also from the irreverence of... schismatics and Separatists'. Clarendon complained that Pym exaggerated the influence of Papists in the Court; and in Parliament he said: 'Papists were the butt against whom all arrows were directed.'[13] Certainly, vehement attacks upon episcopacy as being a form of Popery brought support from moderate men to the bishops' side and the King's.

Episcopacy was still nominally the system in the Church as the 'Root and Branch' Bill which had been passed by the Commons had been abandoned. There was no agreement about the form of government to be substituted and the general dilemma is seen in the remarks of Sir Edward Dering (who had proposed the 'Root and Branch' Bill) during the debate on the Grand Remonstrance :

'Mr Speaker, there is a certain newborn, unseen, ignorant, dangerous, desperate way of Independency. Are we for this Independent way? Nay, sir. Are we for the elder brother of it, the Presbyterian form? I have not yet heard any one gentleman within these walls stand up and assert his thought for either of these ways.' [14]

This is a remarkable indication of the position in the Commons in November 1641, after twelve months' debates upon Church government.

The Bishops' Exclusion Bill was again pressed upon the Lords. It was carried only after Bishop Williams and other prelates had refused to attend the House and had foolishly protested against anything being carried in their absence, their excuse being the brawling mobs outside Parliament. Their action resulted in their imprisonment. Eight days after the Lords passed the Bill Charles felt obliged to give the royal assent (13th February 1642). It was at this time of feverish excitement that the incident of the five members inflamed passions still higher against the King and his supporters.

When the Civil War followed, Baxter declared : 'It was a Parliament of Episcopals and Erastians and not of Presbyterians, who first took up arms in England against the King.'[15] Nearly all the officers of the Parliamentary army were at first, Baxter said, 'Episcopal by profession.' And yet, Baxter added, 'The Bishops themselves have been the grand cause of our church divisions and separations.'

### 6. *Moderate Episcopal Concessions in 1641 resembling Puritan Demands in 1661*

Before the Civil War broke out some of the bishops had offered concessions which might have preserved the unity of the Church and restored its fully Protestant character on the basis of moderate episcopacy. Similar concessions were treated with scant courtesy by the Laudian bishops in 1661 when they were proposed as part of the ministers' programme of Church reform.

On 1st March 1641 the House of Lords appointed a committee

consisting of thirty lay peers and ten bishops, with others added afterwards. From this number a sub-committee was appointed, with Bishop Williams (Lincoln, afterwards Archbishop of York) presiding. Others were Archbishop Usher (Armagh), Bishop Morton (Durham), Bishop Hall (Exeter). The sub-committee drew up a memorandum of 'Innovations in Doctrine', 'Innovations in Discipline', and 'Considerations upon the Book of Common Prayer'.

Among the ceremonies condemned by these bishops were: making the Holy Table an altar, bowing to the east, placing candlesticks, crucifixes, and images in churches, and making kneeling at Communion compulsory.

The most significant concessions suggested by these bishops were : 'To clear the rubric, how far a minister may repulse a scandalous and notorious from the Communion'; to insert an explanation about kneeling; to insert 'some discreet rubric' explaining the sign of the cross upon infants in Baptism, with the possibility of discontinuing it altogether; to delete lessons from the Apocrypha; to amend the rubric where vestments are commanded; to alter the words of the burial service 'in sure and certain hope of the resurrection to eternal life' into 'knowing assuredly that the dead shall arise again'.

On 3rd May 1641 the House of Commons resolved that these concessions were not sufficient.

Still more important were the schemes of 'Limited Episcopacy' offered by Bishop Williams and Archbishop Usher in 1641.

Bishop Williams continued to oppose the exclusion of bishops from the House of Lords but he was clearly in favour of reform in the Church. He offered limited episcopacy including these features :

1. Every bishop to preach every Lord's Day.

2. No bishop to be a justice of the peace (except the Dean of Westminster, an office Williams himself held!).

3. Every bishop to have twelve assistants, four appointed by the King, four by the Lords, four by the Commons, for jurisdiction and ordination.

4. Bishops to be chosen by the King on the nomination of the twelve assistants, with the dean and chapter.

Hindrances to this plan were the retention of temporal offices by bishops, the possibility of bishops and their 'assistants' not co-operating, and the doubt whether Charles would accept the plan and choose acceptable bishops. That the plan was offered, nevertheless, was remembered. In July 1641 Lord Digby and Bishop Williams actually proposed this Bill 'For regulating Bishops and Episcopal Courts'; but events were moving too fast then, and the Bill was not debated in the Commons.

It is interesting to note that this compromise would have been supported by Clarendon at that time. It might have averted strife if it had been offered before May–July 1641. If the bishops had agreed to it in 1660–61 it could have brought unity to the Church then.

A more famous scheme was Archbishop Usher's 'Reduction of Episcopacy unto the Form of Synodical Government received in the Ancient Church'. Although this plan was not made public until 1655, it should be remembered that in 1641 it was considered by the House of Lords' Committee on Religion; it was proposed again by Usher during the negotiations with the King in the Isle of Wight in 1648; it was discussed between Usher and Baxter in 1655; and it was offered by the Puritans in 1660–61.

Detailed reference will be made to this plan later (see pp. 130–3). Briefly, it was a primitive episcopacy, with a fixed (permanent) *primus* among other bishops, and with synods of presbyters associated regularly with the bishops in all acts of jurisdiction, and with dioceses reduced to the size of counties. It is noteworthy that Martin Bucer, friend of Cranmer, had advocated a similar plan. Such proposals had been in the minds of all Puritans of the moderate episcopal party for years past.

Usher's model was unacceptable to the King and Laudian bishops in 1641. The King might have adopted it in 1648, but the Parliamentary Presbyterians who were dominant then refused it. The restored Laudian bishops in 1661 scorned it.

Laudianism had failed before the Civil War began. Limited episcopacy was not accepted in its place. Now the full Presbyterian system was considered.

## NOTES TO CHAPTER III

1. Evelyn, *Diary*, vol. 2, p. 136.
2. Hutchinson, *Memoirs*, p. 71.
3. Samuel Rutherford, *Letters* (1638), p. 546.
4. Morley, *Oliver Cromwell*, p. 60.
5. *Reliquiae Baxterianae*, III, pp. 133–4.

6. Horton, *Life of John Howe*, p. 3.
7. Masson, *Life and Times of Milton*, vol. 1, p. 318.
8. Samuel Rutherford, *Letters*, p. 440.
9. Trevelyan, *England under the Stuarts*, pp. 202–3.
10. Shaw, *History of the English Church, 1640–1660*, vol. 1, p. 32.
11. *Ibid.*, p. 32.
12. Brett, *John Pym*, p. 180.
13. Clarendon, *History of the Rebellion and Civil Wars*, p. 115.
14. Shaw, *History of the English Church, 1640–1660*, vol. 1, p. 101.
15. *A Treatise on Episcopacy*, II, p. 211.

CHAPTER IV

# PRESBYTERIAN UNIFORMITY ATTEMPTED

FROM 1592 until 1640 Presbyterianism had no existence in England. Cartwright's Presbyterianism had been only a passing phase of Puritanism in the Elizabethan Church—academic, entirely clerical in its support, and established only on a voluntary basis for parish discipline in a few places. Before 1640 those who fell under the wrath of the bishops had been upholders of a limited episcopacy and a modified liturgy or of freedom in the use of the liturgy, or else they had been Separatists.

Pym and the Parliamentary Puritans at the outset of the Long Parliament had wanted Elizabethan episcopacy without the Laudian claims and innovations. Only the Laudian bishops' opposition to the will of Parliament and their support for the King when war broke out made it necessary for another form of Church government to be considered and established. Presbyterianism was not advocated until other plans failed.

Baxter was at great pains to make it clear that Presbyterianism had hardly any supporters in England in the early days of the Civil War. As he knew the country districts fairly well he must be taken as a reliable witness for conditions in a large part of England; but undoubtedly Presbyterianism soon won acceptance with many in London, Lancashire, and parts of the eastern counties. Baxter said:

'Though Presbytery [*i.e.*, Presbyterianism] generally took in Scotland, yet it was but a stranger here; and it found some ministers that lived in conformity to the Bishops, Liturgies and Ceremonies (however they wished for reformation). . . . And though most of the ministers then in England saw nothing in the Presbyterian way of PRACTICE, which they could not cheerfully concur in, yet it was but few that had resolved on their PRINCIPLES. And when I came to try it, I found that most (that ever I could meet with) were AGAINST THE JUS DIVINUM OF LAY

ELDERS, and FOR THE MODERATE PRIMITIVE EPISCOPACY, and for a narrow Congregational or Parochial Extent of ordinary Churches, and for AN ACCOMMODATION OF ALL PARTIES, in order to concord, as well as myself.' [1]

Though the position was becoming increasingly confused, episcopacy was still nominally the established government, and it was not formally abolished by the Commons until 26th January 1643.

Since the Scottish Wars the Scottish Treaty Commissioners, with their attendant Presbyterian ministers, had been in constant touch with English Parliamentarians and Puritan ministers in London. Their greatest wish was to see Presbyterianism adopted in England, but they had to admit that, in the words of Baillie, one of their number, 'As yet a Presbytery to this people is conceived to be a strange monster.' [2]

English Puritans felt that the Scottish Commissioners had come like 'drill-sergeants' to teach them to march in step with the Scots. The Scots' constant fear was that the English might adopt another substitute for diocesan episcopacy. Various sects were spreading with astonishing rapidity in the confusion which pervaded London and other towns. Very soon the Scots detected that they had rivals. Notwithstanding this, the General Assembly of the Church of Scotland in 1642, when replying to the English Parliament's communication soliciting support against the King, expressed the hope that: 'The prelatical hierarchy being out of the way, the work will be easy without forcing of conscience to settle in England the government of the Reformed Kirks by Assemblies.' [3]

Alas for Scottish hopes! If they had truly decided to proceed 'without forcing of conscience' or to allow England to 'embrace a new Form' (in the words of their minister, Alexander Henderson) unity could have been preserved. It was Presbyterian uniformity that they really desired. Such uniformity, but of an Erastian pattern, was ultimately to be attempted when Parliament authorized a Presbyterian State Church in England.

Parliament was now responsible for bringing some semblance of order into a sadly disordered Church. Parliament appointed committees for removing 'scandalous ministers' and for dealing with 'plundered ministers'. Ejections by the bishops had been frequent. Parliament followed the same policy. Vacancies caused by the ejection of clergy regarded as unfit in character or incorrigibly Royalist were filled by ministers, in some cases from abroad or from Scotland, not all of them episcopally ordained. Forms of Presbyterian ordination began, with Parliament's approval. It became clear that intolerance and the enforcement of conformity to authority were not the monopoly of the Laudians.

1. *The Westminster Assembly and the Solemn League and Covenant*

Parliament's method for settling the affairs of religion in England was the calling of the Westminster Assembly, which first met on 1st July 1643. It sat for five and a half years, the total number of sessions being 1163. The Assembly generally met for five days each week, and members were paid four shillings per day for attending. Ten Lords, twenty Commoners, and 119 divines were appointed. Some of these divines were convinced supporters of episcopacy, but the few of these who attended at the beginning left after the Solemn League and Covenant was signed. Several bishops (including Archbishop Usher) were appointed, but only one bishop (Westfield) attended, and he only a few times. The laymen included Pym, Vane, and Selden. One of the two assessors was William White of Dorchester, an ancestor of the Wesleys. Three Scottish lords and four Scottish ministers were members. Five of the English ministers were Independents—Bridge, Burroughs, Nye, Simpson, and Thomas Goodwin. Their number increased before the Assembly concluded, and always their influence was greater than their number. The average attendance at the sessions was sixty.

Baxter gave an important description of the composition of the Assembly:

'Those who made up the Assembly of Divines, and who through the land were the honour of the Parliament party, were almost all such as till then had conformed, and took the ceremonies to be lawful in cases of necessity, but longed to have that necessity removed. . . . The matter of Bishops or no Bishops was not the main thing, except with the Scots, for thousands that wished for GOOD BISHOPS were on the Parliament side. Almost all those afterward called Presbyterians, and all that learned and pious synod at Westminster, except a very few, had been Conformists, and kept up an honourable esteem for those Bishops that they thought religious; as Archbishop Usher, Bishop Davenant, Hall, Morton, &c. Those would have been CONTENT WITH AN AMENDMENT OF THE HIERARCHY. . . . The Assembly of Divines at Westminster were all save eight or nine conformable.'⁴

The Erastian policy of the Parliamentary Puritans was seen at once in the limitation of the Assembly's programme to those matters outlined by Parliament.

It was in this year (1643) that the fortunes of the Roundhead armies had fallen so low that Pym determined to seek military aid from the Scots. Representatives of the Westminster Assembly accompanied Parliamentary commissioners to Scotland. It was expected that the Scots' main demand would be the conformity of England to the Presbyterian model; and it was in anticipation of this that anti-Presbyterians (Vane the Parliamentarian and Nye the Independent minister) sought to reduce the terms of the Solemn League and Covenant, which was the means of cementing the new alliance. In this Covenant the parties promised to extirpate prelacy and to bring the English and Scottish Churches into 'the nearest conjunction and uniformity . . . according to the Word of God and the example of the best Reformed Churches'; these phrases did not commit England to follow Scottish Presbyterianism.

Baxter gives an illuminating summary of the situation:

'This Covenant was proposed by the Parliament to the consideration of the Synod [*i.e.*, the Assembly] at Westminster. The Synod stumbled . . . especially at the word "Prelacy". Dr Burgess the Prolocutor, Mr Gataker, and abundance more declared their judgments to be for Episcopacy even for the ANCIENT MODERATE EPISCOPACY, in which one Stated President, with his Presbytery, governed every Church; though not for the English Diocesan frame, in which one Bishop, without his Presbytery, did by a Lay Chancellor's court, govern all the Presbyters and Churches of a Diocese, being many hundreds . . . . Hereupon grew some debate in the Assembly; some being against every degree of Bishops (especially the Scottish Divines) and others being for a Moderate Episcopacy. But these English Divines would not subscribe the Covenant, till there were an alteration suited to their judgments; and so a parenthesis was yielded to, as describing that sort of Prelacy which they opposed, viz. "That is, Church Government by Archbishops, Bishops, Deans and Chapters, Archdeacons, and all other ecclesiastical officers depending on that Hierarchy".... When the Covenant was agreed on, the Lords and Commons first took it themselves, and Mr Thomas Coleman preached to the House of Lords, and gave it them with this public explication, "that by PRELACY WE MEAN NOT ALL EPISCOPACY, but only the form which is here described".' [5]

Accordingly, on 25th September 1643, the Solemn League and Covenant was taken with great dignity by the Assembly at St Margaret's, Westminster. Parliament ordered that it be subscribed throughout England under penalty of fines. Yet Baxter states that he prevented his people at Kidderminster from taking the Covenant lest, he said, it should ensnare their consciences.

Presbyterian uniformity bid fair to bar the way to unity. Writing long afterwards, Baxter made this comment:

'Above all, I could wish that the Parliament and their more skilful hand, had done more than was done to heal our breaches, and hit upon the right way either to UNITE WITH THE EPISCOPAL AND INDEPENDENTS (which was possible, as distant as they are) or at least had pitched on the terms that are fit for UNIVERSAL CONCORD, and left all to come in upon those terms that would.' [6]

These were wise words and expressed a great ideal; but it was expecting almost too much to suggest a union of all sections during the heat of the Civil War.

Meanwhile the Westminster Assembly debated for many weary months the questions allotted by Parliament. Lay elders were proposed by the Scots as an essential for Presbyterianism:

'This is a point of high consequence, and upon no other we expect so great difficulty, except alone on Independency; wherewith we purpose not to meddle in haste till it please God to advance our army, which we expect will much assist our argument.' [7]

Unfortunately for Scottish hopes, the advance of their army was so tardy as to make Scottish Presbyterianism still less popular.

Parliamentary control over the parishes increased. As 1500 of them were vacant a committee of the Assembly was directed to examine candidates, and county committees of ministers were set up to ordain as an interim measure. It was from the date of the passing of this ordinance arranging for ordinations (2nd October 1644) that many non-episcopally ordained ministers took their authority.

As time went on, the graded church courts of the Presbyterian system were accepted in principle by the Assembly. The first important step in establishing them was the election of elders. A commission of 'Triers' was appointed in August 1645 to test the validity of the elections of elders in London. This election marked the official inauguration of the Presbyterian system in England.

2. *'A lame Erastian Presbytery'*

Parliament was unwilling to hand over unfettered control to the Church. This Parliamentary assumption of power was abhorred by the Scots and the growing number of English Puritan ministers who were accepting Presbyterianism as the only practicable substitute for the discarded diocesan episcopacy.

As lay elderships and presbyteries (classes) were being set up, the question of their powers arose. In the Westminster Assembly the Presbyterians fought for the spiritual independence of the Church. Although the few Independents did not believe in State control they feared still more a rigid Presbyterian discipline, and therefore they supported the limitations Parliament wished to place upon the Church. The crucial provision upon which Parliament was insistent was the right of appeal to Parliament from the church courts. To enumerate certain offences, and retain the decision in regard to those not so enumerated, was Parliament's means of controlling the discipline to be exercised by Presbyterian lay elders.

> 'If any person suspended from the Sacrament of the Lord's Supper shall find himself grieved with the proceeding before the eldership of any congregation, he shall have liberty to appeal to the Classical Assembly, from thence to the Provincial, from thence to the National, and from thence to the Parliament.'[8]

This violated the cardinal principle for which all Puritans like Baxter, and not only orthodox Presbyterians, contended—that the pastor alone should have the power of the keys and be the bishop of the flock. Once again the controversy centred around the question : Who had the power of discipline in the parishes?

Civil commissioners were to be appointed in every county to judge the unenumerated offences, and the elders were to act only upon the commissioners' certificates. This, Baillie declared, was done really to keep down the power of the presbyteries for ever, and hold up the head of the sectaries. The Scottish representatives in the Assembly vigorously protested to Parliament and were supported by the London ministers; but the Common Council of the City of London failed to support them at this critical juncture. Baillie revealed the depths of the Scots' disappointment : 'The leaders of the people seem to be inclined to have but a lame Erastian Presbytery.' [9]

These developments showed that Englishmen were no more willing to give unlimited disciplinary power to a Presbyterian system than to Laudian episcopacy. Parliament had stated that 'it could not agree to the granting of an ARBITRARY AND UNLIMITED POWER . . . to near 10,000 judicatories to be erected within this Kingdom.' [10]

Milton, who represented the sober scholarly Englishmen of the period, at first had hailed Presbyterianism as the only logical and truly scriptural alternative to the repressive Laudian system. In 1641 he had said, 'So little is it I fear lest any crookedness or wrinkle be found in Presbyterial government . . . that every real Protestant will confess it to be the only true Church-government.'

In a few years he saw many 'wrinkles'. He declared that 'New Presbyter is but Old Priest writ large' and assailed Presbyterian uniformity in his strenuous sonnets.

Popular feeling can be seen in a lampoon of 1645 :

'When you shall come with this complaint "Your father, the Bishops, made work grievous, and our parochial Presbyters (those lions' whelps) do add thereto; now do you ease somewhat the grievous servitude and heavy yoke put upon us", you may expect . . . an answer like unto that of Rehoboam's. . . . Instead of one High Commission in the whole Kingdom you shall have ONE IN EVERY PARISH under the name of a Parochial Session, besides the general High Commission called the Common Council of Presbyters. Now have you not to shun the smoke skipped into the fire?' [11]

In 1645 the Assembly's Directory for Public Worship was substituted for the Book of Common Prayer, which had been forbidden even for private use. This Directory gave only general directions for worship, with topics for prayer. The Apocrypha was rejected; the sign of the cross in Baptism and the ring in marriage were discontinued; the altar was changed into the Communion Table in the body of the church so that people might stand or sit before it. Though the Directory allowed freedom through the extensive use of extemporaneous prayer, uniformity again was to be observed. The Directory was compulsory.

One thousand ministers who refused to use the Directory lost their benefices. Altogether, 2000 ministers were ejected for various reasons in the years following 1640—causing a great flood of bitterness that was to return and overwhelm the Puritans at the Restoration. The Parliamentary Puritans had made two egregious blunders—they had banned the Prayer Book, and they had ejected 2000 clergymen. Even though one-fifth of the revenues of livings were secured for the sequestered clergy (a consideration that was not given to the Nonconformists in 1662) the desire for revenge had begun.

The Assembly continued its sittings and finally produced the monumental Westminster Confession, which was not adopted by Parliament and so never became a legal document in the English Church. The catechisms followed, and the Psalms. Presbyterian uniformity allowed no choice even with Psalm-tunes; only those of Rous were permitted.

Another important event occurred in 1645. Ordination by 'Classical Presbyters' was directed by Parliamentary Ordinance (8th November 1645) with a form drawn up by the Assembly in the Directory. In its preamble it said: 'Whereas the words Presbyter and Bishop do in Scripture signify the same function', so it followed that ordination without a diocesan bishop was valid. It was the need for providing for regular ordinations in the counties that induced Parliament at length to arrange for the establishment of classes (presbyteries).

## 3. Presbyterian versus Independent

Another vital question arose in 1645—COMPREHENSION. Could Presbyterians and Independents reach an agreement? To deal with this subject a committee of the Assembly met in the Jerusalem Chamber from 17th November 1645 until 9th March 1646. It was called the Committee of Accommodation and consisted of five peers, sixteen Presbyterian or moderate episcopal ministers, and the Independent members of the Assembly, then numbering six. Had they but realized it they were largely deciding the fate of the English Church. If moderate episcopals, Presbyterians, and Independents had united, they might have formed an enduring comprehensive Church. Or, when diocesan episcopacy returned in 1660, there would have been a united body of Puritans to negotiate with the bishops.

Blame for disunity at this stage rests with the Independents, blame for intolerance with the Presbyterians. When the Committee began to consider a scheme of comprehension, the Independents proposed toleration instead. They claimed the right of their congregations to ordain their own ministers and the freedom of their congregations from the Presbyterian classes, with the right to impose their own voluntary discipline within their congregations. These requests the Presbyterian section flatly refused, as it would have meant a separation from the newly established Presbyterian State Church. The disagreement about toleration was even more disastrous. If only toleration had been admitted, the King's cause and diocesan episcopacy would probably have been lost. Through their divisions and their intolerance the Puritans sealed their own fate.

Baxter made this comment concerning Presbyterians at this time: 'They were so little sensible of their own infirmity that they would not have those tolerated who were not only tolerable but worthy instruments and members in the Churches. The RECONCILERS that were ruled by prudent charity always called out to both the parties, that the CHURCHES MUST BE UNITED UPON THE TERMS OF PRIMITIVE SIMPLICITY, and that we have unity in things necessary, and liberty in things unnecessary, and charity in all; but they could never be heard, but were taken for adversaries to the government of the Church, as they are by the prelates at this day.'[12] Unfortunately, 'reconcilers' were not found at the Westminster Assembly. Baxter, one best deserving of the name 'Reconciler' in his day, was only a young army chaplain and country minister in 1645.

Thus to the two blunders of the Presbyterians (prohibiting the Prayer Book and ejecting 2000 parish clergy) was added the third —the refusal of toleration. The Presbyterians found they had to reckon not with the Independents in the Assembly but with their all-powerful ally, the army.

This year of many changes, 1645, witnessed the formation of the New Model Army. In this standing army, regularly paid and thoroughly disciplined, the Independents were well represented. Not merely orthodox Independents but sectaries of all types were increasing everywhere.

Cromwell had kept free from special denominational affiliations. While the war was going on he had written from the field to Parliament: 'The State in choosing men to serve it takes no notice of their opinions.' During the discussions of Parliament and Assembly, in which the army was soon to join, Cromwell wrote to Colonel Hammond: 'I profess to thee I desire from my heart, I have prayed for it, I have waited for the day to see UNION and right understanding between the godly people (Scots, English, Jews, Gentiles, Presbyterians, Independents, Anabaptists, and all). Our brothers of Scotland (really Presbyterians) were our greatest enemies.' [13]

Cromwell had become the voice of the army in urging the widest toleration. 'I would not be willing to see the day,' he declared, 'when England shall be in the power of the Presbytery to impose upon the conscience of others that profess faith in Christ.'

Toleration had been denounced by strict Presbyterians as the 'Great Diana' of the Independents. The Scots, especially, called the sects a hydra-headed monster, and toleration a satanic device for permitting the ravages of that monster.

Independents, especially in the army, freely lampooned Presbyterian ministers as 'priestbyters'. The orthodox Independents themselves had other troubles. Not only Anabaptists but Quakers, Seekers, Ranters, Familists, and Antinomians were found everywhere. Nye and other orthodox Independents in the Westminster Assembly made it evident that they were not contending for universal toleration, but that they would support a national Church that granted limited toleration, that is, toleration to orthodox Independents.

## PRESBYTERIAN UNIFORMITY ATTEMPTED 91

It was through the strife of competing religious parties that toleration found an opportunity. In the luminous sentence of a modern historian (A. E. Pollard), 'Religious toleration has been won through the internecine warfare between various forms of despotism.' Cromwell himself said, 'When shall we have men of a universal spirit? Everyone desires to have liberty, but none will give it.'

The parties had still to reckon with the conquered King. He had become the problem of Parliament and the army, of Presbyterians and Independents. Even before the last great fight at Naseby, in January 1645, Charles and Parliamentary commissioners had negotiated at Uxbridge. There Charles and his advisers had suggested a system of moderate episcopacy, which, under other circumstances, might have been accepted. Bishops were to be retained but their powers made subject to a council of clergy; there was to be freedom in the use of ceremonies; the Prayer Book was to be revised; and toleration was offered. Whether Charles was sincere, and whether he would have acted upon these proposals, we cannot be certain. Nevertheless, the proposals at Uxbridge are of interest because of their resemblance to what Charles II offered in the Declaration of 25th October 1660, the offer which Baxter eagerly welcomed as a basis for unity and peace.

All terms offered at Uxbridge were rejected by the Parliamentary commissioners. They considered that Charles should take the oath of the Solemn League and Covenant, assent to the abolition of the Prayer Book and of episcopacy, and accept the establishment of Presbyterian Church government.

The sincerity of Charles in the later negotiations must be doubted. On 30th September 1646 he wrote to Bishop Juxon when he was with the Scottish army at Newcastle, 'My real authority once settled, I make no question of recovering episcopal government.' He spoke of any promise he might make as 'temporary compliance'. He averred his abhorrence of Presbyterianism as having 'neither lawful priests nor sacraments duly administered'. At this time he was discussing with the Scots and with English Parliamentary commissioners the extent to which Presbyterian Church government might be accepted. His expressed hope throughout was 'to be able to draw the Presbyterians from the Independents to side with him for extirpating one the other, that he should be really King again'.

When fighting had ceased Charles surrendered first to the Scots —with almost blind trust they turned to a King whom they had fought—under a Covenant which pledged them to protect his person. At Newcastle he would not consider more than approving Presbyterianism for three years, the position to be reviewed by an assembly of divines at the end of that period. It was at this time that he wrote to the Queen, 'This damned Covenant is the child of rebellion and breathes nothing but treason so that if Episcopacy were to be introduced by the Covenant I would not do it.'

The Scots were disappointed with the attitude of both King and Parliament, but, when they had been financially reimbursed by their English allies, they withdrew from England. Charles was left to Parliament and the army. Parliament was so rash as to order all officers to take the Covenant and to subscribe to Presbyterianism; the suggestion was also made to send most of the army to fight in Ireland so that Parliament would not be obstructed in its plans in England. The City of London, stronghold of English Presbyterianism, was appointing Presbyterian officers only in the city militia.[14] The New Model Army, with Charles as its honourable prisoner, thereupon occupied London (6th August 1647) and presented terms for the King's acceptance.

The Heads of the Proposals, the army's terms drawn up by Cromwell and his son-in-law, Ireton, included more favourable terms for the Church than Parliament had offered : modified episcopacy, the bishops to have no coercive powers, freedom in the use of the Prayer Book, freedom with regard to the Covenant, and religious toleration. This noble offer could have reconciled England. Again we may see an anticipation of the first generous offers made after 1660.

Baxter's comments about these events are illuminating. Writing with an antipathy towards Cromwell and the New Model Army, he deplored the growth of the sectaries. He observed how Presbyterian chaplains had left the army in order to take the livings from the ejected episcopal clergy. This he blamed largely for the religious condition of the army as the soldiers fell under the influence of the few Independent ministers in the army and lay preachers of the sects.

The soldiers drew up their own plan for the reconstitution of the Kingdom, the Agreement of the People. Its only religious condition of importance was significant—complete toleration.

## 4. The Failure of Parliamentary Presbyterianism

The year 1648 was the high-water mark of Presbyterianism in England. Its church courts were then functioning in London and Lancashire. London had twelve presbyteries for 139 parishes. The London Provincial Assembly had 108 members. Lancashire had nine presbyteries for sixty parishes. The only other provincial assembly that ever met was in Lancashire. A few other counties had presbyteries. Nominally, England was divided by Parliament into congregational, classical (presbyterial), provincial, and national assemblies. No national assembly ever met.

Royalists, and especially clergy deprived of their livings, loosely called all the new ministers 'Presbyterian'. But, apart from Independents of various types, it is necessary to distinguish the main sections that actually existed:

*Rigid Presbyterians* who had been represented by 'Smectymnuus' and very few others in 1641 but had increased greatly during the War. Only those who joined Presbyterian classes and provincial assemblies really came under this heading. The Presbyterian 'Testimonies', a document signed by 900 ministers of London and thirteen counties, showed the main strength of the party in 1647 (this was a petition to Parliament upholding the divine right of Presbyterianism and opposing toleration).[15]

*Parliamentary Presbyterians,* thorough Erastians, who supported a system controlled by Parliament.

*Moderate episcopals* like Baxter who, as we have seen, believed them to be the large majority especially, in the country. These were never connected with the Presbyterian system.

After 1649 the Presbyterian church courts exercised no compulsory discipline. The system was obviously hampered by the numerical weakness of the lay elderships as well as the restrictions Parliament had purposely placed upon presbyteries; and under the Commonwealth the system itself lapsed except on a voluntary basis. The fourth London classis was an example of the failure of the official Presbyterian experiment; its 14 parishes should have had a strength of 14 ministers and 28 elders, but it had only 9 ministers and 21 elders in 1646, and but 5 ministers and 4 elders in 1654.

The failure of Parliamentary Presbyterianism can be attributed to these facts:

(1) Presbyterianism was introduced for political reasons when Scottish aid was necessary for the Parliamentary cause in 1643.

(2) The system was regarded as essentially Scottish, even with the Erastian modifications imposed by Parliament.

(3) England was not prepared for the system. The reformation had run a different course in Scotland. Englishmen would not have been turned away from episcopacy if it had not been for Laudianism.

(4) The intolerance of Presbyterianism made many Englishmen regard it as little better than the Laudian tyranny—particularly if, as orthodox Presbyterians desired, there was to be no check upon the discipline of its courts. The Presbyterian opposition to toleration for the Independents was their last stroke of folly.

(5) The hostility of the New Model Army and the quarrels with the Independents deprived Presbyterians of any hope of stability and acceptance. The parties' quarrels proved the undoing of them all.

(6) After the Second Civil War and the support many Presbyterians gave to the Stuart cause, official Presbyterianism was discredited with the new rulers; and the eventual doom of militant Puritanism altogether was sealed.

It has been estimated that half the English 'Presbyterians' became Royalists in 1648, and many of these conformed to the Church of England at the Restoration. The other half consisted of those who either remained outwardly neutral from the Second Civil War onward (as Baxter) or else, with the Independents, continued to oppose the King—in either case, this half became the Nonconformists in 1662.

In 1648 the protracted negotiations with the dissembling King ended in his flight from Hampton to Carisbrooke. Cromwell then realized the futility of endeavouring to make a settlement with a King whose word could never be trusted. The Scots, on the other hand, hoped that Presbyterian Church government might at last be established through their agreement with the King. And so they came to his aid in the Second Civil War, as they said, 'to deliver the King from sectaries'. A secret treaty between Charles and the Scots contained the promise to establish Presbyterianism for a trial period of three years, with the immediate suppression of the sects.

## PRESBYTERIAN UNIFORMITY ATTEMPTED 95

It was at this very time, when the Scottish invasion was imminent (1st May 1648) that the English Parliament carried without a division the notorious Ordinance which the Presbyterian party had long sought: An Ordinance for the Suppression of Blasphemies and Heresies, prescribing death for Socinians, Anti-Trinitarians and Anti-Scripturists, and imprisonment for Anabaptists, Arminians, Quakers, and those who even denied the Scriptural warrant for Presbyterian Church government. It has, naturally, been regarded as the crowning evidence of Presbyterian intolerance.

It was a tribute to the orderliness of the army that Parliament was not forcibly dissolved at once, but the army's opinion about the danger inherent in a Presbyterian State Church was confirmed. As an officer significantly remarked: 'Episcopacy was the root of the former war; Presbyterianism you will find to be the root of the succeeding.'[16]

The army had become incensed against the King and all who now supported him—old Royalists or Scots or English Presbyterians. Many London citizens allied themselves with the army. In September 1648, a petition of 40,000 opposed monarchy, pressed for justice on those who had caused the Second Civil War, and demanded the repeal of the Ordinance for the Suppression of Blasphemies and Heresies.

In the last few weeks before his death, Charles had again negotiated with English Parliamentary representatives who pressed once more the claims of Presbyterianism—and this after the débâcle of the Second Civil War! At Newport, in the Isle of Wight, Parliamentary commissioners and divines met the King and his few episcopal advisers. Again the King offered a three years' acceptance of Presbyterianism, the Parliamentary negotiators refusing. From another source an important proposal was then made. Archbishop Usher went to Newport and persuaded the King to accept his famous plan of 'Reduced Episcopacy'.[17] The King, who had refused it before, was now willing to accept it—when the Parliamentary commissioners would not. Unfortunately, Usher had no influence with rigid Presbyterians and Parliamentary members. There was no hope for unity in that critical hour.

With the Scots and their English friends vanquished, the army returned to demand retribution on the 'man of blood' whom, in their prayer-meetings, they had found to be the cause of the nation's divisions. First, they 'purged' Parliament of all but the army's friends. In vain the Presbyterians protested against the trial of the King, the London ministers and the Scottish Commissioners pointing to the provisions of the Covenant which safeguarded the King's person. While episcopal Royalists could only lament Charles's execution in secret or from afar, Presbyterian Royalists were the only ones who could openly deplore the tragedy; they continued loyal to a King who had refused to give up episcopacy and the Prayer Book!

Archbishop Usher was in a house that commanded a view of the scaffold on 30th January 1649, but he almost fainted and had to be removed.

An 'Engagement' of loyalty to the Commonwealth was published, this oath really supplanting the Solemn League and Covenant. It was denounced by the orthodox Presbyterian clergy, and also by others like Baxter who refused to take it and who used his influence in Worcestershire against it. To Baxter, Cromwell was 'the usurper'. It was, nevertheless, regrettable that Baxter's political opposition to Cromwell prevented him from co-operating with a great leader who was pledged to the cause of Christian unity and the promotion of godliness.

## NOTES TO CHAPTER IV

1. *Reliquiae Baxterianae*, I, p. 148.
2. Baillie, *Letters*, vol. 2, p. 117.
3. Shaw, *History of the English Church, 1640–1660*, vol. 1, p. 133.
4. *A Treatise on Episcopacy*, II, p. 211.
5. *Reliquiae Baxterianae*, I, pp. 48–9.
6. *Ibid.*, I, p. 73.
7. Baillie, *Letters*, vol. 2, p. 111.
8. *Journal of the House of Commons*, vol. 4, p. 413.
9. Baillie, *Letters*, vol. 2, p. 362.
10. *Journal of the House of Commons*, vol. 4, p. 513; Shaw, *History of the English Church, 1640–1660*, vol. 1, p. 305.
11. Barclay, *Inner Life of the Religious Societies of the Commonwealth*, pp. 194–6.
12. *Reliquiae Baxterianae*, I, p. 103. Written after the Restoration.
13. *Clarke Papers*, vol. 2, p. 52.
14. *Ibid.*, vol. 1, p. 153.
15. Matthews, *Calamy Revised*, p. 553; Shaw, *History of the English Church, 1640–1660*, vol. 1, p. 273.
16. *Clarke Papers*, vol. 2, p. 2.
17. *Reliquiae Baxterianae*, I, p. 62; Orme, *Life and Times of Richard Baxter*, p. 133; *Five Disputations*, p. 216; Clarendon, *History of the Rebellion and Civil Wars*, p. 680; Neal, *History of the Puritans*, vol. 3, p. 441; Morley, *Oliver Cromwell*, p. 271.

CHAPTER V

# EXPERIMENTS IN UNITY WITHOUT UNIFORMITY, 1649-60

## 1. *The Federated Puritan State Churches*

CROMWELL might have allowed a Presbyterian State Church to continue, provided that there was toleration for others, but the opposition of Presbyterians to the execution of the King and to the establishment of the Commonwealth necessitated a new ecclesiastical policy.

The condition of religion in England was very confused in 1649. Many of the soldiers would not support the establishment of any denomination, and with their Parliamentary supporters in the Rump Parliament they began to attack tithes and patronage. The majority of the Independents advocated a 'settled' ministry, recognized by the State, so that order might prevail in the parishes. The practical questions were: What ministers should be recognized by the State? By whom were candidates for the ministry to be examined and ordained? Should congregations other than those officially recognized receive toleration?

With the pressing question of whether the infant republic was to survive against its foes at home and abroad, measures to settle the Church had to be delayed. The existing Presbyterian system meanwhile continued on a voluntary basis, but with declining popularity, and sects of all types flourished.

In 1652 a petition was sent to Parliament by Independent ministers, including John Owen, Cromwell's chaplain, and four of the original five Westminster Assembly Independents. This petition sought the appointment of committees of ministers and laymen for each county to examine candidates for the ministry and also to deal with 'scandalous' ministers and the suppression of atheism. This plan satisfied neither exclusive Presbyterians nor Voluntaryists who opposed the recognition of any denomination as a State Church. Parliament appointed a Committee for the Propagation of the Gospel to consider the whole matter, and, on the presentation of its report in February 1653, it was resolved that tithes be continued and that committees of ministers and laymen in each county be appointed to examine candidates for the ministry.

Opposition to a State-paid clergy had become an obsession with extreme Independents like John Milton. The attack upon tithes proved the undoing of the Little or Rump Parliament in 1653. Cromwell's good sense convinced him that no ministry would be acceptable to the larger denominations at that time without a system of tithes.

Cromwell's ecclesiastical policy has been summed up as: State recognition; State control; State support; State protection; and State penalties.[1]

State recognition was provided by the Instrument of Government (December 1653) by which there were virtually established what may be called the Federated Puritan State Churches. These consisted of Presbyterians, Independents, and Baptists, with complete liberty to all other Christians except Papists and prelatists to form their own congregations outside the State Churches, which were the recognized parish churches.

State control was secured by the appointment of the Committee of Triers (20th March 1654). The 31 ministers in this committee comprised 16 Independents, 12 Presbyterians, 3 Baptists, and with them were 12 laymen. Five were sufficient for approving a candidate for ordination, but not less than nine were required for rejection. This committee presented candidates to livings, the rights of patrons being untouched. Some episcopal ministers were approved by this committee.

County committees of 'Ejectors' were first appointed by the Protector's Government on 28th August 1654 to deal with 'scandalous' ministers. Among the offences for which ejection was provided were the public use of the Prayer Book, unworthy conduct, and heretical opinions. To these deprived clergy, one-fifth of their livings were given—a concession not allowed to the Puritans ejected after St Bartholomew's Day, 1662.

The Committee for Plundered Ministers, which had functioned since 1642, was replaced by Trustees for the Maintenance of Ministers, appointed in 1654. These 'Trustees' controlled the livings that had formerly been in the gift of the bishops. Church rates were retained and the amalgamation of small parishes—

# EXPERIMENTS IN UNITY 99

where advisable—secured adequate stipends for parish clergy. A central fund was also used to supplement the income of poorer clergy.

All these measures indicated a practical and equitable policy to benefit ministers of the three denominations—Presbyterians, Independents, Baptists, with moderate episcopal clergy, not recognized as a denomination but probably predominating—in this comprehensive national Church.

Baxter, no friend indeed of Cromwell, passed this judgement upon his committees, based upon his own observation of their work in the counties:

> 'Because this Assembly of Triers is most heavily accused and reproached by some men, I shall speak the truth of them, and suppose my word will be the rather taken, because most of them took me for one of their boldest adversaries ... and because I was known to disown their power.... The truth is, that though their authority was null, and though some few over-busy and over-rigid Independents among them were too severe against all that were Arminians ... they did abundance of good to the Church. They saved many a congregation from ignorant, ungodly, drunken teachers ... all those that used the ministry but as a common trade to live by and were never likely to convert a soul, all these they usually rejected, and in their stead admitted of any that were able serious preachers, and lived a godly life, of what tolerable opinion soever they were.... So great was the benefit above the hurt, which they brought to the Church, that many thousands of souls blest God for the faithful ministers whom they let in, and grieved when the Prelatists afterwards cast them out again.' [2]

And with regard to ejections, Baxter is equally emphatic in endorsing the work of Cromwell's committees:

> 'In all the counties where I was acquainted, six to one at least, if not many more, that were sequestrated by the Committees, were, by the oaths of witnesses, proved insufficient or scandalous, or both ... and those that being godly preachers were cast out for the War alone as for their opinion's sake were comparatively very few.'

Outside these Federated Puritan State Churches there was a wide toleration, which should have been one of Cromwell's best claims to the gratitude of the English nation. Not even his Parliaments agreed with the breadth of his toleration. The 1654 Parliament desired that the liberty given under the Instrument of Government 'to such as profess faith in Jesus Christ' should be more strictly defined. Accordingly a committee was directed to draw up certain fundamentals for toleration.

Baxter was called from Kidderminster to serve as a member of this committee in London; it was the first occasion on which he had been given such prominence. His liberal suggestions caused dismay to most members of the committee. As fundamentals Baxter proposed the Lord's Prayer, the Ten Commandments, and the Apostles' Creed; and, when he was reminded that Papists and Socinians might then be tolerated, he did not object.

It is interesting to consider whether Baxter retreated from this very advanced attitude. When in audience with Charles II in 1660 he denied a toleration for Roman Catholics, was he then acting from fear of a Romish revival because Charles was suspected of favouring Popery? Or did he regard 'fundamentals' in an academic sense in 1655? Or did he feel less responsibility when advising the Protector whose rule he disliked? It seems impossible to decide, but it is likely that Baxter's attitude was more rigid when faced with a critical situation as in 1660.

These discussions in 1655 were fruitless. Parliament, unsympathetic towards Cromwell, decided that toleration should not extend to atheists, Papists, prelatists, or 'such as shall preach or maintain anything contrary to the fundamental principles of doctrine held forth in the public profession'.

In 1655 Cromwell issued an order forbidding the ejected clergy even to preach privately or to be schoolmasters—an ominous precedent for the Clarendon Code. It was at the request of Archbishop Usher, whom Cromwell regarded as a friend, that this order was treated almost as a dead-letter. Provided that ejected clergy did not manifest Royalist sympathies openly and did not use the Prayer Book publicly, Cromwell in practice showed them the clemency he maintained towards Quakers and other small sects at the opposite ecclesiastical extremity.

The 1655 Parliament was reminded by Cromwell that the greatest benefit of his rule was liberty of conscience, and he re-

EXPERIMENTS IN UNITY                101

proached those who suggested curtailing it: 'What greater hypocrisy than for those who were oppressed by the Bishops to become the greatest oppressors themselves, so soon as their yoke was removed?'

His personal inclination was to permit the use of the Prayer Book; and his daughters were married with the service from the prohibited book.

Archbishop Usher, Bishop Brownrigg, Dr Gunning (afterwards Bishop of Ely and Baxter's opponent at the Savoy Conference in 1661) were some of the Anglican divines who preached in London during Cromwell's rule. Some episcopal clergy were allowed to enjoy their livings without taking oaths or the 'Engagement' of loyalty. Among these were Dr Hall (afterwards Bishop of Chester) and Dr Pearson.

Cromwell greatly respected Archbishop Usher for his learning, his piety, and his eirenical spirit. When he died he was buried in Henry VII's Chapel, at Cromwell's own expense, Cromwell also permitting the use of the Prayer Book at the funeral. Such an act was heartily commended by Baxter.

2. *Baxter's Voluntary County Associations*

As early as January 1651, when Baxter's writings were bringing him into some prominence, he had expressed his burning desire for unity in the preface to the second edition of *The Saints' Everlasting Rest*:

'Will God never put into the hearts of rulers to call together some of the most godly learned moderate and peaceable of all four opinions [meaning episcopal, Presbyterian, Independent, and Erastian] not too many to agree upon a way of union and accommodation and not to cease till they have brought it to this issue—to come as near together as they can possibly in their principles; and where they cannot, yet to UNITE AS FAR AS MAY BE IN THEIR PRACTICE, though on different principles.'

The opportunity Baxter found for partially carrying into effect his principles of Church unity came in the Worcestershire Association, which was formed in 1653 through his leadership and included 54 ministers—or almost half of the 112 parishes of the county.

Remembering that the essential element in Baxter's system of

Church government was discipline we can now see how simply and naturally an association was formed. In a parish, he maintained, the pastor must guard the Table and require parishioners to submit to his discipline. This discipline was not always easily exercised, as Baxter found at Kidderminster where only 600 out of 1800 consented to live under his discipline. If an experienced pastor like Baxter felt it advisable to join with others so that their joint authority might be effective in all their parishes, it was particularly advisable to have such a system in the interests of younger pastors.

Baxter explains his reasons for beginning his Association in these enlightening sentences:

'The state of my own congregation, and the necessity of my duty, constrained me to make some attempt. For I must administer the Sacraments to the Church, and the ordinary way of examining every man before they came I was not able to prove necessary, AND THE PEOPLE WERE AVERSE TO IT; so that I . . . thought that, if all the ministers did accord together in one way, the people WOULD MUCH MORE EASILY SUBMIT, than to the way of any minister that was singular.'

Baxter's Association met at Kidderminster and Evesham monthly. A quarterly meeting for the county met at Worcester with pastors from the five sections. After a sermon there were sometimes disputations upon theological points, with prayer, admonition, and cases of discipline. Persons were actually brought from the parishes for reproof before the pastors, although the excommunication itself was left to the culprit's own pastor after he had been fortified by the associated pastors' opinions. Names of those excommunicated in other districts were notified to the meeting. The Association used spiritual penalties only. It was a voluntary association for voluntary discipline, that is, applied to people who had signified their willingness to accept it.

Baxter felt constrained to advocate this system of associating pastors because of the breakdown in the Presbyterian establishment and the lack of co-ordinated control of parish life. The Presbyterian discipline that had been approved by Assembly and Parliament had depended upon fully maintained elderships and classical courts, with civil support. In actual fact, elders were not forthcoming in many places, few classes and synods met, and this

# EXPERIMENTS IN UNITY

was the position even before the State withdrew its approval for the system.

The Worcestershire Association soon had its counterparts in many counties. By 1657 there were associations in fourteen counties—Cumberland and Westmorland, Cambridge (30 parishes), Cornwall (26 ministers), Norfolk (80 ministers), Nottingham (over 30 ministers), Dorset, Essex, Cheshire, Hampshire, Shropshire, Somerset, Wiltshire, and Devon. The Devonshire Association was the largest and most elaborately organized. It had 109 ministers, with district meetings every six weeks, divisional meetings quarterly, and a county meeting yearly.[3]

In his own Association Baxter was asked to draw up a form of agreement. This was *The Agreement of the Associated Pastors and Churches of Worcestershire*, which Baxter published with the alternative title *Christian Concord*.

The Association's object was set out also in Baxter's later writings:

'I drew up some articles for our consent which might engage us to the most effectual practice of so much discipline as might reduce the Church to ORDER, and satisfy ministers in administering the Sacraments, and stop the more religious people from separation, to which the unreformedness of the Church, THROUGH WANT OF DISCIPLINE, inclined them. . . . Though some few of the ancient Presbyterians were against it . . . most of the godly, faithful ministers, as far as I could learn, were for it.'[4]

Corroboration of the approval given to the plan of county associations is found in the autobiography of a Cheshire minister (Martindale) who gave his reasons for joining a voluntary association when he would not join a Presbyterian system:

'If it be asked how I got satisfaction to act with them now, when I had scrupled some things concerning Classical [=Presbyterian] Government. . . . I answer, the case is not the same. Here was only a VOLUNTARY Association of such as were desirous to advise and assist one another, nor did we look upon ourselves as having any pastoral inspection over one another's congregations.'[5]

Sion College, where the rigid London Presbyterian ministers met regularly until 1659, did not approve the Worcestershire and other associations because they included ministers of various persuasions. Baxter's ideal of unity without uniformity was clearly unacceptable to the instincts of orthodox Presbyterians. Baxter said:

'The chief of the Presbyterian and Independent divines, who were weary of divisions, and willing to strengthen each other's hands, united in these assemblies, though the exasperated Prelatists, the MORE RIGID PRESBYTERIANS and severer sort of Independents kept at a distance.' [6]

'There was not, that I know, one thorough Presbyterian among them [*i.e.*, in the Worcestershire Association] nor did any Independent subscribe, save one. . . . As also some few of the Episcopal way, who never came . . . and resolved to do nothing till they had Episcopacy restored.' [7]

The diversity in the members' principles, which seemed a barrier to those wedded to uniformity, proved the basis of success in practice. The ideal of unity was achieved when men actually co-operated for the promotion of godliness.

'If Episcopacy, Presbytery, or Independency &c, be indeed the way of God, there is no way in the world so likely to set it up as the meeting and loving Association of the Pastors, where all things may be gently and amicably debated.' [8]

'All the rest who joined us were MERE CATHOLICS, MEN OF NO FACTION, nor siding with any party, but owning that which was good in all as far as they could discern it and upon a concord in so much laying out themselves for the great ends of their ministry, the people's edification.' [9]

The pastors in Worcestershire in their Agreement resolved not only to belong to no party but to practise unanimously 'those known truths which the sober and godly of each party are agreed in'; to reprove sin, no matter what material loss they suffered in the process; and to admonish and exclude impenitent sinners. The process of public admonition, for which detailed forms were provided in Baxter's 'Reformed Liturgy' in 1661, is given in general outline in this Agreement. The members of the Association followed Baxter's example at Kidderminster in catechizing and private instruction in home visitation.

The great stress placed upon strict supervision of the communicants' lives can be seen in the Devonshire Association's articles which included: 'That none be admitted into the Association that will administer the Lord's Supper PROMISCUOUSLY TO ALL SORTS GOOD AND BAD.'[10]

Ordinations do not seem to have been carried out by the Worcestershire Association but there are records of many ordinations in the Cheshire, Cornwall, Cumberland and Westmorland, Nottingham, Devonshire, and other associations, especially towards the end of the Protectorate period when the work of the official Committee of Triers was affected by the growing disfavour felt towards the State and its official agencies. Even earlier the practice of associations ordaining indicated that the Federal Puritan State Churches were not supplying the needs of the parishes everywhere.

In Baxter's 'Explication' of the articles of the Worcestershire Association he revealed that some of the pastors who were members had not been episcopally ordained, and that this was a reason why some rigid episcopal divines did not join the Association.[11] Baxter replied to this objection with the practical argument that it was more important to correct drunkards and other sinners in the parishes than to settle details about ceremonies or even validity of ordination.

### 3. *Archbishop Usher's Discussions with Baxter*

Baxter advocated a system of compromise, although he well knew the strength of the divisions among episcopal clergy as well as Presbyterians. With regard to episcopal clergy of various types he had mixed feelings. 'I heartily reverence and desire their union', he declared of Usher, Hall, Morton, and other moderate bishops. On the other hand, there were the 'Cassandrian Papists', as he designated the Laudian clergy, particularly those who would not recognize the other Protestant Churches but yet desired re-union with Rome.

Baxter stoutly maintained that the Church of England itself continued to function during the Interregnum even though bishops and many clergy had been dispossessed. Quoting Cyprian and Occam, he declared that when bishops had fallen into error in past history, the rest of the clergy had been justified in continuing the Church's life without interruption or schism.[12] We may say that Baxter did not make a strong case for the unaltered continuity of the Church of England without episcopal government. Precedents for error or heresy did not apply to all the bishops of the period. Some, like Usher, were held up to admiration by Baxter himself. Nevertheless, as a practical issue, seeing that bishops were not allowed to ordain (at least publicly) during the Commonwealth and Protectorate, Baxter could reasonably contend for the validity of non-episcopal ordinations although he himself did not take part in such ordinations by associations. Baxter hoped that England would adopt one of the modified episcopal systems that the Parliament had considered during the Civil War (see pp. 75, 77-9), more particularly Archbishop Usher's model.

When Baxter was called to London in 1655 to the Committee considering the 'fundamentals' for toleration to be given under the Instrument of Government, he preached before Cromwell and took the opportunity to criticize his Government and to show 'how mischievous a thing it was for politicians to maintain such DIVISIONS for their own ends that they might fish in troubled waters and keep the Church by its divisions in a state of weakness, lest it should be able to offend them'. He proceeded to tell Cromwell the necessity and means of union. In this amazing incident we see the tactlessness of Baxter in a practical situation, and his inability to recognize Cromwell as one who had both the desire and the authority to bring about Church unity (as he had done through the Federated Puritan State Churches). Because of his political opposition to Cromwell he dared to uphold monarchy to the Protector's face.

During this visit to London in 1655 Baxter met Archbishop Usher and discussed Usher's monumental plan not long before it was actually published for all interested to see. The two famous divines visited each other many times and, as Baxter stated, they found they could agree together in half an hour! The proposals Baxter presented to Usher were quite acceptable to him. The essentials were:

'That every pastor be the governor, as well as the teacher of his flock.

'In those parishes that have more presbyters than one, that one be the stated president.

'That in every market town . . . there be frequent assemblies of parochial pastors associated for concord and mutual assistance in their work : and that in these meetings, one be a stated (not temporary) president.

'That in every quarter or diocese there be every year, or half-year, or quarter, an assembly of all the ministers of the county or diocese; and that they also have their fixed (permanent) president; and that in ordination nothing be done without the president, nor in matters of common or public concernment.

'That the coercive power or sword be meddled with by none but magistrates.' [13]

Baxter's proposals conformed to Archbishop Usher's plan (see pp. 130–3). Usher told Baxter that at the Isle of Wight in 1648 he had advocated this plan, and that when asked by Charles for precedents for ordination with the assistance of presbyters he had produced precedents even for ordination by presbyters only. Usher also admitted that a synod should be for agreement, not for controlling pastors; this, Baxter afterwards stated, 'of his own accord he told me confidently'.

'I found in the search of Scripture and antiquity, that in the beginning a governed Church and a stated worshipping Church were all one, and not two several things . . . and I found that Episcopal men (as Bishop Usher himself did voluntarily profess his judgment to me) did hold that every Bishop was independent, as to Synods; and that Synods were not proper governors of the particular Bishops, but only for their CONCORD.' [14]

Baxter often voiced his regret that many Puritan ministers had not properly considered Usher's scheme. No doubt the reason was that very few were 'reconcilers' like Baxter, and only such were genuinely willing to support any scheme of Church government but the one to which they and their party were devoted.

One concession Baxter made rather reluctantly to Usher's scheme. True to the strict Puritan tradition in not approving a negative voice *de jure* for the president or bishop in ordination, yet he was willing to concede that the pastors should resolve *de facto* that they would not ordain without the president.

Macaulay has written about Baxter's discussions with Usher and his friends. Even if one disagrees with Macaulay's terms for Baxter as a 'moderate Presbyterian' and Usher as a 'moderate

Episcopalian' as though they were in different denominations, his general conclusion was clearly correct :

'It did not seem impossible to effect an accommodation between the moderate Episcopalians of the school of Usher and the moderate Presbyterians of the school of Baxter. The moderate Episcopalians would admit that a Bishop might lawfully be assisted by a council. The moderate Presbyterians would not deny that each provincial assembly might lawfully have a permanent President and that this President might lawfully be called a Bishop. . . . But to no such plan would the great body of the Cavaliers listen with patience. The religious members of that party were conscientiously attached to the whole system of their Church. She had been dear to their murdered King. . . . Other Royalists, who made little pretence to piety, yet loved the episcopal Church because she was the foe of their foes. . . . They were so far from being disposed to purchase union by concession that they objected to concession chiefly because it tended to produce union.'[15]

To Bishop Brownrigg, formerly Bishop of Exeter, Baxter proposed in 1655 terms for unity similar to those given to Archbishop Usher. They included the establishment of associations or classes, with a president for life; a provincial assembly every year or every two years, with a standing president or bishop or superintendent; ordination by president and pastors, in the association or the larger body, the assembly. Like Usher, Brownrigg ADMITTED THAT EVERY PASTOR MUST BE A GOVERNOR OF HIS FLOCK.[16]

Had Usher lived until the Restoration, his influence would at least have mollified the temper of the episcopal body as a whole. His personal presence and his advocacy of his plan of modified episcopacy would have carried far more weight than the offering of his plan by the divines to their opponents, the restored bishops. His friendship with Baxter would have introduced a new element into the negotiations of 1660–61.

Usher also knew and approved the offers Baxter made to the Independents through Philip Nye, and they should now be reviewed.

### 4. *Negotiations for Presbyterian and Independent Unity*

It may well be thought that Baxter's discussions with bishops during the Protectorate were largely academic, and that approaches to the Independents were more important and practical. There is no doubt that Baxter was more anxious to come to an understanding with other parties than with the Independents. He disliked Separatism and desired a national comprehensive Church such as he would call 'The Confederate Parish Churches of England'. He disagreed with the Independents' democratic practices of ruling by the majority of the votes of the people in the congregations and regarding ordination as being to a particular congregation. He criticized Independents in these terms: 'Most of them made the people by majority of votes to be church-governors, in excommunications, absolutions &c, which Christ hath made an act of Office, and so they governed their governors and themselves.'[17]

In spite of these differences, Baxter approached Philip Nye, a leading Independent, in an endeavour to find a basis of union for Independents and moderate episcopalians, the so-called 'Presbyterians' Baxter represented. In 1656 or 1657 (no exact date seems to be known) Baxter induced Nye to give 'sufficient concessions for our desired end'. These conditions were that they might have liberty to take Church members out of other parishes, and that they might have all Church power within themselves, in their several congregations. Nye included the right of ordination in individual congregations under this 'Church power'.

Baxter was willing to accept Nye's stipulations, provided that 'Parishes shall be the ordinary bounds, but in necessary cases and no other, you shall except and be free from them', these cases being where scandals would result if Church members were not taken out of the parishes. Synods should exist, not to make laws governing congregations but for consultation concerning church duties, for engaging in spiritual exercises for the members, and for assisting pastors, especially younger pastors, in cases of excommunication. Ordination to be by previous pastors of a congregation or from neighbouring congregations. Baxter afterwards consented to waive the condition of ordination by pastors and by imposition of hands, 'as an extraordinary indulgence to a tender conscience'.

It was to Baxter's credit that he was willing to concede so much to Nye. Nevertheless, there was an air of unreality in these discussions, and Nye, evidently without giving sufficient reason, withdrew from them.

In his correspondence with Nye, Baxter had added terms on which the episcopalians could be included to form a grand union of the three parties. This showed again not only Baxter's catholic spirit and his determination to seek a larger union, but also his willingness to reach terms that might be agreeable to bishops at a time when there seemed little chance of bishops being restored to the Church. It was also for this reason that Baxter endeavoured to persuade Independents that ordination should not be merely to a particular congregation but to a ministry in the universal Church. Baxter told Nye: 'On these terms, in the last two propositions, Bishop Usher, when I propounded them to him, told me, that the Episcopal party might well agree with us, and the MODERATE would, but the rest would not.'[18]

Following this, Baxter published and sent to prominent Independents his Twelve Articles by which 'The Churches in these nations may have a holy communion, peace and concord, without any wrong to the consciences or liberties of Presbyterians, Congregational, Episcopal, or any other Christians.' Probably nothing wider than these propositions has been made in the cause of Christian unity. These Twelve Articles proposed:

1. Ministers 'to have no power of violence' but to exercise pastoral duties according to the Word of God, 'and let no princes or Parliaments make them rules' for preaching, admonishing, or administering Sacraments.

2. Adult members not to trust just to their infant Baptism but to make PUBLIC PROFESSION OF FAITH, after preparation by catechizing.

3. 'Let the young, and ignorant, and ungodly . . . be compelled by some moderate penalty to hear and confer with the teachers, and be instructed and catechized by them.'

4. 'Let *parishes* be the ordinary bounds of Churches, so that all the adult members of the Universal Church . . . within that parish, who do consent, be members of that particular church.'

5. Pastors to have power of 'the keys for binding and loosing within their own congregation'.

6. Communion between particular Churches.

7. Meetings for ministers for such consultation.

8. Matters of discipline, as well as forms of worship, through these associations. 'It will be most regular, and avoid the hurt of the Churches, if ordination of ministers be either performed by

these assemblies, or the ministers to be ordained be here tried and approved, and the ordination to be performed in the Church to which he is ordained by such as they appoint or by the teaching elders of that Church itself, after their approbation of the person.'

9. These associations to choose their presidents or moderators, or leaders given any other suitable designation, and to determine whether temporary or permanent.

10. Magistrates, if convenient, to be present at meetings of association as witnesses only, and also to prevent rumours of disaffection against the State.

11. Larger associations covering more extensive areas to be formed.

12. Only if manifest heresy or corruption enter into these associations should the State intervene.[19]

Not only did these broad principles indicate the extent to which Baxter was prepared to go in an accommodation with other Christians, but his correspondence in 1658 mentions his willingness to co-operate with Anabaptists, provided that they did not denounce infant Baptism (and he would be silent on the subject of re-Baptism). Under these circumstances Baxter was agreeable to the admission of re-baptized persons to Communion.

Baxter strongly resented the criticism that he had been intolerant towards Independents, an attack made against him in later years by the bishops who expelled all Nonconformists in 1662. His words are a definite indication of his position as well as an evidence of what he considered to be the Independents' situation under the Protectorate (and see pp. 45–6) :

'It was the toleration of ALL Sects unlimitedly that I wrote and preached against and NOT (that I remember) of mere Independents.

'Those that did oppose the toleration of Independents, of my acquaintance, did not deny them the liberty of Independency, but opposed Separation, or their gathering other Churches out of parish-churches that had faithful ministers. . . . They [the Independents] commonly had presentations, and the public maintenance; and no subscription, declaration, liturgy, or ceremony, was imposed on them. Again I say, I ASK YOU [the bishops] NO MORE LIBERTY THAN WAS GIVEN THE INDEPENDENTS BY THEIR BRETHREN CALLED PRESBYTERIANS.'[20]

In 1657 the new constitution for the State, the 'Humble Petition and Advice', included the establishment of a national Church, to consist of moderate 'Presbyterians' and moderate Independents. This envisaged a different system from that of the Instrument of Government when all who accepted the 'Christian religion as contained in the Scriptures' had become entitled to public maintenance—what we have called the Federated Puritan State Churches.

The new united national Church, to be recognized by the State, was to have a dogmatic Puritan creed, not the Westminster Confession, which Scotland had accepted, but one that the divines of the 'Presbyterian' and Independent parties would frame. Under the proposed system there would be less toleration than the system of 1654 had allowed: Papists, prelatists, Unitarians, Quakers, blasphemers would all alike be banned.

This proposed new Church establishment of 1657 was the reason for reviving efforts to unite Presbyterians and Independents. We can see the motive for John Howe, Cromwell's chaplain, now discussing Church union with Baxter. Baxter had urged Howe to approach Cromwell about 'healing principles' that would unite episcopalians, Presbyterians, Independents, Erastians, and Anabaptists—Baxter's great vision of a national comprehensive Church. While Howe assented to such a scheme in theory he considered that the union of Presbyterians and Independents was the only practicable question, and one that needed to be settled urgently.

Before approaching Cromwell on this subject, Howe wrote to Baxter in April 1658:

> 'Whether it may not be a more hopeful course to attempt first the RECONCILING ONLY OF THE TWO MIDDLE PARTIES, PRESBYTERIAN AND CONGREGATIONAL? Inasmuch as the extreme parties would be so much startled at the mention of an union with one another (as Anabaptists with Episcopalians, yea, or with Presbyterians), that it might possibly blast the design in its very beginning; but if these two other parties could be brought together first, endeavours might afterwards be used for drawing in the rest (probably with more success); and therefore whether accordingly it were not best to present to his Highness only what might serve that end?' [21]

It is unfortunate that no more evidence seems to be available about the discussions on this attractive subject at this critical stage. Probably they were confined to consultations between Howe and Baxter. Baxter was *persona non grata* with the Protector, and Howe knew the practical difficulties also. Evidently Henry Cromwell, the Protector's brilliant son, was sympathetic to the proposals. Had he succeeded his father he might have seen Church unity effected as well as the prolonging of the new form of government in England.

The dissolution of Parliament early in 1658 put an end to the whole plan for a national Church. The failure of an agreement between the two parties seems to have induced the Independents to confer among themselves and to formulate a declaration of faith as a basis for their denominational purposes. There is no doubt that the Independents at that time preferred to stabilize their own position rather than to seek union.

The Savoy Conference of the Independents opened on 29th September 1658. It consisted of about 200 Congregational ministers and laymen from 120 churches, the laymen predominating. The leaders were John Owen, John Howe, Philip Nye, Thomas Goodwin. As a counterpart to the Westminster Confession they drew up their own Declaration of the Faith and Order owned and practised in the Congregational Churches in England.[22]

Cromwell had not desired the Independents to hold this Savoy Conference. He did not favour any denominational movement but supported efforts to unite Presbyterians and Independents. (The great Protector had breathed his last on 3rd September, a few weeks before the Savoy Conference opened.) Baxter heartily agreed with Cromwell's position in this regard.

'To consummate the confusion, by confirming and increasing the division, the Independents at last, when they had refused with sufficient pervicacy to associate with the Presbyterians (and RECONCILERS too) did resolve to show their proper strength, and to call a General Assembly of all their Churches. The Savoy was their meeting-place. There they drew up a Confession of their Faith, and the Orders of their Church Government. . . . In their propositions of Church Order, they widened the breach, and made things much worse, and more UNRECONCILABLE than ever they were before.'[23]

Still clinging to hopes of unity, Baxter wrote to Richard Cromwell (whom he addressed as a Solomon of peace following his father, a David of war) calling on him to build the temple of harmony by 'a union of the tolerable dissenting parties'.[24] There is nothing to show that Richard Cromwell acted upon this letter or even received it. Unfortunately, the opportunity for union had already passed.

In 1659 the religious as well as the political situation of England became still more confused. In May 1659 John Howe, not naturally given to dolefulness, wrote to Baxter: 'Sir, such persons as are now at the head of affairs will blast religion, if God prevent not. . . . Religion is lost out of England, farther than as it can creep into corners.'[25]

In justice to Baxter, self-styled 'Reconciler', it should be said that he hardly deserves all the criticisms passed upon him for not securing union with the Independents before the Restoration. Even if there were more orthodox Presbyterians after the breakdown of established Presbyterianism than Baxter allowed, and granted also that these were as unlikely to be received into an episcopally governed restored Church as the Independents were, yet it was natural for Baxter to hope for an accommodation with the episcopal parties without the Independents and to bend his energies rather to the union of episcopals and Presbyterians of various types.

Baxter had tried to find an agreement with Nye and Howe. The Independents, on the other hand, had consolidated their own position at the Savoy Conference in 1658. Furthermore, the political differences must be remembered. The Independents were anti-Royalist. Most of the Presbyterians and moderate episcopals had been Royalist since the Second Civil War. After the Restoration there was no prospect of Independents being accommodated in the established Church.

5. *Efforts to unite Episcopal Parties in the Church of England*

Such efforts had absorbed much of Baxter's energy for years past. In the disturbed years before the Restoration he was seeking an accommodation for the moderate Churchmen he represented, especially on the basis he had discussed with Archbishop Usher in 1655. Though the evidence now available is scanty there is support for his belief that these moderate Churchmen desired union with other episcopals in the re-established Church rather than any union outside the establishment.

A significant discussion with Sir Ralph Clare and Dr Hammond arose out of the civil commotions of the times. In July 1659 Baxter was told by Sir Ralph Clare of his deep concern about what might follow the revolts of the army since Cromwell's control had been removed, and also his belief that Anabaptist and Fifth Monarchy fanatics among the disorderly soldiery should be suppressed. Sir Ralph had often troubled Baxter by his demands to receive Communion kneeling, and, as the Royalist squire of his congregation and an upholder of the old prelacy, he had been unsympathetic throughout Baxter's ministry at Kidderminster. It was probable that Baxter was more firmly Royalist in 1659 than he had been ten years before; and the arbitrary actions of army leaders in 1659 were influencing him still more to support the restoration of monarchy. It is certain that Sir Ralph Clare believed that Baxter with his widespread influence among Puritans would be a useful ally in persuading Churchmen to bring back the King.

Sir Ralph Clare induced Baxter to believe that the bishops' party in exile would welcome union with Baxter's friends and with Presbyterians. He told Baxter that he had received information from Bishop Morley and others who were in the councils of the King in Holland, that modified episcopacy would be acceptable to them, and that a 'bare Presidency in Synods, such as Bishop Usher in his "Reduction" did require, was all that was intended', that there would be 'no Lord Bishops, no so large dioceses, much less in persecuting power', and that 'no godly able minister should be displaced'.[26] All this, if sincerely offered, made an excellent basis for uniting the episcopal parties in the Church of England.

It was agreed that Baxter should send proposals to one of the leading episcopal divines in England, Dr Hammond, with Sir Ralph Clare as intermediary. Baxter responded, although he saw the loophole in the suggestions that were made to him—everything would have to be approved by a new Parliament. Hammond's reply also was noncommittal. Still, if Hammond had lived beyond 25th March 1660, Baxter might have received support from him in the fateful negotiations later that year.

In writing to Hammond, Baxter affirmed his hope for an agreement of episcopalians, Presbyterians, and Independents. Obviously he still cherished the vision of a wider union, if this was at all feasible.

Before setting out Baxter's proposals in order, their vital similarity with what he had advocated earlier should be noted—and their similarity with Usher's model and with the offers afterwards made by Baxter and his associates at the Savoy Conference in 1661. Here we see Baxter's programme of reform and unity for the Church of England. Baxter's proposals in 1659 were:[27]

1. Private religious assemblies for edification to be permitted.

2. A godly efficient ministry, for preaching and for catechizing.

3. Preachers not to be forced upon congregations against their consent.

4. Open profession of faith before reception at Communion, as a ratification of the baptismal covenant.

5. Confirmation as a rite to be left an open question for the present.

6. The cross in Baptism, the surplice, kneeling at Communion —to be optional. 'We are certain LEAVING THESE UNNECESSARY THINGS AT LIBERTY . . . IS THE WAY TO UNITY.'

7. The use of the liturgy to be optional, or a new book using Scriptural terms only to be drawn up.

8. Pastors to 'govern' their own flocks, to admonish, call to repentance, absolve, reject, and call Church people to 'avoid' the impenitent.

9. Monthly synods in market towns, with fixed (permanent) presidents for life, the synods being for consultation, that is, about disciplinary cases brought before them without destroying the power of the pastors over their own flocks.

10. Quarterly synods for the county, with fixed president.

11. Ordination and jurisdiction in synods to be with the consent of the members.

12. A National Council of president and two ministers from each county synod.

13. No subscription except to the Scriptures, the Creeds, and Articles of Faith 'expressed in Scriptural terms'.

14. Church discipline to be exercised only by spiritual penalties.

Thus, in 1659, before Baxter met the King, Clarendon, or the restored bishops, and before he consulted with other ministers who were afterwards associated with him in the negotiations, his pro-

EXPERIMENTS IN UNITY 117

gramme of reform and unity for the Church was clearly formulated. It was this programme to which he adhered throughout the next two years, even though for the sake of peace he was willing to reduce it to fewer essentials.

All this was to be in vain. He was to see 'the poor Church of Christ ... like Christ that was crucified between two malefactors, the profane and formal persecutors on one hand, and the fanatic dividing sectary on the other'.[28] Extravagant words, perhaps we say today! But they expressed his abject disappointment when the restoration of unfettered and intolerant episcopacy brought persecution to godly ministers and made the division in the English Church which has remained for 300 years.

## NOTES TO CHAPTER V

1. Stoughton, *History of Religion in England*, vol. 2, pp. 77–91.
2. *Reliquiae Baxterianae*, I, p. 72.
3. Shaw, *History of the English Church, 1640–1660*, vol. 2, pp. 153–64; Neal, *History of the Puritans*, vol. 4, p. 76.
4. *Reliquiae Baxterianae*, I, p. 167.
5. Martindale's autobiography, quoted in Shaw, *History of the English Church, 1640–1660*, vol. 2, p. 442.
6. Neal, *History of the Puritans*, vol. 4, pp. 75–6.
7. *Reliquiae Baxterianae*, I, p. 148.
8. *Christian Concord*, 'Explication', p. 106.
9. *Reliquiae Baxterianae*, I, p. 97.
10. Shaw, *History of the English Church, 1640–1660*, vol. 2, p. 169.
11. *Christian Concord*, p. 42.
12. *Ibid.*, pp. 56–7.
13. *Reliquiae Baxterianae*, I, p. 206.
14. *Ibid.*, II, p. 14.
15. Macaulay, *History of England*, vol. 1, p. 128.
16. *Reliquiae Baxterianae*, II, pp. 172–6.
17. *Ibid.*, II, p. 143.
18. *Ibid.*, II, p. 193.
19. *Ibid.*, II, pp. 194–7.
20. *Ibid.*, III, p. 131.
21. Horton, *John Howe*, pp. 49–50.
22. Walker, *Creeds and Platforms of Congregationalism*, p. 346 et seq.; Matthews, *Savoy Declaration of Faith and Order, 1658*.
23. *Reliquiae Baxterianae*, I, p. 104.
24. Powicke, *Richard Baxter*, vol. 1, p. 138.
25. Horton, *John Howe*, p. 59.
26. *Reliquiae Baxterianae*, II, p. 208; Stoughton, *History of Religion in England*, vol. 3, p. 51.
27. *Reliquiae Baxterianae*, II, pp. 208–9.
28. *Ibid.*, I, p. 103.

CHAPTER VI

# CHARLES II's NEGOTIATIONS WITH ECCLESIASTICAL PARTIES (1660)

## 1. *The Return of the King and the Bishops to England*

BAXTER'S MIND was not free from foreboding even before the King was invited to return. He preached before the House of Commons two days before the invitation to the King was sent on 1st May 1660. Even modified episcopacy, he felt, would be doomed, and the worst might be feared from the reprisals that would follow.

'Every man whose religion is not ceremonious and complemental shall be called a Presbyterian, and every Presbyterian a rebel. And whereas heretofore they had no worse names to call godly men by, than the foolish names of Puritans and Roundheads, henceforth if a man will not be as bad as others, he shall be called an enemy to the Government. And though not one of forty of the ministers ever meddled with the wars, they shall all fare alike if they be not Prelatists.'

'In that sermon . . . I told them that whether we should be loyal to our King was none of our differences, in that we are all agreed. . . . And for the concord now wished in matters of church-government, I told them it was easy for moderate men to come to a fair agreement, and that the late revered Primate of Ireland [Usher] and myself had agreed in half an hour.'[1]

If the opinions of all the clergy could have been tested in 1660, it is probable that the majority (excluding the newly reinstated ministers who had suffered sequestrations in the wars) would have supported Baxter's programme of modified episcopacy. There were, however, other factors at work, far more influential than the preferences of clergymen like Baxter.

The memory of the execution of Charles I stood between the Laudian clergy and those who had opposed the King AT ANY TIME. It mattered nothing that 'Presbyterians' had expressed the utmost abhorrence at the execution, and that many of them had been estranged from Cromwell from then onwards. It was enough for their rivals that they had supported Parliament against the King at the outset, and also that they had agreed with Parliament in banning the use of the Prayer Book to which the King had been so loyal. Though it was certainly not the fault of 'Presbyterians', it was never forgotten that the use of the Prayer Book had been sternly refused, by order of the Rump Parliament, at the burial of the martyred King at Windsor. The new loyalty of 'Presbyterians' to Charles II could not efface these memories. A Royalist summed up the situation : 'The Independents cut off the King's head, but it was the Presbyterians who brought him to the block'—an unjust statement, but typical of the attitude of those who desired vengeance in 1660.

The sequestrations of the Royalist clergy could not be forgotten. Again it mattered little that it was Parliament, and not the Puritan ministers, who had ordered these ejections; or that many of the sequestered clergy had lived scandalous lives and merited ejection for that reason. Royalist supporters alleged that the real reason for clergy being thrust out of their livings was their refusal to give up the Prayer Book.

Presbyterians and moderate episcopalians had to endure a very large share of the odium cast upon all non-prelatical denominations because they were the majority. It was a strange affliction for those who had opposed the sects that they should be linked with them by the Royalists. All Puritans were hated by Royalists because of their strictness, the enforcement of sabbath observance and the suppression of vice. In the Restoration lampoons, the term 'Presbyterian' was generally used for those who upheld morality and opposed licentiousness.

'Presbyterians', having accepted in many cases the ecclesiastical benefits of the Interregnum, could hardly expect a continuance of these favours after the Restoration. The wealthier benefices in London were held by Presbyterian ministers; such facts might well excite the envy of the restored clergy.

Social prestige operated against the 'Presbyterians', even though many of the gentry and some of the nobility were still 'Presbyterians' in 1660. The desertions of aristocratic 'Presbyterians' became numerous under a King who advised Lauderdale to transfer his Church loyalty because 'Presbyterianism was NO RELIGION FOR

A GENTLEMAN'.[2] Titles and political advantages accepted by 'Presbyterian' leaders in high social circles meant the gradual disappearance of the party as a political force.

The Laudian clergy in exile had determined that unmodified episcopacy should be restored. Presbyterianism was not only abhorrent to them politically. With the full connivance of the future Lord Chancellor, Clarendon, they were resolved not to abate any of the claims of the old order in the Church. Morley, afterwards Bishop of Worcester, when acting as agent for Clarendon in his conversations with 'Presbyterian' ministers in the early months of 1660, before Charles returned, stated: 'I engage nor undertake for nothing . . . but only by a friendly and familiar manner of conversing with them, endeavour to gain upon them, and to get an interest in them.'[3]

Before the King returned there was no general advocacy of prelacy in England, but rather the reverse. On 21st February 1660 the surviving members of the Long Parliament were recalled and were addressed by General Monk, who had marched from Scotland to take command of the situation. His reference to the Church was:

'It is most manifest that if it be monarchial in the State, the Church must follow and Prelacy must be brought in, which these nations [England and Scotland], I know, cannot bear and against which they have so solemnly sworn [in the Solemn League and Covenant]; and indeed, MODERATE, NOT RIGID, PRESBYTERIAN government, with a sufficient liberty for consciences truly tender, appears at present to be the most indifferent and acceptable way to the Church's settlement.'[4]

The Long Parliament adopted the Westminster Confession and ordered the Solemn League and Covenant to be placed on the walls of the Commons as well as read in every church in the land once a year. Its Presbyterian bias was also seen in removing John Owen, an Independent, from the deanery of Christ Church, Oxford, and appointing Edward Reynolds (a 'Presbyterian', soon to be made a bishop) in his place. Parliament actually provided for the restoration of the official Presbyterian system by directing that England be divided into classical presbyteries—an indication of the strength of rigid Presbyterianism that has to be remembered when Baxter's disclaimers of its numbers are noted.

Parliament even contemplated re-organizing the army with Presbyterian officers. All this was being done as though nothing was more natural than reverting to the conditions of 1647, before the Second Civil War, with Parliamentary Presbyterianism recognized in England—and as if nothing was so unlikely as the restoration of episcopacy with the King's return a few weeks later.

Milton had formerly written: 'Woe be to you Presbyterians especially, if ever any of Charles's race recover the sceptre! Believe me, you shall pay all the reckoning.' He now repeated his warning: 'Nor let the new-Royalized Presbyterians persuade themselves that their old doings, though now recanted, will be forgotten, whatever conditions be contrived or trusted on.'[5]

On 16th March 1660 the Long Parliament dissolved itself and ordered an election, which was confined to those who had not fought for the King.

Meanwhile the Royalists still in exile were sending flattering offers to 'Presbyterian' leaders. It was whispered that non-episcopal ordinations would be recognized, that restored episcopacy would be modified to meet Puritan wishes, and that the union of episcopal and Presbyterian parties could confidently be expected. The more discerning ministers in England suspected in this talk much insincerity and a bait to gain their support for the Restoration. Bishop Morley's words, quoted above, make this clear.

During the weeks of secret consultations (February–April 1660), some who had been rigid Presbyterians gave up any thought of seeing the Presbyterian system accepted in the new order and began to advocate Usher's plan of modified episcopacy instead. Evidently Dr Manton and other strict Presbyterian London ministers were now of this mind. Though they accepted this plan as a compromise in an emergency, they willingly joined forces with Baxter and his friends, who had advocated this plan for years.

Baxter came to London on 13th April 1660. His long ministry at Kidderminster, though he did not know it then, had closed. He came at the request of the Earl of Lauderdale, the Scottish Royalist and Presbyterian noble, who was anxious to win over the ministers to the King's side. Lauderdale seems to have been sincere in his admiration of Baxter's character and influence.

Baxter's constancy in supporting the Restoration does the more credit to his integrity and courage when he realized what awaited ministers like himself: 'We all look to be silenced and some or many of us imprisoned or banished; but yet we will do our parts to restore the King, because no foreseen consequence must hinder us from our duty.'[6]

The so-called Convention Parliament, which assembled on 25th April 1660, was generally 'Presbyterian' in character. The Earl of Manchester, a noted Presbyterian, presided over the House of Lords. Parliament received letters from the King with the famous Declaration of Breda, which Charles had issued on 4th April. Nothing seemed more satisfactory than the terms of this declaration, but the cautious must have noted the ominous qualification that the promised freedom depended upon an Act of Parliament. The King's words were:

> 'Because the passion and uncharitableness of the times have produced several opinions in religion ... we do declare a liberty to tender consciences, and that no man shall be disquieted or called in question for differences of opinion in matters of religion, which do not disturb the peace of the Kingdom.'

Subsequent events showed that Charles hoped to include toleration for Roman Catholics in his plans. Already the belief was warranted that 'No age produced a greater master in the art of dissimulation.' He prayed aloud in the room adjoining the waiting-room where the Puritan divines who had gone to The Hague could hear him. He had seen that reports were circulated about his faithfulness to the Protestant cause in France. Granted that he was tolerant by nature and opposed to religious persecution, there can be little doubt that he was prepared to make any promises to regain his throne.

Upon receiving this declaration, the Convention Parliament resolved on 1st May to invite Charles to return. A committee was appointed to draw up a dutiful reply, and a deputation of Lords and Commons with attendant ministers went to await upon His Majesty at The Hague. Sir Matthew Hale, Baxter's friend, moved that a committee be appointed to consider the propositions regarding Church government offered to Charles I at the Isle of Wight in 1648 (Usher's modified episcopacy). Hale did this, realizing that it was foolish to forgo some guarantee for the future of the Church. Unfortunately, there was little disposition in Parliament to show any prudence. Monk artfully replied that any delay in recalling the King might give 'incendiaries' an opportunity for raising a flame in the nation. Pepys shows the general feeling at the time was 'that the Presbyterians did intend to have brought him in with such conditions as if he had been in chains',[7] but the debate does not support this view.

All caution was swept aside. The nation would brook no delay; it wanted the King at once, with or without conditions. Thus, without any assurance beyond the vague promise in the Declaration of Breda, England restored the King and with him a form of Church government that was certain to be the full episcopacy for which Clarendon and the exiled Royalist clergy had prepared.

On 2nd May the King was proclaimed, and on that day Baxter preached before the Lord Mayor and Corporation of London. His Royalist sympathies and his forebodings for the Church caused strange conflict in his mind. He hardly shared the hopes of some who 'thought that if we were the means of the King's Restoration, the Prelates would not for shame deny us such liberty as the Protestants have in France'.[8]

The deputation from the two Houses and leading 'Presbyterian' divines (Calamy, Manton, Reynolds, Case, Bowles, Spurstow, and others) went to The Hague to present the formal invitation to the King. They met him on 17th May. Representing various sections of Presbyterians, all the divines realized that episcopacy must be expected, but they wanted promises that it would not be the old prelacy. They were anxious also to prevent toleration for the sects! It is almost inconceivable that these ministers would reveal their dislike of the sects while asking for consideration for their own party. They were equally injudicious in presenting their objections to the Prayer Book. Clarendon narrates that, in their audiences with Charles, 'they were tedious enough in presenting their duties and magnifying the affections of those of their friends . . . . They professed that they were no enemies to Moderate Episcopacy.'

Clarendon, who was, of course, their critic, further relates that they requested the King to set the personal example of abstaining from two practices that offended their party, namely, the use of the Prayer Book and ordering the clergy to wear the surplice. They asked also that the King should permit neither Prayer Book nor surplice in the royal chapel when he landed in England, or, if he desired the Prayer Book, he would use only parts of it and allow extempore prayers to be added. It seems that Charles was roused by such a tactless attitude; and he told the deputation 'that whilst he gave them liberty he would not have his own taken from him'.[9]

The King landed at Dover on 25th May. No bishop was present, but the 'Presbyterian' chaplain of the Mayor of Dover presented Charles with a gold-clasped Bible, which he accepted with protestations of devotion to it. On Sunday 27th May the King reached Canterbury and attended divine service in the Cathedral, the Prayer Book being used. In the great procession that attended the King on Tuesday 29th May, upon his entry into London, there were twelve London 'Presbyterian' ministers in Genevan gowns and bands—the only sombre-looking persons in the colourful parade through the excited metropolis. On the Sunday following the King's entry, Dr Thomas Pierce preached in St Paul's Cathedral and urged the City of London to petition for the restoration of full episcopacy.

Clarendon, always an enemy of the Puritans, even when it was politic to cloak his feelings, had resolved upon his course. 'I would not, to preserve myself, wife and children from the lingering pain of want and famine . . . consent to the lessening any part, which I take to be in the function of a Bishop, or the taking away the smallest prebendary in the Church, or be bound not to endeavour to alter any such alteration.'[10] He regarded it only good policy to appease the 'Presbyterians' temporarily in order to secure the King's Restoration. By appointing a number of political 'Presbyterians' to positions in the King's Council he gradually won them over.

Meanwhile the old order was restoring itself. Incumbents to livings of sequestered clergy were dispossessed, and, upon complaints in some cases being made to the Court, no redress was offered. The ejections were sometimes public and dramatic; for example, in Halifax, the 'Presbyterian' minister was beginning the worship used for the past few years in the parish church when the episcopal vicar appeared at the church door, prepared with surplice and Prayer Book and, approaching the pulpit, insisted upon taking the minister's place forthwith. A royal declaration on 1st June, suspending action against incumbents until Parliament decided, had seemingly little effect. In spite of it, Laudian clergy were returning to their livings and receiving preferments throughout England.

The King appointed ten Presbyterian and moderate episcopal chaplains. These included Baxter, Calamy, Manton, Reynolds, Spurstow, Bates, and Case, but only four of them were called to preach before the King, and these not more than once.

Nine bishops were restored, including Juxon (formerly of London, now translated to Canterbury), revered because of his officiating in the last sad rites with Charles I; Frewin, appointed to York; and Wren, who had been in the Tower since 1642. These nine declared their disapproval of Usher's plan of modified episcopacy in these terms: 'As to Usher's Model of Government, we decline it as not consistent with his other learned discourses on the original of Episcopacy and of Metropolitans, nor with the King's Supremacy in matters ecclesiastical.'[11]

When the actual negotiations for Church government began, an air of unreality was immediately apparent. The Laudian bishops were using delaying tactics until there was more open feeling against the Puritans in the country, and in another Parliament yet to be called. Baxter made a fair comment upon this:

'I think that those men are reprovable who say that nothing but deceit and juggling was from the beginning intended. . . . It was necessary that they should proceed safely, and feel whether the ground were solid under them. . . . How knew they what the Parliament would do? . . . Therefore it was necessary that moderate things should be proposed and promised, and no way was so fit as by a Declaration which being no law is a temporary thing, giving place to laws. And it was needful that the calling of a Synod were delayed, till the Presbyterians were partly cast out, and a way to keep out the rest secured.'[12]

The declaration to which Baxter referred came on 25th October, the synod (the Savoy Conference) the following April, and the ejections little more than a year afterwards.

The newly appointed chaplains were called upon to meet the King at the lodgings of the Earl of Manchester, the Lord Chamberlain, a loyal though rather irresolute Presbyterian. This important interview occurred at the end of June 1660. It followed assurances from Baxter to Manchester and other sympathetic nobles about the possibility of re-union on Usher's plan. Their conversation was reported to the King, who then directed these chaplains to meet him.

In this interview with the King, the Lord Chancellor, the Earl of Manchester, the Earl of St Albans, and others were present. Baxter was chief speaker for the ministers in asking that the Church should be both settled and united by these means:

'1. By making only THINGS NECESSARY TO BE THE TERMS OF UNION.

2. And by the true exercise of CHURCH DISCIPLINE AGAINST SIN.

3. And NOT CASTING OUT THE FAITHFUL MINISTERS THAT MUST EXERCISE IT, nor obtruding unworthy men upon the people.' [13]

These three points, together with Usher's plan of modified episcopacy, represented the essential principles which Baxter consistently advocated for the unity of the Church of England. These, he believed, would promote godliness as well as secure the union of various parties in the Church. He particularly urged that ministers appointed in the Interregnum, provided that they were faithful and efficient, should not be dispossessed. These points, he said, were far more important than any question of ceremonies.

Clarendon refused to allow Baxter to present Usher's plan to the King at this preliminary consultation, but only to offer the three points mentioned.

Baxter, fervently but tactlessly, pleaded with Charles to remember that Cromwell had found it wise to appoint worthy ministers and he (Charles) should not endanger his popularity by allowing less competent men to replace them.

'I told him also that it was not Presbyterians, or any party, as such, that we were speaking for, but for the religious part of his subjects....

'I humbly besought him that he would never suffer his subjects to be tempted to have favourable thoughts of the late usurper, by seeing the vice indulged which they suppressed; or the godly ministers discountenanced whom they encouraged. ... For all his enemies cannot teach him a more effectual way to restore the reputation and honour of the usurpers, than to do worse than they.' [14]

The King returned a gracious answer and pledged himself to bring about a union which 'must not be by bringing one party over to the other, but by abating somewhat on both sides and meeting in the midway'. Such an alluring prospect delighted the ministers. 'Old Mr Ash burst out into tears with joy, and could not forbear expressing that gladness this promise of His Majesty had put into his heart.'[15]

Charles suggested that the London ministers should confer and draw up proposals about Church government and that the other side would bring their suggestions. *The bishops' party never did this.* The ministers duly brought forward their proposals.

2. *'The First Address and Proposals of the Ministers'*

The divines conferred daily at Sion College for two or three weeks. The result was 'The First Address and Proposals', which proposed changes in the liturgy and ceremonies and offered Archbishop Usher's plan of modified episcopacy. Reynolds and Worth (both afterwards conformists and bishops) and Calamy were mainly responsible for the document.

'About Discipline we designedly adhered to Bishop Usher's model, without a word of alteration; that so they might have less to say against our offers as being our own; and that the world might see that IT WAS EPISCOPACY ITSELF WHICH THEY REFUSED . . . and that we pleaded not at all with them for Presbytery, unless a MODERATE EPISCOPACY be Presbytery.'[16]

The Address began with a preface, which was evidently written by Baxter. The other ministers considered that the four points in the preface were irrelevant, but to Baxter's mind they expressed the moral and religious issues the Puritans were defending, namely:

(1) GODLINESS. The practice of religion should not be made 'the common scorn', and Christians meeting together for prayer and sermon-discussion should not be persecuted as they had been.

(2) THE MINISTRY. Each congregation should have a learned and godly pastor, and the law should secure that negligent and scandalous ministers should not be admitted to livings.

(3) PERSONAL PROFESSION BEFORE ADMISSION TO THE LORD'S SUPPER, a personal owning of the baptismal covenant by a profession of faith not contradicted by a scandalous life, 'and that

unto such only, Confirmation (if continued in the Church) may be administered'. If confirmation were continued, pastors should certify their approval of persons to be confirmed.

The requirement of moral and spiritual fitness for Communion, the *sine qua non* of a true Church in the ministers' opinion, is manifest again from Baxter's emphatic statement:

'THE UTTER NEGLECT OF DISCIPLINE ... HAD CAUSED ALL OUR CONFUSIONS; AND IN THIS POINT IS THE CHIEFEST PART OF OUR DIFFERENCE WITH THEM INDEED, AND NOT ABOUT CEREMONIES.'[17]

(4) THE LORD'S DAY. Puritans could not forget that many ministers had been expelled under Laud's régime for not reading the King's *Book of Sports* which permitted games on Sundays.

The Address then proceeded to outline the suggestions for Church government, the liturgy, and ceremonies.

I. CHURCH GOVERNMENT. 'We do not, nor ever did renounce the TRUE, ANCIENT AND PRIMITIVE EPISCOPACY OR PRESIDENCY as it was balanced and managed by a due COMMIXTION OF PRESBYTERS therewith, as a fit means to avoid corruption, partiality, tyranny, and other evils, which may be incident to the administration of one single person.'[18]

The evils of prelatical government existing before 1640 were then set forth:

(1) The size of the twenty-six dioceses in England and Wales made impossible the effective supervision by the bishops.

(2) The bishops deputed the administration of much of their trust, even in matters of spiritual cognizance, to commissaries, chancellors, and officials.

(3) The bishops exercised ordination and jurisdiction without any co-operation or consultation with presbyters, affirming that their episcopal office by divine right was distinct from that of presbyter.

(4) The government of the prelates was arbitrary as seen, for instance, in imposing additional ceremonies not required by law.

To reform these evils, Baxter and his colleagues put forward Usher's 'Reduction of Episcopacy unto the Form of Synodical Government received in the Ancient Church' 'as a GROUNDWORK towards an accommodation and fraternal agreement in this point of ecclesiastical government'.

For this 'fraternal agreement' the ministers asked that suffragans or *chorepiscopi* be chosen by the synods, and that 'the ASSOCIATIONS may not be so large as to make the DISCIPLINE impossible'. Further, that the arbitrary powers of bishops be disallowed, and that no oaths or promises of obedience to bishops be required before ordination or induction.

These requests represented the essential programme for Church reform in 1660–61. Had these been granted, unity could have been restored to the Church, and the great body of ministers in England (all except rigid Independents and smaller sects) could have been comprehended within the national Church. The Church of England would have become a truly national Church, governed by constitutional bishops with their synods. Looking back to 1660–61, it is an unrelieved tragedy that these terms were rejected outright, a tragedy the greater because the chief features have been adopted in Anglican Church government since then. C. A. Briggs has pointed out that *every one of Baxter's proposals has been accepted in the Protestant Episcopal Church in the U.S.A.*[19]

By the same token, the question arises as to why these terms should not permit of re-union in 1962. Presbyterians and denominations with similar polity could be expected to welcome the modified episcopacy proposed by their spiritual forbears three centuries ago. But would all others accept it? Where, in the final analysis, does spiritual authority reside—in the pastor of a congregation or in a diocesan bishop, be he monarchical or constitutional? If it resides in the Church, expressed through council or association or synod, then, again, Baxter's contention is upheld.

II. THE LITURGY. The ministers expressed their belief that a liturgy was lawful, provided that extempore prayers were allowed to supplement the liturgy. As for the Book of Common Prayer, it was stated that it contained 'many things that are justly offensive and need amendment', that it had been abandoned during the Interregnum, and that it had become a source of disunity. The ministers preferred that a new liturgy using Scriptural words should be drawn up by 'learned, godly and moderate divines of both persuasions'. If this was unacceptable, it was asked that at least the Prayer Book should be revised, with alternative forms added.

III. CEREMONIES. The ministers pointed out that ceremonies

not enjoined by Scripture had been discarded in the Reformed Churches on the Continent. 'They are at best but INDIFFERENT, and in their nature mutable, and yet they had been imposed by Prelates as though they were as vital in every detail as the Sacraments themselves.' Paul's teaching regarding things indifferent and about not giving an occasion of offence to weak brethren might well be applied to ceremonies, it was urged. The following requests were made:

(i) Those ceremonies, which had been imposed by prelates to the satisfaction of the Papists, but contrary to all law, be absolutely PROHIBITED: the erecting of altars and bowing towards altars.

(ii) Those which even their defenders could plead to be only 'indifferent and mutable' to be ABOLISHED: the use of the surplice, the use of the cross in Baptism, and bowing at the name of Jesus.

(iii) Others, of human institution, to be made OPTIONAL: kneeling at Communion and the observance of holy days.

As Archbishop Usher's model was appended to the ministers' Address and it was prominent in all the negotiations, its chief provisions are outlined in the following section.[20]

### 3. Archbishop Usher's 'The Reduction of Episcopacy unto the Form of Synodical Government received in the Ancient Church, proposed in the year 1641, as an Expedient for the Prevention of those Troubles which afterwards did arise about the matter of Church Government'

'EPISCOPAL AND PRESBYTERIAL GOVERNMENT CONJOINED'

'By the Order of the Church of England, all presbyters are charged to minister the doctrine and Sacraments and the discipline of Christ as the Lord hath commanded, and as this realm hath received the same....

'Of the many elders, who in common thus ruled the church of Ephesus, there was one President, whom our Saviour, in his epistle to the church, in a peculiar manner styleth the angel of the church of Ephesus; and Ignatius, in another epistle, written about twelve years after, to the same church, calleth the Bishop thereof ... by the Presbytery understanding the company of the rest of the Presbytery or Elders who then had a hand, not only in the delivery of the doctrine and Sacraments, but also in the administration of the discipline of Christ....

'For with the Bishop, who was the chief President (and therefore styled by Tertullian Summus Sacerdos for distinction sake), the rest of the dispensers of the Word and Sacraments were joined in the common government of the Church. And therefore in matters of ecclesiastical judicature, Cornelius, Bishop of Rome, used the received form of gathering together the PRESBYTERY.

'The presence of the clergy being thought to be so requisite in matters of episcopal audience that, in the fourth Council of Carthage, it was concluded that the Bishop might hear no man's cause without the presence of the clergy.

'True it is, that in our Church this kind of Presbyterian government hath been long disused, yet seeing it still professeth that every Pastor hath a right to RULE the Church (from whence the name of RECTOR also was given at first unto him) and to administer the discipline of Christ, as well as to dispense the doctrine and Sacraments.... And how easily this ancient form of government, by the united suffrages of the clergy, might be revived again ... the reader may quickly perceive by the perusal of the ensuing propositions.

'I. IN EVERY PARISH the Rector or the incumbent Pastor, together with the churchwardens and sidemen, may every week take notice of such as live scandalously in that congregation, who are to receive such several admonitions ... and if by this means they cannot be reclaimed, they may be PRESENTED UNTO THE NEXT MONTHLY SYNOD, and in the meantime be DEBARRED BY THE PASTOR from access unto the Lord's table.

'II. Whereas by a statute in the 26th of King Henry VII (revived in the first year of Queen Elizabeth), SUFFRAGANS are appointed to be erected in 26 several places of this Kingdom, the number of them might very well be conformed unto the number of the several RURAL DEANERIES into which every Diocese is subdivided, which being done, the Suffragan (supplying the place of those who in the Ancient Church were called CHOREPISCOPI) might every month assemble a SYNOD of all the Rectors, or Incumbent Pastors within the precinct, and according to the MAJOR PART of their voices conclude all matters that should be brought into debate before them.

'To this SYNOD the Rector and churchwardens might present such impenitent persons, as by admonition and suspension from the Sacrament, would not be reformed; who, if they should still remain contumacious and incorrigible, the sentence of EXCOMMUNICATION might be decreed against them by the Synod, and accordingly be executed in the Parish where they lived. . . . Also the censure of all new opinions, heresies, and schisms which did arise within that circuit, with liberty of appeal if need so require unto the Diocesan Synod.

'III. THE DIOCESAN SYNOD might be held once or twice in the year . . . therein all the Suffragans and the rest of the Rectors or incumbent Pastors (or a certain select number out of every Deanery within that Diocese) might meet; with whose CONSENT, or the major part of them, all things might be concluded by the Bishop or Superintendent (call him whether you will) or in his absence by one of the Suffragans, whom he should depute in his stead to be MODERATOR of that Assembly. . . . And if here also any matter of difficulty could not receive a full determination, it might be referred to the next Provincial or National Synod.

'IV. THE PROVINCIAL SYNOD might consist of all the Bishops and Suffragans, and SUCH OF THE CLERGY as should be elected out of every Diocese within the Province. The Primate of either Province might be the Moderator of this meeting. . . . This Synod might be held every third year, and if the Parliament do then sit . . . both the Primates and Provincial Synods of the land might join together, and make up a NATIONAL COUNCIL.'

Baxter wrote a summary of the 'Address and Proposals of the Ministers' and suggested to his colleagues that it should be presented to the King, to enable him to grasp the ministers' position more easily. In this 'Brief Sum of our Judgment and Desires about Church-Government', Baxter went beyond what the other ministers were willing to concede. They also felt that it was wiser to pin their faith to Usher's model. Baxter yielded to the persuasions and withdrew his paper.[21]

Nothing could better express the Puritan ministers' wishes for Church government than Usher's model. That it was the work of the Primate of Ireland gave the greater weight to this scheme of moderate episcopacy. Every essential Puritan demand for the reform of Church government was included in Usher's plan. For instance:

(i) The pastor's rights over his own flock.

(ii) The primacy of discipline in the congregation, and the necessity for guarding the Lord's Table.

(iii) The rights of pastors in jurisdiction. (It should be noted that ordination was not specifically mentioned by Usher; but he clearly believed that presbyters should be joined with bishops in ordination, as he maintained this in argument with Charles I in 1648 in the Isle of Wight.)

(iv) The graded synodical system, with ministers represented in each synod—all ministers in the lowest, the rural deanery, and elected ministers in higher courts.

(v) The stress placed upon cases of excommunication in the rural deanery (which corresponded to Baxter's county associations), with the sentence executed in the parish by the pastor concerned.

When the ministers took their 'Address and Proposals' to the King they found that the bishops were not present as Charles had led them to expect. Clarendon had evidently met the bishops privately and advised them not to meet the ministers or to make any proposals to them, seeing that they (the bishops) were legally entitled to their authority in the Church. When the ministers were admitted to the royal presence the King received them graciously and promised to arrange a conference with the bishops later. The 'Proposals' were sent to the bishops, who prepared their 'Answer' and this was given to the ministers on 8th July 1660.

During the progress of these negotiations more of the old sequestered clergy were returning to their livings by order of the bishops. Baxter had hoped that certainly those who had been convicted of offences by the old Parliamentary Commission for Scandalous Ministers early in the Civil War would not be restored, but the bishops made no such distinctions. As a result, 695 intruded ministers were deprived of their livings between the King's return and St Bartholomew's Day, 1662. It might well have been expected that those who had taken the place of deceased incumbents might have been exempted, but the bishops were bent on excluding all intruded ministers as soon as possible. Already the bishops were requiring re-ordination and were imposing oaths of canonical obedience and the observance of the liturgy.

All this augured ill for the success of any negotiations. As Baxter said, 'We were all of us to be endured but a little longer.'

On 10th August 1660, Calamy, Manton, and Ash, representing the rigid Presbyterians, wrote to Scotland and informed Scottish ministers that the Presbyterian Church system would certainly not be established in England as the 'general stream and current is for the old Prelacy in all its pomp and weight', and it would also be unwise to ask for toleration for Presbyterians lest 'Papists and Sectaries of all kinds' took advantage of such toleration. They said that the best course was 'MAKING PRESBYTERIANISM A PART OF THE PUBLIC ESTABLISHMENT' by reducing episcopacy to synodical government and mutual accommodation in regard to the liturgy.

The Independents were ignored by the negotiating ministers, who at no time suggested that they be comprehended within the reunited Church of England. Even toleration would depend upon the major party being included in the Church.

An Act for Confirming and Restoring of Ministers was passed by the Convention Parliament, the King's assent being given on 13th September 1660. This enacted that every minister presented to a benefice since 1642 and in possession at the end of 1659 would be adjudged the lawful incumbent, and any minister, formerly ejected and not having declared for the execution of Charles I and not having opposed infant Baptism, would be restored to his benefice before 25th December 1660. When the Cavalier Parliament was elected, it did not accept this settlement.

It was during the debates on this Act that the ministers verbally requested Charles to suspend the restoration of sequestered clergy to livings until their negotiations were concluded with the bishops. They also asked that, at least until a settlement was reached, there should be no compulsory oaths of obedience to bishops and subscription to the liturgy. They further requested that re-ordination would not be required for those ordained by Presbyters only. To these requests Baxter and others added the characteristic point, in accordance with their emphasis upon the spiritual reformation of the nation, that unworthy ministers should not be restored to the churches. The sands were fast running out, but the Puritan divines were true to their principles.

Support for the cause of unity was coming from other quarters. Edward Stillingfleet, a Bedfordshire rector and future famous Bishop of Worcester, published in 1660 his *Irenicum, or, A Weapon Salve for the Church's Wounds*.[22] Stillingfleet advocated that all might agree upon 'a form of government in the

Church as may bear the greatest correspondency to the PRIMITIVE CHURCH, and the most advantageously conducible to the peace, unity and settlement of our divided Church'. He contended that there should be no binding form, as none had been given by Christ for all time, and the reformers had not decided upon one form; the best course was to approximate to primitive practice, and so he suggested a combination of episcopacy and Presbyterianism, with a life President (or bishop), an ecclesiastical senate, smaller dioceses, and provincial synods twice a year. Stillingfleet's proposals showed that some ministers quite unconnected with Presbyterianism in any form shared Baxter's views. He wrote:

'Without all controversy, the main inlet of all the distractions, confusions, and divisions, of the Christian world, has been by ADDING OTHER CONDITIONS of Church-communion than Christ has done. Would there ever be the less peace and unity in a Church, if a DIVERSITY were allowed as to practices supposed indifferent.... The unity of the Church is a unity of love and affection, and NOT A BARE UNIFORMITY OF PRACTICE AND OPINION.... I am sure it is contrary to the primitive practice, and the moderation then used, to suspend or deprive men of their ministerial function for not conforming to habits and gestures, or the like.'

In 1660 also appeared a book by another clergyman, Robert Thorndyke, *The Due Way of composing the Differences on foot, preserving the Church*.[23] He advocated not sacrificing the unity of the whole Church for the sake of comprehending the various sects but uniting the episcopalian and Presbyterian parties only by smaller dioceses, allowing presbyters to act with bishops in ordinations, and amending the Prayer Book while abolishing the Westminster Directory.

Puritan ministers were clearly not singular or unreasonable in their proposals to the bishops.

4. *'The Bishops' Answer to the First Proposals of the London Ministers'*

On 8th July 1660 the ministers received 'The Bishops' Answer to the First Proposals of the London Ministers who attempted the work of Reconcilement'. This answer was even more dogmatic in tone than the ministers' 'Proposals', and it held out no hope of agreement.

The bishops defended the liturgy as being Scriptural and less tedious than the extempore prayers of Puritan ministers. They obviously desired to make the Prayer Book the main battleground, rallying to their support the sentiment of all who cherished its use and who had suffered for it during the Civil War and since.

The 'Answer' suggested that any changes in ceremonies might be left to the King, the bishops knowing full well that there would be no alterations if that course were followed.

Some of the bishops' phrases were slightly more conciliatory than those they were to adopt in the later and more bitter stages of the negotiations. For example, they said, 'Nor are ministers denied the use and exercise of their gifts in praying before and after sermon', and 'If anything in the established Liturgy shall be made appear to be justly offensive to sober persons, we are not at all unwilling that the same should be changed.' Yet they refused extempore prayer and resisted all demands for changes in the liturgy less than a year later. One must accept the reason as being their uncertainty about the situation in July 1660, as contrasted with the developments that followed the election of the Cavalier Parliament and the rise in favour of Royalist clergy.

The bishops stoutly defended episcopacy as being more than a presidency, although they might concede that presbyters be associated with the bishops in ordination and censures. Beyond this somewhat vague statement in their 'Answer' the bishops did not indicate at any time whether they really agreed to presbyters having these rights.

The bishops denied that the existing dioceses were too large or that it was necessary for the diocesan bishop to have personal knowledge of all whom he confirmed. They also joined issue on the question of fact as to whether lay chancellors had exercised spiritual power.

Evidently unable to refute the claims made in Usher's model, the bishops begged the whole question by merely appealing to the perfervid loyalty of the hour by criticizing this brief outline of an ecclesiastical scheme because Usher had not mentioned the King— as if Usher had not been a Royalist, or as if he needed to refer to the King when setting out the powers of the proposed synodical meetings, or indeed would have mentioned the King at all when he published his document in 1655 during the Interregnum. Arguments of this kind showed the futility of the negotiations and the impossibility of receiving any concessions from the Laudian bishops. They did not propose any further discussions with the ministers; indeed they had not met them together at any time. Clearly, the issues were settled as far as they were concerned.

### 5. *Baxter's 'Defence of the Ministers' Proposals'*

The ministers assigned the framing of a defence of their Proposals to Baxter, who wrote it in about one week. Although he was now and always anxious for peace, and sometimes more willing to make concessions for peace than his associates, he was stirred to use stinging arguments in this document. His sincere resentment as well as his natural disputatiousness prevented him from seeing how much better silence could be. When he contended that they owed it to posterity to state their position and to advance every argument for their case the other ministers disagreed. 'They considered that this would but provoke them, and turn a treaty for concord into a sharp disputation, which would increase the discord; and so what I had written was never seen by any man, lest it hinder peace.' [24]

Although this 'Defence' was not published it clearly states that point of view which Baxter and his colleagues were representing.

Baxter's hot, despairing tone shows how unwise it would have been to anger the bishops still further by sending them this 'Defence'. Baxter assailed their sincerity at once. If, as they professed, they were not in disagreement with the ministers about the essential principles of godliness, why had they returned a complete negative to every point in the 'Proposals'?

'To be plain with you ... the great controversy between the hypocrite and the true Christian—whether we should be serious in the practice of the religion which we commonly profess?—hath troubled England more than any other; none being more hated and derided as Puritans, than those that will make religion their business, and make it predominant in their hearts and lives; while others that hate them, take it up in custom, for fashion, or in jest, and use it only in subserviency to the will of man and their worldly ends, and honour it with compliments. RECONCILE THIS DIFFERENCE, and most others will be reconciled.' [25]

Has the issue between pure religion and formalism been more plainly stated? And was not this actually the issue between the two parties as shown in the practical results of their policies? Admitted that the promotion of godliness was desired by many conformists, it yet remains true that it was the supreme concern of all who became Nonconformists; and they could not believe that godliness could be achieved in undisciplined congregations with pastors who were not allowed, whether they desired or not, to be governors of their flocks.

Further, were the bishops sincere in disapproving private meetings for family prayer and sermon-discussion, and alleging that these were, or could be, a danger to the realm? If so, why should not feasts, hunting, races, bowls, be forbidden, because men could plot against the King as easily there?

Where was the sincerity, Baxter asked, in saying that the bishops desired a godly minister for every congregation when hundreds were already being expelled because they had not been ordained by bishops or because they would not subscribe to obey the bishops or their officials?

Could the bishops seriously contend that confirmation, as practised in England then and in the Laudian period, was a sufficient substitute for continual instruction and catechizing?

> 'I was confirmed by honest Bishop Morton, with a multitude more, who all went to it as a May-game, and kneeled down, and he dispatched us with that short prayer so fast, that I scarce understood one word he said; much less did he receive any certificate concerning us, or ask us anything which might tell him whether we were Christians; and I never saw nor heard of much more done by any English bishop in his course of confirmation.' [26]

How could the existing prelatical system be defended as being the same as the primitive episcopacy? Would a general depose all his captains and attempt to exercise discipline himself? When Ignatius contended for one bishop with one altar to rule there alone, but an English bishop ruled one thousand churches, where was the harmony with primitive episcopacy? How much more glaring was the difference when the English bishop gave the keys to lay chancellors who suppressed private meetings, enforced ceremonies, and exercised other disciplinary authority in the Church!

Discipline and Church government, not liturgy and ceremonies, were the main questions at issue.

'YOU KNOW THAT THE DEPRIVING OF ALL THE PARISH PASTORS OF THE KEYS OF GOVERNMENT IS THE MATTER OF OUR GREATEST CONTROVERSIES. No knowing Englishman can be so ignorant that our Bishops have the sole government of pastors and people, having taken all jurisdiction . . . from the particular pastors of the parishes, to themselves alone.' [27]

Baxter pointed out the bishops' damaging admission that having suffragans made it unnecessary to divide dioceses. Actually, there were no suffragans or *chorepiscopi* in England, as Usher's model proposed. Baxter also referred to the significance of the admission that presbyters might assist in ordinations.

To any suggestion that Usher's model did not represent his settled conviction, Baxter pleaded his personal discussions with the Archbishop not long before his death in 1655 and the unmistakable evidence that his model had never been withdrawn.

'Here we leave it to the notice and observation of posterity, upon the perusal of your Exceptions, how little the English Bishops had to say against the Form of Primitive Episcopacy contained in Archbishop Usher's "Reduction", in the day when they rather chose the increase of our divisions, the silencing of many hundred faithful ministers, the scattering of the flocks, the afflicting of so many thousand godly Christians, than the accepting of THIS PRIMITIVE EPISCOPACY, WHICH WAS THE EXPEDIENT WHICH THOSE CALLED PRESBYTERIANS OFFERED, NEVER ONCE SPEAKING FOR THE CAUSE OF PRESBYTERY; and what kind of peacemakers and conciliators we met with, when both parties were to meet at one time and place, with their several concessions for peace and concord ready drawn up, and THE PRESBYTERIANS IN THEIR CONCESSIONS LAID BY ALL THEIR CAUSE, AND PROPOSED AN ARCHBISHOP'S FRAME OF EPISCOPACY; and the other side brought not in any of their concessions at all, but only unpeaceably rejected all the moderation that was desired.' [28]

Nothing could be plainer than the preference of the bishops for dividing the Church: 'This is your conciliation! When it was promised by His Majesty that you should meet us half-way, YOU BRING IN NOTHING!' [29]

Baxter's indignation was justified, but it would have been indiscreet to submit such arguments to the bishops and, still worse, to add that the ministers knew they were to be expelled after negotiations failed. Baxter had been free from any illusion of success, but, though the other ministers did not agree with him in this, he believed that they should not let anyone imagine that silence meant that they had not sought a way of unity. It was for this reason that he wished to publish his defence. 'When we are all silenced and persecuted, and the history of these things shall be delivered to posterity, it will be a just blot upon us if we suffer as refusing to sue for peace.' [30]

During the months of July-August-September, there was much feeling against the Government because of the dispossessing of ministers, some of whom had not taken the place of sequestered clergy, but had filled vacancies caused by death. It was on 13th September that the Bill for Confirming and Restoring of Ministers was sent to the King for his assent; and it was significant that this Bill proposed to recognize ordinations 'by any ecclesiastical persons' as giving a right for confirming the possession of livings. This was evidence that political Puritanism in the Convention Parliament was still active. To counteract these endeavours the King, on Clarendon's advice, decided that Parliament should be adjourned and that effective control should be secured in the Church by the appointment of more bishops during the recess. Between October 1660 and January 1661 all the sees except two were filled, and every appointment was a Laudian bishop. At the same time the King showed a desire to placate Puritan opinion with a show of conciliation in resuming negotiations with the ministers. The King's Declaration was the clearest indication of this turn in the Government's policy.

## NOTES TO CHAPTER VI

1. *Reliquiae Baxterianae,* II, p. 217.
2. Carlyle, *Letters,* p. 297.
3. Bosher, *The Making of the Restoration Settlement: The Influence of the Laudians, 1649–62,* pp. 126, 138.
4. Masson, *Life and Times of Milton,* vol. 5, p. 540; Neal, *History of the Puritans,* vol. 4, p. 204; Stoughton, *History of Religion in England,* vol. 3, p. 48.
5. Masson, *Life and Times of Milton,* vol. 5, p. 680.
6. *Reliquiae Baxterianae,* II, p. 216.

CHARLES II'S NEGOTIATIONS   141

7. Pepys, *Journal*, p. 34.
8. *Reliquiae Baxterianae*, II, p. 216.
9. Clarendon, *Life and Continuation of History of the Rebellion*, p. 909.
10. Quoted in Bosher, *The Making of the Restoration Settlement: The Influence of the Laudians, 1649–62*, p. 137.
11. Plummer, *English Church History, 1649–1702*, p. 53 (footnote).
12. *Reliquiae Baxterianae*, II, p. 287.
13. *Ibid.*, II, p. 231.
14. *Ibid.*, II, pp. 230, 231.
15. *Ibid.*, II, p. 231.
16. *Ibid.*, II, p. 232.
17. *Ibid.*, II, p. 233.
18. *Ibid.*, II, p. 233, and *Documents Relating to the Settlement of the Church of England under the Act of Uniformity, 1662*, p. 15.
19. Briggs, *Church Unity*, p. 98.
20. *Reliquiae Baxterianae*, II, pp. 238–40.
21. *Ibid.*, II, p. 237.
22. See Whiting, *Studies in English Puritanism from the Restoration to the Revolution*, pp. 479–80.
23. *Ibid.*, p. 480.
24. *Reliquiae Baxterianae*, II, p. 242.
25. *Ibid.*, II, pp. 248–9.
26. *Ibid.*, II, p. 250.
27. *Ibid.*, II, p. 251.
28. *Ibid.*, II, pp. 252–3.
29. *Ibid.*, II, p. 258.
30. *Ibid.*, II, p. 259.

CHAPTER VII

## THE KING'S DECLARATION
## (25TH OCTOBER 1660)
## AND HIGH HOPES OF UNITY

THE POSSIBILITY of a re-united Church in England, on a plan that would be practicable in modern times also, was contained in the King's Declaration on Ecclesiastical Affairs. It included a scheme of moderate episcopacy, with concessions regarding the liturgy and ceremonies, and without re-ordination, which could have united nearly all the nation in a liberal and comprehensive Church of England.

This Declaration was more important, and gave much more hope for unity, than the Savoy Conference of April–July 1661, with its unreal exchange of documents and its fruitless debates. Much of the Declaration's value, however, depended upon the degree of sincerity which prompted it. After the disappointments of the long-range negotiations in June and July 1660, the appearance of the King's Declaration raised hopes again; but when these hopes were falsified before the close of the year and Parliament refused to confirm the Declaration, there could be no confidence that any other offers would succeed.

Charles and Clarendon were responsible for the Declaration. Tanner[1] credits Clarendon with the actual drafting. No doubt both of them were willing to offer terms for unity with the Puritans if these could lead to a firmer acceptance of the Royalist regime and if the terms were acceptable to Royalist bishops and clergy. Charles had another motive, namely, toleration, especially for Roman Catholics. To some extent, therefore, Charles and Clarendon were honest in making this attempt to conciliate and comprehend the Puritan ministers in the established Church. Yet some historians reviewing the facts have not felt convinced of their sincerity. Sir James Stephen went so far to make these statements about the Declaration:

'Charles lent his royal name to an experiment of which DECEIT was the basis, and persecution the result.... To maintain the splendour and the powers of Episcopacy, to yield nothing, and yet to avoid the appearance of a direct breach of the royal word, was so glaringly the object of the Court, that wilful blindness only could fail to penetrate the transparent veil of "The Declaration" framed by Clarendon with all the astuteness of his profession, and accepted by the Presbyterians with the eagerness of expiring hope. Baxter was not so deceived. In common with the other heads of his party, he judged the faith of Charles an inadequate security, and refused the proffered mitre of Hereford as an insidious bribe.' [2]

Clarendon gives no positive evidence in his history concerning his personal part in drawing up the Declaration, but there is little reason for doubting that he always deserved his reputation as the implacable enemy of the 'Presbyterians'. Partly because of Charles's unfortunate experiences with the Scots in 1650, Clarendon had had little difficulty in persuading him against attending the French Calvinistic services at Charenton during the exile. Bosher, in *The Making of the Restoration Settlement*, has given impressive evidence of the preparations Clarendon made with the Laudian bishops for the complete establishment of episcopacy, both before Charles returned and in the early weeks after he landed in England. Clarendon's chief motive was to secure support for Charles from all parties. Whatever concessions he proposed were directed towards that purpose, and not through a genuine desire for comprehending the 'Presbyterians' in the established Church.

Though specific evidence is lacking it is highly probable that some of the political 'Presbyterian' leaders then influential at the Court were consulted by Charles and Clarendon in framing the Declaration; these included the Lord Chamberlain (the Earl of Manchester), the Earl of Anglesey, Lord Hollis, and Lord Broghill.

It is difficult to trace the stages at which suggestions were made to Clarendon when the Declaration was being drawn up, before copies of the first draft were circulated among interested persons on 4th September 1660. Evidently private conferences were being held between some of the bishops and the divines at the request of the latter. A slight incident shows the attempts being made to win over the divines, a forecast of the offers of bishoprics later. Baxter states that the divines called the bishops 'My Lords' (some of them had been newly elected though not yet consecrated); and, one of them, Morley, replied, 'We may call you also, I suppose, by the same title.'

On 4th September Clarendon sent copies of the first draft to Reynolds, upon reading Baxter's Petition, felt that its plainness thereupon commissioned Baxter to write a 'Petition to the King upon our sight of the First Draft of the Declaration'. Calamy and Reynolds, upon reading Baxter's Petition, felt that its plainness would give great offence. Three Presbyterian noblemen (the Earl of Manchester, the Earl of Anglesey, and Lord Hollis) were strongly of the same opinion. They urged certain amendments, the divines concurring. Reluctantly, Baxter consented. The Petition, thus amended, was sent to Clarendon, who was so displeased with it that he never called upon the ministers to present it to the King.[3]

Seeing that Baxter's Petition contained Usher's model (as it had been appended to the ministers' 'First Address and Proposals' sent to the bishops in June 1660), it is important to notice that this vital plan of Church government was *never brought before the King,* at least officially, at this or any other time. Therefore it was not mentioned in the King's Declaration.

Instead of accepting Baxter's 'Petition', Clarendon instructed the ministers to draw up any alterations they desired to the draft of the Declaration. The effect of these can be seen in the final form.

Before dealing with the Declaration itself, it is well to consider Baxter's 'Petition', which is the finest record of his position and the best expression of the whole 'Presbyterian' programme for the reform and unity of the Church of England.

1. *Baxter's 'Petition to the King upon our sight of the First Draft of the Declaration'*

Even Baxter's strongest critics never disputed his moral earnestness, which shines through every part of his Petition. His chief concern was that England should have godly pastors. At the outset in his Petition he lamented the expulsions of ministers who had not been episcopally ordained, or were alleged to have refused to take oaths of obedience to bishops, and the substitution of ignorant and scandalous ministers.

The Petition proceeded to forecast that divisions would follow the failure of the negotiations; that godly people would be punished on trumped-up charges of sedition, but actually because they could not pray for a persecuting prelacy; and that, as confusion intensified, 'Papists and others that are intolerable' would be brought forward as fit for a general toleration. Much of this prophecy was true, but fortunately it was deleted upon his friends' advice.

Usher's model was urgently advocated as conformable to Scripture and primitive custom, as guaranteeing discipline in the parishes, and as calculated to unite the great majority in the national Church. In an expunged section, Baxter gave the additional argument that 'not only the Presbyterians, but multitudes of the Episcopal party, and the nobility, gentry, and others that adhered to his late Majesty' had favoured it.[4] Clarendon must have known that this was true and probably he feared to let Usher's model be discussed; certainly he would not suffer it to be debated before the King. Baxter stressed the drastic distinctions between prelacy and the modified episcopacy of Usher's model.

'The Prelacy which we disclaimed is that of Diocesans, upon the claim of a superior order to a Presbyter, assuming the sole power of public admonition . . . excommunicating and absolving (besides confirmation) over so many churches, as necessitated the corruption or extirpation of discipline, and the using of human officers (as chancellors . . .) while the undoubted officers of Christ (the pastors of the particular churches) were hindered from the exercise of their office. THE RESTORATION OF DISCIPLINE in the particular churches, and of the pastors to the exercise of their office therein, AND OF SYNODS FOR NECESSARY CONSULTATION AND COMMUNION OF CHURCHES, AND OF THE PRIMITIVE PRESIDENCY OR EPISCOPACY . . . is that which we humbly offer as the remedy.'[5]

Once more Baxter stated the irreducible minimum he requested for healing and purifying the Church: pastoral discipline; associated synods; and the primitive presidency or primitive episcopacy.

These 'THREE NEEDFUL POINTS' for a reformed Church of England were all to be found in Usher's model, namely:

'1. The Pastors of the respective parishes may be allowed, not only publicly to preach, but personally to catechize . . . admitting none to the Lord's Table that have not personally owned their baptismal covenant by a credible profession of faith and obedience . . . and to deny such persons the Communion of the Church in the Holy Eucharist that remain impenitent.

'2. All the Pastors of each Rural Deanery, having a stated President chosen by themselves . . . may meet once a month' and receive presentments and appeals in case of discipline in the parishes.

'3. That a DIOCESAN SYNOD, consisting of the delegates of the several Rural Deaneries, be called as often as need requireth . . . and that without the *consent* of the major part of them, THE DIOCESAN MAY NOT ORDAIN, OR EXERCISE ANY SPIRITUAL CENSURES ON ANY OF THE MINISTERS.'

The emphasis upon the central requirement—the *consent* of the pastors in spiritual offices including ordination—is again apparent.

The first draft of the King's Declaration was criticized for ignoring inferior synods with their presidents: 'The Bishop which your Majesty declareth for is not episcopus praeses, but episcopus princeps, indued with sole power both of ordination and jurisdiction.' [6] In the first draft of the Declaration a bishop need not even call for 'advice', still less be obliged to accept it.

With regard to the vital principle of guarding the Lord's Table it may be considered that the rubric giving power to repel was sufficient. As it stood this rubric gave directions to 'call and advertise open and notorious evil-livers' not to presume to come to the Lord's Table until true repentance and amendment of life appeared. Archbishop Sheldon (as he became) refused to admit Charles II to Communion because of his notorious immorality; and, considering the extraordinary respect shown the restored King, this refusal even once was greatly to Sheldon's credit. Why, then, were Baxter and his friends not satisfied with this rubric?

(i) They felt that notification of desire to communicate the day before was insufficient time for the pastor. Furthermore, an admonition without the power to deny an impenitent person the Sacrament was useless.

(ii) They knew that it was a most exceptional thing for a person to be repelled while unworthy communicants were constantly being admitted.

## THE KING'S DECLARATION 147

(iii) According to the rubric, the minister had to report his action to the bishop within fourteen days. This made the pastor only 'the Bishop's curate', in Baxter's words. As the bishop could summarily annul the pastor's action the pastor did not possess the power of the keys.

(iv) Baxter and the other Puritans desired a positive action to signify an intending communicant's worthiness; this should be a 'credible profession of faith and obedience to the will of God', the ratifying of the baptismal covenant. Puritans did not agree with the bishops' assumption that all confirmed persons were worthy to communicate.

In a concluding reference to the liturgy and ceremonies Baxter contended that things 'indifferent' or 'unnecessary' should not be forced upon ministers and people. He placed stress upon the admission that these ceremonies were, technically, indifferent; if that was admitted, they should not be made compulsory. He added, 'We doubt not but Peter and Paul went to Heaven without the ceremonies in question.' [7]

Baxter asked the King specifically to include these concessions in the final form of the Declaration:

1. No oath of canonical obedience or subscription to the liturgy to be a condition of ordination or institution to a parish.
2. 'That none be urged to be RE-ORDAINED, or denied institution for want of ordination by prelates, that was ordained by presbyters.'
3. No minister to be deprived of his benefice 'for not reading those Articles of the Thirty-nine that contain the controverted points of Government and Ceremonies'.

*Nothing Baxter requested was granted.* Such was the tension of feeling that his Petition was not even presented to the King by the Lord Chancellor. Instead of this, Clarendon instructed the ministers to prepare 'Alterations' to the draft of the Declaration. These important 'Alterations' were communicated to the Chancellor and read over in the King's presence at an interview on 22nd October. The effect can be seen in the outline of the first draft, the 'Alterations', and the actual amendments to the Declaration set out on the tabulated pages (pp. 153–7).

## 2. The Ministers' Audience with the King on 22nd October

This critical meeting took place at Worcester House, the residence of the Lord Chancellor in the Strand. Those present at this audience were six bishops—Sheldon (London), Morley (Worcester), Gauden (afterwards Exeter), Henchman (Salisbury), Cosin (Durham), Hacket (Lichfield and Coventry), together with other clergy of their party, notably Dr Gunning. There were six 'Presbyterian' divines—Reynolds (afterwards Bishop of Norwich), Baxter, Manton, Spurstow, Wallis, and Ash. Noblemen present included known 'Presbyterians' such as the Earl of Manchester, the Earl of Anglesey, Lord Hollis, as well as Albemarle (Monk).

When the ministers' suggested 'Alterations' were read, the King was adamant in refusing to accept the word *consent* instead of *advice* in the phrases which referred to bishops consulting ministers before ordination or confirmation or passing censures. This was the vital point; it was Baxter's first principle—the pastor must be governor of his flock, and his consent was necessary. The ministers pleaded that unity would be impossible if they were not given the right of consent. 'We were sure that union would not be attained if no CONSENT were allowed ministers in any part of the government of their flocks, and so they should be only teachers ... of the people, whose RECTORS they were called.' [8]

On the other hand, Cosin's words to the King show what the bishops thought about this crucial matter. 'If your Majesty grant this, you unbishop your bishops.' [9]

Bishop Morley interposed to flatter the divines (Baxter in particular), stating that their influence was such that they could win over their people to conformity. He also alluded to Baxter's book, *Five Disputations of Church Government*, only recently published (1659), audaciously asserting that Baxter's writings contradicted his present position and supported the bishops' claims! The discussion passed on to the two questions of prelatical government and re-ordination. Baxter firmly referred Morley to the unanswered arguments in his *Five Disputations* against the English diocesan prelacy and against re-ordination of those ordained by presbyters only.

After long debating in the King's presence about the validity of these ordinations during the Interregnum, Clarendon suddenly produced from his pocket a petition for toleration from the Independents and Anabaptists. He thereupon proposed this significant addition to the King's Declaration : 'That others also be permitted to meet for religious worship so be it they do it not to the disturbance of the peace; and that no Justice of Peace or Officer disturb them.'

That proposal meant toleration for all faiths; not only Baxter, but all present realized that a general toleration would have benefited Roman Catholics more than any others. All present were asked for their opinion. They had noted the evidently premeditated manner in which the subject had been introduced. Prudence silenced them all—all but Baxter, courageous and impulsive. Disregarding the hurried whisper of Dr Wallis that he should say nothing, but let the bishops speak, Baxter uttered a respectful protest against general toleration. Undoubtedly he was obeying his conscience. Possibly he thought also that his speaking might induce the bishops to break silence, and that opposition by both parties to toleration might bring them a little closer. If so, it was a vain hope; the bishops allowed him to accept the odium his speech incurred. Yet what he said was comparatively mild. The 'Presbyterians', he declared, did not ask favours for themselves only and certainly did not desire 'rigorous severity' against any; but some sects were not worthy of toleration, and these included Papists and Socinians to whom (he adroitly remarked) Dr Gunning had referred in the general debate before Clarendon produced the petition. Baxter gave his opinion that his party could not take it upon themselves to support toleration for such religions. To this the King rather petulantly replied, 'That there were laws enough against the Papists', and the meeting ended almost immediately.

Any real interest Charles had taken in the negotiations between bishops and divines ceased after this meeting on 22nd October. He now realized that there was no more prospect of toleration for Roman Catholics from the 'Presbyterians' than from the bishops. Thenceforward the ministers had to reckon with the King's secret but firm opposition to any concession in their favour.

Momentous results had actually depended upon this audience with the King. If the 'Presbyterians' had agreed to toleration, at least specifically for the Independents and Anabaptists for whom the petition had been presented, the King might have favoured their cause sufficiently to have brought concessions from the bishops. Baxter's action not only permanently alienated the King's sympathy; it also strengthened the bishops' position. Moreover, it offended the Independents, most of whom were much closer in spirit to Baxter than the Laudian clergy could ever be. The Independents might easily feel that the 'Presbyterians' were abandoning them and were seeking advantages only for themselves. All this Baxter had feared from the outset.

Nothing distressed him more than the misrepresentations hurled against him from all sides after this meeting on 22nd October. Clarendon, for instance, told the Independents that they had been deliberately refused toleration by Baxter, and it was only with some difficulty that Baxter could eventually make Nye and other Independent leaders realize the true position.

At this stage in his account of the negotiations Baxter explicitly defines where he and his friends stood and particularly reiterates that the term 'Presbyterian' as applied to them was a misnomer. Some like Calamy and Spurstow had been rigid Presbyterians throughout; the initials of these two showed their participation in the Presbyterian production, 'Smectymnuus', in 1641. Baxter and many others were only moderate episcopalians who had never agreed to lay elders and other features of Presbyterianism, and had never been members of any Presbyterian church courts. Baxter makes this abundantly clear:

> 'Any man that was for a spiritual serious way of worship (though he were for Moderate Episcopacy and Liturgy) ... was called commonly a PRESBYTERIAN, as formerly he was called a Puritan, unless he joined himself to Independents, Anabaptists, or some other sect which might afford him a more odious name. And of the Lords, he that was for Episcopacy and the Liturgy was called a Presbyterian, if he endeavoured to procure any abatement of their impositions, for the RECONCILING of the parties. ... And of the ministers, he was called a Presbyterian that was for Episcopacy and Liturgy, if he conformed not so far as to subscribe or swear to the English Diocesan Frame, and all their impositions.
>
> 'I KNEW NOT OF ANY LORD AT COURT THAT WAS A PRESBYTERIAN; yet were the Earl of Manchester (a good man) and the Earl of Anglesey, and the Lord Hollis called Presbyterians ... when I have heard them plead for MODERATE EPISCOPACY AND LITURGY myself. ...

THE KING'S DECLARATION 151

'I leave it on record to the notice of posterity, that to the best of my knowledge THE PRESBYTERIAN CAUSE WAS NEVER SPOKEN OF. . . .

'And for myself, I ever professed my judgment to be so far for Episcopacy, Liturgy, &c, as I have expressed in my "Fifth Disputation for Church Government", and I drew on this Treaty, NOT AS A PRESBYTERIAN, BUT AS A RECONCILER. . . . Never did we write or speak a word (that I know of, who was always with them) for Ruling Elders, nor for the governments of Synods or Presbyteries without BISHOPS OR STATED PRESIDENTS . . . nor for any one thing that is proper to Presbytery.'[10]

In dissolving the meeting of 22nd October the King had left the revision of the words of the Declaration to two divines of each party (not including Baxter), with the Earl of Anglesey and Lord Hollis to settle any points on which these divines could not agree. Baxter had departed from this meeting, feeling that the King's Declaration could not secure peace and unity—because if the pastors' consent was not allowed they would be deprived of all government over their flocks. His conclusion after 22nd October was: 'I was resolved to meddle no more in the business but patiently suffer with other Dissenters.'

3. *The Draft Declaration, the Ministers' Suggested Alterations, and the Actual Amendments*

The revised 'Declaration concerning Ecclesiastical Affairs' was published on 25th October 1660. Baxter first learnt of this by hearing a boy crying in the streets that he had copies of the King's Declaration for sale. At once Baxter bought a copy and went into a nearby shop where he read it with eagerness and surprised delight. The Earl of Anglesey had evidently succeeded in including a number of amendments that the 'Presbyterian' party had desired.

Baxter was greatly relieved to find that the pastor's vital consent was made necessary for confirmation and for admission to Communion, although not for ordination or for episcopal censures. He believed that enough was now conceded to provide a basis of unity at last.

He had been on his way to Clarendon when he bought and read the copy, and when he met Clarendon he stated his expectation that most of the ministers could be brought into the Church if the Declaration became law.

This Declaration needs detailed examination, in this manner:

(1) The draft sent to the ministers on 4th September, this being noted on the following pages as the final form also, except where changes are indicated.

(2) The 'Alterations' submitted by the ministers, after Baxter's controversial 'Petition on sight of the First Draft of the Declaration' had been discarded; where these were accepted and made part of the Declaration, this is indicated.

(3) Actual amendments, either accepted on the ministers' suggestions made privately or brought about by the efforts of the Earl of Anglesey and Lord Hollis.[11]

It should be remembered that Usher's model, which the ministers wished to include in their 'Alterations', and which had been included in their 'Proposals' sent to the bishops in June, and which also had formed part of Baxter's discarded Petition, had NOT been accepted by Clarendon, and through his influence or persuasion it was omitted from the 'Alterations'. Thus Usher's model was not part of the King's Declaration, to the disappointment of the ministers.

The Declaration first expressed the King's devotion to the Church of England, an attachment strengthened by his exile on the Continent where he claimed he had found many who had suspected the Church of England 'as if it had too much complied with the Church of Rome, whereas they now acknowledge it to be the best fence God has yet raised against Popery in the world'. It can be assumed at once that these were the sentiments, not of Charles, but of Clarendon, who was mainly responsible for the Declaration as a whole.

The King went on to acknowledge the 'Presbyterians' ' loyalty and stated that he had incurred much criticism through not enforcing the use of the Prayer Book immediately on his return. His example of moderation had not been followed, he averred, by some who had printed the Declaration that the Scots had forced him to make in 1650. This was evidence of party passions which must be removed before it would be possible to call a conference to settle the state of the Church. He wondered the more at this when the bishops' party and the 'Presbyterian' leaders alike pro-

| FIRST DRAFT (also final form unless amended in right-hand column) | MINISTERS' SUGGESTED ALTERATIONS | ACTUAL AMENDMENTS |
|---|---|---|
| | 'Our purpose is ... to promote the power of godliness' and observance of the Lord's Day. | (Alteration accepted.) |
| Only learned and pious men to be chosen bishops. | Inefficient ministers not to be permitted. | (Alteration accepted.) |
| 'If any Diocese shall be thought too large ... appoint Suffragan Bishops.' | 'Because the Diocese, especially some of them, are ... too large ... appoint Suffragan Bishops.' | (Alteration accepted.) |
| *Ordination, etc.:* | | |
| Ordination and jurisdiction (censures) by the bishops to be undertaken by the *advice* and assistance of the presbyters. | *Advice* and *consent* of the presbyters. | (Alteration disallowed by the King 'because *consent* gave the ministers a negative voice'.) |
| | Lay officials would take no part in excommunication, absolution, or other pastoral matters. | (Alteration accepted.) |
| | Archdeacons to be assisted by 6 ministers (3 nominated by bishop, 3 elected by ministers). | (Alteration accepted.) |
| *Jurisdiction and Confirmation:* | | |
| A number of presbyters should be selected *by the bishop* to assist him and the dean and chapter in ordinations and in the exercise of jurisdiction. | A number of presbyters equal to the number of the chapter and 'annually chosen by the major vote of all the presbyters of that diocese' should assist in all ordinations and acts of jurisdiction. 'Nor shall any suffragan bishop | (Alteration accepted.) |

| FIRST DRAFT (also final form unless amended in right-hand column) | MINISTERS' SUGGESTED ALTERATIONS | ACTUAL AMENDMENTS |
|---|---|---|
| | ordain... but with the advice and assistance' of such elected presbyters, nor exercise jurisdiction without them. | |
| Confirmation to be performed on the *advice* of 'the minister of the place'. | Confirmation 'on the CONSENT of the minister of the place'. | (Alteration accepted.) |
| *Profession of Faith before Communion:* Regarding scandalous persons, the first draft provided only vaguely that 'as great diligence used for the instruction and reformation of notorious and scandalous offenders as is possible'. | The minister 'shall admit none to the Lord's supper, till they have made a credible profession of their faith... and that all possible diligence be used for the instruction and reformation of scandalous offenders, whom the minister shall not suffer to partake of the Lord's table, until they have openly declared themselves to have truly repented and amended'. | (Alteration accepted.) |
| *Church government:* | | In addition to the meeting of the suffragans and their presbytery there should be a monthly meeting in each *rural deanery* consisting of the rural dean and three or four elected ministers to receive 'complaints' from the parishes, and by using admonitions 'to convince offenders'. When reformation did not |

| FIRST DRAFT (also final form unless amended in right-hand column) | MINISTERS' SUGGESTED ALTERATIONS | ACTUAL AMENDMENTS |
|---|---|---|
| | | result, such obdurate cases to be reported to the bishop. *Catechizing* of the young people of each parish to be carried out before confirmation or admission to the Sacrament. |
| *The liturgy:* 'Since we find some exceptions made to many obsolete words, and other expressions... which upon the reformation and improvement of the English language, may well be altered, we will appoint some learned divines, of different persuasions, to review the same, and to make such alterations as shall be thought most necessary, and some such additional prayers....' | 'Since we find some exceptions made against SEVERAL THINGS therein, we will appoint an equal number of learned divines of both persuasions, to review the same, and to make such alterations as shall be thought most necessary, and some additional forms (IN THE SCRIPTURE PHRASE...)... AND THAT IT BE LEFT TO THE MINISTER'S CHOICE TO USE ONE OR THE OTHER.' | (Alteration accepted.) |
| *Ceremonies:* The King's experience abroad where the disputed ceremonies had not been used had convinced him of their value. | | |
| Objectors would have supported the ceremonies if they had been abroad; and many ministers who objected did not consider these ceremonies unlawful. | (Request for deletion of this section.) | (Deleted as requested.) |

| FIRST DRAFT (also final form unless amended in right-hand column) | MINISTERS' SUGGESTED ALTERATIONS | ACTUAL AMENDMENTS |
|---|---|---|
| Every national Church had the right to adopt ceremonies which of themselves 'indifferent' ceased to be indifferent after being 'once established by law'. | | |
| Nevertheless, conscientious difficulties would be considered—for example, kneeling at Communion would be optional until 'a national synod' considered it. | (Proposed addition): 'Provided that none shall be denied the Sacrament of the Lord's Supper, though they do not use the gesture of kneeling in the act of receiving.' | (Addition accepted, but probably only intended to be until the 'national synod' decided as that qualification remained above.) |
| The use of the cross in Baptism, bowing at the name of Jesus, and the use of surplice—all to be *optional*. | Also observance of holy days to be optional. | (Holy days—option refused.) |
| *Oaths and Subscription before ordination:*<br>'Institution and Induction' to be permitted 'without any other subscription [except oaths of allegiance and supremacy] until it shall be otherwise determined by a Synod'. | 'Oath of Canonical Obedience' inserted as well as 'Subscription'.<br>'Ordination' added to 'Institution and Induction'.<br>No reference to decision of a national synod, but an absolute dispensing with subscription to the liturgy and oath of canonical obedience. | (All alterations accepted and substituted for first draft.) |
| | 'No person in the Universities shall for want of such Subscription be hindered in the taking of their degrees.' | (Alteration accepted.) |

| FIRST DRAFT (also final form unless amended in right-hand column) | MINISTERS' SUGGESTED ALTERATIONS | ACTUAL AMENDMENTS |
|---|---|---|
| *Re-ordination:* | 'Lastly, that such as have been ORDAINED BY PRESBYTERS BE NOT REQUIRED TO RENOUNCE THEIR ORDINATION OR TO BE RE-ORDAINED, or denied Institution and Induction for want of ordination by Bishops. And moreover, that none be judged to forfeit their presentation or benefice, or be deprived of it, for not reading of those of the Thirty-nine Articles that contain the controverted points of Church-government and Ceremonies.'[12] | 'Lastly, that none be judged to forfeit his presentation or benefice, or be deprived of it, upon the Statute of the 13th of Queen Elizabeth, chapter the 12th, so he read and declare his assent to all the Articles of Religion, which only concern the confession of the true Christian faith, and the doctrine of the Sacraments comprised in the Book of Articles in the said statute mentioned.'[13] |

fessed their desire for concord : 'they all approve Episcopacy, they all approve a set form of Liturgy'. Now with the return of monarchy, the King said there must be 'a return to Episcopacy, with which the monarchy hath flourished through so many ages.' [14]

A comment must be made about the provision for Church government (given on pp. 154–5 of this study). The clauses given there were not in Baxter's copy of the first draft and not in the 'Alterations' presented by the ministers. There seems to be no evidence available to show how they came to be included in the final form of the Declaration. Yet it is so vitally consistent with the ministers' policy that it must have been verbally proposed by them and included between the meeting on 22nd October and the publication of the Declaration on 25th October, no doubt with the support of the Earl of Anglesey. Also, by comparison with Usher's model, it can be seen that, though the model had not been presented to the King, its essential provisions in the section concerned were adopted in the final form of the Declaration. The influence of Baxter's voluntary associations also can be seen in the provisions in that important section.

### 4. *Was Re-union without Re-ordination proposed?*

The section on re-ordination is so important, especially in its bearing on re-union in modern times, that it is regrettable that every stage of the negotiations between King, Chancellor, and ministers on this particular matter cannot be traced. It is also surprising that more attention has not been focused upon this vital phase of the discussions.

It is true that there is no reference to re-ordination, either requiring it or dispensing with it, in the draft of the Declaration as it appears in *Reliquiae Baxterianae*.[15] The vital sections referring to re-ordination, quoted on page 157 of this study, appear in Baxter's narrative neither in one form nor the other.

It is evident that the King's Declaration in the first draft, as read on 4th September, held out no hope for accepting non-episcopally ordained ministers in the re-united Church. It can confidently be assumed that this represented the true opinion of the Lord Chancellor as well as of the bishops. Some, like Bosher, in *The Making of the Restoration Settlement*,[16] who says, 'The subject was not dealt with in the King's Declaration', have assumed that the subject was not only not dealt with at all in the King's

## THE KING'S DECLARATION 159

Declaration, but have even believed that Baxter did not ask for no re-ordination. The facts are that Baxter asked for the acceptance of non-episcopally ordained ministers in his 'Petition upon our sight of the First Draft of the Declaration' although the 'Petition' was not presented; that he and his colleagues proposed it in their 'Alterations'; and that the provision for the non-requirement of re-ordination was found in the final amendments to the King's Declaration. This final inclusion indicates that the King and Clarendon accepted the request.

There is evidence of the trend of discussions in the volume, *Documents relating to the Settlement of the Church of England by the Act of Uniformity, 1662,* edited by the Rev. George Gould, and published by Kent and Company in 1862 during the bi-centenary commemorations. It is even stated there that the original draft of the Declaration contained the generous promise dispensing with re-ordination and assuring ministers against deprivation for not reading the disputed Articles dealing with Church government. This point, however, must be regarded as incorrect for the following reasons. Firstly, Baxter's discarded Petition, as we have seen, expressed their 'fear and grief' because the first draft was silent on the subject of re-ordination, and in that Petition he proceeded to urge the King not to require re-ordination. This would not have been mentioned if the first draft had actually made the promise. Secondly, the fact that the ministers included the request for not requiring re-ordination in their 'Alterations' indicates conclusively that the new clause emanated from them.[17]

The confusion surrounding the subject is deepest in regard to the difference between the form of the ministers' request for no re-ordination and the form in which no re-ordination appeared in the final form of the Declaration. Why was the ministers' plainly worded statement abandoned? And why was the permission for no re-ordination as given by the Act of 1571 substituted?

No reference to the subject being debated in the audience with the King on 22nd October seems to have been found, but the volume *Documents relating to the Settlement of the Church of England by the Act of Uniformity, 1662* states that the final provision was inserted to comply with the 'Presbyterian' ministers' own request.[18] Again, Baxter gives no hint of this in his narrative. The ministers must have considered that there was wider and surer benefit in the Act of 1571 which stated:

'Every person under the degree of a Bishop, which does or shall pretend to be a priest or minister of God's Holy Word and Sacraments, by reason of ANY OTHER FORM of Institution, Consecration, or Ordering, than the Form set forth by Parliament in the time of Edward VI . . . shall in the presence of the Bishop . . . of some one diocese where he has or shall have ecclesiastical living, declare his assent, and subscribe to all the Articles of Religion (1562) WHICH ONLY CONCERN THE CONFESSION OF THE TRUE CHRISTIAN FAITH AND THE DOCTRINE OF THE SACRAMENTS. . . .'[19]

Most of those who benefited by the Act of 1571 were Romish priests who had not been ordained according to the form added to the Book of Common Prayer, and who were thus enabled to hold or receive livings without re-ordination according to that form upon their making the simple subscription of assent to the Thirty-nine Articles. Although, therefore, the Act of 1571 was almost certainly not designed to benefit Protestant ministers ordained on the Continent in Elizabethan or earlier times by non-episcopal Reformed Churches, yet actually there were instances of such Protestant ministers receiving livings in England without re-ordination (see pp. 34–8).[20]

It may be concluded that the negotiating ministers in 1660 considered that the conditions at the Restoration had some similarities to those which obtained in 1571. Most of the so-called Presbyterian ministers like Baxter had been episcopally ordained, but it seems unthinkable that they suddenly decided to ignore the needs of their brethren who had been ordained by 'Presbyterian' classes or voluntary associations or Cromwellian committees, and equally improbable that they withdrew the first definite provision for no re-ordination in favour of the Act of 1571 if this Act gave them less benefit.

It may be thought possible that the King and Clarendon refused the plain exemption from re-ordination and substituted the benefits of the Act of 1571 because the latter might narrow the entrance for presbyterially ordained ministers by requiring acceptance of ALL of the Articles, including those stipulating government by bishops; but, actually, in giving the benefits of the Act of 1571, the Declaration was providing for those who would accept the Articles dealing with the faith and the Sacraments only. It must be found that the ministers believed that, just as ex-Romish priests received the benefits of the Act of 1571, so these benefits could legally be extended to ministers presbyterially ordained during the extraordinary period of fifteen years when bishops could not regularly ordain in England, provided that they accepted the Articles mentioned.

All this depended upon Parliament ratifying the King's Declaration. There was always a grave doubt whether Parliament would do this; and the bishops were certain to use all their influence against ratification.

The Act of 1571 stipulated a date before which subscription to the Articles without re-ordination would be required. If the King's Declaration had been ratified and a date fixed for all ministers to subscribe to the Articles, re-union would have been effected without re-ordination.

In view of all the forces in Church and State arrayed against the non-episcopally ordained clergy, this offer, so generous as it seemed, may have only academic interest now. Nevertheless, this matter must have been extensively discussed at the time, and Baxter must have regarded it as an indispensable condition for re-union.

5. *Failure—at the Nearest Approach to Unity*

The King's Declaration was the most favourable point the negotiations reached. In fact, 25th October 1660 was the most hopeful day for re-union in the history of religion in England since the Reformation. It was therefore the more disheartening that these bright hopes suddenly raised were so soon dissipated and the record of the national Church stained with the persecution of her dissenting children.

After the publication of the final Declaration, Baxter was in private conference with the Lord Chancellor on several occasions; this was an indication of Clarendon's desire to win the support of a divine with so much influence. Baxter said he would endeavour to persuade the ministers to accept the terms of the Declaration, provided that the liturgy was altered as promised in the Declaration and the Declaration was confirmed by Parliament.

After the Declaration had been issued, bishoprics and deaneries were offered to leading divines. This was generally regarded as an attempt to weaken the Puritan party by removing their leaders. Reynolds accepted the See of Norwich on 'a profession directed to the King . . . that he took a Bishop and presbyter to differ not ordine but gradu, and that a Bishop was but the chief presbyter, and that he was not to ordain or govern but with his presbyters' assistance and consent, and that thus he accepted of the place, and as described in the King's Declaration'.[21]

Baxter was offered the bishopric of Hereford, but he declined it after a few days' deliberation. His good sense as well as his honour forbade him making such terms with his conscience as Reynolds had done. He realized also that he would compromise his future advocacy of the cause to which he had devoted all his energies.

'I feared that this Declaration was BUT FOR A PRESENT USE, and that shortly it would be revoked or nullified. And if so, I doubted not, but the laws would prescribe such work for Bishops, in silencing ministers, and troubling honest Christians for their consciences, and ruling the vicious with greater lenity . . . as that I had rather have the meanest employment amongst men. And my judgment was fully resolved against the lawfulness of the OLD DIOCESAN FRAME.'[22]

In his letter to Clarendon declining the bishopric, Baxter stated that he could more easily work for the desired unity of the Church if he had no personal advantage to gain. He generously mentioned other divines who might be appointed. Baxter's enemies should have recognized his entire freedom from mercenary or worldly motives of any kind.

The See of Coventry and Lichfield was offered to Calamy, who had been closer to orthodox Presbyterianism than the other leaders; it was felt by his associates that his acceptance would have been quite inconsistent. Manton, Bates, and Bowles refused deaneries. Incidentally, there is no evidence of Baxter's having been ordained only a deacon being regarded as a difficulty; seeing that bishops had been consecrated *per saltum* in Scotland it is probable that Baxter would have been consecrated bishop without being ordained priest.

The offers to Baxter and others were the only visible effect of the Declaration. Baxter placed on record that *none of the promises in the Declaration was ever carried out*. No suffragan bishops were appointed. No meetings of rural deaneries were held. No advice or assistance was ever asked from presbyters by the bishops when ordaining or exercising jurisdiction or inflicting spiritual censures. No consent of a minister was sought before confirmation. No test was imposed before admitting anyone to Communion.

Before the last days of 1660 the hopes of a settlement had diminished. Perfervid Royalist feeling had risen everywhere, and it was being expressed in the counties in the squires' hatred of the strict clergy. When these squires had full opportunity in the Cavalier Parliament in the following year, there was no suggestion of any concession whatever. Yet it was the Convention Parliament, with its many 'political Presbyterians', that refused to ratify the Declaration—an action to which reference will be made later.

Baxter knew the working of the old prelatical system too well to expect anything but the silencing of the ministers. He felt it none the less his duty to strive always for unity. He was charitable enough, too, to allow that not all the episcopal representatives in the discussions were guilty of double-dealing or 'that nothing but deceit and juggling was from the beginning intended'.

'The land had been but lately engaged against them. . . . Therefore it was necessary that moderate things should be proposed and promised; and no way was so fit as by a Declaration, which being no law, is a temporary thing, giving place to laws. And it was needful that the calling of a Synod [the Savoy Conference] was delayed, till the Presbyterians were partly cast out, and a way to keep out the rest secured. And if when all these things were done . . . severities were doubled in comparison of what they were before the Wars, no man can wonder that well understood the persons and the causes.' [23]

The *weaknesses* of the King's Declaration were :

(1) It purported to represent the King's personal attempt to honour the promise he had made at Breda that he would consider tender consciences, and it could be regarded as being nothing more.

(2) It did not represent the opinions of the bishops at any point. Clarendon's policy of appeasement was behind it, and he had the assistance of the 'Presbyterian' lords and their ministers'

suggestions given in writing and also in private consultations. Bishops were indeed present at Worcester House on 22nd October when the ministers' 'Alterations' to the first draft were read; and it is possible that those bishops knew of the final revisions before the publication on 25th October. Even so, there was nothing to indicate what concessions, if any, they would support. While the *utmost* the Presbyterians could expect was seen in the final form of the Declaration, the bishops were still free to ignore it *in toto* in any conference with the divines as well as in Convocation and Parliament. Bosher quotes, in his *The Making of the Restoration Settlement*,[24] statements from less rigid bishops like Gauden and Henchman, showing the Declaration to be only an expedient to allay 'Presbyterian' feeling until a synod settled the constitution and worship of the Church.

(3) The Declaration had no effect whatever unless ratified by Parliament.

(4) The liturgy and ceremonies loomed larger in the eyes of the Laudian clergy than the most important sections in the Declaration, which dealt with pastoral duties, discipline, and Church government generally. Any amendments to the liturgy were specifically reserved until the Savoy Conference dealt with them. In this regard, therefore, the Declaration guaranteed nothing.

(5) Hopeful and generous though the terms of the Declaration were, the most rigid 'Presbyterians' were not satisfied. The Independents who were not included in the benefits, and who properly felt that they were being deserted by the major party, would likewise not support the Declaration. The Laudian bishops and clergy would certainly obstruct it altogether. Where was the party with sufficient unity and with enough influence outside a conference to secure acceptance and confirmation of the Declaration?

The *advantages* of the Declaration, which Baxter saw, were:

(1) The scheme of Church government it envisaged would be a precedent for the future. Baxter still hoped that what the King was willing to grant in 1660 might be offered again. Whether the Savoy Conference succeeded or not (although it reviewed only the liturgy and ceremonies), it was theoretically arguable that the essentials of Church order in the Declaration might be brought forward in later years.

(2) The 'Presbyterian' leaders had been given a status through the negotiations for the Declaration that would be of value to their cause if future efforts for unity were made.

(3) The 'Presbyterian' party had twelve months' suspension of the law before conformity might be required regarding the liturgy and ceremonies. (Actually, *this was the only benefit*.)

When the Declaration was issued, a meeting was called for the London ministers 'called Presbyterian' to discuss the question of returning thanks to the King. Some were reluctant to do this, lest they be thereby committed to accepting all the terms of the Declaration, especially in regard to government by archbishops and bishops, which rigid Presbyterians deemed contrary to the Solemn League and Covenant. Baxter argued with his usual vigour that the bishops to whom the Declaration referred would be very different from the old prelates against whom the Covenant had been designed in 1643. He believed that allowing pastors the spiritual government of their congregations was worth almost everything else in the Declaration; this always represented the minimum but sufficient demand Baxter made.

Long afterwards, in reviewing the situation in 1660–61, Baxter confirmed the fact that this was the indispensable requirement for unity when he wrote:

'Here I tell posterity that if we could have but got our Prelates to have confirmed us to BUT ONE WORD which the King granted us, pro tempore, in his Declaration . . . viz. that the confirmation as a solemn transition from Infant Church-state into the Adult should be but by the MINISTER'S CONSENT (as knowing his people better than the Bishop that never before saw them or heard or examined them) it had healed one of the greatest of our breaches; but our concord was not thought worth this little price.'[25]

A considerable number of the London ministers agreed with Baxter and drew up 'The Humble and Grateful Acknowledgment of many ministers of the Gospel in and about the City of London, to his Royal Majesty for his gracious concessions in his Majesty's late Declaration concerning Ecclesiastical Affairs'. Among the signatories were those who afterwards were members of the Savoy Conference: Samuel Clark, Thomas Case, Thomas Jacombe, William Cooper, John Rawlinson, William Bates, and Arthur

Jackson. This 'Acknowledgment', made on 16th November, noted particularly these benefits from the Declaration :

1. Ordination and censures to be only with the advice of presbyters.
2. The abolition of lay chancellors.
3. The restored power of pastors in their own congregations.
4. The monthly meeting of rural deaneries.
5. The promise of a revised liturgy with additional forms, and no punishment of those not using the liturgy until revision.
6. Ordination, institution, and induction without subscription to the whole of the liturgy or oath of canonical obedience.
7. Leaving certain ceremonies optional, these including kneeling, the cross in Baptism, bowing at the name of Jesus, and the surplice.

The 'Acknowledgment' added the hope that re-ordination would not be required. This may support an inference that the ministers did not regard the application of the Subscription Act of 1571 to the conditions of 1660 as sufficient; but it rather indicates that those who held livings in 1660 had been led to expect that the benefits of the Act of 1571 would be given to them if the Declaration was ratified.

All expectations and all doubts about benefits from the Declaration were speedily settled by the vote of the Convention Parliament.

After the House of Commons, on 9th November, had unanimously given thanks formally to the King for the Declaration, a Bill 'For making the King's Majesty's Declaration effectual' was introduced on 28th November before a full House. It was clear that the supporters of the bishops had determined to join battle with the 'Presbyterians' in a crucial test as there was opposition at once. Some members took the ground that it was dangerous to give to a royal declaration the subsequent effect of law. Others disingenuously praised the Declaration but opposed making its provisions legal. Others were influenced by the King's action in adding a clause giving general toleration after the Declaration was published on 25th October; evidently there was much concern about the danger of tolerating both Roman Catholics and anti-monarchist sects. Another circumstance, which may have operated in some members' minds, was Clarendon's statement that a conference would be called to deal with the liturgy in any case; and some members may therefore have been disposed to leave matters to that conference without passing a law to ratify the promises in the Declaration.[26]

The chief reason for the Bill's defeat, however, was the insincerity of the Court party. The Bill needed a large body of sincere sponsors (especially when the provision for a general toleration had been added), and these were lacking. The Secretary of State, William Morrice, who represented the Court, spoke 'ambiguously' and finished his speech by advising the rejection of the Bill. It was credibly stated that Clarendon and others of the King's ministers secretly persuaded members to vote against the Bill. As a result of this attitude of the Court party, the Bill was rejected on the second reading by 183 votes to 157. The 'Presbyterian' minority was, nevertheless, a large one—when it is remembered that many Royalist squires had been brought from the country to vote against the Bill, and also that some Independent members opposed the Bill because of the opinions of the 'Presbyterians' about toleration.

Sir Matthew Hale, Baxter's friend, who had framed the Bill, was elevated to the Bench and thus prevented from advocating moderate episcopal claims in Parliament in future.

This vote of the Commons showed that the 'Presbyterians' ' fate was sealed and negotiations with the ministers would henceforth be almost worthless. The Court party must be regarded as never having genuinely desired accommodation with the Puritans. Clarendon himself had ceased to think of concessions as the weeks passed and the importance of the Puritan parties declined. He felt that, with the mounting tide of Royalist passions everywhere, they could be ignored. The history of the whole period clearly shows that Clarendon never moved from the policy he had accepted during the exile, that he was determined to restore full episcopacy, that he was trifling with the ministers in the negotiations, and that he viewed with equanimity their future expulsion from the Church. Certainly the Cavalier Parliament of Puritan-hating squires in the following year would see to it that the breach in the Church became permanent.

We can see now the changes the King's Declaration would have made in the Church of England. There would have been a constitutional episcopacy at once. There would have been monthly meetings of rural deaneries and annual meetings of synods. Confirmation would have necessitated the consent of pastors. A credible profession of faith would have been needed before admission to Communion. Unrepentant sinners would have been repelled after rural deaneries considered their case. Bishops would have had the assistance of presbyteries in ordination and jurisdiction. There might have been an alternative liturgy, or at least additional forms to the liturgy, and optional ceremonies—provided always that the Savoy Conference fulfilled the expectation foreshadowed in the Declaration.

Whether all this would have been practicable is another question. The autocratic bishops of those days were not accustomed to consulting with their clergy. Most Englishmen were not in favour of a system that would give so much power to clergy to repel from Communion. In spite of the burning sincerity of the ministers in seeking to raise the standards of moral and spiritual life, it is arguable that their disciplinary rigidity was unwise, even in an age much less complacent about these matters than ours. If freedom had been given in forms of worship, there might have been complications. In parishes where Puritan ministers had used freedom before the abolition of the Prayer Book, and in many places since then, there were many people who preferred uniformity and the Prayer Book.

One of the most important results would have been the continuance of ministers in office without taking oaths of obedience to bishops or subscribing to use the whole liturgy; and, it seems, their continuance without re-ordination if they had been ordained by presbyteries or Cromwellian committees or county associations during the Interregnum.

A Church of England, united on the basis of the King's Declaration, would have been free from excessive ritualism. It would have satisfied all who feared the encroachments of alleged Romanist patterns. It may well have been possible also that the arid deism and the spiritual barrenness of a large part of the Church in the eighteenth century would have been avoided, and the evangelical revival of that century might have developed as a natural outcome of the life of the united Church itself and with the full co-operation of bishops and clergy and not have involved the secession of Methodism, which again reduced the strength of the established Church. Unfortunately, all dreams of reform vanished when the hopes raised by the King's Declaration were destroyed.

## NOTES TO CHAPTER VII

1. Tanner, *English Constitutional Conflicts, 1603–1689*, p. 226.
2. Stephen, *Essays in Ecclesiastical Biography*, pp. 347–8.
3. *Reliquiae Baxterianae*, II, p. 274.
4. *Ibid.*, II, p. 267.
5. *Ibid.*, II, p. 268.
6. *Ibid.*, II, p. 269.
7. *Ibid.*, II, p. 272.
8. *Ibid.*, II, pp. 276–7.
9. See Bosher, *The Making of the Restoration Settlement*, p. 186.
10. *Reliquiae Baxterianae*, II, p. 278.
11. *Ibid.*, II, pp. 259–64; and *Documents Relating to the Settlement of the Church of England by the Act of Uniformity, 1662*, pp. 63–78, 98–101.
12. *Reliquiae Baxterianae*, II, p. 276; and *Documents Relating to the Settlement of the Church of England by the Act of Uniformity, 1662*, pp. 77, 101.
13. *Ibid.*, p. 77.
14. *Reliquiae Baxterianae*, II, p. 262.
15. *Ibid.*, II, pp. 259–64.
16. Bosher, *The Making of the Restoration Settlement*, p. 274.
17. *Reliquiae Baxterianae*, II, p. 276; and *Documents Relating to the Settlement of the Church of England by the Act of Uniformity, 1662*, pp. 77, 101.
18. *Ibid.*, p. 77 (footnote).
19. Gee and Hardy, *Documents Illustrative of English Church History*, p. 478; and Sykes, *Old Priest and New Presbyter*, p. 98.
20. *Ibid.*, pp. 99, 100.
21. *Reliquiae Baxterianae*, II, p. 283.
22. *Ibid.*, II, p. 281.
23. *Ibid.*, II, p. 287–8.
24. Bosher, *The Making of the Restoration Settlement*, pp. 191–2.
25. *A Treatise on Episcopacy*, p. 76.
26. Green, *A Short History of the English People*, p. 587.

CHAPTER VIII

# BAXTER AND THE BISHOPS AT THE SAVOY CONFERENCE, 1661

CHARLES had issued his Declaration to keep faith with his promise at Breda. He called the Savoy Conference to honour the promise in the Declaration that there would be a synod to consider Prayer Book revision. The Declaration had yielded nothing and the Conference was to prove fruitless.

Although the Savoy Conference has received more attention from historians than the earlier negotiations it actually had less significance. It was concerned only with the liturgy and ceremonies, which, to Baxter and his colleagues, were not comparable in importance with the questions of Church government and discipline. The ministers were also embarrassed by the fact that the Prayer Book and the disputed ceremonies had become symbols of loyalty to the King and the Church. Seeing also that the Declaration had been nullified by Parliament, and that hopes of reform in government and discipline had completely failed, it was idle to look to the Savoy Conference for any agreement concerning the liturgy and ceremonies.

Probably no one believed that the bishops would make the Conference an honest attempt to revise the Prayer Book as Puritans had desired. The bishops' ranks had been reinforced. Seven new bishops had been consecrated on 2nd December 1660. They were Cosin (Durham), Gauden (Exeter), Walton (Chester), Sterne (Carlisle), Laney (Peterborough), Lloyd (Llandaff), Lawes (St David's). At their consecration, the preacher was Sancroft, the future Archbishop of Canterbury, famous at the Seven Bishops' Trial in 1688 and as leader of the non-jurors afterwards; at this time he was domestic chaplain to Cosin, and in his sermon he said: 'Blessed be this day in which we see the phoenix arising from her funeral pile, and taking wing again; our holy mother, the Church, standing up from the dust and ruins in which she sat so long, remounting the Episcopal throne, bearing the keys of the Kingdom of Heaven with her, and armed with the rod of discipline.' This proved to be the rod of discipline for Nonconformist ministers and people.

Supporting the bishops was the newly elected Cavalier Parliament. Clarendon's expectations had been fulfilled, and the supporters of prelacy had swept the polls everywhere, except in London and a few towns. Only fifty members in the Cavalier or Pension Parliament were not completely bound to the old episcopal order. All members had to take Communion according to the Prayer Book service on the assembling of Parliament. 'The most profane, swearing fellows that ever I heard in my life', was the comment of Pepys on the new Parliament, all of whom had taken Communion. The majority of members were country, Puritan-hating squires. Men of this type had opposed the Laudian bishops because of their authoritarian attitude before 1640, but now, joining forces with the restored parsons, they hotly attacked the 'Presbyterians'. Both squires and sequestered clergy remembered the repressive acts, including the heavy taxation and fines levied on Royalists, during the Interregnum.

The Convention Parliament in 1660 had ordered the Solemn League and Covenant to be read in all churches and affixed to the wall of the House of Commons. The Cavalier Parliament in 1661, by 228 votes to 113, ordered the Covenant to be burnt by the common hangman. Even the Convention Parliament, for the various reasons noticed, had not been willing to give effect to the King's Declaration. There was no likelihood of any sympathy for the bishops' critics from the Cavalier Parliament.

Presbyterians, Independents, and all sects had become objects of suspicion for other reasons. The ridiculous rising of Fifth Monarchy men in January 1661 was used by the Royalists as an excuse for harassing all Puritans. Accusations of disloyalty were hurled against the most respectable 'Presbyterians'. Baxter, known for his loyalty, nevertheless suffered the indignity of his private correspondence being seized in transit and taken to the Lord Chancellor. The position was deteriorating and concessions for unity less likely than ever.

## 1. *The King's Warrant*

On 25th March 1661 the King's Warrant was issued for the fateful Conference. It recalled the promise made in the Declaration to appoint an equal number of learned divines of both persuasions to review the liturgy. The Warrant directed the bishops and divines named: 'to advise upon and review the Book of Common Prayer. . . . And if occasion be, to make such reasonable and necessary alterations, corrections, and amendments therein . . . as shall be agreed upon to be needful or expedient for the giving satisfaction to tender consciences, and the restoring and continuance of peace and unity in the churches.'

The bishops' party included Accepted Frewen (Archbishop of York), Gilbert Sheldon (London, and Master of the Savoy), George Morley (Worcester), John Cosin (Durham), John Warner (Rochester), Henry King (Chichester), Humphrey Henchman (Salisbury), Robert Sanderson (Lincoln), Benjamin Laney (Peterborough), Bryan Walton (Chester), John Gauden (Exeter), and Richard Sterne (Carlisle). The episcopal assistants were Dr John Earle (Dean of Westminster), Dr Peter Heylen, Dr John Hacket, Dr John Barwick, Dr John Gunning, Dr John Pearson, Dr Thomas Pierce, Dr Anthony Sparrow, and Herbert Thorndike.

Frewen took little part. Sheldon, although exerting much influence when present, seldom attended. Morley, who was personally acquainted with Baxter, was bitter in his tone and unswerving in his opposition. Cosin, the ripest scholar in his party, upheld the strongest opinions of Laudian episcopacy. Pearson was one of the cleverest debaters on his side. Gunning became Baxter's keenest antagonist, especially towards the end of the controversies. Gauden had conformed to the Cromwellian ecclesiastical establishment, although a convinced episcopalian; he was the most moderate of the bishops during the discussions.

The 'Presbyterian' divines are shown, with a number of details concerning their ordination, positions, and subsequent relation to conformity, on pages 175-7. Together with their assistants or substitutes they numbered 21, all representative of 'Presbyterian' parties, especially in London. Of these 21, 13 had been episcopally ordained; 6 had evidently been presbyterially ordained; 2 seem to have no record to show the nature of their ordination; 6 had been members of the Westminster Assembly; 3 had, with two others, written 'Smectymnuus' for Presbyterianism in 1641; 4 did not attend, and 2 others attended only two or three sessions; 16 were ejected under the Act of Uniformity; and 5 conformed (one, Reynolds, being already a bishop, and another, Conant, changing to conformity some years after ejection).

There were many younger ministers in England not episcopally ordained; and it is natural that most of the Savoy divines, being older men, had been episcopally ordained before the Interregnum began.

More than half of the twenty-one were orthodox Presbyterians and had belonged to Presbyterian church courts. Hardly any of them but Baxter fully merited his favourite designation of moderate episcopal or mere Catholic. Where, then, is there support for his oft-repeated contention that most of the non-prelatical clergy were moderate episcopal and not orthodox Presbyterian? The explanations probably are, firstly, that all of the twenty-one in the list (except Baxter, Newcomen, Collinges, and the University ministers) were London ministers, and London had been the stronghold of orthodox Presbyterianism from the First Civil War onwards; and, secondly, that Baxter could properly claim many former orthodox Presbyterians as converts to moderate episcopacy, especially when there was no likelihood of anything else being considered by the bishops. After the expulsions of 1662, moderate episcopal ministers merged with true Presbyterians. All of the sixteen (out of twenty-one) 'Presbyterians' at the Savoy Conference, who were ejected and did not subsequently conform, styled themselves as 'Presbyterian' when licensed under the King's Declaration of Indulgence in 1672 as entitled to preach—Baxter alone excepted.

Baxter had desired to be omitted from the commission, as he knew that his outspokenness made him an irritant to the bishops; what he did not realize, perhaps, was that he was often an embarrassment to his colleagues. 'Overdoing is undoing', his own maxim, was never better illustrated than by some of his disputes at the Savoy Conference. Of the other ministers, Bates, Jacombe, Newcomen, and Clark took frequent and capable part in the discussions.

There was an air of unreality in the Savoy Conference from the outset. It did not touch the chief issues, such as discipline and Church government. In an agenda confined to the liturgy and ceremonies there was no possibility of agreement, but only of widening the breach between the parties.

At once it was clear that the bishops were determined to concede nothing. After Baxter's death in 1691, Archbishop Tillotson advised Matthew Sylvester, Baxter's friend and executor: 'Be sure to give a clear account of the transactions at the Savoy of which he [Baxter] hath told me he had a fuller account amongst his papers than any yet extant, and how truly he foresaw and told what would follow, on the course they took.'[1] Tillotson, as a young clergyman, had been a spectator of the Savoy Conference and had felt sympathy with Baxter then.

Bishop Burnet, no friend of the Restoration bishops, it is true, was nevertheless not unfair in his estimation of their policy at the Savoy Conference :

'The Bishops and their party knew that the Presbyterians were possessed of most of the greatest benefices in the Church, chiefly in the city of London and the two universities; that many of them had gone into the design of restoring the King with as much zeal and readiness as any; that they were men of great credit in several places, and very influential in the election of members of Parliament; and that some of them still retained their old leaven and confirmed animosity against the Church; and therefore, to divest them of their livings, as well as preclude them from any claim of merit or power of doing ill, they thought it advisable, instead of using any methods to bring them in, to apply the most effectual ones to KEEP THEM OUT of the bosom of the Church, and accordingly prevailed with the King to fix the terms of conformity on what THEY HAD BEEN BEFORE THE WAR, WITHOUT MAKING THE LEAST ABATEMENT OR ALTERATION.' [2]

The King's Warrant had been issued on 25th March, and had limited the Conference to four months from that date. Yet the Conference did not begin until 15th April. Furthermore, Convocation was called by summons on 11th April as though it was assumed that the Conference could not affect what Convocation itself would do. In the elections to Convocation, ministers ordained only by presbyteries were declared unfit. Sheldon, Bishop of London, omitted Baxter and Calamy from those elected in London to Convocation, not because of their ordinations; he had a right to omit two from the number, but his action was significant.

Sheldon showed what was the bishops' policy at the beginning of the Savoy Conference when he said that, as the 'Presbyterians' had asked for the Conference and they sought to amend the liturgy, they should set out their complete proposals in writing.

## 2. SKETCH OF THE 'PRESBYTERIAN' MINISTERS AT THE SAVOY CONFERENCE, 1661

| Names (in alphabetical order) | Whether attended | Party description | Ordination | Other particulars | Whether ejected or conformed in 1662 |
|---|---|---|---|---|---|
| 1. Richard Baxter | Yes | — | Episcopal—deacon, 1638 | Chaplain to King, 1660. Offered bishopric of Hereford. | Ejected |
| 2. Edmund Calamy | Yes | Orthodox Presbyterian | Episcopal—priest, 1626 | Wrote 'Smectymnuus' (1641). Member of Westminster Assembly. Went to Breda to meet Charles, May 1660. Chaplain to King, 1660. Offered bishopric of Lichfield and Coventry. | Ejected |
| 3. Thomas Case | Yes | Orthodox Presbyterian | Episcopal—priest, 1626 | Member of Westminster Assembly. Went to Breda to meet Charles, May 1660. Chaplain to King, 1660. | Ejected |
| 4. Samuel Clark | Yes | Orthodox Presbyterian | No record—probably episcopal | Admitted to benefice, 1643, by Committee for Plundered Ministers. Held curacies from 1620. Moderator, London Presbyterian Provincial Assembly. | Ejected |
| 5. Thomas Conant, D.D. | No | Orthodox Presbyterian | Presbyterial (at Salisbury) 1652 | Vice-Chancellor of Oxford and Regius Professor of Divinity. | Ejected, but conformed later. Re-ordained, 1670. |

| Names (in alphabetical order) | Whether attended | Party description | Ordination | Other particulars | Whether ejected or conformed in 1662 |
|---|---|---|---|---|---|
| 6. Arthur Jackson | Yes | Orthodox Presbyterian | Episcopal— priest, 1620 | At the head of London ministers who presented King with Bible when he entered London, May 1660. | Ejected |
| 7. Thomas Manton, D.D. | Yes | — | Episcopal— deacon,1640; perhaps priest, 1660 | Was scribe at Westminster Assembly. Went to Breda to meet Charles, May 1660. Chaplain to King, 1660. Offered deanery of Rochester. | Ejected |
| 8. Matthew Newcomen | Yes | Orthodox Presbyterian | Episcopal— licensed curate, 1635 | At Visitation 1636 did not show orders, which he said he had received from Bishop of Ely. Wrote 'Smectymnuus' (1641). Member of Westminster Assembly. | Ejected |
| 9. Edward Reynolds | Yes | — | Episcopal | Accepted bishopric of Norwich, 1660. | Conformed |
| 10. William Spurstow, D.D. | Yes | Orthodox Presbyterian | Episcopal— rector, 1638 | Wrote 'Smectymnuus' (1641). Member of Westminster Assembly. Chaplain to King, 1660. | Ejected |
| 11. Anthony Tuckney, D.D. | No | Orthodox Presbyterian | Episcopal— vicar, 1635 | Member of Westminster Assembly. Master of St John's College, Cambridge. | Ejected |
| 12. John Wallis, D.D. | Yes | — | (No record) | — | Conformed |
| *Assistants or Substitutes:* | | | | | |
| 1. William Bates, D.D. | Yes | — | Evidently presbyterial | Vicar, 1649. Chaplain to King, 1660. Offered deanery of Lichfield. | Ejected |

| Names (in alphabetical order) | Whether attended | Party description | Ordination | Other particulars | Whether ejected or conformed in 1662 |
|---|---|---|---|---|---|
| 2. John Collinges, D.D. | Yes | Orthodox Presbyterian | Evidently presbyterial | Vicar, 1645. | Ejected |
| 3. William Cooper | Yes | Orthodox Presbyterian | Episcopal | Vicar, 1640. | Ejected |
| 4. Roger Drake | No | Orthodox Presbyterian | Evidently presbyterial | Elected by parishioners, 1650. | Ejected |
| 5. Thomas Horton | No | — | (No record) | — | Conformed |
| 6. Thomas Jacombe | Yes | — | Evidently presbyterial | Elected by vestry, 1649. | Ejected |
| 7. John Lightfoot, D.D. | Only once or twice | — | Evidently episcopal | Master of Catharine Hall, and Vice-Chancellor, Cambridge. (Prebendary of Ely, 1668.) Member of Westminster Assembly. | Conformed |
| 8. John Rawlinson | Yes | — | Episcopal | Rector, 1643. | Ejected |
| 9. Benjamin Woodbridge, D.D. | Only three or four times | — | Evidently presbyterial | Admitted by Committee for Plundered Ministers, 1643. Said to have been re-ordained by Bishop of Salisbury, 1665, but appears as nonconformist licensed preacher, 1672. | Ejected |

(SOURCES: Matthews, *Calamy Revised* and Gordon, *Freedom after Ejection*)

The bishops had always refused to offer suggestions, declaring that they were the defendants and the ministers must prove their case against the liturgy as it stood. Bishop Burnet's narrative also has this comment: 'Bishop Sheldon saw well enough what the effect would be of obliging them to make all their demands at once, that the number would raise a mighty outcry against them as a people that could never be satisfied.'

Some of the ministers objected to Sheldon's demand because the terms of the Warrant were that they meet together and confer. Baxter dissuaded those who thought of abandoning the Conference altogether from taking this action; indeed, he saw advantages for his party in adopting Sheldon's method because they would be able to agree among themselves in private while preparing their proposals and, by committing their representations to writing, they would avoid misinterpretation in future years.

It was thereupon agreed that the ministers' 'Exceptions' should be brought in at one meeting, and their additions to the liturgy at another. The latter task was left to Baxter, and he isolated himself for a fortnight to attempt the stupendous task of writing what proved to be a whole liturgy to be offered as an alternative to the Prayer Book. The rest of the ministers conferred on the subject of the 'Exceptions' they would present against the Prayer Book.

3. *Baxter's 'Reformed Liturgy' presented to the Savoy Conference*

In his fortnight's seclusion Baxter drew up an entire liturgy, although, according to the terms of the King's Warrant, he could call it only the additions or alterations to the Prayer Book. He did this, not only to show that he was in favour of liturgy, but also in order that there might be an alternative service available if the Declaration of 25th October 1660 became operative at any future time.

Another important reason was that a complete liturgy allowed Baxter to include matters of discipline, the crucial point that had been offered in the King's Declaration but which the Savoy Conference had not been directed to examine. 'I PUT IN THE FORMS AND ORDERS OF DISCIPLINE, partly because else we should never have had opportunity therein to express our minds, and partly because indeed it belongeth to the integrity of the work, and TO SHOW THE DIFFERENCE BETWEEN THEIR KIND OF DISCIPLINE in Chancellors' Courts, and OURS BY PASTORS IN CHRISTIAN CON-

GREGATIONS.'³ For this reason it was one of the most important presentations of the whole programme for Church reform that Baxter and his colleagues offered.

Those historians who have condemned Baxter as presumptuous in writing his own liturgy have not sufficiently recognized that he offered it, not as a substitute for the Prayer Book, but as an alternative form for optional use. It was probably too diffuse and prolix to be acceptable for general use and one could not imagine it being acceptable today. Yet no one should fail to acknowledge the sublimity of its conception and its thoroughly Scriptural character. The typical Puritan stress upon use of Biblical language is seen in the amazing list of texts throughout this liturgy, the margin of which is filled with at least one text for every line.

It would be unseemly to praise Baxter's awe-inspiring opening of worship:

'Eternal, incomprehensible, and invisible God, infinite in power, wisdom, and goodness, dwelling in the light which no man can approach, where thousand thousands minister unto Thee, and ten thousand times ten thousand stand before Thee, yet dwelling with the humble and contrite, and taking pleasure in Thy people: Thou hast consecrated for us a new and living way, that with boldness we may enter into the holiest, by the blood of Jesus, and hast bid us seek Thee while Thou mayst be found; We come to Thee at Thy call, and worship at Thy footstool....'

The same characteristics are seen in the first phrases of the 'Confession of Sin and Prayer for Pardon and Sanctification':

'O most holy, righteous, and gracious God, Who hatest all the workers of iniquity, and hast appointed death to be the wages of sin, but yet for the glory of Thy mercy hast sent Thy Son to be the Saviour of the world, and hast promised forgiveness of sin through His blood, to all that believe in Him, and by true repentance turn unto Thee, and that whosoever confesseth and forsaketh His sin, shall have mercy....'

Incidentally, this confession and prayer for pardon would take nearly ten minutes to read; and the alternative confession and prayer, added by Baxter for use 'when brevity is necessary', is almost half as long.

With regard to the prayer for the King, no one should have questioned the loyalty of Baxter and his friends when these were the words he used :

'Almighty God . . . Who by Thy special providence hast set over us Thy servant Charles, our King; crown him with Thy blessings, and satisfy him with Thy goodness. Save him by Thy right hand, and defend him against such as rise up against him. . . . Make him an angel of God to discern between good and evil. . . .'

Comment upon that petition, in view of Charles's known immoral habits, is superfluous; but Baxter, in his sincere loyalty, added :

'Let all his Majesty's subjects duly submit to him and obey him, not only for wrath, but for conscience' sake. . . .'

The General Prayer would require nearly ten minutes, with a 'Thanksgiving for Christ and His gracious benefits' only slightly shorter.

'The Order of Celebrating the Sacrament of the Body and Blood of Christ' has some remarkable sections showing sacramental doctrine which some may not have expected to find among Puritans. The bread and wine were directed to be solemnly brought to the Table, according to the custom of Geneva and Scotland; and the fraction of the bread, and the libation of the wine, were included in the dignified ritual. A few extracts from the service must be given to make Baxter's position clear :

'The Lord's Supper is a holy sacrament instituted by Christ, wherein bread and wine being first by consecration made sacramentally, or REPRESENTATIVELY, the body and blood of Christ, are used by breaking and pouring out to represent, and commemorate, the sacrifice of Christ's body and blood, upon the Cross once offered up to God for sin . . . and they are received, eaten, and drunk by the Church, to profess that they willingly receive Christ Himself to the ends aforesaid. . . .

'It being the renewing of a mutual covenant that is here solemnized, as we commemorate Christ's sacrifice, and receive

Him and His saving benefits, so we offer and deliver to Him ourselves. . . .

'These are to be admitted, by the pastors, IF THEY . . . HAVE MADE A PERSONAL PROFESSION OF FAITH, repentance, and obedience; and are members of the Church, and not justly for heresy or scandalous sin, removed from its present communion.

'SEE HERE CHRIST DYING IN THIS HOLY REPRESENTATION. BEHOLD THE SACRIFICED LAMB OF GOD, THAT TAKETH AWAY THE SINS OF THE WORLD. IT IS HIS WILL TO BE THUS FREQUENTLY CRUCIFIED BEFORE YOUR EYES. . . . Let no trembling, contrite soul draw back, that is willing to be Christ's upon His covenant terms, but believe that Christ is much more willing to be yours. . . . SEE HERE HIS BROKEN BODY AND HIS BLOOD, the testimonies of His willingness . . . RECEIVE NOW A CRUCIFIED CHRIST HERE REPRESENTED. . . .'

Would that in spirit, if not in these words, modern communicants could always be led in such a prayer of penitence and adoration as Baxter wrote:

'Most holy God, we are as stubble before Thee, the consuming fire. How shall we stand before Thy holiness, for we are a sinful people . . . When we were lost, Thy Son did seek and save us. . . . Heal our backslidings, love us freely, and say unto our souls, that Thou art our salvation. . . . Though we are unworthy of the crumbs that fall from Thy table, yet feed us with the bread of life, and speak and seal up peace to our sinful, wounded souls. . . .'

In the 'Prayer of Consecration' these words were used:

'Sanctify these Thy creatures of bread and wine, which according to Thy institution and command, WE SET APART TO THIS HOLY USE, THAT THEY MAY BE SACRAMENTALLY THE BODY AND BLOOD OF THY SON JESUS CHRIST.'

The minister's declaration follows:

'THIS BREAD AND WINE BEING SET APART, AND CONSECRATED TO THIS HOLY USE BY GOD'S APPOINTMENT, ARE NOW NO COMMON BREAD AND WINE, BUT SACRAMENTALLY THE BODY AND BLOOD OF CHRIST.'

In breaking the bread before the people, the minister would say :

'The body of Christ was broken for us, and offered once for all to sanctify us. Behold the sacrificed Lamb of God, that taketh away the sins of the world.'

With regard to the distribution it is stated :

'Let none of the people be forced to SIT, STAND, OR KNEEL, in the act of receiving, whose judgment is against it.'

The strong Puritan conviction that Baptism, as well as the Lord's Supper, must be safeguarded and administered only to those worthy or the children of believing parents can be seen in 'The Celebration of the Sacrament of Baptism'.

'Let no minister, that is therein unsatisfied, be forced against his judgment, to baptize the child of open atheists, idolaters, or infidels, or that are unbaptized themselves, or of such as do not competently understand the essentials of Christianity . . . nor of such as never, since they were baptized, did personally own their baptismal covenant, by a credible profession of faith and obedience, received and approved by some pastor of the Church, as before confirmation is required, and in His Majesty's Declaration . . . .'

The next paragraph makes an exception :

'If both the natural parents are infidels, excommunicate, or otherwise unqualified, yet if any become the PRO-PARENTS and owners of the child, undertake to educate it in the faith of Christ . . . let it be done by a minister whose judgment doth approve it, but let no minister be forced to it against his judgment.'

Again Baxter contended for the essential rights of the pastor. The parents were required to answer questions concerning their own faith and their adherence to their own baptismal covenant as well as to give a promise that they would instruct the child in the meaning of the covenant. The prayer is significant :

'We beseech Thee let this child grow up in holiness; and when he comes to years of discretion let Thy Spirit reveal unto him the mysteries of the gospel, and . . . cause him to renew and perform the covenant that he hath now made. . . .'

The most significant section of all is: 'Of Pastoral Discipline, Public Confession, Absolution, and Exclusion from the Holy Communion of the Church'. That Baxter asked the bishops to accept such a service, or even allow it as an alternative to the Prayer Book, is an evidence of his unswerving adherence to his convictions. Their differences were never resolved at this vital point, the authority of the pastor. Nevertheless, Baxter shrewdly alluded to the King's Declaration, in his preface to this section of his liturgy:

'His Majesty's Declaration concerning Ecclesiastical Affairs, determineth that all public diligence be used for the instruction and reformation of scandalous offenders, whom the minister shall not suffer to partake of the Lord's table, until they have openly declared themselves to have truly repented. . . . If the scandalous offender continue impenitent, or unreformed, after due admonitions and patience, let the pastor in the congregation, when he is present, rebuke him before all. . . . If yet the offender remain impenitent, let the pastor openly declare him unmeet for the communion of the church, and require him to abstain from it. . . . But before this is done, let no necessary consultation with OTHER PASTORS, or concurrence of the church, be neglected. . . .'

Both the 'Form of Public Admonition' and the 'Form of Confession' are extremely lengthy, the latter including these statements:

'I have deserved to be forsaken of the Lord, and cast out of His presence and communion of saints, into desperation, and remediless misery in hell. . . . I humbly beg of the congregation that they will earnestly pray, that God will wash me thoroughly from mine iniquity, and cleanse me from my sins, that He will forgive them, and blot them out. . . .'

A long prayer for a sinner impenitent, full of the most awesome phrases is given. Also a 'Form of Rejection' from the Communion of the Church which includes these words:

'Jesus Christ, the King and Lawgiver of the Church, hath commanded . . . that we keep no company, if any that is called a brother, be a fornicator, or covetous, or an idolater, or a railer, or a drunkard, or an extortioner, with such a one, no, not to eat. . . .

'We do therefore, according to the laws of Christ, declare him unmeet for the Communion of the Church, and reject him from it . . . and we leave him bound to the judgment of the Lord, unless his true repentance shall prevent it.'

A 'Form of Absolution and Reception of the Penitent' states, *inter alia* :

'I declare to you the pardon of all your sins in the blood of Christ, if your repentance be sincere. And I exhort and charge you that . . . you return not to your vomit, or to wallow again in the mire, when you are washed . . . but obey the Spirit, and keep close to God in the means of your preservation.'

Our aversion today to such procedures and terms should not prevent us recognizing the importance which Baxter placed upon guarding the Lord's Table.

This monumental liturgy was never used. It was scorned by the bishops; it has been derided by Baxter's critics ever since. All should admit that only a spiritual genius, steeped in the knowledge of Scriptures and the doctrines of the Reformation, could have produced such a massive work in a fortnight.

Dr Johnson, though opposed to Dissenters, spoke of Baxter's liturgy as 'one of the finest compositions of a ritual kind that he had ever seen'.[4]

To assert, as some have done, that Baxter wrecked the Conference by submitting his liturgy is to overlook the fact that the bishops found many other causes for dismissing the requests of the 'Presbyterian' divines.

### 4. *Baxter's 'Exceptions to the Prayer Book'*

After Baxter's fortnight of seclusion, he rejoined the other ministers to find them only beginning to draw up their 'Exceptions'. A few of them were opposed to the use of the Prayer Book as a whole. Others wished to include matters in their 'Exceptions' that Baxter felt could not well be substantiated.

'From the beginning I told them I was not of their mind, who charged the Common Prayer with false doctrine, or idolatry, or false worship in the matter of substance, nor that took it to be a worship which a Christian might not lawfully join in, when he had not liberty and ability for better; and that I always took the faults of the Common Prayer to be, chiefly, DISORDER and DEFECTIVENESS; and so, that it was a TRUE WORSHIP THOUGH IMPERFECT; and imperfection was the charge that we had against it (considered as distinct from the Ceremonies and Discipline).... And I think this was the mind of all our brethren, save one, as well as mine; and old Mr Ash hath often told me that this was the mind of the OLD NONCONFORMISTS and that he hath often heard some weak ministers so disorderly in prayer, especially in Baptism and the Lord's Supper, that he could have wished that they would rather use the Common Prayer.'[5]

In that important statement Baxter clarified his position. He criticized only the imperfections of the Prayer Book, and in doing so he was true to the tradition of the older Puritans for the past one hundred years and parted company with the orthodox Presbyterians of the recent period.

Impulsive, self-confident, as always, Baxter now drew up his own list of suggestions when he found that his colleagues were so dilatory. Baxter's 'Exceptions'[6] need not be examined in detail here; it was never presented to the bishops.

The gravamen of Baxter's complaint was the lack of orderly sequence in the Prayer Book, and the tautology of many of the prayers. His chief objections were:

(1) The Creed and the Decalogue should precede Confession and Absolution.

(2) The Confession referred to our sins of omission and commission without any expression of repentance.

(3) The Collects for Peace and for Grace were pointless.

(4) The Litany was worse even than Morning Prayer in frequently returning to petitions already expressed.

(5) 'The Prayer on Christmas Day determineth that Christ was born as on that day, when the world of learned men are not agreed of the month or year, much less the day.'[7]

(6) Most of the Collects for the various days had no definite relation to the particular days.

(7) The continued repetition of prayers to be delivered from

adversities made it appear that this was the chief concern of the Church, whereas Christians know that they have to suffer tribulations as followers of their Lord.

(8) Objections to the Communion Service included these:

The exhortation to all and sundry to communicate was unworthy.

'It is the greatest disorder of all, that every parishioner shall communicate at least thrice in the year, WHETHER HE BE FIT OR UNFIT.'

The Prayer of Consecration should not 'BEGIN IN A PRAYER AND END IN A NARRATIVE'.[8]

'It is disorderly for the minister to receive the Sacrament in both kinds himself before the other ministers or people do receive it in either.'

(9) 'In Baptism it is the greatest disorder, that ministers must be forced, though against their consciences, to baptize all children without exception; the children of atheists, infidels ... or impenitent fornicators, or such like.'

Children should be dedicated to God by believing parents.

Objection is taken to not requiring the parents to be present and to leaving the baptismal covenant to godparents who cannot accept real responsibility for the children's Christian education.

(10) Objection was taken to the cross in Baptism.

(11) It was very dangerously stated that children were regenerated by Baptism.

(12) Confirmation should not be administered until a 'CREDIBLE PROFESSION OF FAITH' was made. It was not a sufficient condition merely that the Creed, the Lord's Prayer, and the Decalogue should be recited.

Even when reviewing the Prayer Book, Baxter was concerned most of all with matters of discipline and the conformity of prayers and ceremonies to spiritual truth and the promotion of godliness. Altogether, hundreds of detailed criticisms were given by Baxter against the liturgy. Baxter's colleagues could see, even if he did not, that such a list would give the bishops extreme annoyance. They were right; Baxter's 'Exceptions' did not show the way to peace.

5. *The 'Exceptions to the Prayer Book' presented by the Ministers*

On 4th May the ministers again met the bishops in conference and presented their 'Exceptions'. As these reveal the general position of Church-reformers during the period they merit close study.

From the opening phrases this document conforms to the programme of reform which Puritans had proposed from Elizabethan times, in the Millenary Petition of 1603, and onwards to 1661. The Prayer Book was regarded as a valuable, but imperfect, expression of reformed worship. It was urged that, after one hundred years' use of the Book, a revision might well be attempted, 'especially considering that many godly and learned men have FROM THE BEGINNING all along earnestly desired the alteration of many things therein'.[9]

The key to the ministers' attitude is the request that 'nothing doubtful or questioned' should be included in the acts of worship in which all worshippers were obliged to join. John Hales, the Latitudinarian to whom Puritans could appeal as unbiased, was quoted:

'To load our public forms with the private fancies upon which we differ, is the most sovereign way to perpetuate schism to the world's end. . . . Wheresoever false or suspected opinions are made a piece of church-liturgy, HE THAT SEPARATES IS NOT THE SCHISMATIC.'[10]

There followed an allusion to the wisdom with which the first reformers won over many Papists by making as few changes as possible in the old liturgy. Similar wisdom in 1661 could win all Protestants in England to the established Church at a time when, it was said, Protestant unity was desirable in the face of renewed Roman aggression. The event showed how impervious the bishops were to expediency being a reason for revision.

The ministers' document then dealt with the alleged disorderliness of the Prayer Book. Repetitions and responses by minister and congregation, it was said, caused a confused murmur. In principle also, it was submitted, the minister alone should offer the prayer and the people merely respond 'Amen'. The ministers declared: 'Scripture makes the minister the mouth of the people to God in prayer.'[11] It was suggested that 'One methodical and entire form of prayer' was preferable to many collects with repetitions.

'The Confession is very defective, not clearly expressing original sin, nor sufficiently enumerating actual sins . . . but consisting only of generals.' Baxter also had said this, with many instances.[12]

Fasting in Lent was opposed. Saints' days might be observed as festivals but not as holy days and should not be made equal in importance to the Lord's Day. Other characteristic Puritan requests were stressed: the prohibition of lessons from the Apocrypha, the use of 'minister' instead of 'priest' and 'Lord's Day' instead of 'Sunday'.

With regard to ceremonies, specific objection was taken to their being imposed upon clergy and people, seeing that opinions had differed since the beginning of the Reformation about the use of the surplice, the 'transient image of the Cross' in Baptism, and the obligation to receive Communion kneeling which had not been the custom for several centuries in the early Church.

The ministers questioned the right of the bishops to impose 'human' institutions. Even their advocates had admitted that these ceremonies were 'indifferent'. Reference was made to Paul's rule that no stumbling-block or occasion of offence should be laid before a weak brother. At the very least, there should be liberty to use or to discard such ceremonies as conscience dictated.

A pathetic plea was made that matters which had caused grievous disunity in England 'for above a hundred years' should no longer be made compulsory.

'We do therefore most earnestly entreat the right reverend fathers and brethren, to whom these papers are delivered . . . to join with us in importuning His Most Excellent Majesty, that His most gracious indulgence, as to these ceremonies, granted in His royal Declaration, may be confirmed and continued to us and our posterities. . . .'[13]

The ministers contended that in the first 300 years of Church history there was no record of any liturgy with which comparison might be made, as directed in the King's Warrant, and that for several centuries after that period there was no case of any liturgy being actually imposed.

The remainder of this lengthy document consisted of a detailed list of 'Exceptions to the Rubric', clause by clause. Among these, by far the most important related to Communion and Baptism. Where some critics of the ministers have seen only their complaints about details, they have overlooked the interests which

Baxter and his colleagues were passionately seeking to serve—the spiritual quickening of the nation and the maintenance of proper discipline in congregations through allowing the pastors their rights as governors of their flocks. This vital plea emerges again:

'We desire the MINISTER'S POWER BOTH TO ADMIT AND KEEP FROM THE LORD'S TABLE, may be according to His Majesty's Declaration, 25th October, 1660, in these words:

' "The minister shall admit none to the Lord's Supper till they have made a credible profession of their faith, and promised obedience to the will of God . . . and that all possible diligence be used for the instruction and reformation of scandalous offenders, whom the minister shall not suffer to partake of the Lord's table until they have openly declared themselves to have truly repented and amended their former naughty lives, as is partly expressed in the Rubric, and more fully in the Canons." '

The ministers here referred not only to the expectations raised by the King's Declaration but to the intentions of the rubric and the canons which were not being carried into effect. The rubric allowed twenty-four hours or less for notifying a person's desire to communicate, but the ministers regarded this as inadequate.

A sermon, it was considered, should be made compulsory before the administration of the Lord's Supper. In delivering the elements, the minister should 'use the words of our Saviour as near as may be' rather than the existing form, and they should not be required to repeat the words to each communicant in the singular number. Very strong objection was taken to requiring every parishioner to communicate at least three times in the year, irrespective of his worthiness.

Kneeling should be optional, seeing that Christ and the apostles were seated at a table; and the Act 1 & 2 Edward VI did not compel kneeling. It was also urged that the Black Rubric, 5 & 6 Edward VI, should be re-inserted, stating that kneeling did not imply adoration of the elements. The event proved that this was the only request of any consequence that was recognized in the 1662 revision of the Prayer Book; and even so, it was through Parliament's action, and not because of the ministers' opinion, that the Black Rubric was re-inserted after Convocation had voted against it.

The 'Exceptions' also contended that a minister should not be forced to baptize the infant of persons who were atheists or living in open and notorious sin. Grave objection was taken to requiring godparents to enter into a covenant which should be made by the parents themselves. In loyalty to their principles the ministers asked that any phrase which seemed to signify baptismal regeneration should be clarified. 'We cannot in faith say, that every child that is baptized is regenerated by God's Holy Spirit.'[14] Private Baptism should be discouraged. The amendment of the Catechism was urged, to agree with the suggested alterations in the rubric for Baptism; it was misleading to state that baptized children have been 'undoubtedly saved'. Also God's covenant was made with actual believers, not with sureties like godparents who made promises on behalf of infants.

Throughout the 'Exceptions' the Puritan essentials of personal faith and godly living were emphasized. The recital from memory of the Lord's Prayer, the Ten Commandments, and the Catechism should not be the qualification for confirmation, 'for it is often found that children are able to do . . . this at four or five years old'.[15] The ministers asked that the terms of the King's Declaration should particularly be observed on this point: 'That Confirmation be rightly and solemnly performed by the information and CONSENT OF THE MINISTER of the place.' When the rubric stated that only bishops might confirm, this implied that confirmation was higher than Baptism which deacons might perform, or the Lord's Supper. Was there not danger also that the imposition of hands as a sign certifying God's bestowed grace might seem to constitute confirmation another sacrament? Finally, the ministers asked that the lack of confirmation should not debar a person from Communion.

In the marriage service the ministers asked that the ring should be optional. They even expressed the opinion that the Triune Name should not be used in solemnizing matrimony lest this seem to make it a sacrament. The suggestion that newly married persons should not be obliged to receive Holy Communion was one of the few suggestions adopted by the bishops.

The words used in absolution, it was urged, should be in harmony with reformed tradition; instead of 'I absolve thee', the minister should declare, 'I pronounce thee absolved if thou dost truly repent and believe.'

Communion to the sick should be administered only on evidence of repentance. Nor should a minister be forced to commit every person's body to the ground 'in sure and certain hope of resurrection to eternal life' when some had lived and died 'in open and notorious sins'.

In spite of the details being somewhat tedious, the 'Exceptions' are invaluable as expressing the moral and spiritual principles maintained by English Puritans for one hundred years past, in harmony with reformed standards on the Continent and in Scotland. They firmly believed that a national Church should not assume that every person born within the realm was entitled to the full privileges of membership in Christ's Church, provided merely that Baptism and confirmation had been administered. The Independents had formed their own 'gathered' congregations because proper conditions of membership were not observed in many parish churches. Now, as late as May 1661, when the tide had turned strongly in favour of the bishops and a persecuting parliament, a few Churchmen like Baxter, 'generals without an army' perhaps, still fought the hopeless battle for a comprehensive Church that would be loyal to the principles of the Protestant Reformation.

It has been noticed that the new Cavalier or Pension Parliament met on 8th May, four days after these 'Exceptions' were given to the bishops at the Savoy Conference. On 8th May also, Convocation assembled at London and York but adjourned until 31st July. With the changing ecclesiastical and political scene the Savoy Conference was almost destined to be abortive.

6. *Baxter's 'Petition for Peace and Concord presented to the Bishops with the proposed Reformation of the Liturgy'*

Shortly after the ministers' 'Exceptions' had been delivered to the Conference, Baxter drew up a 'Petition for Peace and Concord' and urged his colleagues to present it as an earnest of their despairing efforts to reach a peaceful and just settlement. Baxter states: 'Because I foresaw what was like to be the end of our Conference, I desired the brethren that we might draw up a plain and earnest Petition to the Bishops to yield to such terms of peace and concord as they themselves did confess to be LAWFUL to be yielded to.'[16]

This 'Petition' was accepted by the ministers with hardly a verbal alteration. At the same time Baxter's 'Reformed Liturgy' was adopted with very few emendations, and both were presented to the bishops.[17] Baxter does not give a date for the presentation of the two documents but he mentions that they were given together and that this was *before* the bishops' 'Answer'. Baxter indeed added that it was 'A GOOD WHILE AFTER' that the bishops gave their 'Answer' and he could hardly have been mistaken about the sequence of events; and the 'Answer' was given by the bishops about the middle of the period of sessions, perhaps early in June, certainly long before the expiry of the warrant on 25th July. Bosher, in *The Making of the Restoration Settlement*, quotes Dr Ferne, who was not a member of the Savoy Conference, in a letter that stated that Baxter's liturgy was not brought forward until the first week of July, and a letter from Dr Hacket, a member, on 8th July, which seems to infer that that liturgy might have been received not long before.[18] On the assumption that it was Baxter's liturgy that so greatly affected the bishops that they decided that the Conference would be futile, and believing that this liturgy was received much later than Baxter indicates in his sequence of events, Bosher absolves the bishops from blame for the breakdown of the Conference. It may well be, however, that Baxter was correct in his sequence of the presentation of documents and this would mean that his liturgy was in the hands of the bishops much earlier than July. In any case the bishops' attitude was determined by other considerations and there is other evidence to show clearly that they were opposed to the Puritan divines from the beginning, and that it was generally recognized that the Conference was futile and that the ministers were certain to be expelled.

Baxter was now deputed to read the lengthy 'Petition' he had written. One gathers that the bishops' vexation during its reading was occasioned less by the time it occupied than by the devastating condemnation of their attitude. They were unlikely to be patient during such an unanswerable appeal to their consciences, such an exposure of the consequences of the expulsion of godly ministers throughout England, such an emphasis upon the moral and religious standards that meant everything to men like Baxter but meant little to some of the prelates.

The main request in the Petition was that the bishops might accept the alterations and additions to the liturgy which the ministers had tendered (this being another piece of evidence that

Baxter's liturgy was presented at that time) as ALTERNATIVE forms that might be left to the discretion of parish clergy.

'Seeing that we cannot obtain the Form of Episcopal Government, described by the late reverend Primate of Ireland, and approved by many episcopal divines, we may at least enjoy those benefits of reformation in DISCIPLINE, and that FREEDOM FROM SUBSCRIPTION, OATHS, and CEREMONIES, which are granted in the Declaration.' [19] (25th October 1660.)

Here is the essence of the 'Presbyterian' programme of reform for the national Church. The reformers desired, first, to see the adoption of Usher's model of primitive episcopacy; but, failing that, they would have been satisfied with these minimum requests:

1. Freedom to use an *alternative liturgy*.
2. The right of pastors to exercise *discipline* in their own churches.
3. Freedom of ministers from subscribing to use the whole of the Prayer Book and particular ceremonies to which some objected.
4. Freedom from swearing canonical obedience to diocesan bishops.

*The King's Declaration had promised these specific reforms.* The ministers were entitled to expect those promises to be honoured, but the months of negotiations and the Savoy Conference itself made it clear that the bishops were unwilling to concede even one of these basic reforms.

Nothing could be more emphatic than Baxter's summing up: 'Were those TWO granted (the CONFIRMATION OF THE GRANTS IN HIS MAJESTY'S DECLARATION, with *the liberty of the "Reformed Liturgy" offered you*, and the RESTORING OF ABLE, FAITHFUL MINISTERS to a capacity to be serviceable in the Church of England, without forcing them against their consciences to be RE-ORDAINED) how great would be the benefits to this unworthy nation!' [20]

Any imputation against Baxter and his colleagues of neglecting their non-episcopally ordained brethren is false. The restoration of ALL ministers expelled from their livings for lack of episcopal ordination was urged: 'That it be not imputed to them as their unpardonable crime, that they were born in an age and country which required ORDINATION BY PAROCHIAL PASTORS, without Diocesans; and that RE-ORDINATION (whether absolute OR HYPOTHETICAL) be NOT MADE NECESSARY to the future exercise of their ministry. But that AN UNIVERSAL CONFIRMATION MAY BE GRANTED OF THOSE ORDAINED AS AFORESAID.' [21]

The bishops were reminded that they were contemplating the expulsion of ministers for refusing to comply with forms '*Indifferent in your own judgment*'. Would not the bishops see that there must be conscientious convictions in men for whom nonconformity would entail expulsion while compliance would bring prosperity? How could the bishops still say, 'It is not conscience, but obstinacy or singularity'?

'Do you think the Lord that died for souls, is better pleased with RE-ORDINATION, SUBSCRIPTION, and CEREMONIES, than with the saving of souls, by the means of His own appointment? Concord in Ceremonies, or re-ordination, or oaths of obedience to Diocesans . . . do not so much conduce to men's salvation as the preaching of the Gospel doth, by able, faithful, and laborious ministers.' [22]

The bishops seemed deaf to that pleading.

More than that. Baxter appealed to the fact that there would not be enough competent ministers in England if nonconformists were driven out. If the bishops could fill all the parishes with ministers both willing to conform and worthy of their office, Baxter and his fellow-petitioners would be silent.

The bishops might expel ministers who would not accept the whole of the existing liturgy, but, if they did so, they were acting at variance with the practice in the early Church for centuries. They might expel those who were willing to accept primitive episcopacy, an alternative liturgy, and the system of discipline set forth in the King's Declaration; but, if they did this, they were doing what bishops like Usher and Hall would have utterly condemned.

The Laudian bishops in 1661 might insist upon re-ordination, but in so doing they would be adopting a novel attitude, 'a thing that both Papists and Protestants condemn . . . not only the former Bishops of England were against it, but even the most fervent adversaries of the Presbyterian way, such as Bishop Bancroft himself'. [23]

One can imagine how Baxter's heart burned as he called upon bishops to consider 'when your souls are most seriously thinking of the day of your accounts',[24] and how the bishops must have reacted to such plain speaking. He quoted Matthew xviii. 5, 6, with these words, 'Bear with us while we add this terrible passage', and added, 'Consider . . . how Christ will take it, to have His servants . . . cast out of the ministry, or church, for an unavoidable dissent in things indifferent.'[25]

The history of the previous one hundred years in England had shown the disaster occasioned by imposing forms and ceremonies, and Baxter saw much worse ahead; and this could be avoided if the bishops would remember that 'It must be the primitive simplicity of faith, worship and discipline, that must restore the primitive charity, unity and peace.'[26]

The 'Petition' concluded with a moving appeal the like of which no body of English bishops had ever received:

'Grant us but the freedom that Christ and His apostles left unto the Churches; use necessary things as necessary, and unnecessary as unnecessary . . . and tolerate the tolerable, while they live peaceably. . . . But if you reject our suit, we shall commit all to Him that judgeth righteously. . . . Come, Lord Jesus! Come quickly! Amen.'[27]

7. *'Answer of the Bishops to the Exceptions of the Ministers'*

The only satisfaction the ministers received was this document, the 'Answer' to their 'Exceptions'. Though the time allowed for the Conference was passing, the bishops evidently did not intend to debate the controversial points. After much delay they returned their 'Answer', as Baxter observed, 'without any abatements or alterations at all that are worth the naming'.[28]

The bishops contented themselves mainly with upholding the Prayer Book as the best guarantee for preserving peace and unity in the Church. They argued that the onus was upon the ministers to prove that the liturgy was actually sinful and unlawful. The mere fact that many persons did not wish to use it was no proof, especially when an appeal to numbers, the bishops said, showed that far more were devoted to it. It would be impossible to frame public prayers that would satisfy the consciences of all men, but the bishops were satisfied that the existing liturgy conformed to Scripture and to the usages of antiquity.

Replying to criticisms against the forms of prayer, the bishops considered that 'Devotion is apt to freeze or sleep, or flat in a long continued prayer', and therefore many short prayers were preferable, as worshippers were 'therein often called upon and awakened by frequent "Amens" and responses'. The bishops also contended that private opinions expressed in tedious extemporaneous prayers were often mischievous. They were probably influenced by the abuse of extemporaneous prayer by some of the extreme sectaries whose faults were charged against Baxter and orthodox Puritans.

The bishops also defended fasting in Lent, the observance of saints' days, the use of the words 'priest' and 'Sunday', and the three disputed ceremonies, the surplice, the cross in Baptism, and kneeling at Communion. The main argument in favour of these three, apart from their decency and fitness, was that only superior persons could judge their convenience and inferiors had nothing to do but obey: 'Pretence of conscience is no exemption from obedience . . . and we must not perform public services undecently or disorderly for the ease of tender consciences.' Those who objected, it was said, were either ignorant or obstinate, and they put their own stumbling-block in their way. Paul's injunction did not apply, because he spoke only of waiving his own opinion rather than offend his brother, but not of breaking the laws and practices that the Church had a right to make and enforce. The surplice was ancient and helped to preserve reverence; the cross signified that Christians were not ashamed of the cross of Christ; kneeling at Communion was decent and reverent.

The bishops ignored the crucial question of admission to the Lord's Table and dismissed the protest against the rubric which compelled all parishioners to communicate at least three times a year.

In regard to Baptism, the bishops emphatically disagreed with the ministers' objection. They disapproved giving ministers the power to decide whether the parents who brought infants to Baptism were fit and proper persons or were notorious sinners and unbelievers. As strongly as Baxter had pleaded for the power of the keys to be given to pastors, so firmly did the bishops refuse to yield any such authority. The whole of these controversies, ultimately, centred around this question of authority—the bishop alone, or the pastor supported by synods or associations in which bishop and clergy acted together?

On a sounder principle the bishops contended that every infant should be baptized, declaring: 'It is an erroneous doctrine, and the ground of many others, and of many of your exceptions, that children have no other right to Baptism, than in their parents' right. . . . Our Church concludes more charitably, that Christ will favourably accept every infant to Baptism, that is presented by the Church according to our present order.'

However, the bishops were adamant upon the retention of the teaching of baptismal regeneration. 'Seeing that God's Sacraments have their effects, where the receiver does not put any bar against them (which children cannot do), we may say in faith of every child that is baptized, that it is regenerated by God's Holy Spirit.'

It was argued that the effect did not depend on the infant's faith or on that of parents or godparents, but upon the ordinance of Christ. It was only necessary in confirmation that the baptized person perform the conditions of repentance and faith for which the godparents had been sureties.

Confirmation, it was asserted, must be reserved to a bishop, 'to bless being an act of authority'. Clearly, the maintenance of episcopal authority was regarded as of paramount importance.

The giving of the ring in marriage was defended. It was assumed that all persons marrying ought to be fit to receive the Sacrament; but, in spite of the bishops' assumption, Parliament afterwards decided to make Communion optional on the marriage-day.

The bishops wished it taken for granted that persons to be buried had repented; 'it is better to be charitable, and hope the best, than rashly to condemn'.

The Puritans, over-strict and rigid as they must be regarded today, were seeking to secure essential spiritual principles: that only the children of believing parents should be baptized, only those who made a credible profession of faith should be admitted to Communion, and that faith and godliness should be required for full Christian burial. The bishops, on the other hand, emphasized the ordinances which persons accepted or rejected on their own responsibility. One may ask, Which was the higher conception? Which party contained the true 'High' Churchmen?

The bishops even went so far as to indicate their intention to make an alteration in the Prayer Book against the ministers' principles—that the Catechism should state, 'that children being baptized have all things necessary for their salvation, and dying before they commit any actual sins, be undoubtedly saved, though they be not confirmed'.[29] Whatever may be our modern opinion, such a proposal from the bishops roused the sternest protest from Baxter; and on this point he subsequently declared: 'That of forty sinful terms for a communion with the Church party, if thirty-nine were taken away, and only that rubric, concerning the salvation of infants dying shortly after their Baptism, were continued, YET THEY COULD NOT CONFORM.'[30]

Baxter was justified in describing the abatements in the bishops' 'Answer' as almost nothing. The only concessions, other than a few verbal alterations to the liturgy, were:

(1) The use of the last translation for the passages chosen for the Epistles and Gospels.

(2) The font to be placed where the congregation could hear better.[31]

(3) A longer time for signifying the names of communicants, the rubric in future to read, 'at least some time the day before'.

(4) 'That the power of keeping scandalous sinners from the Communion may be expressed in the Rubric according to the 26th and 27th Canons; so the minister be obliged to give an account of the same immediately after to the Ordinary.'

The bishops also gave a direct negative to the ministers' most important request—the recognition of the pastor's rights foreshadowed in the King's Declaration.

8. *'The Rejoinder of the Ministers to the Answer of the Bishops'*

Upon receiving the bishops' 'Answer', the ministers felt that they must make a reply though this would necessarily involve, in part, recapitulating their former 'Exceptions'. Baxter was entrusted with writing the formidable 'Rejoinder'. Shutting himself up in the home of Dr Spurstow at Hackney, he accomplished this feat in eight days.

With only ten days left before the expiration of the four months set by the King's Warrant, the ministers pleaded with the bishops to discuss together the points raised by the 'Answer' and the 'Rejoinder', 'as tended to the ends which are mentioned in the King's

Declaration and Commission'. The bishops, however, had consistently declined to discuss any of the objections in open conference, and the interchange of documents without discussion had clearly proved useless.

Baxter has recorded his opinion that most of the bishops and their assistants at the Conference did not peruse the 'Reformed Liturgy' he had written or any other papers submitted to them, and that they were ignorant of their contents beyond the parts read openly in Conference. The letters quoted by Bosher in *The Making of the Restoration Settlement* give evidence that there was more consideration given than Baxter believed, but this outside the Conference.[32] When asked to review the suggestions and say how much they were willing to accept, the bishops refused. Their point always was that the ministers must prove the necessity for making alterations, and then they, the bishops, must be the judges. In vain did the divines refer to the King's Declaration and the Warrant, which stated the ends desired as 'giving satisfaction to tender consciences, and the restoring and continuance of peace and unity in the Churches', with the method expressed therein, namely 'to make such reasonable and NECESSARY ALTERATIONS, corrections, and amendments therein, AS SHALL BE AGREED UPON TO BE NEEDFUL OR EXPEDIENT for the giving satisfaction to tender consciences'.

The bishops rested their case upon the words 'necessary' and 'as shall be agreed upon'. They did not concede that changes were necessary. The ministers pointed out that the clauses could bear only this construction—that changes were assumed to be necessary to achieve the purpose of giving satisfaction to tender consciences and restoring the unity of the Church. Thus the Conference reached an impasse on the meaning of the word 'necessary'. The utmost that the bishops would allow was a disputation as to whether 'any alteration was necessary to be made'. Baxter and his party pointed out that such a disputation could hardly be concluded in the few days remaining and this would still leave the real issues untouched. 'But we spoke to the deaf; they had other ends, and were other men, and had the art to suit the means unto their ends.'

Many of the divines decided to withdraw from such a barren and pitiful employment, but Baxter contended that they should not refuse lest they be misrepresented and the blame for the breakdown of the Conference be laid against them.

Before noticing the fiasco with which the Savoy Conference ended, the ministers' 'Rejoinder' claims attention. This huge document comprised 148 pages, and, with the exception of the short preface written by Calamy, it was composed by Baxter in eight days.

In the preface Calamy pointed out that bishops before the Civil War had been willing to grant some of the things which now the bishops would not consider; these included the cross in Baptism, and the word 'minister' instead of 'priest'. Calamy reminded the bishops that even the Scottish liturgy in 1637, the cause of the Bishops' Wars, had used the word 'minister'.

In the body of this massive document, Baxter expressed resentment at the charge that the ministers showed ingratitude to the King when they asked for freedom from the use of the entire liturgy. Actually, the King had directed both parties to confer concerning necessary alterations. Baxter laid great stress upon no liturgy having been given by the apostles and none being known in the sub-apostolic Church. If unity in worship had required a uniform liturgy, such forms could have been expected in Scripture or in the early Church. Nor had the primitive Church known kneeling at Communion, the cross in Baptism, or the surplice.

The bishops had contended for the liturgy in order to secure peace, but actually it had produced discord in Scotland and elsewhere, and it had been the cause of Puritan migrations to America and the persecutions by bishops' courts before 1640. Neither did the liturgy in itself secure a Church against heresies as it had been argued; no country had been so free of heresies as Scotland, where there had been no such liturgy.

> 'We must say, that the way to make us think the Bishops to be so wise, and careful guides and fathers to us, is not for them to seem wiser than the apostles, and make those things of standing necessity to the churches' unity, which the apostles never made so, nor to forbid all to preach the gospel, or to hold communion with the Church, that dare not conform to things UNNECESSARY.'[33]

Baxter mentioned the ministers' distress because of the bishops' condemnation of extemporaneous prayer. If their reason was a dislike of private opinions being expressed in prayer, such opinions would far more likely be found in sermons. The aversion many persons felt to the Prayer Book would be increased if they knew that it was to be used in order to shut out other prayers because those prayers would be 'ministers' private conceptions'. Judges and physicians were not compelled to give their decisions in forms read from a book; and, if divines were to be limited to reading printed prayers, work 'such as a schoolboy may do as well as they', the result would be a ministry which would be indolent and ignorant if not worse. If nothing but a set liturgy without extempore prayer was the means of reaching unity in the Church, then the bishops were seeking 'to unite us all in a dead religion'.[34]

Baxter returned to the quotation from the Latitudinarian John Hales, esteemed by the bishops, in his treatise on 'Schism'. 'To load our public forms with the private fancies upon which we differ is the most sovereign way to perpetuate schism.... Wheresoever false or suspected opinions are made a piece of church-liturgy, he that separates is not the schismatic.' Yet the bishops were 'laying the Church's unity upon unnecessary things'.[35] Usher, Williams, and other bishops had been willing to make alterations to the liturgy in 1641, he reminded his opponents.

The ministers were not asking for complete liberty to be given to a clergyman to select or omit parts of the liturgy as he chose, but that extemporaneous and appropriate prayers could be permitted.

'We would avoid both the extreme that would have no forms, and the contrary extreme that would have nothing but forms.... You would deny us and all ministers THE LIBERTY OF USING ANY OTHER PRAYERS BESIDES THE LITURGY.'

Baxter dreaded the quenching of the prophetic spirit through limiting all utterances to the reading of set forms. He also made it clear that exception was not being taken to the mere reading of books of the Apocrypha in church, but to reading them as lessons as though they were of equal value with the canonical Scriptures.

Throughout this massive 'Rejoinder', which no one expected to be noticed when the Conference was ending through effluxion of time, and when agreement was manifestly impossible, Baxter's tactlessness and his incorrigible disputatiousness were evident. In referring to the bishops' defence of many repetitions in the liturgy and what the ministers considered lack of orderliness, and then to the bishops' scornful reference to ministers' extemporaneous 'conceived prayers', his unfortunate comment was : 'This shows us the wonderful power of prejudice.' [36]

While preferring the word 'minister', Baxter did not scruple so much about using 'priest' as the English equivalent for 'presbyter', provided the meaning was not misconstrued. He took graver objection to 'Sunday', as a term applied by heathens, instead of 'the Lord's Day', the Scriptural term.

Baxter argued for the superiority of a continuous 'conceived prayer'. He further criticized the Confession as being general and vague : 'We complain . . . that there is nothing but generals in so great a part of your prayers.' [37] The bishops had imagined that the reformers' main objections were to three things—the surplice, the cross in Baptism, and kneeling at Communion. Baxter made it clear that to abate these three ceremonies would not satisfy the ministers who regarded provision for extemporaneous prayers as essential, and added : 'As the proverb is, you may as well think to make a coat for the moon, as to make a liturgy that shall be sufficiently suited to the variety of places, times, subjects, accidents, without the liberty of intermixing such prayers or exhortations as alterations and diversities require.' [38]

Baxter used the argument that his party would certainly not support the expulsion of any minister who used the surplice, or made the sign of the cross in Baptism, or forced all to receive Communion kneeling—even though their opinion as to the disorderliness of such proceedings was at least as strong as the bishops' opinion about their desirability.

He particularly objected to the cross in Baptism as an unnecessary sign and one likely to be misinterpreted. If that sign must be used to indicate that we are not ashamed of Christ's cross, why not 'make laws that everyone is publicly to taste vinegar and gall, as a sign that we are not ashamed of, but resolved . . . to follow Christ, that did so. . . . If milk were to be publicly drunk by all, in profession that we will feed on the sincere milk of His word . . . or if we were to put on an helmet and other armour, in token that we will be his soldiers to the death.' [39]

Baxter was perfectly serious when drawing these grotesque analogies. Why, he asked, should the bishops make the using of any sign, such as the cross in Baptism, a requisite test of a minister's fitness? Christ made no laws for 'postures, and vestures, and words, and teaching signs of this nature'; and He said nothing about leaving officers to make such ceremonies obligatory. Baxter indignantly repudiated the suggestions that Puritans were ignorant, or did not study the arguments in favour of ceremonies, or that their 'tenderness of conscience' was actually unreasoning obstinacy about inconsequential matters, or that the cause of divisions in the Church was 'lust and inordinate desires of honour, or wealth, or licentiousness' when, as a matter of fact, the Puritan ministers' integrity was well known and also their refusal of bishoprics and other preferments in the Church.

With regard to kneeling, Baxter repeated the Puritan fear that the posture might imply adoration, seeing that Romanists had taunted the Church of England with agreeing with transubstantiation because of this ceremonial in the Communion Service.

Baptism should not be regarded as allowing the minister no discretion. He should not be obliged to baptize all children, irrespective of their parents' attitude; and parents, not godparents, should bring the children. Since only those personally fit should receive Communion, so only godly parents could undertake a covenant on their children's behalf in Baptism. 'What is the infant's title to baptism, if it be not found in the parent? Assign it, and prove it when you have done, as well as we prove their right, as they are the seed of believers, dedicated by them to God, and then we promise to consent.' [40]

The central position of the reformers was re-affirmed. It was fatal to assume always that persons were fit for either of the Sacraments without due inquiry and proof. No godly minister could exercise office day by day on pure assumptions, administering Baptism, confirmation, Communion, performing marriage services, and officiating at burials, declaring always that everyone without exception was acceptable.

> 'Indeed! Will you phrase and modify your administrations upon such a supposition, that all men are such as they ought to be, and do what they ought to do? Then take all the world for saints, and use them accordingly, and blot out the doctrine of reproof, excommunication, and damnation from your Bibles .... You say that whosoever desireth the Sacrament ... must in

charity be presumed to be penitent. But where hath God commanded or approved so blind and dangerous an act as this?'[41]

*The greatest demand of Puritan reformers was a pastor's personal examination of the worthiness of his people so that God's sacred ordinances were used for the worthy only.*

This remarkable document ended with these scathing words against the bishops: 'We must say, in the conclusion, that, if these be all the abatements and amendments you will admit, YOU SELL YOUR INNOCENCY, AND THE CHURCH'S PEACE FOR NOTHING.'[42]

## 9. *The Complete Failure of the Conference*

Even if the Savoy Conference had reached a satisfactory agreement about the Prayer Book, it would not have produced unity when its agenda did not include the essential questions: Church government by absolute prelacy or modified episcopacy and Church discipline by diocesan bishops or by pastors and synods.

The discussions on the Prayer Book were doomed to failure with the futile method of exchanging bitter documents and the bishops' refusal to settle disputed points openly. In justice to the bishops, however, certain matters must be remembered. It had been a principle established at the Reformation that every national Church should impose ceremonies that were not believed contrary to the Word of God; and the bishops in 1661 believed they were acting in consonance with that principle. On the other hand, the reformers were contending not that the special ceremonies in dispute were sinful in themselves, but that it was sinful to impose them. The negotiations of 1660–61 were concerned with the question of whether such freedom regarding the Prayer Book and ceremonies was compatible with the constitution of the Church of England. The bishops could well maintain that such freedom was unknown in England. On the other hand, the standpoint of High Churchmen has been that, although the Prayer Book had been designed to accommodate as many Papists as possible within the Church of England in the previous century, yet it should not be amended in any way that would satisfy Puritans who were already in the Church and who desired to remain within it. Clearly there were other influences at work to harden the bishops' hearts against Puritans in 1661.

If these extrinsic influences—political considerations—had not affected the issue, the bishops might have heeded the plea for the Church to achieve unity without uniformity and to prove itself a comprehensive Church. Usher and other bishops had been very sympathetic with this ideal. But now the sea of hatred had flowed between sequestered clergy and the Puritans; and because of these extra-ecclesiastical circumstances the Church was rent in twain by the Act of Uniformity of 1662.

Some modern apologists for the bishops have admitted that they refused to treat with the ministers on an equal footing or to listen to any appeals for concessions. Some of these writers have referred to the Puritan ministers in general as 'malcontents' and have described their requests as 'the Puritan wail, which had been going on for a hundred years, against set forms and ceremonial' as if, in any case, that was the essential programme of proposed reforms. Ridicule and misrepresentation of the Puritans have not been confined to writers in the seventeenth century.

Baxter mentioned an incident indicating the attitude of the bishops. Sterne, Bishop of Carlisle, had impressed Baxter as honest and serious though a silent member of the Conference. Baxter had been appealing to the bishops not to drive out so many ministers 'through the nation' because of ceremonies admittedly indifferent, when Sterne turned to the other bishops and remarked on Baxter's expression 'the nation'. 'He will not say "In the Kingdom" lest he own a King.' No one should have suspected Baxter of being a secret republican, but the incident gave evidence of the disposition of a bishop to find the flimsiest excuse for condemning Baxter.

When only ten days remained, and some of the divines had left, disheartened, it was agreed that formal debates should take place on the lawfulness of the 'impositions'. Pearson, Gunning, and Sparrow debated with Baxter, Bates, and Jacombe. Concerning this procedure, Baxter has written : 'I told them over and over ... that to keep off from personal conference until within a few days of the expiration of the Commission, and then to resolve to do nothing but wrangle out the time in disputing, as if we were between jest and earnest in the schools, was, in the sight of all the world, to defeat the King's Commission, and the expectations of many thousands who longed for unity and peace. But we spoke to the deaf.'

At this stage, Bishop Cosin produced a paper from an unknown superior person suggesting that controversy in the Church might cease if 'anything in the doctrine, or discipline, or the Common Prayer, or ceremonies' could be shown to be 'contrary to the Word of God'. If proof could be given, Convocation should be asked to consider the matter with a view to healing the divisions in the Church. This sounded plausible enough, and Baxter was asked by Bishop Cosin to supply an answer. Lest misrepresentations occur, Baxter submitted a paper as from Bates, Jacombe, and himself. In this, he gave eight instances of practices contrary to Scripture but directed in the Prayer Book:[43] FORCING ministers (1) to baptize with the transient image of the cross; (2) to wear the surplice; (3) to give Communion to none that would not receive it kneeling; (4) to pronounce all baptized infants as regenerate; (5) to deliver Communion 'unto the unfit'; (6) to absolve the unfit; (7) to give thanks for all persons buried; (8) to subscribe that there is NOTHING in the Prayer Book, the Book of Ordination, and the Thirty-nine Articles contrary to the Word of God.

Great harm came from the reporting of these closing debates to the King, Clarendon, and the Court. It was stated that Baxter had condemned the ceremonies as sinful when he was contending that IMPOSING them was sinful. Some who had previously manifested friendliness towards Baxter resented his alleged statements. Some High Church writers ever since have borne Baxter a grudge through the same misrepresentation. It was at the episcopal party's suggestion that the debates took place about the sinfulness, or otherwise, of IMPOSITION. He was quite willing to accept kneeling as lawful but he opposed requiring ministers to repel communicants who would not receive kneeling; such an obligation upon ministers was 'sinful'.

Bates, one of the ablest coadjutors, secured an interesting admission from Dr Gunning during these closing discussions. Bates suggested that if the bishops insisted upon the cross and the surplice, they might also introduce holy water and candles and other Romish ceremonies in the same way. To this Gunning answered, 'Yes, and so I think we ought to have more, and not fewer, if we do well.'[44]

The public were admitted into the last week's debates, most of them being supporters of the episcopal disputants. Tillotson, the future Archbishop of Canterbury, was one of the few sympathetic towards Baxter and his friends. Baxter was frequently baited, to the merriment of the public, and he was subjected to constant interruptions from Bishop Morley. Nothing annoyed Morley more than being reminded that the Nonconformists were certain to be expelled after the failure of the Conference. At one stage also, Morley taxed Baxter and his party with having cast out their opponents from benefices, and added that they should not complain if similar treatment were meted out to them; Baxter's reply was that he had never supported the ejection of any except scandalous or incompetent ministers of any party. Bishop Walton of Chester admitted that Baxter had written against ejecting him.

It is profitless to dwell upon this pitiful closing scene—England's leading divine, tactless though he was, using his powers of logic in fruitless debates and conscientiously pursuing his task to the very end while being held up to ridicule before an audience largely biased.

In the course of these closing debates, Gunning delivered a paper 'full of insulting words' (so Baxter afterwards wrote). To this he drew up 'The Reply to the Bishops' Disputants'. The only value of this document was its summarizing again the essentials for which Baxter and his associates had been wearily contending.

On the second last day the Bishop of Lincoln was put into the chair; he angrily declared that Gunning had prevailed in his debate with Baxter. On the last day Bishop Cosin asked the audience, nearly all of them supporters of the bishops, whether Gunning had proved that Romans xiv and xv did not refer (as Baxter had submitted in his Reply) to cases such as receiving Communion. The audience declared that Gunning had won. And so the Conference ended abruptly.

Even if the Savoy Conference had not been abortive, any recommendations it might have made could only have been submitted to Convocation and Parliament, where the Puritans could now expect no consideration. As it was, the King's Commission was returned with this brief report for both parties: 'That we were all agreed on the ends, for the Church's welfare, unity, and peace . . . but, after all our debates, were disagreed of the means.'

Baxter's writings show that he would have been willing, for the sake of peace, to admit as non-essentials some things which he had opposed in the closing debates. Knowing the hopelessness of the position, he had been struggling to represent the ministers' case for the sake of posterity. Unfortunately, he had created the impression that the Puritan party consisted of precisians who opposed union on technicalities or through sheer obstinacy. His boldness and pertinacity had resulted in his being blamed by many for the failure of the Conference. Honestly he recorded against himself : 'I thought that the day and cause commanded me those two things, which then were objected against me as my crimes, viz. speaking too boldly, and too long. And I thought it a cause that I could comfortably suffer for; and should as willingly be a martyr for charity as for faith.' [45]

The result would have been the same. Was Baxter unfair in making these comments upon the bishops' attitude?

'So had these men rather 1,800 godly faithful ministers were silenced at once, and 100,000 godly Christians kept out of the Church's communion and persecuted, than one ceremony should be cast out of the Church, or left INDIFFERENT, or one line reformed in their Common Prayer.' [46]

'To prefer this genuflexion in the reception of the Sacrament, before our brethren's communion with Christ and His Church in the Sacrament, and before the preaching of the Gospel by all those ministers that will be hereupon laid by, is to prefer sacrifice before mercy, yea, AN UNNECESSARY CEREMONY before sacrifice and mercy.' [47]

After the Conference, the ministers met together to consider drawing up their petition to the King. They waited upon Clarendon for advice, and it was immediately evident that Clarendon had been offended by Baxter's obstinacy at the Conference. It was represented to Baxter that he had been 'severe and strict', like 'a melancholy man and made these things sin which others did not'.[48] Clarendon disapproved the terms of the 'Petition' which Baxter had composed on behalf of his brethren. In this opinion their friend, the Lord Chamberlain (the Earl of Manchester), concurred : 'too pungent', 'too vehement, and such as would not well be borne' were his comments. Baxter thereupon deleted the passages disapproved. Manchester also advised the ministers that it would be better for them if Baxter were absent from their audience with the King. Baxter did not hesitate and prepared to leave though his brethren wished to be loyal to him. Manchester then, fearing he had been too critical, prevailed on Baxter to return and to stand with the deputation while Manton spoke on behalf of the petitioners.

To the ministers' protestation that the failure of the Conference did not lie at their door and that the differences did not concern the vital questions of Church order, the King returned the question, 'But who shall be judge?' Who indeed! There was none in that generation. The only answer could be Baxter's prophetic statement at his last trial in 1685, 'These things will surely be understood one day.'

This 'Petition to the King' was a temperate protest against the conduct of the Savoy Conference. It pointed out that the Conference had entirely failed to carry into effect the promises of the King's Declaration that there should be 'mutual approaches', and 'necessary alterations' of the Prayer Book. The event had proved that the bishops had decided that they were the bank and the ministers the boat that must be pulled to the bishops' immovable position (in Baxter's metaphor). Thus, not a single controverted point had been conceded.

It was remarkable that Pepy's wrote on 26th July 1661, two days after the closing of the Savoy Conference: 'The King now would be forced to favour Presbyterianism or the city would leave him.'

Even as late as 24th June 1662, when the Act of Uniformity had been passed, and only a short time would elapse before the ejection of ministers, Pepys gave his opinion: 'I confess I do think that the Bishops will never be able to carry it so high as they do.'

The fact was that the City of London no longer was predominant. The country squires and restored parsons were now in power with their hot memories of the Civil War, with its fines and sequestrations, and they would certainly not spare the rejected 'Presbyterians'.

*Reasons for the Failure of the Savoy Conference*

(1) The bishops opposed the giving of any concessions. There can be no doubt that they were bent upon excluding their rivals from the Church unless they conformed to their wishes. The King's Declaration had given ground for hoping that a comprehensive Church might be possible (and hence Baxter's short-lived elation upon receiving the Declaration), but the bishops them-

selves had never approved any of its provisions and they had never deviated from demanding uniformity and from excluding all who would not conform. When the King's Declaration was annulled by Parliament, no hope remained for any concession to the ministers' views.

This is indicated not only by the bishops' policy at the Conference that the ministers should bring forward their objections (Baxter did not demur to that procedure), but by their scorn for the suggestion of the 'mutual approaches' indicated in the Declaration, their refusal to discuss any points in open conference (the academic debates in the closing days being of a different order), and also their delays. Far from agreeing with the conditions in the King's Warrant that there should be consultations about the matters needed to restore peace and unity, they refused to consult together. They evidently thought nothing of the Church's peace and unity if these necessitated any concession.

The evidence is inescapable that the negotiations in the months before the Conference, as well as the conduct of the Conference itself, were insincere methods of procrastination until the bishops were in full control of the Church throughout the land, and until the Cavalier Parliament had followed the Convention Parliament and ensured the bishops' triumph.

Bishop Sheldon said after the Conference, 'Now we know their mind, we will MAKE THE DOOR SO NARROW THAT THEY WILL BE KNAVES IF THEY CONFORM.' Later, when taxed with having made the door so narrow that multitudes had been forced out of the Church, Sheldon declared, 'If we had thought so many of them would have conformed, we would have made it straiter.'[49] The bishops were more resolved upon excluding ministers than Clarendon was, and the sharpest Acts against them were passed at their instigation after Clarendon had fallen from office.

It was not strange that Baxter said the bishops (in Tertullian's phrase) had made SOLITUDE and called it PEACE.

(2) The wars and the bitterness engendered in the Interregnum militated against the possibility of any success at the Conference. If the wars had not taken place, many of the reforms desired in 1661 would have been accepted. In 1641 not only Puritans but several of the bishops would have accepted limited episcopacy and also modifications in the Prayer Book.

Politics have directed religious persecutions very often in history. Even mild Presbyterian Royalists seemed 'stained with the King's blood' in the eyes of the exiles and others who had suffered in the King's cause. When 'Presbyterians' who were enjoying the livings of sequestered clergy avowed their loyalty, they were asked what their loyalty had cost them. The hatred against Cromwell as well as against Committees of Plundered Ministers rebounded on the 'Presbyterians', who were treated as if they were sectaries and republicans. Some, like Baxter, had never been orthodox Presbyterians in any degree and had not benefited in status or income by any ecclesiastical changes. It could not be urged openly against them that they had supported Parliament against the King in the First Civil War, for Monk and many nobles and gentry now acceptable at the Court had done the same, some of them until very shortly before the Restoration. The motive of political animosity may have been concealed, but it was a major reason for opposing any concessions in religion.

(3) There was little unity among the Puritans. Generally speaking, the representatives at the Savoy Conference agreed, but there was no united body of Puritans.

First, the Independents were not included or considered. Baxter might well maintain that no accommodation was possible for them when the situation was so unfavourable even for moderate episcopals and Presbyterians. He could also claim that he was seeking the restoration of unity within the Church of England, whereas the Independents did not desire union with a national Church. Looking back over the history of dissent, we may dispute Baxter's judgement that expediency should have ruled against considering the Independents in 1661. The divisions in Nonconformist ranks after 1662 were the fruit of the neglect of unity before then.

Even among 'Presbyterians' there was little unity. In voluntary county associations various degrees of moderate episcopal clergy and some Presbyterians had worked harmoniously though not all had joined. Now, in face of a common foe, they did not close up their ranks. One result was that the ministers' contentions at the Savoy Conference were mainly negative, and they became the victims of the bishops' tactics, being held up to hatred as the would-be mutilators of the Prayer Book. The one positive contribution of the party at the Conference was Baxter's 'Reformed

Liturgy', and it was not enthusiastically supported by all the ministers.

(4) There were too few 'reconcilers' (Baxter's term) among the ministers themselves. Though Baxter's manner was provocative, his motives were sincere, and we know he was more disposed than his colleagues were towards concessions that did not infringe conscientious feeling. Many in his party not only thought reconciliation impossible but did not seek it.

True it is that the Savoy Conference must be considered in the light of many years' wranglings among ecclesiastical parties. The Parliamentary Presbyterians had not sought unity when they had the power in 1645–47. They had banned the Prayer Book entirely, and they had ejected almost as many rectors as the number of Nonconformists soon to be expelled. Similarly, there had been rivalry between 'Presbyterians' and Independents for years past. The Puritan ministers came as defeated men to seek an accommodation with the Laudian victors in 1661 and found them no more disposed towards conciliation than their own parties had been in the heyday of their power.

The disputes at the Conference also showed that obstinacy was not the monopoly of one side, and that the 'Presbyterian' divines were quite as disputatious as their opponents. Both sides had grown so accustomed to coercion that unity without uniformity was little more than an ideal found only in the mind of Baxter and very few others. Baxter might complain with justification that the bishops would 'open the church doors so wide as that moderate loyal Romanists may come in ... rather than ... a few inconsiderable Puritans',[50] but his own party as a whole had shown little desire to open any doors.

(5) Baxter's tactics spoilt the case for his own side, even if the bishops had been disposed to consider it at all. His admission that he had spoken 'too boldly and too long' indicated this. He seemed at the Savoy Conference almost incapable of keeping silent, and his honest loquacity and pertinacity made him sometimes embarrassing to his friends and always objectionable to his foes.

Others in his party must, however, share some of the blame. Their list of objections to the Prayer Book had outgrown what was anticipated at Breda, and it was a tactical blunder to include minute details in the liturgy together with matters of importance.

(6) The ministers' opposition to toleration had forfeited them

the sympathy of the King. They should have realized that he was their only slender hope, but Baxter had irritated him in the audience on 22nd October. The King had no great love for the bishops and he would have helped any party that supported general toleration. Baxter believed the bishops were already secretly favouring the Romanists; but their public acts did not support his suspicion, and both the bishops and the parliaments repeatedly refused toleration for Papists even when they knew the King desired it.

Without the King's sympathy the ministers had no prospect of success from a conference which had been called merely to fulfil his promise in the Declaration.

(7) Puritans in general had become almost as unpopular with Parliament and the nation as they were at Court. The licentiousness of the Restoration period could be given as a proof of the need for the discipline the Puritans desired, but over-strictness had antagonized the general body of Englishmen.

Charles II's Parliament was determined to use some of the powers for which the Long Parliament had fought against his father. Parliament would not endure attempts by Charles to help either Romanists or Puritans, as it thought he was doing by his Declaration. As Macaulay declared, Parliament now was more zealous for episcopacy than the bishops themselves. The previous generation of country squires had heard Puritan 'lecturers' with approval, and had hated the Laudian clergy; the Restoration squires had turned from sober Puritans and their preaching. The common people, the villagers, and town rabble alike derided Puritans with impunity under the new régime. The Savoy Conference could not succeed in the atmosphere of perfervid Royalism and anti-Puritanism sweeping England at that time.

(8) The decline of the 'political Puritans' had taken away the ministers' support at the Court. Royal favours and political promotions had drawn nobles and gentry away from a cause that was swiftly becoming more and more unpopular. In the background, the disbanding of the army made Royalists breathe more freely and feel that their policies in Church and State could be followed without hindrance.

(9) The Savoy Conference was held one year too late. Had it taken place soon after Charles returned in May 1660, there might have been a different result. At that time there was talk every-

where of rewarding the 'Presbyterians' for bringing back the King, and the restored bishops were walking warily. In July 1661, the bishops (in Pepys's phrase) 'carried themselves high' and knew they had the majority of Englishmen with them. They could now have their revenge without let or hindrance.

Baxter had feared, even before May 1660, that ejections would follow the Restoration. The Savoy Conference had effectively dismissed any faint prospect of unity, and the Act of Uniformity barred and bolted the door.

10. *A Summing up of Baxter's Proposals for Church Unity*

The indispensable conditions Baxter required can be seen through the many details and the considerable repetition found in the series of documents he wrote during the negotiations of 1660–61, and which have been reviewed in the foregoing pages. In a hopeless situation, and with ejection imminent, few troubled to study, still less to record, the irreducible minimum which Baxter had offered for unity. His programme for the Church's welfare passed almost into oblivion. Today we may turn to Baxter's own record of his proposals and learn some lessons for our own times.

We have, first, to remove a basic misunderstanding. Because the Savoy Conference dealt with objections to the Prayer Book, it has been supposed by many that the Nonconformists left the Church of England because they were not satisfied with the liturgy and ceremonies of the Church. That is not so.

The Nonconformists left the Church because the RIGHTS of the parish clergy, and their FREEDOM in certain vital matters, were not allowed by the bishops.[51] The essential PASTORAL RIGHTS Baxter claimed were these:

(1) *The right to receive or repel communicants*

The formal authority given in the rubric was not being exercised, and, in any case, a clergyman could act only under the direction of the bishop, to whom he had to report any case of unfitness in a communicant. Baxter insisted over and over again that he and other ministers would not submit to be bishops' curates. They must govern, they must have a 'credible profession of faith and obedience' from every communicant, they must have the power of discipline and excommunication.

Usher would have allowed this, as his 'Reduction of Episcopacy' clearly showed, but no bishop at the Restoration would do so. If these Laudian bishops had granted the pastor's right, they would have changed entirely the relationship of bishop and parish clergy, and they would have tacitly accepted the vital alteration from diocesan prelacy to modified episcopacy, the parochial episcopacy with synodical government which Baxter believed to be both Scriptural and the practice of the primitive Church. In this essential divergence of view between the AUTHORITY OF THE PASTOR and the AUTHORITY OF THE PRELATE lay THE ROOT-CAUSE OF THE SEPARATION OF NONCONFORMIST MINISTERS FROM THE CHURCH OF ENGLAND in 1662.

(2) *The right to approve or disapprove of confirmands*

So strongly did Baxter claim that the minister must have the deciding voice in this matter that he regarded the word *consent* in this connexion, in the King's Declaration, as the most vital concession, sufficient in itself to enable 'Presbyterian' ministers to remain in the Church of England. Again, Baxter's party was determined that a sacred act signifying a person's entering the adult-stage of Church membership should not be a formality but should necessitate the parish clergyman's approval of the confirmand's fitness.

(3) *The right to baptize or refuse Baptism*

Here also the ministers were not satisfied to be virtually puppets, required to baptize all children, irrespective of their parents' belief, and accepting merely the word of godparents. In this regard the ministers took up a harsh attitude, and were denounced by the bishops for penalizing infants for their parents' unfitness, and modern opinion would support the bishops, at least in expecting godparents to be substitutes for unworthy parents so that no children would be denied the ordinance. Yet the ministers were adamant, believing that they had the right to decide who should receive the benefit of a Sacrament.

(4) *The right to decide whether persons were fit to be absolved,* and finally fit to have pronounced over their burial that they had died 'in sure and certain hope' of resurrection.

Once again the ministers maintained a most rigid position, but it was consistent with their refusal always to use sacred words and perform sacred acts without sufficient warrant, and consistent too with their insistence that only the pastor should declare the blessings or the censures of the Church upon the conditions given in God's Word.

With those four rights there were associated four freedoms for parish ministers, namely: the minister's freedom to dispense with the surplice; his freedom to use, or not to use, the cross in Baptism; his freedom to give Communion to persons whether kneeling or not; and his freedom to be ordained and instituted without being required to subscribe to the whole of the Prayer Book or to swear canonical obedience.

Baxter had made it clear that he was not condemning the surplice, the sign of the cross, or the custom of kneeling. He opposed these ceremonies being *imposed* upon ministers. The fourth point was just as vital; repeatedly he declared that the Church could not be united by insisting upon *unnecessary* things, that is, by requiring ministers to subscribe to every part and detail of the Prayer Book and to give complete obedience to bishops. To surrender here meant forfeiting all the authority of the pastoral office.

In addition to the above, *reduced episcopacy* was always regarded by Baxter as indispensable for the unity of the Church, as far as he was concerned. Usher's scheme of modified episcopacy was not discussed at the Savoy Conference, for the reasons we have seen, but it had been most prominent in the previous negotiations. The reasons Baxter always advanced for Usher's model of reduced episcopacy were: Usher's form of episcopacy secured pastoral discipline; it provided for synods or associations in which pastors were consulted about discipline and jurisdiction; and it was (in Baxter's firm belief) a true primitive episcopacy.

Lastly, Baxter pleaded for the appointment of godly and efficient ministers as the indispensable means for the reformation of religion in England. This included no re-ordination for non-episcopally ordained ministers, provided that they were faithful and capable.

These terms would have enabled the majority of the ministers and their people to remain within the Church of England, and would have brought reformation as well as unity and peace to the Church and nation.

The consistency of the Puritan demands throughout the period and the exact nature of the terms can be traced in the pages that follow.

II. A SKETCH OF PROPOSALS FOR REFORM : 1603, 1641, 1660, 1661

| | *Millenary Petition* (1603) | Archbishop Usher's 'Reduction of Episcopacy' (advocated by Usher, 1641; offered by ministers, 1660) | 'First Address and Proposals of the ministers' (July 1660) | The King's Declaration (25th October 1660) (final form) (see pp. 153–7 for first draft and alterations) | *Ministers' 'Exceptions to the Prayer Book'* (Savoy Conference, 1661) |
|---|---|---|---|---|---|
| (1) SYSTEM OF CHURCH GOVERNMENT: *Powers of pastor* | 'None be excommunicated without consent of the pastor.' | 'Every pastor hath a right to rule the church and administer the discipline of Christ.' | Pastor's approval necessary for confirmation, etc. | Pastor's consent required for confirmation, for Communion, etc. | Pastor's rights over discipline 'to admit and to keep from the Lord's Table', confirmation, Baptism. |
| *Modification of episcopacy* | | Increased number of suffragans or *chorepiscopi* to equal number of rural deaneries. | No arbitrary power of diocesan bishops. Suffragans or *chorepiscopi* chosen by synods. 'Ancient and primitive Episcopacy or Presidency' with 'a due commixtion of presbyters'. | Because some dioceses were too large, suffragan bishops to be appointed. Suffragans and presbyters to act together. | |
| *Synods* | | (1) Monthly synod of suffragan and rectors to vote on questions of discipline brought by rectors, to excommunicate as | Usher's scheme approved and requested | (1) Monthly meeting or rural synod. Rural deans and elected clergy, receiving complaints from parishes. | |

| | Millenary Petition (1603) | Archbishop Usher's 'Reduction of Episcopacy' (advocated by Usher, 1641; offered by ministers, 1660) | 'First Address and Proposals of the ministers' (July 1660) | The King's Declaration (25th October 1660) (final form) (see pp. 153–7 for first draft and alterations) | Ministers' 'Exceptions to the Prayer Book' (Savoy Conference, 1661) |
|---|---|---|---|---|---|
| | | decided in synod and executed in parishes. (2) Diocesan synod, once or twice a year, with bishop or superintendent presiding. (3) Provincial synod, bishops, suffragans and elected clergy; primate to be 'moderator', every third year. (4) National council of both provincial synods. | | Suffragans and presbyters meeting. (2) Diocesan synod, with delegates from rural synods. | |
| Ministers' powers of ordination and jurisdiction | | Ministers' consent, or major part of them' for concluding 'all things' in synods. | (Usher's proposals urged.) | 'Advice and assistance' (King refused 'consent') of ministers. Presbyters equal to number of chapter, chosen annually by all presbyters, to assist in all ordinations and jurisdiction. | |

|  | Millenary Petition (1603) | Archbishop Usher's 'Reduction of Episcopacy' (advocated by Usher, 1641; offered by ministers, 1660) | 'First Address and Proposals of the ministers' (July 1660) | The King's Declaration (25th October 1660) (final form) (see pp. 153–7 for first draft and alterations) | Ministers' 'Exceptions to the Prayer Book' (Savoy Conference, 1661) |
|---|---|---|---|---|---|
| (2) CHURCH DISCIPLINE: *Tests before Communion* | 'Examination ... before the Communion.' | Rector and churchwardens to notice those who live scandalously every week, report them to monthly synod; in meantime pastor to debar from Table. | Communion only 'after credible profession of faith'. | Minister to admit none until 'credible profession of their faith'; not to suffer any to partake until repentance. | (Same as the King's Declaration.) |
| *Excommunication by lay officials* | To be forbidden. |  |  | To be forbidden. |  |
| *Godly and efficient ministers* | To be appointed. |  | To be appointed. | To be appointed. |  |
| *Oaths of obedience to bishops and subscription to liturgy before ordination* | 'Not to subscribe but according to law, to the Articles of Religion and the King's Supremacy only.' |  | Not to be required. | Not to be required. | Not to be required. |

| | Millenary Petition (1603) | Moderate Episcopal Suggested Concessions (House of Lords Committee—Williams and Usher—1641) | 'First Address and Proposals of the ministers' (July 1660) | The King's Declaration (25th October 1660) (final form) (see pp. 153-7 for first draft and alterations) | Ministers' 'Exceptions to the Prayer Book' (Savoy Conference, 1661) |
|---|---|---|---|---|---|
| (3) THE LITURGY: Liturgy in general | 'Longsomeness of Service to be abridged.' | | Lawful if agreeable to the Word of God, but request for extempore prayer, and revision of Book with Scriptural words. | Because objections to several things, review of Book by Savoy Conference, with 'additional forms . . . in Scriptural phrases . . . left to minister's choice to use one or other' (*e.g.*, additions). | To consist of nothing doubtful; to omit repetitions, responses, in favour of 'one solemn prayer'. Extempore prayer and alternative liturgy requested. |
| Communion service | | | | | Christ's words to be used. Rubric against adoration to be restored. No requirement of three times yearly communicating. |
| Communion at wedding service | | | | | Not to be compulsory as not all were fit. |
| Baptismal service | | | | | Ministers not forced to baptize children of unbelievers. Parents to make profession of faith for their children. Not baptismal regeneration. |

| | Millenary Petition (1603) | Moderate Episcopal Suggested Concessions (House of Lords Committee—Williams and Usher—1641) | 'First Address and Proposals of the ministers' (July 1660) | The King's Declaration (25th October 1660) (final form) (see pp. 153–7 for first draft and alterations) | Ministers' 'Exceptions to the Prayer Book' (Savoy Conference, 1661) |
|---|---|---|---|---|---|
| *Burial service* | | Alter 'in sure and certain hope' to 'knowing assuredly that the dead shall rise again'. | | | 'Sure and certain hope of resurrection cannot be said of all. |
| *Term 'Priest'* | To be corrected. | | | | 'Minister', not 'priest'. |
| *Lessons from the Apocrypha* | 'Canonical Scriptures only to be read.' | Delete Apocrypha. | | | Delete lessons from the Apocrypha. |
| *(4) Ceremonies: Confirmation* | 'To be taken away as superfluous.' | | 'If continued... only to those who make credible profession of faith' and with 'approbation of the pastors'. | Only with 'consent' of the ministers. Rural deans and assistants to see that young persons are carefully instructed. | (King's Declaration requirements repeated.) |
| *Cross in Baptism* | 'To be taken away.' | Explain with 'discreet' rubric or discontinue. | To be abolished. | Optional. | Optional. |
| *Ring in marriage* | To be 'corrected'. | | | | |
| *The surplice* | 'Not to be urged.' | Amend rubric commanding vestments. | To be abolished. | Optional. | To be 'left indifferent to be used or forborne'. Optional. |

|  | Millenary Petition (1603) | Moderate Episcopal Suggested Concessions (House of Lords Committee—Williams and Usher—1641) | 'First Address and Proposals of the ministers' (July 1660) | The King's Declaration (25th October 1660) (final form) (see pp. 153–7 for first draft and alterations) | Ministers' 'Exceptions to the Prayer Book' (Savoy Conference, 1661) |
|---|---|---|---|---|---|
| Kneeling at Communion |  | To be explained; to be optional. | Not to be imposed against conscience. | Optional. | That it 'may be left free'. |
| Bowing at the name of Jesus | 'No minister charged to teach their people to bow.' |  | To be abolished. | Optional. |  |
| The altar |  | Holy Table not to be made an altar. | Laws forbidding to be enforced. |  |  |
| Bowing to altar |  | Condemned. | Laws forbidding to be enforced. |  |  |
| The Lord's Day | To be 'not profaned'. |  | 'Effectual course . . . for sanctification of the Lord's Day.' | 'To be applied to holy exercises.' | Term 'Sunday' not to be used. |
| Saints' days | 'Rest upon Holy days not to be so strictly urged.' |  | Not to be imposed. | To be declared indifferent. | Not to be observed. |
| Ceremonies in general |  |  | 'At best but indifferent and in their nature mutable.' |  | Should be optional because held sinful and unlawful by some, unnecessary by others, and burdensome. |

# NOTES TO CHAPTER VIII

1. Powicke, *Richard Baxter, under the Cross, 1662–1691*, p. 294.
2. Burnet, *History of his own Time*, p. 41.
3. *Reliquiae Baxterianae*, II, p. 306.
4. Luckock, *Studies in the History of the Prayer Book*, p. 176.
5. *Reliquiae Baxterianae*, II, p. 307.
6. *Ibid.*, II, pp. 307, 308–13.
7. *Ibid.*, II, p. 310.
8. *Ibid.*, II, p. 312.
9. *Ibid.*, II, p. 316.
10. *Ibid.*, II, p. 317.
11. *Ibid.*, II, p. 317.
12. *Ibid.*, II, p. 319.
13. *Ibid.*, II, p. 320.
14. *Ibid.*, II, p. 327.
15. *Ibid.*, II, p. 329.
16. *Ibid.*, II, p. 334.
17. *Ibid.*, II, p. 334.
18. Bosher, *The Making of the Restoration Settlement. The Influence of the Laudians, 1649–62*, pp. 227–8.
19. *Documents Relating to the Settlement of the Church of England under the Act of Uniformity, 1662*, p. 177.
20. *Ibid.*, pp. 177–8.
21. *Ibid.*, p. 177.
22. *Ibid.*, p. 183.
23. *Ibid.*, p. 187.
24. *Ibid.*, p. 188.
25. *Ibid.*, p. 189.
26. *Ibid.*, p. 196.
27. *Ibid.*, pp. 199–200.
28. *Reliquiae Baxterianae*, II, p. 334.
29. Proctor and Frere, *New History of the Book of Common Prayer*, p. 200.
30. Luckock, *Studies in the History of the Prayer Book*, p. 250.
31. Proctor and Frere, *New History of the Book of Common Prayer*, p. 188.
32. Bosher, *The Making of the Restoration Settlement*, pp. 227–8.
33. *Documents Relating to the Settlement of the Church of England under the Act of Uniformity*, p. 216.
34. *Ibid.*, p. 230.
35. *Ibid.*, p. 233.
36. *Ibid.*, p. 259.
37. *Ibid.*, p. 267.
38. *Ibid.*, p. 269.
39. *Ibid.*, p. 281.
40. *Ibid.*, p. 321.
41. *Ibid.*, pp. 334, 338.
42. *Ibid.*, p. 345.
43. Proctor and Frere, *New History of the Book of Common Prayer*, p. 192.
44. *Reliquiae Baxterianae*, II, p. 340.
45. *Ibid.*, II, p. 364.
46. *Ibid.*, II, p. 344.

47. *Reliquiae Baxterianae*, II, p. 360.
48. *Ibid.*, II, p. 365.
49. *Bicentenary Lectures*, p. 52, quoted by Principal A. M. Fairbairn; Plummer, *English Church History, 1649–1702*, p. 64, the Anglican author accepting Neal, *History of the Puritans*, vol. 4, pp. 332–3.
50. *Practical Works*, vol. 4, p. 695.
51. See also *A Treatise on Episcopacy*, II, pp. 126–9.

CHAPTER IX

# THE DESTRUCTION OF UNITY
# BY THE ACT OF UNIFORMITY (1662)

THE stage was now set for the expulsion of those who would not submit to the bishops' authority. Sheldon, who became Archbishop of Canterbury in 1663, declared that the purpose of the Act of Uniformity was to compel the Puritan ministers to be Nonconformists or 'knaves' and he regretted only that the door to conformity had not been made narrower to exclude still more (see p. 210).

The growing hostility towards the Puritans could readily be seen in other events. At the coronation on 23rd April 1661, while the Savoy Conference was in session, no 'Presbyterian' minister, not even one of those who had been appointed royal chaplains, had any part in the service. The King and Bishop Sheldon went to the theatre to see Baxter and Calamy lampooned personally in Ben Jonson's play, *Bartholomew Fair*; this was recorded by others as well as Pepys, who was not edified by seeing the royal party enjoying jokes from a public stage at the expense of the two leading Puritan divines.

Not only the bodies of Cromwell's mother and daughter, but those of noted Presbyterians (Dr William Twisse, prolocutor of the Westminster Assembly, and Dr Stephen Marshall, one of the 'Smectymnuus' writers) were taken from their tombs in Westminster Abbey and buried in a common pit. Typical ridicule against the Solemn League and Covenant was that shown at Bury St Edmunds, where a copy of the Covenant was fastened to an effigy of Cromwell's chaplain, Hugh Peters, with a copy of the Westminster Directory of Public Worship also tied to the effigy, which was led through the streets and publicly burnt.

### 1. *The Bill before Parliament*

While the Savoy Conference was still in session, Parliament appointed a committee to prepare the Bill for the compulsory use of the Prayer Book. This Bill was passed by the House of Commons on 9th July 1661, before the conference had concluded, and was sent at once to the House of Lords. At that time Convocation had not begun to consider the Book, and yet the Commons were prepared to order assent to be given by all clergy to a liturgy still to be revised. The House of Lords, perhaps more conscious of the proprieties, delayed dealing with this Bill until the Savoy Conference had ended, and also until the bishops had taken their places again in the House, as they did on 28th November 1661.

In January 1662 the impatient Commons urged the Lords to deal with the Bill. On 25th February Clarendon read a message to the Lords from the King transmitting the Book as revised and approved by Convocation. The King himself was suspected of indifference towards the Bill. It was on 3rd March that he summoned the Commons to attend him and addressed them in words intended to reassure them of his devotion to the Church and its liturgy.

'Gentlemen, I hear you are very zealous for the Church . . . and even jealous that there is not expedition enough used in that affair. . . . But I must tell you I have the worst luck in the world if, after all the reproaches of being a Papist, whilst I was abroad, I am suspected of being a Presbyterian now I am come home. . . . I am as much in love with the Book of Common Prayer as you can wish . . . and you may be confident I had as much desire to see a uniformity settled. . . .'[1]

In the House of Lords some abatement of the requirements of uniformity was proposed. For example, on 17th March 1662 the Lords (Clarendon actually proposing this) agreed to ask the King to exempt ministers from expulsion under the Act of Uniformity if their only objections were to the surplice and the cross in Baptism. This proposition was rejected by the Commons on 22nd April. It was also significant that it was in the House of Lords (9th April 1662) that there was a proposal that dissenting clergymen should have an allowance of one-fifth from their livings. This was introduced by the ministers' friend, the Earl of Anglesey. When the Lords accepted this amendment, the Commons on 26th April, by 94 votes to 87, refused to agree. The Commons also voted against a suggestion that the King might make provision for the deprived clergy. Through their manager, Mr Serjeant

Charlton, the Commons gave their reason for opposing the Lords' proposal: 'It was one thing to allow a differing religion in a nation; another thing to allow men to receive profits for [sic] that Church unto which men would not conform.' [2]

The more liberal attitude in the Lords was evident also from their willingness to require from ministers only an assent to the *use* of the Prayer Book and not an assent to all its contents, an accommodation that Baxter would have approved. The Commons summarily swept aside all such concessions and demanded 'unfeigned assent and consent' to everything in the Book.

The harshest part of the Act was the requiring of assent before St Bartholomew's Day, instead of Michaelmas, the date first proposed. The changed date was fixed by the House of Lords, and approved by the Commons on 17th April by 96 votes to 87. The closeness of voting on important amendments is evidence of the willingness of many, even in the Cavalier Parliament, to press less heavily on the Nonconformists. Had Michaelmas been agreed upon, the ejected clergy would have received their tithes for the half-year, but at St Bartholomew's Day they were obliged to leave without the income to which they were entitled as well as with no prospect of other means of support in the future. It was recalled that the clergy ejected by the Long Parliament for loyalty to the liturgy, or for other reasons, had been given one-fifth of their livings.

The King's own desire was to suspend the operation of the Act for three months, but upon the insistence of Clarendon and Sheldon he relented. The royal assent was given on 19th May 1662, the day on which Parliament was prorogued. When both Houses assembled before the King, the Speaker of the House of Commons addressed him in words significant not for the usual fulsomeness of the references to the 'most religious King' but for bitterness towards Nonconformists.

> 'May it please your most excellent majesty. The glorious body of the sun doth exhilarate the soul of man with its light, and fructify the earth by its heat. In like manner, we ... acknowledge these frequent accessions to your royal presence do both comfort our hearts, and influence our actions. ... We cannot forget the late disputing age, wherein most persons took a liberty ... to trample upon the discipline and government of

the Church. The hedge being trod down, the foxes and the wolves did enter; the swine and other unclean beasts defiled the temple. At length it was discerned, the SMECTYMNIAN PLOT did not only bend itself to reform ceremonies, but sought to erect a popular authority of elders, and to ROOT OUT EPISCOPAL JURISDICTION. . . . Then the forms of Common Prayer, which as members of the public body of Christ's Church were enjoined us, were decried as superstitious, and in lieu thereof nothing, or worse than nothing, introduced.'³

After presenting the Bill for Uniformity for the King's assent, the Speaker added : 'We hope the GOD OF ORDER AND UNITY WILL CONFORM the hearts of all the people in this nation, to serve Him in this ORDER AND UNIFORMITY.' The Laudian theory was again being applied, it being assumed that the 'God of unity' would conform the people to uniformity.

### 2. *The Requirements of the Act of Uniformity*

'St Bartholomew might seem to be the patron saint of Christian enormities.'⁴ Apart from the infamous massacre of the French Huguenots on that day, it has been notorious in England. It was on 23rd August 1645, the eve of St Bartholomew's Day, that the Book of Common Prayer was forbidden by the Long Parliament and the Westminster Directory of Public Worship substituted. On St Bartholomew's Day, 1662, the country squires in the Cavalier Parliament, as well as bishops and parsons who had been loyal to the liturgy, did not forget what Puritans had done in the heyday of their power. Now they had ample revenge; and, not content with this, they libelled their opponents in words placed in the preface to the Act of Uniformity, words which, Dr R. W. Dale of Birmingham recalled at the bi-centenary in 1862, were still standing on the Statute Book of England :

'A great number of people in divers parts of this realm, following their own sensuality, and living without knowledge and due fear of God, do wilfully and schismatically abstain and refuse to come to their parish churches, and other public places where Common Prayer, the Administration of the Sacraments and preaching of the Word of God is used. . . . And by the great and scandalous neglect of the ministers in using the said Order or Liturgy . . . many people have been led into factions

## THE DESTRUCTION OF UNITY 229

and schisms, to the great decay and scandal of the reformed religion of the Church of England, and to the hazard of many souls.'[5]

The political aims of the bishops' party were seen in the provisions of the Act requiring clergymen not only to swear that there was nothing in the liturgy and ceremonies repugnant to the Word and to give 'unfeigned assent and consent to all and every thing contained and prescribed in and by the Book of Common Prayer', not only to swear canonical obedience to the bishops, but also to declare:

'That it is not lawful upon any pretence whatsoever, to take arms against the King [and to] abhor that traitorous position of taking arms by his authority against his person [and that there was] no obligation from the Solemn League and Covenant to endeavour ANY CHANGE or alteration of government, either IN CHURCH or Government.'[6]

The Act endorsed episcopal ordination for all clergy. Indeed a new offence in English history was created by the Act, it being punishable for the Sacrament to be administered by anyone not a priest episcopally ordained, with a fine of £100.

Clarendon himself is witness to the lack of precedent for not recognizing non-episcopal ordination under any circumstances in the Church of England. Referring to this clause in the Act of Uniformity, Clarendon wrote:

'This was new; for there had been many, and at present there were some, who possessed benefices with cure of souls, and other ecclesiastical promotions, who had never received orders but in France or in Holland; and these men MUST NOW RECEIVE NEW ORDINATION, which had been always held unlawful in the Church, or by this Act of Parliament must be deprived of their livelihood, which they enjoyed in the most flourishing and peaceable time of the Church.'[7]

The event proved that some ministers were willing to receive re-ordination. Some bishops carried the new policy to the extent of demanding from presbyterially ordained clergymen an explicit repudiation of their past ordinations before they were re-ordained.[8] A modern Anglo-Catholic historian refers to Bishop Hall of Chester doing this and justifies it because those ministers had been set apart only for preaching but had not been ordained 'priests'.⁹

An indication of the decidedly Protestant attitude of Parliament was seen in the restoration of the Black Rubric from the 1552 Book after its omission in 1559; this rubric explained that kneeling at Communion did not signify adoration of the elements. Convocation had decided against re-inserting this in the Prayer Book, but Parliament was determined to oppose anything capable of interpretation as an evasion in Romanist interests. Thus Parliament, if more zealous for episcopacy than the bishops, as Macaulay declared, was also more Protestant.¹⁰

Copies of the new Prayer Book were not available anywhere until a few days before St Bartholomew's Day, 1662. In some parts of England ministers were ejected for not accepting a book that had not reached them. The date of the official approval of the Prayer Book, forming the schedule to the Act 'as a true and perfect copy of the orginal', was 13th December, nearly four months after the ejections had taken place.

The details of the new Prayer Book have been discussed in many works and need not be given here. Of the nature of the alterations, it has been stated that they 'seemed designed to convince the Nonconformists that, instead of any wish to admit them . . . there was a distinct and settled desire to restrain and exclude them. So strongly did they themselves feel this conviction, that it was proposed on their behalf, in the House of Lords, that the existing Liturgy should be continued, and all the corrections made in Convocation should be abandoned.' ¹¹

Some Anglican historians have admitted that the ministers ejected in 1662 were punished for holding opinions that had been accepted in the Church of England for the previous one hundred years. For example, Abbey and Overton state that by the Act of Uniformity the Church 'lost the services of some of the most devoted of her Puritan sons, men whose views were in many cases IN NO WAY DISTINGUISHABLE FROM THOSE WHICH HAD BEEN HELD WITHOUT REBUKE BY SOME OF THE MOST HONOURED BISHOPS OF ELIZABETH'S TIME'.¹²

### 3. *The Expulsion of the Nonconformists*

The frequently quoted approximate number of ejected ministers is 2000. The records for England and Wales indicate the

## THE DESTRUCTION OF UNITY

following numbers as probably correct: ejected in 1660-61, 324; ejected in 1662, 1873; ejected (uncertain dates), 152; silenced, 98; the total being 2447.[13]

All of these 2447 were ministers holding office or benefices in the Church of England. Apart from these, Independents, Baptists, and smaller sects outside the establishment were persecuted together with their hitherto more favoured fellow-Puritans. About 254 of the 2447 ejected conformed at later dates. Approximately 7000 clergy conformed in 1662.

Of the moderate episcopal Nonconformists, Baxter said: 'They are the soberest, and most judicious, unanimous, peaceable, faithful, able, constant ministers in this land, or that I have heard or read of in the Christian world.' Both the moderate men whom Baxter had represented and the more rigid Presbyterians were subsequently registered as 'Presbyterian', except Baxter himself, who adhered to the title of mere Nonconformist. Men of this kind had been the heart of the Puritan movement for the previous hundred years, and had formed the party that had constantly sought to reform the Church from within and striven for unity as well as purity of religion. These were the men whom Baxter again represented, in writing to his old antagonists, Bishops Morley and Gunning, in his 'True and Only Way of Concord' (1679), reminding them of the negotiations in 1660-61:

> 'We never treated with you for Presbyterian government, or Independent, but for unity and peace; nor did we herein offer you any worse than Archbishop Usher's form of the primitive Episcopal government . . . and I never heard of the name of Episcopal Presbyterians . . . till of late.'[14]

About 400 ejected ministers were Independents who had held parish appointments under the Commonwealth and Protectorate. In Wales over 90 of the 106 ejected were Independents, an indication of the strong bias of the principality towards Congregationalism.

The unusually high standard of scholarship among the ejected clergy is a striking feature. At least 1285 were University men, 733 having been at Cambridge (where 68 had held Fellowships), 513 at Oxford (36 Fellowships), 32 in Scotland or at Harvard or Trinity College, Dublin. Of the 733 Cambridge men, 155 came from Emmanuel, 'most Puritan of Colleges'.

Many of the men who accepted expulsion rather than dishonour had been episcopally ordained—at least 420 of them before the Civil War; and of these, 72 had held their livings for over twenty years. At least 45 of those ejected had received episcopal ordination between May 1660 and St Bartholomew's Day, 1662, it being considered that they had taken this step because of the encouragement of the King's Declaration of 25th October 1660.

Because of the manifest sufferings of the ejected Nonconformists, the bishop's party felt constrained to refute charges of extreme harshness by pointing to the numbers of Royalist clergy expelled by the Long Parliament and its committees. Bishop Bramhall said:

'Let Mr Baxter sum up into one catalogue all the Nonconformists . . . ever since the Reformation who have been cast aside or driven away . . . those who in these late intestine wars have been haled away to prison, or chased into banishment by his party in three places alone, in London and the two Universities, or left to the merciless world to beg their bread, for no other crime than loyalty, and because they stood affected to the ancient rites and ceremonies of the Church of England, and they shall double them for number.' [15]

Yet Bramhall elsewhere admitted that many of those sequestered under the Long Parliament and Protectorate had been ejected for political reasons.[16] Some of them had been expelled for proven immorality or incompetence; and no such charges were made against any minister ejected in 1662. The late Bishop Hensley Henson declared: 'The Anglican of the Restoration was a religious persecutor inspired by political panic, the Puritan of the Commonwealth was a persecuting social reformer inspired by religious fervour.'[17] Hallam's *Constitutional History*[18] sums up the position: 'The Church of England had, doubtless, had provocations; but she made retaliation much more than commensurate to the injury. No severity comparable to this cold-blooded persecution had been inflicted by the late powers, even in the ferment and fury of a civil war.'

John Wesley's great-grandfather, Bartholomew Wesley, was ejected and died shortly afterwards, still in middle life, gravely affected by his sufferings. His son, John Wesley, ejected from Winterbourne Whitechurch in Dorset, was imprisoned several times and fined; when he died the vicar of Preston (Dorset) would not permit his body to be buried in the church.[19] Samuel Annesley, maternal grandfather of John and Charles Wesley, was another of the ejected clergy; he was a cousin of the Earl of Anglesey, the friend of Baxter and the ministers in their negotiations with the King, and an advocate of consideration for them in Parliamentary debates in 1662.

Sunday 17th August 1662, the last Sunday on which Nonconformist ministers could preach in parish churches, was a day of consternation and sorrow in many quiet country parishes, and still more in London and larger towns where most of the Nonconformists had ministered to considerable congregations. Baxter did not wait until August. To make his position clear he made public his refusal to subscribe soon after the Act of Uniformity received the royal assent. On 25th May he preached his last sermon as a clergyman of the Church of England.

4. *Indulgence refused and Harsher Laws passed (1663-70)*

Before the end of 1662 Charles endeavoured to remove the harshness of the Act of Uniformity and to grant an indulgence by his Declaration of 26th December. In this he referred to his promises at Breda, and to the fears of some of his subjects that he had 'added straiter fetters than ever, and new rocks of scandal to the scrupulous, by the Act of Uniformity'. He averred that it was zeal for the maintenance of 'the true Protestant religion' that was the Parliament's motive for the Act of Uniformity, but he wished to mitigate the penalties of the Act, and would ask Parliament to pass legislation such 'as may enable us to exercise that power of dispensing, which we conceive to be inherent in us'. Charles was not only tolerant by nature, but he indicated in his Declaration his desire to include Roman Catholics in the benefits of his indulgence because of their loyalty to the Crown in the wars.

In addressing Parliament, the King supported his Declaration with these words :

'He would not have them infer that he meant to favour Popery . . . nor that I intend them [Papists] to hold any place in the Government, for I will not yield to any, no, not to the Bishops themselves, in my zeal for the Protestant religion, and my liking the Act of Uniformity; and yet if the Dissenters will behave themselves peaceably and modestly under the Government, I could heartily wish I had such a power of indulgence to use upon all occasions, as might not needlessly force them out of the Kingdom, or staying here, give them cause to conspire against the peace of it.'

The King's protestation was addressed to Parliament in vain. On 23rd February 1663 the Lords, it is true, voted in favour of making the Declaration into a Bill for the benefit of Protestants only, although Clarendon opposed this. The Commons, without waiting for a Bill to come from the Lords, drew up an address to the King. After the customary flattery, they offered the King the advice that the Declaration would establish schism by a law, and 'be a cause of increasing sects and sectaries' until they would demand 'a general toleration which your Majesty hath declared against, and, in time, some prevalent sect will, at last, contend for an establishment, which, for aught can be foreseen, may end in POPERY'.

Charles was appeased with a grant, and was urged to put the laws against Roman Catholics in operation. Clarendon's outspoken opposition to this Declaration contributed to his eventual estrangement from the King. The Lord Chancellor had felt so keenly the threat to the Church and the possibility of Popish advantages that, despite his illness, he had gone to the Lords and advocated the withdrawal of the Bill that would have approved applying, in part, the King's Declaration.

When the King had issued this Declaration, the Independent, Philip Nye, visited the King at Whitehall. The result was so encouraging to him that he spoke to Baxter about toleration. Baxter, however, refused to support the Declaration, shrewdly discerning that its real intention was to benefit Roman Catholics. Unfortunately, this incident revived the recriminations between Independents and 'Presbyterians', the former believing that they had been deliberately neglected in the negotiations of 1660–61.

Baxter states that those Independents (and some Presbyterians) who criticized him at first for his policy at the Savoy Conference did so because they thought he conceded too much, rather than because they were not included in the negotiations; and later Baxter felt assured that all unbiased men recognized the justice of his position in 1660–61. The definite evidence of this from Inde-

## THE DESTRUCTION OF UNITY

pendents was expressed in Baxter's statement: 'The Independents confessed that we had dealt faithfully and satisfactorily; and indifferent men said that reason had overwhelmed the cause of the Diocesans, and that we had offered them as much as left them without excuse. And the moderate Episcopal men said the same.'[20]

The possibility of toleration having passed, the position of the ejected clergy and their people became more distressing, and harsher laws were soon to add to their sufferings. Nonconformist congregations shared the religious disabilities of their pastors, who, however, were generally in financial distress also. The Nonconformist laymen were only one-twentieth of the population, while their ministers represented two-ninths of the English clergy. The disproportionate numbers of laymen and ministers showed that many of the people had not been willing 'to suffer affliction with the people of God'.

Nothing could quench the devotion of those who suffered for conscience' sake, or remove the enduring effects of their piety. Puritan piety and family religion continued in many homes. Puritan moral standards affected far more than the expelled ministers and their people and gave eventual rise to the term, 'the Nonconformist conscience'. For the present, the moral temperature of England had fallen sadly, and iniquity abounded in high places. Nor was this only a reaction from Puritan strictness as secular historians have often surmised. Baxter and his fellow-Puritans had toiled for the revival of godliness and had fought social evils for many years before the Restoration. Now, with the scandal of the Restoration Court as an example, moral laxity increased in the nation and was rather half-heartedly rebuked by the Church. Macaulay's comment was not unfair: 'The clergy, for a time, made war on schism with so much vigour that they had little leisure to make war on vice.'[21] Those preachers who could have had more influence against vice had been silenced.

The Corporation Act in 1661 ensured that there would be no 'Presbyterian' magistrates to give local support to Nonconformist ministers after the Act of Uniformity was passed. Baxter states that only one man out of thirteen aldermen and twenty-five burgesses at Kidderminster was willing to keep his office under the Corporation Act, although not more than three of them had ever taken the Solemn League and Covenant which the corporation had to abjure.

The first Conventicle Act of 1664 followed the attempt of the King to grant an indulgence; every effort he made on behalf of Roman Catholics led to a fresh Parliamentary persecution of Nonconformists as well as Roman Catholics. This Act made the punishment for the third offence a fine of £100 or transportation, with death if the person convicted returned to England. Husbands whose wives were present at conventicles were to be fined, even if they themselves had not worshipped there.

The Five Mile (or Oxford Oath) Act of 1665 was the most outrageous measure of political persecution. It was a purely political test for ministers, the preamble of the Act stating that Nonconformist ministers 'have settled themselves in divers corporations in England . . . taking an opportunity to distil the poisonous principles of schism and rebellion into the hearts of His Majesty's subjects, to the great danger of the Church and Kingdom'.

The title of the Act was 'An Act for Restraining Nonconformists from Inhabiting Corporations'. It deliberately forced ministers to reside in sparsely settled districts where they could not even earn a livelihood by teaching. The House of Commons considered an amendment to force all Englishmen to take the Oxford Oath—against taking up arms, and against endeavouring any change in the government of the Church or State. Only by a majority of three votes was this sweeping amendment defeated.

The Second Conventicle Act of 1670 (Pepys said) angered the people of London and 'not all the forces in London could put down the great Presbyterian gatherings'. This Act was directed against 'seditious Sectaries and other disloyal persons', a clear appeal to Royalist emotions and a branding of Dissenters as disloyal. Two features were particularly infamous: one-third of all fines were to be paid to informers, who were thereby encouraged to pry upon their neighbours, and the Act stated that its provisions were to be interpreted in the sense most favourable to informers and most opposed to persons found in conventicles. To such a depth had British justice sunk. Charles received £300,000 from a grateful Parliament after he gave his assent to this Act, and he promptly prorogued Parliament.

All the bishops except two (Wilkins of Chester and Rainbow of Carlisle) had voted for the Second Conventicle Act, the most vindictive part of the Clarendon Code. Archbishop Sheldon particularly was delighted with the suppression of conventicles. Coleridge can be cited in his exposure of the Archbishop's conduct :

'This was the incendiary! this Sheldon, the most virulent enemy and poisoner of the English Church. . . . I look on Gardiner as canonizable compared with Sheldon. Much as I love the Church of England, I have no hesitation in asserting, as my belief, that nothing in the history of the Inquisition was equally wicked, as the conduct of Sheldon and the court after the Restoration.' [22]

We must regard Coleridge's comparisons as unbalanced, but still retain our condemnation of the bishops for the imprisonment of many ministers and thousands of worshipping Christians, and for the division of the Church of England for 300 years past.

The only apology for the Clarendon Code—and the only benefit from the Puritan persecutions—that some historians can find have been expressed by Trevelyan :

'It was not merely vengeance; the Clarendon Code was also a measure of policy against the revival of the Roundhead party.'

'Laud's religion triumphed . . . through the action of the Parliament of squires whose right to pronounce upon religion he and Charles I had died rather than acknowledge.' [23]

'It may at least be questioned whether the religious settlement of the Restoration has not led to more religious, intellectual and political LIBERTY than would have resulted from a wider extension of the boundaries of the Established Church. If the plan to "comprehend" Baxter and the moderate Puritans had succeeded at the abortive Savoy Conference of 1661, the Quakers, Baptists, and more advanced sects, who must still have been left outside, might have been too isolated and inconsiderable ever to enforce the claim of toleration for themselves. . . . Our TWO-PARTY SYSTEM IN POLITICS flourished so long and so vigorously because RELIGION ALSO was based upon the two great parties of PRIVILEGED and UNPRIVILEGED.'

Trevelyan's assessment, nevertheless, gives only one of the consequences. There was another side, and no one has assessed the loss to the Church of England in sterner and surer terms than another historian, the Anglican clergyman J. R. Green :

'The expulsion of these men was . . . the definite expulsion of a great party which from the time of the Reformation had played the most active and popular part in the life of the Church. It was the close of an effort which had been going on ever since Elizabeth's accession to bring the English Communion into closer relations with the Reformed Communions of the Continent, and into greater harmony with the religious instincts of the nation at large. . . . By its rejection of all but episcopal orders, the Act of Uniformity severed it as irretrievably from the general body of the Protestant Churches, whether Lutheran or Reformed. . . . With the expulsion of the Puritan clergy, all change, all efforts after reform, all national development, suddenly stopped. From that time to this the Episcopal Church has been unable to meet the varying spiritual needs of its adherents by any modification of its government or its worship.' [24]

The bishops had claimed that to admit Baxter's principles would have changed the character of the Church of England. They were right. It would have taken away the bishops' arbitrary powers. It would have ended the sacerdotal pretensions of Laudianism. It would have anticipated the modern constitutional episcopate. It would have made the Church of England tolerant within and without. It would have strengthened immeasurably the evangelical effectiveness of the Church. It would have fortified it against future schism and so built up its impact on the nation's spiritual life that the Methodist secession would not have occurred. It would have retained the Protestant character of the Church. Baxter's acuteness saw the issues involved and the motives of the bishops—as he told Bishops Morley and Gunning in 1679:

'I doubt not but you still think . . . how much more desirable it is to open the church doors so wide as that moderate loyal Romanists may come in, as they did in Queen Elizabeth's first years, and to reconcile them by nearer approaches or concessions, rather than to *go further from them, to unite with a few inconsiderable Puritans.*' [25]

To have admitted Baxter's reforms would also have made a truly national Church. It would have allowed diversity with unity. It would have retained room for the development of forms

THE DESTRUCTION OF UNITY 239

of worship. It would have secured closer relationship with the life of the people, making the Church the vitalizing and cleansing force the nation needed. It would have resisted the growth of the modern secular spirit. It would have meant that the battle for the nation's soul in this secular age would have been fought in the only successful way, unitedly. The event showed that secularism, while banishing religious persecution from English society, was to weaken the hold of religion itself upon the conscience of the nation and to bring about the moral confusion that an 'uncertain, divided and lethargic Church' cannot overcome.

At the same time there would have been beneficial effects for the Puritans themselves if they had been comprehended in the national Church. They would have lost their dogmatic harshness and censoriousness. They would have been saved from the arid disputatiousness and spiritual inertia which produced eighteenth-century deism and Arianism.

The bishops obviously gave little, if any, thought to the possible effect of their actions upon the future history of England. They were bent upon excluding their rivals who 'carried with them the spiritual light of the Church of England'.

## NOTES TO CHAPTER IX

1. *Documents Relating to the Settlement of the Church of England under the Act of Uniformity, 1662*, pp. 416–17; Clarendon, *Life and Continuation of the History of the Rebellion*, p. 1076.
2. *Documents Relating to the Settlement of the Church of England under the Act of Uniformity, 1662*, p. 449.
3. *Ibid.*, pp. 454–5.
4. Morley, *Oliver Cromwell*, p. 404.
5. Gee and Hardy, *Documents Illustrative of English Church History*, p. 601.
6. *Reliquiae Baxterianae*, II, p. 393.
7. Clarendon, *Life and Continuation of the History of the Rebellion*, p. 1077.
8. Stoughton, *History of Religion in England*, vol. 3, p. 259.
9. Whiting, *Studies in English Puritanism from the Restoration to the Revolution*, p. 15.
10. Macaulay, *History of England*, vol. 1, p. 139.
11. Cardwell, *Conferences*, pp. 386–8; Vaughan, *English Nonconformity*, pp. 313–14.
12. Abbey and Overton, *The English Church in the Eighteenth Century*, p. 3.
13. For records of numbers see Matthews, *Calamy Revised*; Lyon Turner, *Original Records of Early Nonconformity under Persecution and*

*Indulgence;* Whiting, *Studies in English Puritanism from the Restoration to the Revolution,* p. 12; *Essays Congregational and Catholic* (A. Peel, ed.), p. 296.

14. *Practical Works,* vol. 4, p. 694.
15. Bramhall, *Vindication,* pp. 166–7, quoted by Plummer, *English Church History, 1649–1702,* pp. 63–4.
16. Whiting, *Studies in English Puritanism from the Restoration to the Revolution,* pp. 6–7.
17. *Ibid.,* p. 282.
18. Hallam, *Constitutional History,* vol. 2, p. 474.
19. Matthews, *Calamy Revised,* p. 521.
20. *Reliquiae Baxterianae,* II, p. 380.
21. Macaulay, *History of England,* vol. 1, chapter 2.
22. Coleridge, *Notes on English Divines,* pp. 22–45.
23. Trevelyan, *History of England,* p. 450.
24. Green, *A Short History of the English People,* p. 589.
25. *Practical Works,* vol. 4, 'True and Only Way of Concord', p. 695.

CHAPTER X

# BAXTER'S CONTINUED EFFORTS FOR UNITY AFTER 1662

1. *The Nonconformist Baxter a Communicant in Parish Churches*

NOTHING shows more clearly the sincerity of Baxter's catholic spirit than his persistent advocacy of Christian unity under persecution, supported by his practice of attending parish churches for worship and Communion.

Unlike some who opposed the liturgy entirely, unlike those who desired a completely non-episcopal form of government, Baxter had much in common with the established Church. Like John Wesley, he did not secede from the Church. Unlike John Wesley, he did not lead a movement that claimed to be within the Church but was organized separately; the repressive measures against his party made any such project impossible even if it had appealed to his temperament. Hoping against hope, he still sought the reunion of moderate men within the national Church. He recognized the following parties in the Church of his day :[1]

*Episcopal conformists.* These were of two kinds. 'Some lately sprung up, that follow Archbishop Laud and Dr Hammond, hold that there are no . . . churches lower than Diocesan . . . and so that the parish-churches are no churches properly, but part of Churches . . . . This party called themselves the Church of England, 1658, 1659. . . . And these seemed uppermost in 1660, 1661 . . . and were the men I disputed with.'

'The other Episcopal Conformists are they that follow the REFORMERS, and hold the doctrine of the Scripture as only sufficient to salvation, and as explicatory of it, the Thirty-nine Articles. . . . These take the parish-pastors for true rectors, and the parish-churches for true churches but subordinate to the Diocesans, and to be ruled by them.'

*Episcopal nonconformists* 'are for true parish-churches and ministers, Reformed, without swearing . . . or subscribing to any but sure, clear, NECESSARY things . . . desiring that every presbyter be an overseer of the flock . . . and that godly Diocesans may . . . have the oversight of many ministers and churches, and all these be confederate. . . . That this was the judgment of the Nonconformists that treated for peace in 1660 and 1661, is to be seen from their printed proposals, in which they desired Archbishop Usher's Model of the Primitive Episcopacy joined with the Synods of Presbyters.'

*Presbyterians* 'are for parish-churches, guided by elders, some teaching, and some only ruling, and these under Synods of the like class, without Diocesan or parochial superiors; and all under a National Assembly of the same, as the supreme church power'.

*Independents* 'are for every Congregation to have all church power in itself, without any superior church-government over them, whether Bishops or Synods, yet owning Synods for voluntary concord'.

Baxter contended that all these sections, except the Independents, belonged to the true Church of England and could be united as 'THE CONFEDERATE PARISH-CHURCHES OF ENGLAND that have able godly pastors, want nothing, which Christ or His apostles, or the Universal Church of Christ for 600 years (yea or to this day) did ever make or judge necessary to the being of ministers or Church'.[2]

Therefore Baxter felt impelled to partake of Communion regularly at the local parish churches at Acton and elsewhere after 1662. His conscientiousness was clearly revealed in his determination to go as far as he could with conformists and yet exclude himself from the conforming ministry. He sought purposely 'to separate from them NO FURTHER THAN THEY SEPARATE FROM GOD'.[3]

Some Presbyterians and all Independents opposed Baxter's policy of 'occasional conformity' with parish churches. The bitterness of persecution was driving the Independents farther from the possibility of any communion with the established Church; it was even inducing them to rid their own services of any liturgical elements. John Owen went so far as to declare: 'All liturgies, as such, are false worship.'[4] The title of John Owen's last work indicated the Independents' position at that time : 'Twelve Arguments against any Conformity of members of Separate Churches to the National Church.' This was circulated in manuscript after Owen's death in 1683, and the title of Baxter's book, *Catholic Com-*

*munion*, which contained a refutation of Owen's position, represented Baxter's principles.[5]

When John Owen in 1667 wrote his 'Catechism for Independency', Baxter noticed that he had given up 'two of the worst of the principles of popularity', acknowledging that the people have NOT the power of the keys, and that they give not the power of the keys, or their office-power to the pastors.[6]

Baxter had previously been in communication with Owen and believed that, if unity between the two sections could be effected at all, it could most hopefully be attempted with his, Owen's, guidance. It is clear that these discussions with Owen were only of a preliminary nature and referred only to general considerations, but Baxter pursued the questions and in his reply (16th February 1668) plainly stated:

'The great things which hinder the Presbyterians and Moderate Episcopal men from closing with you, are principally these.

'1. Because they think that your way tends to destroy the Kingdom of Christ, by dividing it [any party of Christians being allowed to form a congregation].

'2. Because, while you seem to be for a stricter discipline than others . . . your usual practice tendeth to extirpate godliness out of the land, by taking a very few . . . and making them the Church . . . and by neglecting the souls of all the parish else. . . . They think that PARISH-REFORMATION TENDETH TO THE MAKING GODLINESS UNIVERSAL, and that your SEPARATION tendeth to dwindle it to nothing.'[7]

Whether Owen was affected by Baxter's frankness (what he called Baxter's 'chiding letter'), or whether he had little interest in the effort, the fact remains that these discussions were fruitless.[8] After Owen had retained Baxter's terms for more than a year, he returned the papers, merely giving this statement, 'I am still a well-wisher to these mathematics' (*i.e.*, academic discussions).

In his dislike of the Separatists' principles, Baxter blamed them for most of the woes that had fallen upon England from 1642, the opening of the Civil War, onwards. 'It was the Separating Party that all over the land set up ANTI-CHURCHES in the towns that had able godly ministers, when they had nothing imposed on them to excuse it, neither Bishops, Liturgies, nor Ceremonies. So that

Churches became like cockpits, or fencing-schools, to draw asunder the Body of Christ.'[9]

It is noteworthy that episcopal Nonconformists like Baxter would not take part in any ordinations lest they should thereby seem to condone or perpetuate schism. Evidently Baxter did not approve this practice even after the Declaration of Indulgence was withdrawn in 1673 and persecution was renewed.

Similarly, Baxter did not baptize or administer Communion after his ministry at Kidderminster ceased in 1660. As the hopes of comprehension faded, other episcopal Nonconformists began to do both, and also to use tests and exercise discipline in their congregations, as well as to ordain lest their ministry fail of successors.

Meanwhile, moral standards were deteriorating while ridicule was publicly heaped upon Dissenters. Ardent, old-fashioned Royalists like Evelyn were disgusted at the orgy of vice that followed the example of the Court, a Court corrupted by French customs adopted during the Exile and afterwards. Sycophantic clergymen who did little to correct the manners of the Court took part in the mummery of 'the King's evil' and solemnly repeated the Gospel words: 'He put His hands on them and healed them' when 'the most religious King' touched the diseased who were brought before him at this ceremony.

The lampooning of the Puritan divines, a habit that was countenanced in the highest social circles, was inspired by political hatred as much as by the ribald wit of the ungodly. *Hudibras* and other plays called Dissenters 'Presbyterians'. We have seen that the King and bishops attended the theatre when Puritan leaders were held up to scorn on the stage. The sermons and prayers of these ministers were pitilessly parodied. They were often represented as hypocrites. 'Jack Presbyter' was a term used for anti-Royalists in the doggerel of the period. A typical example was the poor rhyme:

'A Presbyter is such a monstrous thing
That loves democracy and hates a King.'[10]

When mobs broke up Nonconformist services in 'conventicles', and in doing so were sometimes led by parish clergy as well as constables, they declared that they were attacking rebels and anti-Royalists.

Trevelyan has shown that, behind the squires' antipathy towards Nonconformists was another factor, the new social cleavage in the national life. Dissent continued, and finally increased, in the towns where many wealthy traders and craftsmen were loyal to the persecuted cause; but most of the country clergymen conformed and retained their social status and their alliance with local squires, evidence of 'the strict and remarkable influence of CLASS on religious observance in England'.[11]

It was remarkable that soon after the downfall of Clarendon in 1667 a suggestion came from the friends of the 'Presbyterians' in Parliament for making it possible for them to return to the Church. In 1667 a Bill of Comprehension was prepared by Sir Robert Atkins (afterwards Lord Chief Baron of the Exchequer). In this Bill it was proposed that 'Presbyterian' ministers were to be allowed to preach in any church, to administer the Sacraments, and also to be eligible for appointment to parish churches, upon these conditions: subscribing to those Articles 'which only concern the confession of the true Christian faith and the doctrine of the Sacraments'; reading the Common Prayer before the sermon, or leaving the reading to another minister if the 'Presbyterian' minister so desired; leaving optional the three ceremonies, the surplice, the cross in Baptism, and kneeling at Communion; the oath abjuring the Solemn League and Covenant not to be required.

Although this proposed Bill was not brought before the House, it is notable that it was contemplated, that the proposal was made so soon after the Act of Uniformity—and that it was made by laymen. One wonders whether the attitude of the bishops might have been altered to any degree if laymen had been given an opportunity to take part in the 1660–61 negotiations. It is true that the 'Presbyterian' earls had done their best to support the ministers during the earlier negotiations of that period. Now there were still a few Parliamentarians in 1667 prepared to advocate receiving Nonconformist ministers back into the Church on most accommodating terms.

Bishop Wilkins of Chester was a supporter of this policy of comprehension. He had married Cromwell's sister. He was one of the two bishops who voted against the Second Conventicle Act later (in 1670). While he held his seat on the Bench of Bishops from 1668 until his death in 1672, he came into prominence in further discussions about re-union.

2. *Baxter's Negotiations with Bridgman and Bishop Wilkins, 1668—and the Hindrance of Re-ordination*

This second attempt seemed to have a little more prospect of success. The leader on this occasion was Sir Orlando Bridgman, the Lord Keeper, who was supported by Sir Matthew Hale, the Lord Chief Baron, Baxter's faithful friend and neighbour at Acton. The Earl of Manchester, as an old 'Presbyterian' before 1662, was favourable. Bishop Wilkins made the actual proposals for the conformists. Baxter, Manton, and Bates were the unofficial representatives of nonconformity.

Baxter has related his part in some detail and has made it clear that he regarded as the danger the suggested toleration of Papists, a point raised so frequently that he felt it must be inspired by the King and his friends. Sir John Baber, Bridgman's intermediary, introduced the question of tolerating Papists at a preliminary meeting when Bridgman was not present.

At the first formal interview, Bridgman told Baxter and Manton that the actual scheme of comprehension contemplated could not include Independents and other sects. It becomes evident that Baxter was offering a wide scheme of re-union, in accordance with his own desire to include Independents if possible. He states:

'I told him, that I did think we could offer such terms, no way injurious to the welfare of any, which might take in both Presbyterians and Independents and all sound Christians, into the public established ministry. He answered, that that was a thing that he would not have; but only a toleration for the rest.'

At the second meeting Bridgman was represented by two divines (Bishop Wilkins and Burton, Bridgman's chaplain). Baxter states that he then found that Wilkins was 'author of the proposals and of the whole business'.

The terms Wilkins proposed were as follows:

(1) THAT NON-EPISCOPALLY ORDAINED MINISTERS BE ADMITTED to the Church after a ceremony including the imposition of hands,

with such words as these: 'Take thou authority to preach the Word of God and to administer the Sacraments in any congregation of the Church of England where thou shalt be LAWFULLY APPOINTED thereto.'[12]

(2) That clergymen who had taken the Oath of Allegiance and Oath of Supremacy be required only to subscribe their profession of 'the doctrine, worship and government established in the Church of England, as containing all things necessary to salvation' and their promise to 'continue in the communion of the Church of England, and not do anything to disturb the peace thereof'.

(3) Kneeling at Communion, the surplice, the cross in Baptism, and bowing at the name of Jesus, to be optional.

(4) If the liturgy were revised, a minister should publicly read the liturgy, declaring his assent to the lawfulness of USING it.

(5) Alterations might include: no lessons from the Apocrypha; no insistence upon having godparents for Baptisms; no reference to baptismal regeneration; no imputation that all persons over whom the burial service was read were saved; and allowing one continuous prayer, and not requiring repetitions or responses.

Such generous suggestions were surprising, especially in view of the violent feelings that had been aroused for years past; but the possibility of sufficient support for the proposals was another matter.

Baxter's own words about the crucial point, RE-ORDINATION, are illuminating:

> 'The hardest knot that we found before us was somewhat proposed like a re-ordination. And our reasons against that nullity of the silenced ministers' ordination being many and great . . . and satisfying . . . Dr Wilkins whom we were to treat with, we were constrained . . . to accept of such terms as might satisfy both parties, without contradicting the judgment of either, so as to put them upon supposed sin.'

It is apparent that Baxter did not object to a form of re-ordination, provided that there was no repudiation of the former ordination. Even Bishop Cosin had stated his willingness to ordain presbyterially ordained ministers with this formula as the prefix: 'IF THOU HAST NOT BEEN ORDAINED.'

*Baxter's proposals* were the following :

(1) Non-episcopally ordained ministers 'to have leave to give in their profession, that they *renounce not their ordination,* nor take it for a nullity, and that they take this as the magistrate's licence and confirmation' (that is, they were to take their appointment to a parish as an act under the establishment).

Bishop Wilkins refused to accept this first condition, 'where was our greatest stop and disagreement', Baxter plainly commented.[13] So strongly did Baxter feel on this point that he gave a separate paper with 'Reasons why we cannot Consent to Re-ordination'. The first reason was enough :

'We dare not causelessly consent to the use of such words as imply an UNTRUTH, viz., that such as were ordained by lawful pastors, and the presidents of their Synods, are not lawful ministers of Christ.'

To this list of reasons Baxter appended his personal affirmation :

'And I, Richard Baxter, must profess, that having eight years ago, written a treatise purposely to prove the validity of the late ordination by the Synods or Presbyteries in England (though I never practised any myself) and having openly called for some confutation of it, I never could procure any to this day. And therefore am the more excusable if I err (though I was myself ordained by a Bishop).'[14]

(2) Assent to be only to thirty-six Articles, omitting the three dealing with ceremonies and prelacy.

(3) No oath or promise from ministers, except fidelity in their ministry and allegiance to the King.

(4) Freedom for ministers to use 'a competent number of the ruined churches', those ruined after the Fire of London, 1666, upon their promise to preach no heresy, and to use the Common Prayer or the Westminster Directory or the alternative liturgy offered by Baxter at the Savoy Conference.

Another method would be to allow 'each party' in the Church to have its own minister about whose ordination it was satisfied. In the same parish church, therefore, it might be permissible for a dissenting party to have its own assistant apart from the incumbent, to officiate for half of the day, and to administer the Sacrament separately to his own party in the same church.[15] Such a naïvely impracticable scheme was entirely unacceptable, of course.

(5) A suspended minister to have the right of appeal from the bishop to the civil courts. This condition was withdrawn later.

(6) Pastors to have disciplinary rights over communicants, with a novel suggestion (unacceptable to Bishop Wilkins and withdrawn) that names of those owning their baptismal covenant be entered in the parish registers, such persons to be admitted to Communion 'without any further examination', provided their lives were consistent; those who scoffed at religion to be excluded.

(7) Alterations to the liturgy. Ministers not to be obliged to baptize children of atheists, etc., or to require godparents; words implying baptismal regeneration to be altered although 'sacramentally' might be added to 'regenerate';[16] alteration of words of the burial service; holy days to be left indifferent; kneeling at Communion, the surplice, and the cross at Baptism, to be left optional.

After further discussions with Bishop Wilkins, the conditions were taken to Sir Matthew Hale, with the consent of Lord Keeper Bridgman. It was understood that Hale would embody them in a Bill of Comprehension to be submitted to Parliament.

With regard to the crucial matter of re-ordination, it was suggested (and Baxter agreed) that, instead of his insisting that there should specifically be no renunciation of a former ordination, the form of admission to a parish should be: 'Take thou LEGAL authority to preach the Word of God and administer the Holy Sacraments in any congregation of England where thou shalt be lawfully appointed thereto.'

Baxter added the reason: 'That so the word LEGAL might show that it was only a general licence from the King that we received .... For the paper which I gave in against re-ordination convinced Judge Hale, and Dr Wilkins, that the RENUNCIATION OF FORMER ORDINATION IN ENGLAND WAS BY NO MEANS TO BE EXACTED OR DONE.'

It was extremely doubtful whether Baxter's reasons and the addition of the word 'legal' would have satisfied the bishops of that day.

These secret discussions produced no result. Baxter states that Hale did not do more than make a draft of a Bill, 'but it was never more called for, and so I believe he burnt it'.

Baxter had also suggested to Hale and Wilkins a form of subscription to the Scriptures and thirty-six Articles for Independents and others outside the scheme of comprehension so that they would receive toleration.

Alarm soon arose as news of these negotiations leaked out. Bishop Wilkins, it seems, had told Bishop Ward of Salisbury, who informed other bishops. When Parliament met on 6th February 1668, a vote expressly directed that the King strictly enforce the Act of Uniformity. The Commons also declared: 'That if any people had a mind to bring any new laws into the House about religion, they might come, as a proposer of new laws did in Athens, with ropes about their necks.'

In spite of this, on 10th February, the King in his speech from the throne recommended Parliament to secure 'a better union and composure in the minds of my Protestant subjects in matters of religion'. Parliament's response was to urge the King to issue a proclamation enforcing the laws against conventicles; this was in consequence of excited reports about seditious utterances in various conventicles.

It was remarkable that, in the debates that followed, there were found some to advocate comprehension and toleration. By 176 votes to 70, the Commons voted against the King's proposal to consult such persons as he chose in order to unite his Protestant subjects. Hallam has called this the first instance 'of a triumph obtained by the Church over the Crown in the House of Commons'.[17]

The King's persistent desire for comprehension and toleration could be seen in his audience with Manton and other 'Presbyterians' in the autumn of 1668. Baxter was not present, owing to illness, but he was told by Manton of the seeming sincerity of the King's reiterated assurance that he would do his utmost to unite the 'Presbyterian' party with the established Church.

In 1670, Morley and other bishops, alarmed at the activities of Papists at Court, made it known 'that they greatly desired that some of the Presbyterians [as they called even the episcopal nonconformists] might by some abatement of the new Oaths and Subscriptions have better invitation to conform in other things ... but after long talk there is nothing done'.[18]

In the same year Baxter wrote secretly to the 'best of the conforming ministers' asking them to petition for abatement of Oaths and Subscriptions, retaining only acceptance of the Scrip-

BAXTER'S EFFORTS FOR UNITY 251

tures, the doctrinal part of the Thirty-nine Articles, the Oaths of Allegiance and Supremacy, with liberty to preach for those who would not read the liturgy. 'But I could get none to offer such a petition.' [19]

It was after the failure of all these efforts that the Second Conventicle Act was introduced. Although carried in the Commons by 144 votes to 78 (28th April 1668), the Bill had not passed in the Lords, beyond a first reading, when Parliament was prorogued in March 1669 until the next year. The Conventicle Act of 1664 had expired, and the new Act did not actually become law until 11th April 1670. As already noticed, only Wilkins and Rainbow among the bishops voted against an Act that marked the lowest level to which the Church sank in its measures against Nonconformists.

Manton was imprisoned under this Conventicle Act. Baxter had been imprisoned a few months before for not taking the Oxford Oath (Five Mile Act) and for preaching to his neighbours in his own house at Acton.

Later in the year 1670 Baxter was approached by the Earl of Lauderdale (once a 'Presbyterian', and now a member of the Cabal Ministry) with a remarkable offer—that he should conform and be appointed to a bishopric in Scotland or to a collegiate position there.[20] It was upon Lauderdale's invitation that Baxter had left Kidderminster for London in April 1660 to win support among the ministers for the Restoration. This offer of a Scottish bishopric could not have been made now without the King's permission.

In an interview, Lauderdale indicated to Baxter that it was proposed to remove the oath of canonical obedience and 'all impositions of conformity' in Scotland, with the ministers sitting together with the bishops and moderators in presbyteries or synods. Baxter refused the offer, making his physical condition a sufficiently truthful and courteous reason. Instead, he begged Lauderdale 'leave to preach for nothing', and added: 'If I be sent to Newgate for preaching Christ's gospel, for I dare not sacrilegiously renounce my calling to which I am consecrated, per sacramentum ordinis, if I have the favour of a better prison, where I may but walk and write, these I should take as very great favours.' [21]

Baxter's earnestness and his distress concerning the 'divided and distracted condition' of the English Church are evident from another letter sent to the Earl of Lauderdale at this time.[22] In this he suggested another conference for reconciliation :

'That if there were first a command from his Majesty to the Bishops of Chester and Norwich on one side, and two peaceable men on the other, freely to debate and offer such expedients as they think most proper to heal all our divisions, they would soon agree. And when they had made that preparation, if some more such moderate divines were joined to them' (Baxter then named many, including Stillingfleet, Tillotson, Pierson, Wallis, and Barlow on one side, with Conant, Langley, and others), 'they would quickly fill up, and confirm the concord'.

Nothing whatever came of all Baxter's efforts.

### 3. *The King's Declaration of Indulgence, 1672*

At last the King intervened. His Declaration of 1672 claimed 'that supreme power in ecclesiastical matters which is not only inherent in us but hath been declared and recognized by several Statutes'.

Though short-lived, this relief gave the Nonconformists opportunities for exercising their ministry and also enabled them to take stock of their position. Great numbers were released from prison. Crowds flocked to hear preachers who had been silenced for ten years.

Under the Declaration it was necessary for preachers to be licensed and to state their denomination. Baxter applied for a licence, but upon the express condition that he 'might have it without the title of Independent, Presbyterian, or any other party, but only as a NONCONFORMIST'. In stating the case for granting his licence, Baxter declared, 'My judgment of Church-government is for that form of episcopacy which is described in Ignatius and Cyprian and was the usage then of the Christian Churches.'

On 27th October 1672 the licence was issued to 'Richard Baxter, a Non-conforming Minister'. He began preaching in London, but he did not administer the Sacraments as he had done at Kidderminster, not only because he had no church appointed to him, but also that he might not offend conformists or hinder any prospects of re-union. It was at St James's market-house that he preached to multitudes; he gave details of how a serious accident was narrowly averted one day in the crowded galleries. The liturgy he frequently used, maintaining his Kidderminster practice. Outside this building he put up his 'profession', the notice being dated 30th January 1674 : 'We meet not under colour or pretence of any religious exercises in other manner than ACCORDING TO THE LITURGY AND PRACTICE OF THE CHURCH OF ENGLAND.' [23]

Baxter was at some pains to make his attitude towards the established Church conciliatory as well as consistent with his principles. 'I openly told them that we met NOT AS A SEPARATED DISTINCT CHURCH but for the time to supply the notorious necessities of the people and as helpers of the ALLOWED ministry.' [24]

Baxter and other ministers of his acquaintance made Salters' Hall their centre for week-day lectures. Independent preachers made Pinners' Hall their centre.

Nonconformist preaching-places had to be licensed in the same way as preachers were licensed. In ten months 3500 licences were issued. Roman Catholics were allowed to worship in their own homes under the Declaration.

Presbyterians and Independents brought addresses of gratitude to the King, though the Independents felt the more grateful. The King, moved by their thanks, gave pensions to some ministers. Baxter was offered £100 per annum but promptly refused it. Burnet gives as the King's motive the winning of ministers' support for the toleration of Roman Catholics.

On 14th February 1673, Parliament declared the King's Declaration invalid, the vote in the Commons being 168 votes to 116. In the course of this debate, some members advocated bringing in a Bill for uniting Protestants, others supported toleration. It was again evident that laymen were more liberal than the bishops.

On 18th February, the House in Committee definitely considered providing for a scheme of comprehension embracing all who would accept the doctrines of the Church of England and take the Oaths of Allegiance and Supremacy—the requirements for assent and consent to the Prayer Book to be removed. This scheme, together with toleration for other Dissenters, took shape in a Bill, which was read a third time on 17th March. The usual charge of disloyalty against the Dissenters was made by the opponents of the Bill, one of them saying : 'If you pass this Act, you give away the peace of the nation. A Puritan was ever a rebel. These Dissenters made up the whole army against the King. The destruction of the Church was then aimed at. Pray God it be not so now.'

After the Commons had approved a measure which held out so much hope for unity, the Lords introduced amendments that were unacceptable to the Commons; delay then ensued, and nothing was done before Parliament was again prorogued.

Parliament then passed an Act of a very different character. This was the notorious Test Act, which secured all civil posts, all commissions in the navy and army, and education in the universities only for those who received Communion in the Church of England. The Dissenters were not alone in deploring a device for making the most sacred rites of the Church a test for aspirants for office and preferment.

The number of those who declared themselves Roman Catholics and resigned after the passing of the Test Act caused alarm in the Church and Parliament. These defenders of the established Church would have been still more deeply disturbed if they had known that their King had been negotiating with the Pope in 1662-63, and with the Pope and the French King in 1669-72, offering to bring the Anglican Church into submission to Rome by changing its doctrines and ritual to conform with those of the Roman Church;[25] and also if they had realized the extent to which Charles was becoming the paid ally and vassal of Louis XIV.

The proposals for comprehending the Presbyterian party within the Church had been evidence of the general desire to strengthen the Church of England against the encroachments of Papal pretensions in England, rather than a belated determination to restore the Dissenters to their place within the Church of the nation.

*4. The Distribution of Dissent in 1672*

Lyon Turner has minutely investigated the records showing the distribution of Nonconformists during this period. He has reproduced the Episcopal Returns for 1669, showing 1138 Nonconformist preachers in England and Wales, 1234 Nonconformist conventicles, 70,875 people attending these conventicles.[26] Turner believes more worshippers attended than the bishops showed in their Returns; certainly, as time went on, and especially as persecution ceased, the membership of Dissenting causes increased.

The counties returning the largest numbers in the 1669 returns were:

| | | | |
|---|---|---|---|
| Somerset | 168 preachers, | 155 conventicles, | 12,315 worshippers. |
| London | 44 preachers, | 53 conventicles, | 9,860 worshippers. |
| Norfolk | 64 preachers, | 53 conventicles, | 4,192 worshippers. |
| Wiltshire | 75 preachers, | 60 conventicles, | 3,841 worshippers. |
| Yorkshire | 62 preachers, | 88 conventicles, | 3,340 worshippers. |

In these 1669 Returns, the Nonconformists' denominational distribution was as follows:

| | | | |
|---|---|---|---|
| Presbyterian | 845 preachers, | 500 conventicles, | 41,998 worshippers. |
| Congregational | 299 preachers, | 203 conventicles, | 14,092 worshippers. |
| Baptist | 234 preachers, | 278 conventicles, | 6,078 worshippers. |
| Quakers | 165 preachers, | 318 conventicles, | 10,731 worshippers. |

The Presbyterians were strongest in the south-west of England, and next followed the south-east, including London:

| | | | |
|---|---|---|---|
| Somerset | 129 preachers, | 129 conventicles, | 10,285 worshippers. |
| Wiltshire | 70 preachers, | 24 conventicles, | 2,490 worshippers. |
| London | 33 preachers, | 32 conventicles, | 5,610 worshippers. |

Congregationalists were strongest in the eastern counties, and then in London, with Wales proportionately very strong:

| | | | |
|---|---|---|---|
| Norfolk | 57 preachers, | 31 conventicles, | 2,985 worshippers. |
| London | 10 preachers, | 10 conventicles, | 1,500 worshippers. |
| Wales | 38 preachers, | 25 conventicles, | 2,160 worshippers. |

The line of demarcation between Presbyterian and Congregationalist ministers tended to disappear, and this acted to the detriment of Presbyterianism. The strict Presbyterian system could not be followed easily under persecution, because synods and presbyteries could not be held. In Norfolk there were 14 Presbyterian classes with 104 congregations in 1645; in 1672 there were 43 Presbyterian ministers licensed in that county; in 1717 there were only 18 Presbyterian congregations.[27]

Especially when many of those termed 'Presbyterians' were actually moderate episcopalians, it was only natural that, with the fading of their hopes of comprehension within the established Church, some should turn towards Independency rather than to rigid Presbyterianism, which they had never espoused. Lancashire had been a centre of Presbyterianism, but all the churches of that denomination in Lancashire today have arisen since the seventeenth century; those called Presbyterian in Lancashire before 1700 have become either Congregational or Unitarian.[28]

The Returns under the Declaration of Indulgence, 1672, are still more instructive. 'Teachers and Householders for Nonconformist places of worship in England and Wales' showed the following leading totals:[29]

| Presbyterian (2590) | | Congregationalist (1182) | | Baptist (412) |
|---|---|---|---|---|
| Devonshire | 233 | Norfolk | 77 | |
| Somerset | 205 | Suffolk | 75 | |
| Lancashire | 146 | London | 68 | |
| Yorkshire | 137 | Bedfordshire | 62 | |
| Essex | 131 | Yorkshire | 59 | |
| London | 116 | Devonshire | 59 | |

Calamy gives the numbers of licences issued under the Declaration of Indulgence, 1672, for England only, as:[30]

854 Presbyterian
385 Congregationalist
202 Baptist

Of these preachers, 940 had been ejected in 1660–62; their distribution was (in 1672):

730 Presbyterians
189 Congregationalists
16 entered as belonging to both denominations
5 Baptists

This affords additional evidence of the smaller number of Independent ministers who had been in the establishment before 1662, and also the growth of their denomination after 1662. Lyon Turner quotes an investigator of the position about 1685:

'There was practically little difference between a Presbyterian and an Independent church in those days, except in one important particular. In the latter the minister was appointed by the whole body of the members; in the Presbyterian Church he was chosen by trustees. This may have had something to do with the rapid spread of negative theology in the Presbyterian churches, and with the decadence which followed it.'[31]

In connexion with the licences in 1672 it is interesting to notice that in Worcestershire, Baxter's county, there were 11 Presbyterian teachers and 34 teachers and householders, 7 Congregational teachers and 18 teachers and householders, no Baptist teacher and only 1 Baptist householder. In London the 62 Presbyterian teachers included such famous names as Dr Samuel Annesley, Dr William Bates, Edmund Calamy, Edmund Calamy Junior, Dr Thomas Jacombe, Dr Thomas Manton, Matthew Sylvester; and the 33 Congregationalists included Dr John Owen, Dr Thomas Goodwin, and Philip Nye.

The religious census in 1676 in the province of Canterbury was not calculated to show Dissenters in the most favourable light, the bishops being now disposed towards proving that under persecution the Dissenters could be expected to decline. The totals in the census were:

|  |  |
|---|---|
| Conformists | 2,123,362 |
| Nonconformists | 93,154 |
| Roman Catholics | 11,870 |

### 5. Baxter's Proposals to the Earl of Orrery and Bishop Morley, 1673

The Earl of Orrery (formerly Lord Broghill) had been a 'Presbyterian' noble and a friend of the ministers in the 1660–61 negotiations. Towards the end of 1673 he sent a request to Baxter for proposals that 'would satisfy the Nonconformists so far as to UNITE US ALL AGAINST POPERY'. The Earl stated that he knew many who were in favour of this enterprise, especially the new Lord Treasurer, Sir Thomas Osborne (afterwards Lord Danby), and Bishop Morley of Worcester, whom Baxter had no reason to trust overmuch. When Baxter, on 15th December 1673, sent his papers to the Earl they were returned with Bishop Morley's comments. These comments were such as to show Baxter the futility of the proceedings and the bishop's 'deceitful snares'.[32]

The most important part of Baxter's propositions was the permission for all preachers to exercise their ministry upon a legal authorization, without re-ordination.

'Let not those who are ordained by Presbyters be put to renounce their ordination, or be re-ordained, but, only upon proof of their fitness for the ministry, receive by word, or a written instrument, a LEGAL AUTHORITY to exercise their ministry in any congregation ... where they shall be lawfully called.'

The following three special provisions also were submitted:
(1) The Sacraments to be 'received by none but volunteers' (thus abolishing the formality of expecting persons to receive

Communion in order to qualify for office in the State, as well as allowing pastors to decide those who were fit).

(2) Ministers to be allowed 'to preach in those churches where the Common Prayer is read by others'. This (Baxter said) 'would take in all, or almost ALL THE INDEPENDENTS ALSO'. This impracticable scheme had been proposed by Baxter to Bridgman and Bishop Wilkins in 1668.

(3) 'The door left open' to amend the form of Church government, preferably by adopting Usher's model of modified episcopacy or with, at least, a system which allowed ministers to meet in rural deaneries and confer about the discipline of the Church.

In all these matters Baxter was consistent with the principles he had advocated throughout his life. He also suggested that no oath be required upon ordination or institution except the Oaths of Allegiance and Supremacy, and subscribing to the doctrines of the Church contained in the Thirty-nine Articles according to the 1571 Act, together with a special subscription against encouraging rebellion. Provided that 'the greatest part of the Liturgy be sometimes (as once a quarter, or half a year) used by himself, and every Lord's Day ordinarily . . . either by himself, or by his curate or assistant', no minister should be punished for omitting the use of the liturgy. Baxter again emphasized the responsibility of the parish ministers to decide who should be baptized, to require parents to be sureties for their children's baptismal covenant, to guard the Lord's Table, to use sacred words at the burial service only when they could conscientiously do so.

Thus Baxter made it as clear as ever that the fundamental dispute between the episcopal party and the Nonconformists concerned the rights of the pastor, and not ceremonies. To Bishop Morley, Baxter wrote: 'There are, I still see, GREATER MATTER THAN CEREMONIES THAT WE DIFFER IN.'[33]

Bishop Morley shrewdly attacked Baxter about proposing a scheme that would include the Independents, when he stated: 'If Independents may be taken in by us now, why did not you take them in when you were in power, but preach and write so much as you did against toleration of them? But you that would have us dispense to all things now, would yourself dispense with nothing then.'[34]

Baxter made the best rejoinder possible. He himself had not

been 'in power', and he had not been one of the Parliamentary Presbyterian party or Cromwell's party later. Furthermore, he said:

'It was the toleration of ALL sects UNLIMITEDLY that I wrote and preached against, and not of mere Independents. ... We never denied the Independents the liberty of preaching lectures, as often as they would, nor yet the liberty of taking parish-churches; they commonly had presentations, and the public maintenance, and no subscription, declaration, liturgy or ceremony was imposed on them. Again I say, I ASK YOU NO MORE LIBERTY THAN THAT GIVEN THE INDEPENDENTS BY THEIR BRETHREN CALLED PRESBYTERIANS.'[35]

In these discussions there is no evidence that Morley was sincerely seeking unity. The only reason for his giving any consideration to Baxter's proposals was to prevent Nonconformists, as he thought, falling 'into the Papists' hands' and being used as their tool in the schemes for complete toleration and their own rise to power in England.

Immediately following these abortive discussions, a Bill was proposed by some members of the House of Commons to 'take off our oaths, subscriptions and declarations, except the Oath of Supremacy and Allegiance, and Subscriptions to the doctrine of the Church of England, according to the 13th of Elizabeth' (1571). Baxter states that, when information of this proposal was given to Bishop Morley, he took steps to prevent the Bill being brought forward in Parliament.[36] On 24th February 1674 the King prorogued Parliament; and any faint hope of some relief for the Nonconformists was dispelled again.

### 6. *Negotiations with Tillotson and others, 1675–80*

In April 1675 two episcopal advocates of better terms for Nonconformists—Tillotson (then Dean of Canterbury) and Stillingfleet —met Baxter, Manton, Bates, and Poole to consider the possibility of re-union. Tillotson and Stillingfleet were acting with the knowledge of Bishop Morley and Bishop Ward. Tentative terms that were drawn up by Baxter ('An Healing Act', he termed it) were submitted to those bishops, who promptly disapproved them. Tillotson thereupon withdrew, and wrote the following apology to Baxter (11th April 1675):

'I am unwilling that my name should be used in this matter; not but that I do most heartily desire an accommodation, and shall always endeavour it; but I am sure it will be a prejudice to me, and signify nothing to the effecting of the thing which, as circumstances are, cannot pass in either House without the concurrence of a considerable part of the bishops, and the countenance of his Majesty, which at present I see little reason to expect.'[37]

Baxter's terms ('An Act for the Healing & Concord of his Majesty's subjects in matters of religion') were similar to those advocated in 1673 in the discussions with the Earl of Orrery. The suggestion he made to avoid re-ordination was:

'Whereas many persons having been ordained as presbyters by parochial pastors in the times of usurpation and distraction, hath occasioned many difficulties; for the present remedy hereof, be it enacted—That all such persons as before this time have been ordained as presbyters by parochial pastors only, and are qualified for that office as the law requireth, shall receive power to exercise it, from a Bishop by a written instrument (which every Bishop in his Diocese is hereby empowered and required to grant) in these words and no other: To A.B. of C. in the county of D., Take thou authority to exercise the office of a Presbyter, in any place and congregation in the King's Dominions whereto thou shalt be LAWFULLY called.'

At this point Baxter made a shrewd comment upon his proposal:

'And this practice sufficing for PRESENT concord, no one shall be put to declare his judgment, whether this, or that which he before received, shall be taken for his ordination, nor shall be urged to speak any words of such signification; but EACH PARTY BE LEFT TO JUDGE AS THEY SEE CAUSE.'[38]

It is not without interest that this is a solution of the problem of re-ordination which some in modern times have advocated.

In 1680 John Howe met Bishop Lloyd (of St Asaph) at Tillotson's house and was asked by him what would satisfy the Dissenters and make union possible. Howe replied, 'If the law were so framed as to enable ministers to attempt PAROCHIAL REFORMA-

TION', which was confirmation in itself of the first principle for which Baxter had always striven.

On 18th November 1680 a Bill for Comprehension was introduced in the House of Commons, but it was soon dropped. It was entitled, 'An Act for Uniting His Majesty's Protestant Subjects', and it would have required subscription only to the doctrines of the Church, leaving ceremonies optional.

About the same time a Bill for Toleration, to benefit Protestant Dissenters only, was actually passed. The fear of Popery among episcopal Parliamentarians had inspired it. Charles was more openly defying Parliament than before, and he arranged that this Bill should not be presented for his assent before the prorogation of Parliament.

One of the greatest disappointments to Baxter, Howe, and other friends of Stillingfleet was the change in his attitude towards Dissenters after 1680. His authorship of *Irenicum: or, A Weapon Salve for the Church's Wounds* (1659), and his support for schemes of comprehension after the Restoration had not prepared them for the change when he became Dean of St Paul's. In 1680 Stillingfleet published a sermon on 'The Mischief of Separation', virtually a reply to Baxter's 'Nonconformist's Plea for Peace' (1679). It is true that, in opposing separation, he made suggestions for unity, these including a revision of the Prayer Book, subscription to thirty-six doctrinal Articles only, and leaving optional kneeling at Communion and the cross in Baptism.

The Church had become more definitely Protestant because of the fear of resurgent Romanism. The bishops were now as determined as any Nonconformists to oppose concessions to them. It was the boast of their party, in the words of a writer of the period, that the Church of England maintained the middle path between 'the meretricious gaudiness of the Church of Rome and the squalid sluttery of fanatical conventicles'.[39]

The tide was still moving strongly against Dissenters during the last four years of Charles's reign, the period of his unchecked absolutism. The violence of the Whigs (who favoured toleration for Dissenters) in fighting for the Exclusion Bill, which sought to prevent James, an avowed Roman Catholic, from succeeding his brother, and which roused the fiercest Tory loyalty for the royal family, worked against the cause of toleration and made schemes of comprehension unthinkable.

## NOTES TO CHAPTER X

1. *Reliquiae Baxterianae*, App. IV, pp. 71–2.
2. *Ibid.*, App. IV, p. 79.
3. *Ibid.*, III, p. 74.
4. Powicke in *Essays Congregational and Catholic* (A. Peel, ed.), p. 300.
5. 'Catholic Communion' (1684), II.
6. *Reliquiae Baxterianae*, III, p. 62.
7. *Ibid.*, III, p. 67.
8. Orme, *Life and Times of Richard Baxter*, vol. 1, p. 35.
9. *Reliquiae Baxterianae*, App. IV, p. 77.
10. Whiting, *Studies in English Puritanism from the Restoration to the Revolution*, p. 427.
11. Booth, *Life and Labour in London*, vol. 7, 'Religious Influences', p. 47; Trevelyan, *England under the Stuarts*, p. 343.
12. *Reliquiae Baxterianae*, III, p. 25.
13. *Ibid.*, III, p. 34.
14. *Ibid.*, III, p. 38.
15. *Ibid.*, III, p. 24.
16. *Ibid.*, III, p. 32.
17. Hallam, *Constitutional History*, vol. 2, p. 70.
18. *Reliquiae Baxterianae*, III, p. 84.
19. *Ibid.*, III, p. 87.
20. *Ibid.*, III, p. 75.
21. *Ibid.*, III, p. 92.
22. *Ibid.*, III, p. 93.
23. *Ibid.*, III, p. 254.
24. Wilkinson, *Richard Baxter and Margaret Charlton*, p. 133.
25. Trevelyan, *England under the Stuarts*, p. 366.
26. Lyon Turner, *Original Records of Early Nonconformity under Persecution and Indulgence*, vol. 3, pp. 114 *et seq*.
27. Whiting, *Studies in English Puritanism from the Restoration to the Revolution*, p. 63.
28. *Ibid.*, p. 63.
29. Lyon Turner, *Original Records of Early Nonconformity under Persecution and Indulgence*, vol. 3, pp. 716 *et seq*.
30. Matthews, *Calamy Revised*, p. xv.
31. Lyon Turner, *Original Records of Early Nonconformity under Persecution and Indulgence*, vol. 3, p. 731.
32. *Reliquiae Baxterianae*, III, p. 109.
33. *Ibid.*, III, p. 126.
34. *Ibid.*, III, pp. 130–1.
35. *Ibid.*, III, p. 131.
36. *Ibid.*, III, p. 140.
37. *Ibid.*, III, p. 157.
38. *Ibid.*, III, p. 159.
39. Quoted by Inge, *Outspoken Essays*, 1st Series, p. 107.

CHAPTER XI

# TOLERATION WITHOUT UNITY (1689)

1. *The Church and Dissent brought closer by James II's Rule and the Revolution of 1688*

NONCONFORMISTS suffered brief but bitter persecution under James II. Baxter's trial by Jeffreys, a travesty of justice unsurpassed in modern English history, has been given in detail.[1]

The charge against the aged Baxter was one of sedition, founded upon a distorted interpretation of his *Paraphrase of the New Testament*. The complete indictment gave many quotations from this book which indicated that Baxter, because of his sympathy for silenced ministers, had sharply censured the bishops and laid himself open to misrepresentation.[2] Jeffreys raged shamelessly against eminent counsel retained by Baxter's friends for his defence.

When he was told by one of the counsel (Pollexfen) that Baxter believed in episcopacy, and his book produced in court was in favour of it, Jeffreys declared, 'I will see none of his books. It is for primitive episcopacy, I will warrant you—a bishop in every parish. Pox take 'em, we know their bishops well enough.'

Counsel reminded the Judge, 'My lord, Mr Baxter was a commissioner, appointed by the King at Savoy, to settle ecclesiastical affairs, and he never offered anything for agreement and accommodation but Archbishop Usher's Reduction of Episcopacy, and nothing at all against liturgies, as such.'

Jeffreys retorted: 'It is no matter what he or Bishop Usher offers. Our Church is established, and we will bate nothing.'

When Baxter himself stated, 'My lord, I have been so moderate with respect to the Church of England that I have incurred the censure of many Dissenters upon that account,' Jeffreys broke out in unbridled ridicule, 'Baxter for bishops! A merry conceit indeed.'

To the quotation in which Baxter had written about respect due to 'those truly called to be bishops among us', the shrewd and merciless Judge replied, 'Aye, this is your Presbyterian cant! Truly called to be bishops! That is himself and such rascals—called to be bishops of Kidderminster and other such places. Bishops set apart by such factious, snivelling Presbyterians as himself. . . . According to the saying of a late learned author, "And every parish shall maintain a tithe-pig metropolitan".'

Browbeating counsel and refusing to hear them further, Jeffreys summed up to the jury in a wild harangue, declaring that Baxter was an arch-rebel and a plot was meditated against the King. 'Gentlemen, for God's sake don't let us be gulled twice in an age.'

While he was remanded for sentence, Baxter wrote to the Bishop of London:

> 'Being by episcopal ordination vowed to the sacred ministry and bound not to desert it . . . I knew not how better to serve the Church than by writing a Paraphrase of the New Testament. . . . I have lived in its Communion, and conformed to as much as the Act of Uniformity obliged one in my condition. I have drawn multitudes into the Church, and written to justify the Church and ministry against separation. . . .'

Baxter went on to ask the Bishop as his diocesan to present a petition to James II. Jeffreys is reported to have urged that Baxter's punishment include being whipped through the streets of London, but his brother-judges overruled him. The sentence was a fine of 500 marks, with imprisonment till it was paid. Under this burden Baxter (now 70 years of age) was imprisoned for seventeen months. Only an act of clemency by the King in remitting the fine procured his eventual release.

Dr F. J. Powicke, in his definitive biography of Baxter, after carefully weighing Baxter's words, has endorsed Baxter's opinion about the sympathies of the Restoration bishops with many of the Roman Catholic practices. Before they became alarmed at the growing influence of Romanists in the Court, they had been more sympathetic with Romanist doctrines and ceremonies than with the Dissenters' principles. In his last important book—*Against the Revolt to a Foreign Jurisdiction* (1691)—Baxter amassed evidence to prove that these sympathies were one reason for the bishops' antagonism to Puritan proposals in 1661 and ever since. Baxter declared that in 1661:

> 'Dr Gunning and others told us plainly that they had a GREATER PARTY THAN WE ARE TO CONSIDER, THAT MUST NOT BE ALIENATED TO PLEASE US; and when Dr Bates said that

TOLERATION WITHOUT UNITY (1689)    265

abundance more of the Popish ceremonies might be introduced by the same reasons as were pleaded for those imposed, Dr Gunning answered, they must have more and not fewer. And Dr Morley told me that he had good reason to BELIEVE THAT MOST OF THE ROMAN CHURCH ON THIS SIDE THE ALPS [*i.e.* France] WOULD HAVE JOINED WITH US, were it not for the stumbling-blocks that Calvin had laid in the way.' ³

The bishops under James II had to revise their attitude in the face of the imminent danger of the King's absolutism and their own eclipse.

Before James had reigned three years his precipitous defiance of the law in appointing Roman Catholics to Government positions, to the Army and the University, revealed to Churchmen the danger to the established Church. Their alarm increased with the revocation of the Edict of Nantes and the arrival of Huguenot refugees in England. A crisis had arisen for all Protestants. Even then, if James had not foolishly presumed upon the loyalty of bishops and their clergy by requiring that they read his Declaration of Indulgence from their pulpits, he might still have carried all before him.

When the King had issued his first Declaration of Indulgence, a few dissenting ministers prepared an address of thanks to the King for giving freedom of worship. In this movement Baxter and others resolutely refused to join; they refused to accept from a Roman Catholic king advantages outside the law that would have drawn them farther away from Protestant conformists. Both then and later, the Dissenters' actions brought approval from many bishops.

James went on to demand that the Church publish his second Declaration giving freedom of worship and abolishing the provisions of the Test Act. When Archbishop Sancroft and six other bishops professed both their loyalty and their inability to read the King's declaration contrary to law, James petulantly broke out, 'This is a standard of rebellion. Did ever a good Churchman question the dispensing power before? Have not some of you preached for it and written for it?' ⁴

The excitement throughout the land was tremendous. Those who had been most subservient among the clergy opposed the King. All knew that, if they capitulated, the power of the Church and the power of Parliament would have been lost. Samuel Wesley (father of John and Charles), stout Churchman and perfervid loyalist, preached on the text, 'Be it known unto thee, O King, that we will not serve thy gods, nor worship the golden image which thou hast set up.'[5] Baxter from his pulpit praised the bishops and clergy who had defied a law-breaking sovereign. A deputation of ten Nonconformist ministers visited the seven prelates imprisoned in the Tower.

Is there a more stirring piece of descriptive prose in English literature than Macaulay's account of the historic trial of the seven bishops for their 'seditious libel'? Through those moving times the Dissenters were, heart and soul, in support of the Church that had pitilessly crushed them for nearly thirty years. After the acquittal, Archbishop Sancroft in his pastoral letter called upon the clergy to treat their Dissenting brethren with great tenderness, to try to persuade them to conform, but in any case to make common cause with them for the defence of the Reformed faith —and no Churchman had been more hostile to Dissenters than Sancroft himself, before that short-lived day of goodwill and gratitude!

When James had fled and William of Orange reached London, the Dissenting ministers, led by Howe (Baxter, to his great regret, being debarred by illness from attending), presented addresses of loyalty. Their language was impeccable in its discretion. All they sought was 'the defence and propagation of the Protestant interest throughout the world'. To this William replied, stating his desire for 'a firm union among Protestants'. By this he meant comprehension in the English Church. At last there was a king who desired the fulfilment of the unity for which Baxter and others had ardently longed. But, once more, the majority of the bishops and the conformist clergy were opposed, and hopes of unity were soon dashed to the ground again. In 1689, as in 1661, the bishops would brook no concessions to the Nonconformists.

It was soon apparent that the bishops as a body could not be enthusiastic about a foreigner, a Dutch Calvinist king. Twelve out of fourteen bishops in the House of Lords voted against William and Mary receiving the Crown. Eight bishops (including the Primate, Sancroft, and the saintly Ken of Bath and Wells), with over 400 clergy, declined to take the Oath of Allegiance; and, with the secession of these non-jurors, the established Church experienced another schism.

## 2. The Bill for Comprehension

William III had a threefold policy for the Church: toleration, comprehension by changes in ritual and polity, and the abolition of the Test Act so as to enable all Protestants to hold office.

How could William carry out his policy for comprehension? Only with the support of Churchmen. Macaulay estimates that the clergymen who favoured comprehension were not more than one-tenth of the whole, and they were Low Churchmen and Latitudinarians. Among laymen, perhaps one-half favoured comprehension, but they were Whigs and acted for political reasons. Macaulay declares that there were not twenty 'Presbyterian' members in the Commons at this time and, if Dissenters at heart, they were communicants in the Church of England.

Not only was there the prejudice of three decades against comprehension, but the position of the Dissenters had changed. What might have been possible in earlier years was more difficult in 1689. Baptists, Quakers, and others had added to the number of the sects. Conformists pleaded that there were now so many varieties in Dissent that not all could be absorbed into the Church.

The outlook, therefore, was not at all favourable for re-union. Nevertheless, the expected Bill was introduced in the Lords by the Secretary of State, the Earl of Nottingham, on 11th March 1689.

The real value of the Comprehension Bill is found in its vindication of all that Baxter had upheld. It may still set a model for a possible re-union of the English Church today.

Re-ordination, the Gordian knot in all negotiations, was avoided in the Comprehension Bill. A minister, previously ordained by presbyteries, had merely to receive an extended commission from the hands of a bishop with these words: 'Take thou authority to preach the Word of God, and administer the Sacraments, and to perform all other ministerial offices in the Church of ENGLAND.' [6]

Subscription to the Thirty-nine Articles was not explicitly required. Instead, a declaration was to be made: 'I do approve of the doctrine and worship and government of the Church of England by law established, as containing all things necessary to salvation; and I promise, in the exercise of my ministry, to preach and practise according thereunto ... and to conform to the worship and government thereof as established by law.'[7]

The Bill contemplated a commission of thirty divines to revise the liturgy and canons, and the event showed that this was the only fruitful section.

Unfortunately, the advocates of the Comprehension Bill in the Lords were lukewarm, and its opponents unrelenting. The old familiar objections were raised to any concessions to Puritans. The debates raged again around ritual and ceremonies. Any relaxation of requiring episcopal ordination was summarily dismissed.

With many excisions, the Comprehension Bill was sent by the Lords to the Commons. Actually, the Commons had begun to consider their own Comprehension Bill, introduced by a few supporters. This complication gave an excuse for delay until Convocation met. Neither of these Comprehension Bills was ever mentioned in Parliament again.

Since 1689, Parliament has never considered a measure to comprehend Nonconformists within the Church of England.

3. *Tillotson's Plan for Re-union*
*(Jerusalem Chamber Commission, 1689)*

Insufficient attention has been given to the truly surprising concessions offered by the Jerusalem Chamber Commission of episcopal leaders.[8] Its recommendations included many of the reforms that Baxter had continually advocated—and the significant fact is that these now came from Anglican divines, a contrast indeed to the Savoy Conference of 1661! No Presbyterians, no Dissenters, but a commission of Anglicans proposed substantial relief, and did so voluntarily—and recommended a scheme that could have united the majority of English Churchmen.

The appointment of this Commission was the only part of the abortive Comprehension Bill to which effect was given. An attempt had been made in the Commons to include laymen in the Commission, but the thirty members were bishops and other prominent divines. The ten bishops included Compton of London, Trelawny of Exeter, and Burnet of Salisbury. Ten of the twenty other divines afterwards became bishops, prominent among them being Stillingfleet, Tenison, and Tillotson, the last two future archbishops of Canterbury. Tillotson, the most renowned preacher

TOLERATION WITHOUT UNITY (1689)     269

among the conformists, had a dominating influence in the Commission.

The Commission's authority stated:

'Whereas the particular forms of divine worship, and the rites and ceremonies appointed to be used therein, being things in their own nature indifferent and alterable . . . and whereas the Book of Canons is fit to be reviewed . . . and particularly there is not sufficient provision for the removing of scandalous ministers. . . . We therefore . . . for the reconciling as much as is possible of all differences among our good subjects . . . have thought fit to authorize you . . . to prepare such alterations of the Liturgy and Canons. . . .'

Tillotson had just declared his own opinions in a document dated 13th September 1689.[9] In this he proposed the following: the controverted ceremonies to be optional; the liturgy to be revised; only a general subscription to the doctrine, discipline, and worship of the Church to be required, with a promise to teach accordingly; NO RE-ORDINATION for those ordained in foreign Reformed Churches; future ordinations at the hands of bishops in England; those ordained by presbyters in England in the past, NOT TO BE OBLIGED TO RENOUNCE THEIR ORDINATION, but to receive imposition of hands from a bishop with the words: 'If thou art not already ordained, I ordain thee.'

The Commission met in the Jerusalem Chamber from 3rd October to 18th November 1689. At the first session some of the High Church members withdrew at once, stating that they did not see any necessity for alterations in the liturgy and canons. Not more than seventeen of the thirty members met at any session afterwards; the quorum was nine, and sometimes the quorum was only slightly exceeded. Yet even that number represented some of the leading Anglicans of that period, and it was from them that this plan for re-union was proposed.

The recommendations of the Commission included:

(1) AVOIDING RE-ORDINATION. Four meetings were occupied with this question. It was finally decided to accept the hypothetical form of ordaining that Tillotson had urged already. It was, and still is, open to grave difference of opinion as to whether such freedom of interpretation is justifiable. The Commission's statement was:

'Whereas it has been the constant practice of the ancient Church to allow no ordination of priests, *i.e.* presbyters, or deacons, without a Bishop, and that it has been likewise the constant practice of this Church, ever since the Reformation, to allow none that were not ordained by Bishops WHERE THEY COULD BE HAD; yet in regard that several in this Kingdom have of late years been ordained only by Presbyters, the Church being desirous to do all that can be done for peace, and in order to the healing of our dissensions, has thought fit to receive such as HAVE BEEN ORDAINED BY PRESBYTERS ONLY, to be ordained according to this Office with the addition of these words . . .

"IF THEY SHALL NOT HAVE BEEN ALREADY ORDAINED". By which she retains her opinion and practice, which makes a Bishop necessary to the giving of Orders when he can be had; so she does likewise leave all such persons as have been ordained by Presbyters only the FREEDOM OF THEIR OWN THOUGHTS CONCERNING THEIR FORMER ORDINATIONS. It being withal expressly provided that THIS SHALL NEVER BE A PRECEDENT FOR THE TIME TO COME, and that it shall only be granted to such as have been ordained before the . . . day. . . .'[10]

Those from foreign Reformed Churches who were 'in that imperfect state that they cannot receive ordination from Bishops', were to be received by an imposition of hands, with the words:

'Take thou authority to preach the Word of God, and to minister the holy Sacraments IN THIS CHURCH, as thou shalt be LAWFULLY APPOINTED thereunto.'

It is noteworthy that this form, and the form suggested in the Comprehension Bill, provided for giving authority in 'this Church' or 'the Church of England', and not, as in the Prayer Book forms for the Ordering of Deacons and Priests and the Consecration of Bishops, 'in the Church of God'. THIS AVOIDED THE IMPUTATION OF INVALIDITY TO A FORMER ORDINATION.

(2) CEREMONIES, etc. The wearing of the surplice was to be optional; kneeling was to be optional; and the cross in Baptism was to be optional. Lessons from the Apocrypha would not be used. The terms 'Minister' instead of 'Priest' and the 'Lord's Day' instead of 'Sunday' would be used. Children 'may be baptized

upon the engagement of the parents only' as an alternative to the use of godparents.

A direct form of interrogation would be provided in the Order for the Visitation of the Sick.[11]

The burial service would not include words assuming that the dead person's soul was saved, but use only general terms ('a firm belief of the resurrection of the dead at the last day, in which they who die in the Lord shall rise again to eternal life. . . ').

Forty-two new Collects were written, and 598 alterations, covering ninety pages, were proposed in the liturgy, these chiefly the work of Tenison, future Archbishop of Canterbury.

After all this, no result whatever was seen. The concessions proposed by the Commission were not even brought before Convocation.

Calamy stated that he would have entered the Church if the Commission's proposals had been carried into effect, and he believed he spoke for at least two-thirds of the Dissenters.[12]

The fact, unfortunately, was that it was well-nigh impossible to put back the clock. In 1662 the issue of Church unity in England had been settled.

### 4. *Convocation and the Hardening against Dissent*

Tillotson and other Low Church and Latitudinarian divines did not represent the great body of the Church, especially the country clergy who had not relented in their hostility towards Dissenters. There were various causes for a hardened attitude towards any proposal for comprehension.

(1) The hard core of High Church opposition to Nonconformity was the one unchanging factor from the time of Bancroft and Laud onwards and the Revolution had done nothing to change it.

(2) In 1689 there was a reaction from the glow of goodwill felt towards Dissenters when the Church of England was in danger, especially when the seven bishops were being tried.

(3) Ecclesiastical and doctrinal differences between Churchmen and Dissenters were summed up in the problem of ordination. High Churchmen would not abate one jot of their insistence upon re-ordination, and the devices proposed by 'men of latitude' were acceptable to few.

(4) The dislike of William III, as a foreigner and one whose

coldness contrasted unfavourably with the affability of Stuart kings, was increased by Churchmen's antipathy towards his Dutch Calvinist principles. He was reported as regarding all forms of Protestantism as alike. His unpopularity with most Churchmen affected any schemes of comprehension that he was known to favour.

(5) The defection of 400 non-jurors caused grave concern. If at this juncture Nonconformist ministers had been received into the Church of England, it was quite likely that more High Churchmen would have followed the non-jurors, and there would have been a still greater schism in the Church.

(6) Resentment at the attitude of Scottish Presbyterians at this time also hardened Anglican Churchmen against English Nonconformists. News came from Scotland of Presbyterians, now restored as the established Church of Scotland, destroying copies of the Prayer Book and driving out episcopal clergy. 'All these things were published up and down England, and much aggravated, and raised the aversion that the Church had to the Presbyterians so high, that they began to repent their having granted a toleration to a party that, where they prevailed, showed so much fury against those of the Episcopal persuasion.[13] (The Toleration Act in England had just been passed, and is discussed in the next section.)

(7) There was a fear of the effects of diversity in practice if this was allowed in the Church as part of the plan of comprehension. In spite of the exaggeration of some of the following statements, they represented the fears of some about what might follow abandoning uniformity in worship.

'Some will kneel at the Sacrament, some stand, some perhaps sit; some will read this part of the Common Prayer, some that —some, perhaps, none at all. In the same cathedral you shall see one prebendary in a surplice, another in a long coat, another in a short coat or jacket; and in the performance of the public services some standing up at the Creed, the Gloria Patri, and the reading of the Gospel, and others sitting, and perhaps laughing and winking upon their fellow-schimatics, in scoff of those who practise the decent order of the Church.... So that I dare avouch, to bring in a COMPREHENSION IS NOTHING ELSE BUT, in plain terms, TO ESTABLISH A SCHISM IN THE CHURCH BY LAW.'[14]

## TOLERATION WITHOUT UNITY (1689)

(8) Nonconformists were not united among themselves. Most of the Presbyterians desired comprehension, but very few of the Independents and other sects did. It was said that some Presbyterian ministers did not want to give up comfortable London churches for the uncertainty of their position if they were absorbed in the established Church. It might have been more accurate, and charitable, to say that these Nonconformists felt themselves separated, evidently permanently, from the Church as they had seen little evidence of a change of heart in the establishment.

It was on 16th April 1689 that Parliament asked the King to summon Convocation. Macaulay described the reaction in these words:

'The clergy were everywhere in a state of violent excitement. They had just taken the oaths [of allegiance to William and Mary] and were smarting from the earnest reproofs of Nonjurors, from the insolent taunts of Whigs, and often undoubtedly from the stings of remorse. The announcement that a Convocation was to sit for the purpose of deliberating on a plan of comprehension roused all the strongest passions of the priest who had just complied with the law, and was ill satisfied or half satisfied with himself for complying.... He had an opportunity of signalizing his zeal for that Church whose characteristic doctrines [e.g. non-resistance] he had been accused of deserting for lucre. She was now, he conceived, threatened by a danger as great as that of the preceding year. The Latitudinarians of 1689 were not less eager to humble and to ruin her than the Jesuits of 1688.' [15]

Except for his touch of rhetorical exaggeration, Macaulay made the situation clear.

Convocation sat from 21st November to 16th December, following the meetings of the Jerusalem Chamber Commission. In the Upper House of Convocation there was rather a conciliatory spirit, but in the Lower House no thought whatever of compromise with Dissenters was entertained. The Lower House even considered asking the non-jurors to return, and could barely be persuaded to send a respectful address of loyalty to the King. In reply to the lukewarm address Convocation sent to William, it was asked again to consider comprehension on the basis of the Commission's recommendations but it made no response to this at any time.

When Parliament was dissolved in January 1690, Convocation did not meet again for ten years. And so the downfall of the Stuarts brought no more hope for the unity of the Church of England than their Restoration in 1660. Macaulay's comments are apt:

> 'So ended, and for ever, the hope that the Church of England might be induced to make some concession to the scruples of the Nonconformists. A reform, such as, in the days of Elizabeth, would have united the great body of English Protestants, would, in the days of William, have alienated more hearts than it would have conciliated. The schism which the oaths had produced was, as yet, insignificant. Innovations such as those proposed by the Royal Commissioners would have given it a terrible importance.... If the compositions of the doctors of the Jerusalem Chamber had taken the place of the old Collects, if clergymen without surplices had carried the chalice and the paten up and down the aisle to seated communicants, the tie which bound [some laymen] to the Established Church would have been dissolved.... The new sect [of non-jurors], which as yet consisted almost exclusively of priests, would soon have been swelled by numerous and large congregations.' [16]

There was justification for the belief that there would have been a large High Church schism if comprehension had been offered to the Dissenters in 1689.

Green, in his *A Short History of the English People,* regards the failure of unity at this stage as a blessing, in its political consequences; the Church, generally politically conservative, might have blocked reforms more successfully if its strength had been increased by absorbing the Nonconformists—whereas the Dissenters were generally advocates of political progress and they continued that policy after 1689.[17] On the other hand, it was also arguable that the leaven of liberalism in ecclesiastical and political life might have leavened the whole lump. Green, nevertheless, asserts that, 'With religious forces on the one side and on the other, England has escaped the great stumbling-block in the way of nations where the cause of religion has become identified with that of political reaction.'

### 5. *Toleration for Protestant Dissenters granted by Parliament*

The Toleration Act had been passed before the events in the Commission and Convocation, to which reference has just been made. This Bill was introduced into the Lords by the Earl of Nottingham on 14th March 1689, concurrently with the ill-fated Comprehension Bill.

There seemed to be a note of apology in the very title of this Act —not, officially, a Toleration Act at all, but 'An Act for exempting their Majesties' Protestant subjects dissenting from the Church of England from the penalties of certain laws'. The Act stated that existing laws were not to be construed to apply to those who took the Oaths of Allegiance and Supremacy, and who subscribed to a Declaration against Transubstantiation. A Nonconformist minister was allowed to preach, provided that he subscribed to thirty-four Articles, the thirty-fourth, thirty-fifth and thirty-sixth concerning Church government being omitted, with part of the twentieth and part of the twenty-seventh (concerning infant Baptism) in the case of Baptists. Special provisions were made for Quakers, who could not conscientiously take oaths. Roman Catholics and Unitarians were specifically debarred from all benefits of the Act.

The Commons brought forward their own Toleration Bill on 8th April, but on 18th April they received the Bill from the Lords. This was passed on 15th May. One suggestion made in debate would have given only a trial period of seven years for toleration— so grudgingly did some wish to concede freedom of worship. Royal assent was given on 24th May 1689.

Macaulay has written eulogistically about the ease with which toleration was given.[18] He was correct in pointing out that the persecutions of four generations ceased with hardly a protest, that the necessity for exile beyond the seas for freedom of worship had now ended, and that no longer would Protestant Dissenters be imprisoned—as, for example, John Bunyan had been in 1660 for 'devilishly and perniciously abstaining from coming to Church to hear divine service'. Modern English-speaking Christians might sometimes remember that this was the reason given for imprisoning Bunyan, perhaps England's greatest religious genius.

The Dissenting ministers went to the Quarter Sessions everywhere to swear and to sign assent to the Articles as required by the Toleration Act. It was characteristic of Baxter that he gave a detailed explanation of his interpretation of the Articles—including his disapproval of the damnatory clauses of the Athanasian Creed, and his larger hope for the ultimate salvation of those who had lived virtuous lives but died without an opportunity to know Christ as Saviour.[19] It was not only typical of Baxter's scrupulous nature and his verbose style that he did this; it revealed also the touch of liberalism and modernity in his theological outlook. He concluded his subscription and interpretation with these words:

> 'If I have hit on the true meaning, I subscribe my assent; and I thank God that this National Church hath doctrine so sound. I pity those who write, preach, or practise, contrary to the Articles which they subscribe; and that accuse those who refuse to subscribe them, take those for sinners who take not them for pastors, alleging that their wickedness nulleth not their sacramental administration.'

6. *Attempts to unite Presbyterians and Congregationalists, 1691*

Most Anglicans regarded toleration as ample concession to Dissenters. It would not have been allowed if it had not been for the Revolution and the co-operation of Dissent with conformity in rejecting James II. An influential thinker like Locke also had convinced many reasonable men that the State should not force conscience in religion unless for reasons of State; and the winning of political liberty in 1688 had shown the incongruity of refusing religious liberty.

Tolerated, but refused comprehension, the two main bodies of the Dissenters began to consider unity between themselves. Common sufferings had drawn them closer, and now a common opportunity had come with toleration.

The first step was a practical one. A common fund was instituted in London on 1st July 1690 to sustain the ministry of Nonconformist ministers and to train students for the ministry. John Howe, formerly Independent but now regarding himself as Presbyterian, and Matthew Mead, Congregationalist, were chiefly instrumental in establishing this fund.[20] The trustees were seven Presbyterian ministers (Howe, Bates, Annesley, Daniel Williams, and three others) and seven Congregationalists. This common fund con-

# TOLERATION WITHOUT UNITY (1689)

tinued for three years, after which Congregationalists gradually left and formed their own fund.

Howe then went further and suggested that Presbyterian and Congregational ministers should in future be called 'THE UNITED BRETHREN'. He was influenced by Baxter's Worcestershire Association of the Cromwellian period, and in this new venture he had the aged Baxter's fervent approval. The basis of federation was drawn up mainly by Howe and entitled 'THE HEADS OF AGREEMENT'. This was accepted by between eighty and one hundred London ministers. The chief sections of this important document were these:

THE HEADS OF AGREEMENT ASSENTED TO BY THE UNITED MINISTERS IN AND ABOUT LONDON, FORMERLY CALLED PRESBYTERIAN AND CONGREGATIONAL

'We declare against intermeddling with the National Church-Form.

'Imposing these terms of Agreement on others is disclaimed.

'To reduce all distinguishing names to that of UNITED BRETHREN.

'That each particular Church hath right to choose their own Officers; and being furnished with such as are duly qualified and ordained according to the Gospel Rule, hath authority from Christ for exercising government, and of enjoying all the ordinances of worship within itself.

'In the administration of Church power, it belongs to the Pastors and other Elders of every particular Church . . . to rule and govern; and to the brotherhood to consent. . . .

'That ordinarily none shall be ordained to the work of this ministry, but such as are called and chosen thereunto by a particular Church.

'That in so great and weighty a matter as the calling and choosing a Pastor, we judge it ordinarily requisite, that every such Church consult and advise with the Pastors of neighbouring congregations.

'When all due means are used, according to the Order of the Gospel, for the restoring an offending and scandalous brother; and he notwithstanding remains impenitent, the censure of Excommunication is to be proceeded unto.

'That none of our particular Churches shall be subordinate to one another.'

Ruling elders, functions of synods, and choice of doctrinal standards were left open questions:

'Whereas divers are of opinion, that there is also the Office of Ruling Elders, who labour not in word and doctrine, and others think otherwise, we agree, that this difference make no breach among us.

'We agree, that in order to concord, and in any other weighty and difficult cases, it is needful, and according to the mind of Christ, that the Ministers of several Churches be consulted and advised with about such matters....

'That a Church acknowledge the Scriptures to be the Word of God, the perfect and only rule of faith and practice, and own either the doctrinal part of the Articles of the Church of England, or the Confession or Catechism compiled by the Assembly at Westminster, or the Confession agreed on at the Savoy' (in 1658).[21]

This important venture had the following characteristics:

(1) It was an attempt to realize the principle of UNITY WITHOUT UNIFORMITY.

(2) It was inspired by Baxter's principles and practice, although restricted to two denominations, and going beyond the loose structure of the voluntary county associations of the Interregnum.

(3) It left certain matters open questions.

(4) Its tendency was Congregational although controversial points of Church government were avoided.

It was natural that the tendency should be away from the graded Presbyterian system of church courts, which had not been practicable under persecution.

Congregationalists had conceded that it was the right of pastors and elders to ordain, and that pastors of neighbouring churches should be consulted about choosing ministers. Presbyterians gave up still more in having no system of graded courts and in recognizing the existence virtually of a 'gathered' Church; the failure of comprehension had led them to this.

The agreement thus effected in London was called 'THE HAPPY UNION', and at its inauguration on 6th April 1691, Matthew Mead, the Congregational minister, preached upon the text, 'Two sticks made one' (Ezekiel xxxvii. 19).

In the same year, Richard Baxter breathed his last. On 8th December 1691 his long life and ministry closed with words revealing his devout spirit, 'When Thou wilt, what Thou wilt, and how Thou wilt.'

To the end Baxter had been consistent. In his pulpit prayers, a visitor in 1689-90 noted, Baxter included the King, the royal family, Parliament, the Churches of the East, Convocation, the need for reconciling Protestants so that 'party nor sect be never heard any more among them'.[22] In his last hours his prayers were for Christian unity. True to his lifelong practice he had felt bound to express himself about the new development in Presbyterian-Congregational unity, by writing, a few months before his death, a book entitled, *Church Concord; containing a dissuasive from unnecessary divisions and separations; the real concord of the* MODERATE INDEPENDENTS WITH THE PRESBYTERIANS *instanced in ten seeming differences; with the terms necessary for concord among all true Churches and Christians* (1691). This was typical, in its contents and the involved title.

The great apostle of Christian unity in his century had the satisfaction of seeing a federation of Presbyterian and Congregational ministers consummated—and he did not live to see its speedy dissolution.

'The Happy Union' was ruptured through doctrinal disputes in which most of the Presbyterian and Congregational ministers took opposing denominational sides. Dr Daniel Williams, a staunch Presbyterian scholar, had succeeded Baxter as a lecturer at Pinners' Hall. In 1692 (with the written support of Howe and Bates in the preface of his book) he attacked views that he regarded as Antinomian. In the acrimonious debates that followed, Williams and his friends were denounced as Arminians. The Congregationalists were generally orthodox Calvinists. The Presbyterians who sided with Williams were sometimes called 'Baxterians' because of the moderateness of their Calvinism and their repudiation of absolute reprobation.

Many Congregational ministers withdrew from the union in 1693 and claimed Pinners' Hall as their headquarters. Williams and his party (fifty or sixty in number) met, first at Dr Annesley's meeting-house, still calling themselves 'The United Ministers'. A few of these Presbyterians were already being suspected of leaning towards Unitarianism.[23] Salters' Hall became this party's headquarters.

Recriminations dragged on, and, although Williams gave a final statement of pacification in 1699 and ended the discussions, all hope of unity had gone—at least in London.

In the counties some associations continued. The most famous of these was the Exeter Assembly of Divines. Others eventually became Congregational 'County Unions'; others, Presbyterian courts. Not only was the influence of 'The Heads of Agreement' seen in the counties when it had ceased in London, but in America where the Congregational, and a large section of the Presbyterian, Churches took this document for their model of government.[24]

### 7. Renewed Hatred of Dissent

Baxter had upheld and practised occasional conformity, which he called 'a healing custom', during the darkest days of persecution. 'Presbyterians' had been more prominent than other Nonconformists in this practice because of their desire not to separate farther than necessary from the established Church.

However, occasional conformity was practised by many Dissenters because of the Test Act, merely to obtain or retain office in the State or corporations, and this roused the ire of many stout Churchmen. The strength of Dissent can be seen from the number of Nonconformist Lord Mayors of London in this period. One of them, in 1697, attended Pinners' Hall meeting-house regularly, and always in civic state, although he practised occasional conformity also.

In actual fact the increase in the numbers of Dissenters was disturbing Churchmen, who made occasional conformity the excuse for their antagonism. In the census of 3rd May 1688, Dissenters numbered 108,678, or 1 to 22·8 of conformists.[25] The estimates of over 200,000 in 1712, and nearly 300,000 in 1715, are not exact, but undoubtedly such increases did occur under toleration.[26] When toleration came, 2418 Dissenting places of worship were licensed—far more than in 1672.

The most bitter outbursts against Dissenters broke out in Queen Anne's reign. She had been welcomed to the throne with High

TOLERATION WITHOUT UNITY (1689) 281

Church ballads, some with the refrain 'Down with the Presbyterians'. Her loyalty to the High Church party was well known. The loyal address presented at her accession by Dr Williams and a deputation of Presbyterians, Independents, and Baptists was received by her in complete silence.

Occasional conformity became the bone of contention. In the Commons on 4th November 1702 a Bill was introduced proposing that any person holding any office, even the most menial, who attended a conventicle after receiving Communion in an Anglican church should be dismissed, and fined £100 and £5 for every day in employment afterwards, with permanent incapacity for any future public appointment. Amendments from the Lords were accepted only after long conferences in which Archbishop Tenison and Bishop Burnet were prominent in the cause of pacification. In 1703 a second Bill for dealing with occasional conformity, with penalties lower than proposed the year before, passed the Commons (233 votes to 140) but was rejected in the Lords (71 votes to 59; 14 bishops voting to reject, 9 bishops in favour). The following year another Occasional Conformity Bill was accepted in the Commons (179 votes to 31), but rejected in the Lords (71 votes to 50). The measure was not revived until the time of Tory re-ascendancy in 1711. Before then London was in a fever of excitement caused by the trial of the eccentric Churchman, Dr Sacheverell, who had preached against Dissenting academies for teaching 'hellish principles of fanaticism, regicide, and anarchy'. Several Dissenting meeting-houses, even in London, were burnt by the mobs at this time, and effigies of leading Dissenting ministers were burnt. The cry was raised everywhere, 'The Church is in danger.'

In 1711 the Occasional Conformity Act was passed at last. As a result most of the Dissenters who held office gave up their attendance at Dissenting worship; but it was anticipated that the Act would be repealed with the return of the Whigs after George of Hanover succeeded Anne. In the meantime, the 1714 Schism Bill represented the climax of the Tory and High Church persecution of Dissent; it was carried in the Commons by 237 votes to 126, and in the Lords by 77 to 72. This forbade any person to teach in a school or privately unless he had obtained a licence from a bishop, with a certificate that he had communicated in the Church of England during the previous year. The aim was to prevent the education of Dissenters' children by Dissenters, and to stifle Dissent altogether. The Queen signed this Bill on 25th June 1714; it was to become effective on 1st August.

On the very morning of 1st August, Bishop Burnet met Thomas Bradbury, Congregational minister of Fetter Lane Chapel, as he was walking through Smithfield on his way to preach and told him that the Queen was very low. Burnet arranged to send a messenger who would drop a handkerchief in the gallery of the chapel if the Queen passed away that morning. Before the end of his sermon Bradbury saw the signal and startled his congregation by including in his closing prayer a fervent petition for the new sovereign, George I. The Dissenters were saved.

## NOTES TO CHAPTER XI

1. Macaulay, *History of England*, vol. 1, pp. 376–9; Orme, *Life and Times of Richard Baxter*, vol. 1, pp. 445–64; Lloyd Thomas, Appendix 1, pp. 257–63, to the Everyman edition of Baxter's autobiography, and based upon the account of an eye-witness sent to Sylvester and recorded by Calamy.
2. Orme, *Life and Times of Richard Baxter*, vol. 1, pp. 446–50.
3. *Against the Revolt to a Foreign Jurisdiction*, p. 319, quoted by Powicke, *Richard Baxter, Under the Cross 1662–1691*, p. 215.
4. Macaulay, *History of England*, vol. 1, p. 772.
5. *Ibid.*, vol. 1, p. 774.
6. *Ibid.*, vol. 2, p. 283.
7. *Ibid.*, vol. 2, p. 283; Skeats and Miall, *History of the Free Churches in England*, p. 111.
8. Sykes, *Old Priest and New Presbyter*, pp. 132–3, deals with the proposals for waiving re-ordination 'as reflecting contemporary opinion among men of latitude'.
9. Proctor and Frere, *New History of the Book of Common Prayer*, p. 208.
10. *Ibid.*, p. 220; Sykes, *Old Priest and New Presbyter*, pp. 132–3.
11. Proctor and Frere, *New History of the Book of Common Prayer*, p. 218.
12. Calamy, *Life*, quoted in Skeats and Miall, *History of the Free Churches in England*, p. 119.
13. Burnet, *History of His Own Time*, p. 319.
14. Abbey and Overton, *The English Church in the Eighteenth Century*, p. 172, quoting the writings of Dr South, a contemporary divine.
15. Macaulay, *History of England*, vol. 2, p. 577.
16. *Ibid.*, vol. 2, p. 590.
17. Green, *A Short History of the English People*, p. 651.
18. Macaulay, *History of England*, vol. 2, p. 280.
19. *Practical Works*, vol. 4, pp. 1043–5; Orme, *Life and Times of Richard Baxter*, pp. 487–92.
20. Gordon, *Freedom after Ejection*, pp. 164 *et seq*.

21. Walker, *Creeds and Platforms of Congregationalism*, pp. 455 *et seq*.
22. Coomer, *English Dissent under the Early Hanoverians*, p. 36.
23. Gordon, *Freedom after Ejection*, p. 158.
24. Skeats and Miall, *History of the Free Churches in England*, p. 138.
25. Bebb, *Nonconformity and Social and Economic Life, 1660–1800*, p. 33.
26. *Ibid.*, p. 38.

CHAPTER XII

# SOME OF THE EFFECTS OF DISUNITY IN THE EIGHTEENTH CENTURY

1. *The Disabilities of Dissent and of the Establishment*

BOTH sides suffered from the Revolution Settlement. The losses to the established Church may have been less obvious at first, apart from the numerical loss. Nonconformists were only one in twenty-two of the population in 1700, but they had grown to one in eight in 1800, and were nearly one-half in 1851, largely due to the rise of the Methodists.

The losses of the establishment in the eighteenth century were rather spiritual than numerical. Much evangelical zeal and scholarship, godly living and earnest preaching, found at their best in seventeenth-century Puritanism, had been lost to the Church. The Church, it is true, had some virtues to its credit to balance the scandals of pluralities, absenteeism, and the worldliness that disgraced some Churchmen; but religion was undoubtedly at its lowest ebb after the Church had vanquished Dissent in the early eighteenth century.

The established Church suffered because its most sacred rites were tests for official advancement. The Corporation and Test Acts had not merely divided Church and nation. They had opened the door to formalism and hypocrisy. It was little wonder that foreigners visiting England observed how religion was ridiculed in many places; the beliefs of the Church were held only lightly or were discarded altogether because, with many men, they were only a badge of fashion and political expediency. Not all the godlessness and shameless vice that were rampant in both the highest and lowest social circles could be charged against the Church, even though many bishops and parish clergy were not zealous in pursuing their sacred calling; but the Church that represented religion before the world had to accept a major part of the responsibility for the nation's moral decline.

Had not disunity largely contributed to the feebleness of the Church in this age?

'Never has a century risen on Christian England so void of soul and faith as that which opened with Queen Anne, and which reached its misty noon beneath the second George. . . . The memory of BAXTER AND USHER possessed no spell, and calls to revival or reform fell dead on the echo. . . . The Puritans were buried, and the Methodists were not born.'[1]

The Church also had lost the strength to resist the sacerdotal claims of the High Church party. Under a cloud during the early years of the Hanoverians because it was Tory politically, this party gradually regained influence. The disunity of English Protestantism had resulted in many who could have combated its sacerdotal extravagances being permanently outside the Church.

The Church had now developed such a readiness to exclude earnest evangelical preachers that, later in the century, it continued the work of division by showing the Methodists the same attitude it had adopted towards the Dissenters.

Dissenters indeed had paid a heavy price for their fidelity to conscience. They were excluded from public office and from university education. They were treated as 'only half citizens'.[2] They were subjected to the snobbery that was practised towards 'bodies that were unfashionable in a country where snobbery is the rival religion to Christianity'.[3] Loyal Dissenters patiently endured their political and social disabilities and their staunchness was not unworthy of their Puritan forbears. Also, through their habits of personal piety, their moral influence was out of proportion to their numbers.

Yet there were losses of a more subtle nature in eighteenth-century Dissent; the contrast between the Dissenters of that age and the Puritans of Baxter's becomes evident.

It is true that the advent of the Hanoverian dynasty brought relief at the most critical points. The Schism Act was not enforced, and both that Act and the Occasional Conformity Act were repealed in 1719; even then most of the bishops in the House of Lords opposed repeal. No longer actively persecuted, Dissent lost its distinctive spirit, which had sustained it through its most fiery trials. What was to be the future for Dissent? Was it to be merely an opposition to establishment, a denial of episcopacy? There was now no uniform pattern in Dissent, and the denominations became more disunited—Presbyterians soon divided, Baptists were of varied types, and only the Congregational Churches preserved their chief characteristics.

As the years went by, the effect of separation became more marked at the vital point of education. Nothing had done more harm than this shrewdest stroke of the Dissenters' enemies; some families conformed only because they desired university education for their children, and some young Dissenters changed after receiving their education in the excellent Dissenting academies (these deserters included Archbishop Secker, Bishop Butler, and Samuel Wesley).

Several decades passed before wealthy Dissenters received relief from another miserable form of persecution. In London men were sometimes deliberately chosen to serve as sheriffs, although they could not hold the office unless they took Communion in the Church of England, and, upon declining office on these terms, they were heavily fined. Finally, in 1767, the House of Lords ruled against the practice, six out of seven Law Lords concurring. In a notable judgement, Lord Mansfield declared that it was not a crime for a man to be a Dissenter or to refuse to take Communion; in the sternest terms he denounced persecution as being 'against natural religion, revealed religion, and sound policy'.

It was natural that much of the energy of Dissenters should be given to agitating for the withdrawal of their political and social disabilities. In 1732 the 'Dissenting Deputies' were formed to press for repeal of the Test and Corporation Acts. Walpole was sympathetic but unwilling to incur political unpopularity by repeal. In 1723 he had introduced the *Regium Donum*, the payment of £1000 annually to widows of Dissenting ministers, partly as an inducement to Dissenters not to seek repeal. Several attempts in Parliament met with failure. It was not until 1812 that the Five Mile and Conventicle Acts were repealed, and in 1828 the Test and Corporation Acts.

The Trust Deeds of new chapels called 'Presbyterian' or 'Protestant Dissenting' required adherence to thirty-five of the Articles, in accordance with the provisions of the Toleration Act. It is difficult to decide in many cases whether a chapel was Presbyterian or Congregational, especially because there was no Presbyterian ecclesiastical organization in England. This made it easier for Presbyterian chapels and ministers to become unorthodox in doctrine.

SOME OF THE EFFECTS OF DISUNITY 287

In 1772 a Bill came before Parliament to dispense with a subscription to the thirty-five Articles in order to give relief to Unitarians, and to enable them to hold meeting-places legally. It was in this debate that Lord Chatham used his stinging phrases about the Church of England having 'a Calvinist creed, a Popish liturgy, an Arminian clergy'. Rejected at that time, the Act was passed in 1779. This measure gave an indication of the growth of Unitarianism.

It was in regard to orthodoxy that eighteenth-century Dissent showed the most marked decline from the standards of Baxter's age, and here can be seen the gravest consequence of the failure to preserve unity in the Church.

2. *The Ravages of Heresy and Inertia*

One of the greatest modern Nonconformists, Alexander McLaren, has used these terms concerning the decline of the formerly Orthodox Dissenters in the eighteenth century: 'Arianism and Unitarianism spread like dry-rot among the Presbyterians.'[4] While it is true that the Puritans of the previous century had too often been wedded to theological disputes with sometimes exaggerated logical distinctions, no one could have foreseen that the descendants of Baxter, Owen, and Howe would fall into arid intellectualism and doctrinal heterodoxy.

Under toleration, some Dissenters felt free to pursue any theological phantasy. They acted as though their denial of the forms of Church government in the established Church could justify their quarrelling also with its doctrinal standards. Many Presbyterians, appointed by trustees to churches that had no credal bases or covenants binding them to sister churches, ventured upon the verge of Arianism. 'Arianism is not a platform, it is a slope,' it was said.[5] This became so marked that by 1716 there was an instance of a Presbyterian ordination taking place without requiring a subscription to any creed.[6]

The most notorious theological controversy, the Exeter and Salters' Hall dispute, raged around the question of subscription to creeds as against the claim that the Trinitarian belief should be expressed in Scriptural terms only. In 1719 two Presbyterian ministers in Exeter, Peirce and Hallet, objected to the terms of the Westminster Confession and substituted Scriptural terms; local Presbyterian ministers supported them, Congregationalists opposed them. The Devon and Cornwall Assembly, which had been a consultative body only, called upon its members to sign the first of the Thirty-nine Articles as a proof of Trinitarian orthodoxy. When nineteen refused, the Assembly resolved that, as a check against Arianism, no ministers in their district should be ordained without subscribing to the first Article or to the fifth and sixth Answers to the Westminster Catechism.

Meanwhile, the case had been referred by Exeter ministers to a conference of Dissenting ministers at Salters' Hall, London. The debate concerned the question of whether the preface in the letter of advice should contain a subscription by all London ministers to the first Article as a proof of Trinitarianism. To this many (chiefly Presbyterians) objected and favoured Scriptural terms only. 'The Bible won by four votes', 73 to 69, declared a Presbyterian observer, Sir John Jekyll, Master of the Rolls. When this vote was being taken, the cries were raised: 'You who are against persecution, come upstairs,' and 'You that are for the Trinity, stay below.' To this sorry pass had disputing Dissenters been brought. Thomas Bradbury, Congregational minister at Fetter Lane, had been the moving spirit for the orthodox party, and he took his followers to a separate meeting. It has been noted that at least eighteen of the seventy-three voting for Scriptural terms afterwards conformed to the Church of England; Calamy's comment was that those who would not subscribe to the first Article were willing later to accept all the Thirty-nine Articles.

Heresy had now rent the denominations asunder. Drysdale, in *History of the Presbyterians in England,* divided the London Dissenting ministers and showed that Congregationalists were more orthodox than Presbyterians:

Presbyterians (85): 50 non-subscribers, 26 subscribers, 9 neutral.

Congregationalists (35): 7 non-subscribers, 23 subscribers, 5 neutral.[7]

In many parts of England the effects of these disputes could be seen. It was assumed that congregations would have to decide their theological standards for themselves. From this controversy of 1719 can be dated the rise of Arianism among the Presbyterians, the beginning of Unitarianism as a distinct denomination among the Free Churches—and still another division in England.

From 1719 to 1730 the situation deteriorated still further. In the latter year, London Dissenting ministers were divided thus:

Presbyterians (44): 19 Calvinists, 12 Baxterians (moderate Calvinist), 13 Arminians.
Congregationalists (28): 28 Calvinists.
Particular Baptists (16): 7 Calvinists, 9 Antinomians.
General Baptists (8): 5 Arminians, 3 Socinians.[8]

It has been pointed out that 'Arminian' at that time meant Arian, and not the orthodox sense of Arminian or as used by Methodists later.

Dr Powicke, Baxter's biographer, strongly contends that the unorthodox (Arianizing) Churches were as evangelistic as orthodox Dissenters and that, in stressing 'good works', they were as earnest for moral uplift as for theological consistency.[9] He also gives evidence to prove that fewer unorthodox churches than orthodox became extinct in this period; sixteen out of forty-nine orthodox churches in London ceased to exist in a few years after 1719, while thirteen out of twenty-five unorthodox churches closed down in the same period, with statistics from other parts of England more in favour of the orthodox. It seems that, quite apart from whether one section or the other was more viable, Dissenting churches of ALL types were withering during the eighteenth century. Orthodoxy alone could not save them. Unorthodoxy held no better prospect of continuing vigour. Practically independent of each other, the Churches lived to themselves, they had very little concern for the unchurched world around them, they had no missionary passion whatever. A deadly inertia had settled upon Dissent. Together with the establishment it needed the reviving breath of the Evangelical Revival.

Much has been written about 'the frightful seepage in English moral life' at this time.[10] Though both the establishment and Dissent had failed, the stronger condemnation may be passed upon the spiritual successors of the Puritans. Baxter, throughout his life, had pleaded for a revival of godliness in the nation by evangelical preaching. Where was such preaching in a divided and decadent Church, established or Nonconformist? In the middle of the eighteenth century, Chief Justice Blackstone stated that he often went deliberately to all the leading churches in London to hear their preachers, but he had not heard a sermon 'that had more Christianity in it than a speech of Cicero's, and that it would have been impossible for him to tell whether the preacher was a Mohammedan or a Christian'.[11]

The 'battle for the nation's soul' has always called for Christian unity as well as freedom from heresy and inertia.

### 3. *The Decline of the Presbyterians*

Whether Presbyterians in the eighteenth century were descendants of Baxter's episcopal Nonconformists or of the formal Presbyterians, all of that name declined considerably in this period. The causes for their decline revealed reasons why Congregationalists maintained their ground and even gained at the expense of their old rivals. In 1715 there were 1107 Dissenting congregations, about one-half Presbyterian, with Congregationalists more than one-quarter. In 1772 there were only 300 Presbyterian (both orthodox and otherwise) and 400 Congregational congregations. The reasons for the Presbyterian decline were:

(1) Presbyterians had lost the principles of CHURCHMANSHIP so conspicuous in Baxter, who had followed the Genevan traditions of High Churchmanship. He said: 'If the Papists will idolize the Church, shall we therefore DENY IT, DISREGARD IT, OR DIVIDE IT?'[12]

Always Baxter had exalted the Church and declared that it must be a national Church. The Presbyterians in the eighteenth century had lost the ideal of a national Church, though they could not be blamed for being outside the establishment. They became satisfied with separate congregations like the Independents.

'One of the explanations which accounts for the failure of eighteenth-century Nonconformity is the fact that all parties neglected the doctrine of the CHURCH.... Neglect of united action by the Dissenters and their lack of interest in the Catholic ideals of Ministry, Worship and Sacraments in connexion with the visible Church was a sad contrast to THEIR FINE CHURCHMANSHIP of the previous century.'[13]

(2) Presbyterians suffered from lack of organization or 'covenants' between the churches of their denomination, which could have retained their standards even without the graded court system. With some concerted action they could have checked heresy and other ills. Without fixed doctrinal standards they were

left open to Deism, Arianism, and Rationalism, in many cases. Of course, they were not entirely blameworthy. They had hoped against hope for re-union with the establishment. The possibility of such re-union had even been mentioned in the trust-deeds of Presbyterian chapels after 1689.[14] Although, gradually, orthodox Presbyterian congregations became loosely associated, it was not until 1876 that the Presbyterian Church of England was formed.

(3) Departing from conventional beliefs and denying all authority became the distinctive characteristic of many eighteenth-century Presbyterian ministers. Whereas their forbears made episcopacy their objection, these Presbyterians scorned the thought of doctrinal orthodoxy. The former had refused to accept uniformity in ceremonial and worship, the latter saw no reason for uniformity in creed and teaching. Esteeming their scholarship, dearly won through their Dissenting academies, Presbyterian divines often pursued their inquiries in theology and philosophy in a spirit of rationalism and disallowed the authority of revealed religion. The academy at Warrington became as famous for science as any University of that time; Priestley and all its other tutors eventually became Arians or Unitarians.

(4) Presbyterian ministers could believe and preach as they pleased if they were supported by the trustees of their buildings. In England these trustees were not checked by a system of presbyteries and synods. The congregations had no power to influence the situation. Unless endowments were conditioned by detailed doctrinal tests, ministers could rely upon general endowments from wealthy merchants in a previous generation, and could continue with their own unorthodox teaching, in spite of the opposition of their congregations.[15] In contrast with this strange development, the Congregational churches placed the seat of authority in the church-meeting, which chose the minister. Without the use of trustees, who in English law controlled the property and could exclude an orthodox minister if they chose, the Congregationalists generally maintained orthodoxy and avoided the anomalies of the eighteenth-century Presbyterian position.

(5) Presbyterianism did not continue the exacting tests for membership advocated and used in Baxter's day. Infant Baptism and moral conduct were sufficient, without a 'public confession of faith'. Attending Presbyterian worship in the eighteenth century

resembled hearing a public lecture, with few, if any, obligations of belief or duty following.

Some Presbyterian churches became Congregational as time went on, especially when Arianism was spreading, and they found that they could obtain orthodox ministers more easily from the Congregationalists.

Even those Presbyterians who did not fall away to Unitarianism remained unmoved by the Evangelical Revival, which warmed the heart of England later in this century. It was rather strange that it was from clergymen in the established Church, the Wesleys and their ordained colleagues, that the Revival came. Baxter's evangelical passion and moral earnestness appeared again in the Wesleys. The Dissenters contributed nothing, and they received less stimulus from the Revival because of the theological barrenness and spiritual deadness into which they had fallen.

The expulsion of the Methodists had some similarities to the expulsion of the Nonconformists in 1662, though no Parliamentary legislation was launched against them. The established Church again drove out its most zealous sons. Without dwelling upon the faults of the seventeenth and eighteenth centuries, we see clearly enough the effects of our disunity upon the religious life of England in 1962. We can deplore our inheritance of disunity; we cannot excuse its continuance any longer.

## NOTES TO CHAPTER XII

1. James Hamilton, *Christian Classics*, vol. 4, p. 222, quoted by Drysdale, *History of the Presbyterians in England*, p. 546.
2. Barker, *Britain and the British People*, p. 86.
3. Brogan, *The English People*, p. 127.
4. Alexander McLaren in *The Ejectment of 1662*, p. 23.
5. Quoted in Coomer, *English Dissent under the Early Hanoverians*, p. 68.
6. *Ibid.*, p. 68.
7. Drysdale, *History of the Presbyterians in England*, p. 525.
8. Skeats and Miall, *History of the Free Churches in England*, p. 267; Coomer, *English Dissent under the Early Hanoverians*, p. 78.
9. Powicke in *Essays Congregational and Catholic*, p. 306 *et seq.*
10. Father Piette, *John Wesley in the Evolution of Protestantism*, p. 110.
11. Skeats and Miall, *History of the Free Churches in England*, p. 352.
12. *The Reformed Pastor*, p. 183.
13. Colligan, *Eighteenth Century Nonconformity*, quoted by Coomer, *English Dissent under the Early Hanoverians*, p. 123.
14. Barclay, *Inner Life of the Religious Societies of the Commonwealth*, p. 588.
15. Moffatt, *Presbyterian Churches*, pp. 66 *et seq.*

CHAPTER XIII

## CAN THERE BE UNITY WITHOUT UNIFORMITY TODAY?

WHILE it is impossible to apply all of Baxter's programme to the modern situation, it is instructive to find how many of our principles and plans for re-union follow the proposals of the Puritan pioneer. The substance of Baxter's ecclesiastical principles, as set out at the commencement of this study, can be examined and compared with present-day issues.

1. *A United Evangelical Church for a Divided World*

We must be stirred by Baxter's constant dissatisfaction with disunity, though few of us may approach his profound sorrow at the inconsistency and ineffectiveness of a divided Church. With Baxter, we feel it is a reproach to the Body of Christ that we face a pagan world with rival Christian denominations. We realize the futility of preaching the gospel of reconciliation to a divided world when we ourselves are divided.

Not only is the Scriptural metaphor of the 'One Body' powerfully influencing Christian thought, but there is a growing realization that the Church must show that it is the FAMILY OF GOD. Only as the Church is true to its calling as the Family of God can it lead mankind to become a Family of Nations under God.

No one Church adequately represents one nation today, and still less can any Church appeal to the world community of nations.

All Churches have something to offer, something to receive. For example, Nonconformity is now willing to learn the theological truth and the practical advantages of constitutional episcopacy in forms that resemble Baxter's and Usher's principles.

Baxter's first principles were that every minister should be a bishop of the flock, and that there should be effective parish discipline. No longer is this a matter for contention, because the pastoral responsibility of clergy and ministers is recognized in all Churches, even if it is subject to the supervision of bishops or presbyteries. No clergyman today would be regarded as a bishop's curate or a half-pastor as in Baxter's day. In every denomination there are certain tests of membership and of fitness for receiving Holy Communion. These may be by no means as rigid as those Baxter advocated; but neither would we countenance the formalism against which he fulminated, the admission of all and sundry to the Holy Table.

It is not necessary to consider how various denominations, or the re-united Church of the future, should exercise this discipline. The Puritan discipline, with its inquisitorial supervision and stern punishments, would be obviously unacceptable, and yet all Churches know that church members must respect the standards that Christ and His Church demand. The spirit of Puritanism, through calmer and kinder channels, must find its appropriate equivalent in the re-united Church.

Even Matthew Arnold said of Puritan discipline in general: 'As a stage and a discipline, and as means for enabling that poor, inattentive and immoral creature—man—to love and appropriate, and make part of his being, divine ideas, on which he could not otherwise have laid or kept hold, the DISCIPLINE OF PURITANISM has been invaluable; and the more I read history, the more I see of mankind, the more I recognize its value.'[1]

### 2. *A Constitutional Episcopacy*

Baxter's parochial episcopacy would satisfy no one in negotiations for re-union today as the proper form of 'historic' episcopacy. In spite of his strong arguments from the authorities he quoted in the early history of the Church, only diocesan episcopacy would be considered now.

In nothing has there been a greater change since 1662 than in the altered attitude of bishops themselves. It is apparent that some of Baxter's ideals have been realized. Episcopal Churches in English-speaking countries have constitutional, and not monarchical, bishops as Baxter knew them. Smaller dioceses in England, as the Puritans often requested, have been established, many suffragans have been appointed, and there is close contact between bishops and their clergy and people. Usher's synodical scheme, in its essential features, has been instituted. It is not now the bishop alone, but the BISHOP-IN-SYNOD, who is the constitutional ruler of the diocese.

At the highly controversial Kikiyu Conference, in 1918, when

CAN THERE BE UNITY WITHOUT UNIFORMITY? 295

Anglo-Catholic principles prevailed, it was the stoutest contender for High Church Anglicanism, in the person of Bishop Weston of Zanzibar, who declared: 'Episcopacy need not involve us in a monarchical, diocesan episcopate. Many bishops may serve one local church. The bishops should be freely elected, and should rule with the clergy and laity. Nor is it essential that we hold any one view of episcopacy on the doctrinal side, provided the fact of its existence and continuance be admitted.'[2]

Surely we hear echoes of some of Baxter's principles in those statements.

In discussions concerning re-union it has been the Anglican section that has often emphasized, not only that bishops now act constitutionally, but also that, in Anglican Churches outside England, bishops are chosen by synods; that bishops in theory may act with their presbyterate in ordinations; and that they give heed to the call of the Church in appointing parish clergy. Anglicans have conceded that the re-united Church must have 'elements of presbyteral and congregational order' as 'permanent elements in the order and life of the United Church'. The contentions of the moderate episcopal party represented by Baxter in the 1660-61 negotiations, therefore, have been vindicated in the opinions of many modern Anglican leaders.

## 3. *Baxter's Association of Pastors*

It is by no accident that the church that bears Baxter's name in Kidderminster is the Baxter Congregational Church. His Communion Table and chair are there. Strange to say, when a rift took place near the end of the eighteenth century and a Unitarian section left Baxter Congregational Church, it took Baxter's massive pulpit, which stands in the vestry of the 'New Meeting' Church (see frontispiece in this book). One may hope that this pulpit will some day stand again in the parish church of Kidderminster.

It is also significant that most of Baxter's biographers have been Congregational scholars, and that his spirit and policy have been understood best in that denomination. It may be that the genius of modern Congregationalism, with the developments in its government, which have happened since the far-off days of Independency, indicates how Baxter's principles can be applied in the re-united Church which, as Anglican leaders readily admit, will include Congregational elements.

Similarities can be seen in the local Congregational model. Although Baxter's own church was a parish church of the establishment, and he strongly denounced the Independents for creating 'gathered' churches, his ministry, actually, resembled that of a modern Congregational minister. Discipline, which was so essential in his ministry, was exercised only over those who accepted it, in spite of his claiming the whole community as his parish. Certainly he wielded authority over communicants such as no minister of any Protestant denomination would now use. Nor did he give to his people the powers of a Congregational church-meeting. Were he alive today, maybe he would change his opinion of Independent Church government in some particulars, and he would not object to the 'democratic theocracy' which has been the glory of Congregationalism. We can imagine how Baxter would have approved the High Churchmanship of those who maintain, in the words of R. W. Dale, that 'Only those who are in Christ have any right to be in the Church.' Orme, in quoting Baxter's account of the system he followed in his church at Kidderminster, declared that this 'shows that Baxter was the minister of a voluntary congregation, and pastor of a separate church, whose discipline was neither aided nor restrained by the civil powers, though Baxter was supported by the funds which belonged to the Establishment'.[3]

Baxter's voluntary county associations of pastors could be compared with the Congregational county unions of England today. Writing before the formation of the Congregational Union of England and Wales, Orme stated that Baxter's system was not strictly episcopal, Presbyterian, or Independent, but that it corresponded more with the Congregational system than with any other.[4]

Baxter's system, since his lifetime, has been described as MODIFIED INDEPENDENCY. His own term, of course, was MODERATE EPISCOPACY. Congregational county unions may not only remind us of Baxter's voluntary county associations, but, strengthened with the Presbyterian elements found in presbyteries and synods, may provide a pattern for wider re-union projects.

Furthermore, Baxter's ideal of 'THE CONFEDERATE PARISH CHURCHES OF ENGLAND' may be said to have been realized in part,

CAN THERE BE UNITY WITHOUT UNIFORMITY? 297

that is, as far as a non-established denomination could express it, in the formation of the Congregational Union of England and Wales in 1831.

Apart altogether from details of Church organization, the spirit of Baxter lives again in the teaching of modern Congregationalists as expressed in the throbbing words of Bernard Manning:

'What is it that makes the Church different from all other societies, that makes the preaching of the Word different from all other speech, that makes the sacramental rites different from all other significant acts? It is GRACE. Then it is NOT EPISCOPACY OR THE LACK OF EPISCOPACY.... To classify the work of GRACE as sometimes valid and irregular, sometimes valid but irregular, sometimes invalid and irregular, to ask if grace may be invalid though regular, this (it is the distinctive contribution of Congregationalism to make clear) is frivolity in the holy of holies.... It has been ours to assert positively the full-toned orthodox faith without legal bonds, to show that by removing its legal bonds its divine excellence stands forth the more plainly. Orthodoxy without legalism, churchmanship without clericalism.... To convey this treasure to a dying world and a living Church... that I believe to be the call of this Council to us.'[5]

4. *Extension of Orders (Supplemental Ordination)—
but no Re-ordination*

Baxter, an episcopally ordained clergyman, always stoutly defended the validity of presbyterial ordination and opposed re-ordination (pp. 34–9 and other parts of this study). He welcomed the promises in the King's Declaration of 25th October 1660 that those not episcopally ordained would not be required to accept re-ordination, upon certain conditions (pp. 158–61). As in 1660–61 and in 1689, so now it is admitted that only episcopal ordination will be acceptable after re-union has been consummated. The problem has always been the recognition of past non-episcopal ordinations or the use of certain ceremonies and formulas that will avoid the repudiation of past ministries and yet secure a future ministry that all parties concerned will accept as valid.

Among the proposals offered in Baxter's time were:

(1) The conferring of AUTHORITY:

(*a*) LEGAL authority for a presbyterially ordained minister to exercise his ministry in a church or parish to which he was lawfully appointed.[6]

OR (b) Authority 'IN THE CHURCH OF ENGLAND', with no other reference to circumstances past or present, but with the inference that what was required was this specific authority to minister within the Anglican Church after another ministry (Comprehension Bill, 1689—pp. 267-8 of this study. This simple form was also advocated by Tillotson for ministers presbyterially ordained in foreign Reformed Churches (pp. 269-70).

The granting of authority BY A BISHOP has been suggested by Anglican representatives.[7]

Baxter appended a condition to his suggestion, that accepting such legal authority should be subject to the minister's profession that there was no renunciation of his previous ministry; his proviso was disallowed by Bishop Wilkins (1668). It is improbable that conferring legal authority, or making the authorization of a bishop sufficient, would satisfy the scruples of many Anglicans today.

(2) ORDINATION 'SUB CONDITIONE', using the hypothetical formula, 'If thou art not already ordained'.[8] Although suggested in 1689, and also in 1925 when some Anglican leaders approved this method and preferred it to others, it is difficult to believe that many would feel satisfied with this hypothetical formula.[9] Reference to this will be made later.

It is a heartening feature of negotiations in recent years, and an encouraging evidence of the difference in the attitude of leaders of episcopal Churches after 300 years, that two other methods have been suggested, both preferable to the foregoing proposals from Baxter's time:

(1) MUTUAL RE-COMMISSIONING. The episcopally ordained clergymen who have made these proposals or who have assented to them have freely acknowledged that they would be willing to receive a commissioning from ministers who have not been episcopally ordained. The doubt is whether all, or many, episcopally ordained clergymen would really believe that they were receiving any spiritual grace or authority that they did not already possess.

(2) EXTENSION OF ORDERS (SUPPLEMENTAL ORDINATION). Greater hope has been found in this suggestion because the fact is that no ministry at present is complete in its scope; that is, it is only being exercised within its own denomination, no matter what

## CAN THERE BE UNITY WITHOUT UNIFORMITY? 299

were the words used in ordination, and irrespective of any contention that the wording and intention were that the ordination was to 'the Christian ministry' or within 'the Church of God'. The extension of orders would actually give authority to exercise a wider ministry, to serve in a larger combined denomination.

Some pronouncements upon the question or re-ordination are enlightening. First, there was the 1920 Lambeth Conference Appeal:

> 'Bishops and clergy of our Communion would willingly accept from these authorities [of other Communions, and provided that other terms had been satisfactory settled] A FORM OF COMMISSION OR RECOGNITION which would commend our ministry to their congregations. . . . It is our hope that the same motive would lead ministers who have not received it to accept a commission through episcopal ordination, as obtaining for them a ministry throughout the whole fellowship. In so acting no one of us would possibly be taken to repudiate his past ministry. We shall be publicly and formally seeking ADDITIONAL RECOGNITION OF A NEW CALL TO WIDER SERVICE IN A RE-UNITED CHURCH.'[10]

For the first time since the Churches separated in 1662, Anglican and Free Church representatives met together at Lambeth, on 6th July 1923. The two archbishops and eleven bishops representing the Church of England delivered an epoch-making statement upon the nature of Free Church ministries which they regarded 'as being within their several spheres REAL MINISTRIES in the Universal Church'. They added that they were 'prepared to say that . . . ministries which imply a sincere intention to preach Christ's word and administer the Sacraments as Christ has ordained, and to which authority so to do has been solemnly given by the Church concerned, are REAL MINISTRIES OF CHRIST'S WORD AND SACRAMENTS IN THE UNIVERSAL CHURCH'.[11]

That, at least, was a vindication of what Nonconformists and their forbears had maintained before and after 1662. It was the clearest recognition of non-episcopal ministries that Anglican leaders have given. Some may believe that there has been a decline in the warmth of that recognition since that time; others may consider that, especially in the discussions of the World Council of Churches, new and wider opportunities have arisen for further exploration. True it is that the Lambeth Conference of 1930 disregarded what the bishops had stated in 1923 and modified that pronouncement by stating that 'real ministries' are not necessarily 'sufficient ministries', and that Free Church ministries required 'due authority' in order to be, spiritually, fully effective.[12]

It was on another occasion (19th June 1925) that Anglican representatives at this joint conference made two alternative suggestions for overcoming the difficulty concerning re-ordination. As already indicated, these were:

(1) 'A solemn authorization [to] be conferred by the laying on of hands by a bishop' ('the lack of this authority, the main defect in the Free Church ministries'), the words being: 'Take thou AUTHORITY, now committed unto thee by the imposition of our hands, for the office and work of a Priest (or Presbyter). . . .'

The other plan was preferred by these Anglican leaders:

(2) 'ORDINATION SUB CONDITIONE—an act of episcopal ordination prefaced and governed by a condition expressed in some such words as "If thou art not already ordained".'

In support of this proposal, it was stated that:

'It would recognize, as a matter of fact, that there is a doubt on one side; it would not require or involve any acknowledgment of the validity of that doubt from the other side. It would be following a practice which has long been familiar in the Church with regard to the Sacrament of Baptism. . . .'

There follows the historical allusion which covers the precedents mentioned in this study:

'There are PRECEDENTS for it in England IN THE SIXTEENTH AND SEVENTEENTH CENTURIES, and the resolutions of the Lambeth Conference recommend its use in certain cases even of episcopal ordination.'[13]

For the still better method of mutual re-commissioning support came from Canada about the same time. In May 1921 a committee appointed by the Bishop of Montreal agreed with a committee of the presbytery of Montreal in adopting forms of mutual re-commissioning. These forms can be compared with the suggestions for granting authority in the Church of England, made in 1689. Canadian Presbyterians were to be presented to the bishop, who would say:

'Forasmuch as terms have been arranged between the Church of England in Canada, and the Presbyterian Church in Canada . . . and as it is necessary that there should be in this united Church a Ministry that shall be acknowledged in every part thereof, it is our purpose now to give to these our brethren, by the laying on of our hands, a commission to the office of priesthood, it being clearly understood that herein there is no repudiation of, or reflection on, their past ministry, to which they were set apart by the Holy Spirit, whose call led them to that Ministry and whose power enabled them to perform the same.'

Presbyterian ministers would then kneel, and the bishops with the priests present would lay hands upon them, using the usual words of ordination. The moderator would follow with the same prefatory declaration as the bishop had used, and the Anglican clergy would come forward to receive commissioning by laying on of hands from the moderator and other presbyters, their statement including these words:

'We now by the laying on of our hands admit to a WIDER exercise of the Ministry of the Word and Sacraments.'

Afterwards the moderator would address the Anglican clergy with the words:

'In the name of the Lord Jesus Christ, the only King and Head of the Church, and by authority of this Presbytery, I invite you to take part with us in this Ministry, and admit you to all the rights and privileges thereto pertaining.' [14]

These Canadian suggestions are, of course, only of academic value because in 1925 most of the Presbyterians formed, with Methodists and Congregationalists, the United Church of Canada; and discussions for union with the Anglican Church in Canada, since 1925, have been desultory and discontinued.

In Australia, efforts were made to cut the Gordian knot of re-ordination. An inter-Communion group in Sydney, consisting of representatives of several denominations, and an Anglican–Methodist conference in Melbourne, both in 1939, discussed a declaration to be given by ministers of episcopal as well as non-episcopal churches:

'I, believing myself to be called and ordained to a real ministry . . . am yet conscious of a desire for that wider, fuller, and more effectual ministry in a re-united fellowship. . . . I am humbly prepared to receive the MUTUAL laying on of hands with prayer, so that ALL to whom I may lawfully minister within this re-united fellowship may know without scruple or doubtfulness, that I have been fully ordained and commissioned. . . . I do freely and willingly assent to give and to receive, and to bestow and to SHARE . . . such further authority. . . .'

The suggested formula, for mutual recognition, read:

'Receive the Holy Ghost for the FULFILMENT OF WHATEVER MAY BE NEEDFUL in thine ordained ministry as Priest or Minister in the Church of God. Take thou authority to preach the Word of God, to exercise the ministry of reconciliation, and to minister Christ's Sacraments in the congregations whereunto thou shalt be FURTHER called or lawfully appointed.'

It was the vagueness of conferring 'whatever may be needful', with the likelihood of varying interpretations almost nullifying the act, that led to no practical result from these discussions in Australia.

Immediately after Lambeth 1920, Bishop Headlam, in *Doctrine of the Church and Re-union*, contended that Anglican and Free Churches should recognize each other's Orders as valid, and 'each Church should give to the ministers of the other Church authority to minister to its people'. He also found precedents in the orders conferred *per saltum* in 1610 and 1662 when episcopacy was re-established in Scotland, with bishops consecrated although their own ordinations had been only presbyterial.

The resolutions adopted by the Annual Assembly of the Federal Council of the Evangelical Free Churches, on 18th September 1923, may well be recalled in this connexion. These resolutions stated:

'We are dealing to-day NOT WITH THE ANGLICANISM OF THE RESTORATION, which deliberately desired to EXCLUDE Nonconformists and which penalized them, but with the Anglicanism of the Lambeth Appeal, which earnestly seeks re-union and

CAN THERE BE UNITY WITHOUT UNIFORMITY? 303

which approaches Nonconformity with friendship. . . . IF THE CHURCH OF ENGLAND IN THE SEVENTEENTH CENTURY COULD RECEIVE MINISTERS FROM CERTAIN REFORMED CHURCHES WITHOUT EPISCOPAL ORDINATION and yet did not thereby lose its Catholic identity, then it could and can—so far as principle goes —in the twentieth century admit, BY SOME METHOD OTHER THAN ORDINATION, those whom, despite their not having had episcopal hands laid upon them, it has just formally and fully RECOGNIZED AS BEING REALLY IN THE MINISTRY of Christ's Word and Sacraments in the Universal Church.' [15]

For 300 years the Church in England has waited for this example of uniting episcopal and non-episcopal ministries. In South India the re-united Church has accepted the historic episcopate, without approving any one theory of the episcopate, and without implying any invalidity or irregularity in the Orders of the uniting Churches. The recognition of non-episcopally ordained ministries during the interim period of thirty years is worthy of similar acceptance in re-union movements in other parts of the world; it is surely worthy of the approval of all who have striven for unity for the past 300 years. One could imagine Baxter's surprise and gratification at the consecration *per saltum* of new bishops upon the inauguration of union in South India in 1947, with the consequent episcopal ordination of those entering the presbyterate thenceforward. Still more, Baxter, who had been one of the first to recognize in Christian missions a compelling argument for unity, would have rejoiced that a missionary Church had such spiritual intensity of life and such whole-souled devotion to Christian unity that it was leading the world towards re-union.

It is unnecessary to traverse the many documents available regarding the proposals for unions elsewhere, especially in Ceylon and in North India and Pakistan. It is noteworthy that, while these support the methods of mutual commissioning or supplemental ordination, in other places there is growing approval of Bishop Newbigin's contention that the 'bridge-period' used in South India is theologically sound and that it avoids the misconceptions that one party or another may have concerning the act of re-commissioning in future years. Over and beyond the question of the method for avoiding re-ordination there is the influence of Indian Christian Churches determined, at all costs, to give a united witness to their Lord in the face of a pagan world. They are shaming the rest of Christendom.

While, in 1962, we are pursuing the path of re-union, we should remember that, 300 years ago, there were pioneers in this cause like Baxter, earnestly desiring a ministry that would gain general acceptance but always sturdily respecting past ordinations. Baxter indicated this when he wrote, 'By Ordination we mean not . . . a mere ecclesiastical confirmation of former ordination, in a doubted case', and gave, among the various 'Reasons why we cannot consent to re-ordination' :

'We dare not consent to the taking of God's Name in vain, by using holy expressions, and a divine ordinance, either as a scenical form, or to confirm an error. . . . We dare not so far harden the Papists, and honour their cause, nor tempt the people to Popery, as to seem to consent, that their Churches, Ministry and Baptism is true, and the Protestant Ministry, Churches and Baptism is false; nor dare we teach them, if (which God forbid) they should get the power of governing us, to call us all again to be re-ordained.' [16]

### 5. *Diversity of Worship*

Where are practical approaches towards union to begin? Surely, in worshipping together the Christian Churches will come closer to each other. Also, in studying each other's forms of worship, it is often found that the differences are much less than has been supposed.

The seventeenth century has something to teach the twentieth century, in the necessity for some freedom in forms of worship, and also in the benefits of a liturgy, especially with alternative forms. The Puritan reformers were the pioneers in both respects, and, though they were stifled in 1662, their contentions have been justified.

We are convinced today that we need not be committed to the invariable use of mattins and evensong every Sunday, on the one hand, or to the entirely free service of traditional Nonconformity, on the other. The spiritual descendants of Baxter today are serving the cause of unity by fusing both elements as he did. One of the remarkable developments in Church worship has been the changed attitude of Nonconformists, who have learnt the value of liturgical

CAN THERE BE UNITY WITHOUT UNIFORMITY? 305

worship and have published books of worship for use in their churches, while Anglicans have allowed for extemporaneous prayers in their worship.

Baxter's reactions could be surmised if he could have known that in 1938 a joint conference of Anglican bishops and Nonconformist representatives would have issued this statement:

'Some of the very PROPOSALS MADE BY THE NONCONFORMISTS AND REJECTED BY THE BISHOPS AT THE SAVOY CONFERENCE IN 1661 were themselves proposed by the Bishops in 1927, e.g., parents permitted to act as sponsors at Baptism, the substitution of the word "honour" for "worship" in one of the vows of the Marriage Service, and more important, some provision for prayer by the Minister in his own words. So also, on the Nonconformist side, few would be found to-day to resist the use of the word "Sunday" as at least an alternative to "The Lord's Day"; to insist upon retiring collections only; to oppose the saying of the Litany in the body of the church; to object to the reading of any part of the Apocrypha in church, or to refuse to observe some Holy Days, for example Christmas Day and Good Friday. . . . It is also now improbable that Anglicans would think it necessary to insist upon the universal adoption through a United Church of such practices as the use of the surplice, the use of the sign of the Cross in Baptism, or kneeling to receive the elements at Holy Communion.' [17]

There could be no more striking summary of the changed attitudes than this official statement from the 1938 joint conference. We can hope for unity when bishops in modern days reveal so frankly their devotion to unity without uniformity, and when both sides have learned so much from each other.

The same spirit has been manifest in the conditions of union in the Church of South India, including these statements:

'In its public worship the united Church must retain for its congregations freedom either to use historic forms or not to do so as may best conduce to edification and to the worship of God in spirit and in truth. . . . A presbyter in charge of any congregation may introduce experimentally the use of an alteration in the accustomed form of worship of that congregation, or a new form of worship, after giving due notice thereof to the congregation, and shall report any such action to the Bishop of the diocese.'[18]

Once again South India has shown the way and has also profited by the principles of the Puritans 300 years ago.

### 6. *A National Comprehensive Church*

In general terms Baxter's principles would meet with wide acceptance today. It may be that the pressure of a pagan society outside the Churches had induced Nonconformists to see that a truly national Church is needed to mould the life of the nation. The crucial question is not now one of formal establishment or disestablishment, as Scotland has proved. To the extent, at least, that the State should recognize the place of religion as the nation's acknowledgment of God and as the basis of an ordered society, to that extent a national Church may be advocated.

In 1938 the joint conference of representatives of the Church of England and the Free Churches made this statement:

'Free Churchmen, while still emphasizing the need for the "gathered" Church of fully committed Christian disciples, are coming to understand and appreciate more than they did the value of such a CORPORATE RECOGNITION BY THE NATION OF CHRISTIANITY as being in a true sense THE NATIONAL RELIGION. The Church of England, on the other hand, while continuing to value its opportunities as a National Church and retaining its sense of mission to the whole people of England, no longer identifies the leaven with the lump or a congregation of Christ's flock with the whole body of parishioners.'[19]

Professor C. A. Briggs claimed for the Protestant Episcopal Church in the United States that it exemplified this COMPREHENSIVE SPIRIT and had accepted the best elements from other Churches—a remarkable fact for an episcopal Church in full communion with Canterbury. He said:

'It is the glory of the Protestant Episcopal Church of America that it has gradually incorporated the best features of Presbyterianism and Congregationalism, so that those who stand for the old historical Puritanism find in it a BETTER TYPE OF PRESBYTERIANISM, one nearer the IDEALS OF THE SEVENTEENTH CENTURY PURITANS, than in those ecclesiastical bodies which without sufficient reason perpetuate the Presbyterian schism.... The mother Church opens her arms to welcome back all her children under the one banner of Church Unity, and on a platform which NO ANCIENT PRESBYTERIAN COULD HAVE REFUSED.' [20]

In any land, it is generally realized, the national Church of the future must be a COMPREHENSIVE CHURCH. It must allow for varieties of worship and practice such as Baxter advocated. No more encouraging documents have been issued in English Church history than *A Sketch of a United Church* (1935) and *Outline of a Reunion Scheme for the Church of England and the Evangelical Free Churches of England* (1938). Here we find the comprehension which the Anglicans sternly refused in 1662 and in 1689.

'Our IDEAL OF REUNION is one of UNITY WITH VARIETY. It does NOT MEAN ABSORPTION by any existing body, nor would it involve a flat and meagre uniformity; rather it would conserve, and make more widely available, the spiritual treasures at present cherished in separation.' [21]

Although it was recognized in these Anglican–Free Church discussions that the diocese must be the unit of church-life in the re-united Church, Baxter's voice is surely echoed in this pronouncement:

'There is no reason why the Episcopate should not, if circumstances so require, be exercised by more than one person in a diocese.... In the Diocesan Synod the Bishop would take his place along with the Presbyters and representatives of the Laity.... The Bishop would not have any final authority in legislation or administration apart from the concurrence of Presbyters and Laity.' [22]

There could be no more startling contrast than this statement, set alongside the rigid and autocratic words of the Anglican prelates who scornfully refused Baxter's proposals for Church reform. In fact, bishops now would go beyond Baxter's contentions in some respects. Not only would presbyters be associated with bishops in ordinations in the re-united Church, 'but the laity should have a share in the process by which a candidate is approved for ordination.' [23]

Historians with a secularist outlook have found satisfaction in recording the failure of an English theocracy, whether Puritan or Anglican, to control the nation's beliefs and practices in the seventeenth century. Some of them have rejoiced in the growth of SECULARISM to a dominating position in English society since 1688. Its effect on public and private morality in 1962 can hardly please any historian or any other intelligent person. Would a NATIONAL COMPREHENSIVE CHURCH, based upon spiritual unity, have prevented the deterioration of England's moral and spiritual condition? If it is not too late to make the venture, in the interests of national stability as well as for the sake of the Kingdom of God, it must be obvious that ONLY SUCH A UNITED AND COMPREHENSIVE CHURCH can win the 'battle for the nation's soul'.

## 7. Uniformity no longer contemplated

The history of the Church in England has proved that no plan of Church union requiring rigid uniformity in details of doctrine and worship can succeed. Standards in the existing denominations have to be interpreted liberally. Ministers and members are allowed a certain latitude, subject always to the jurisdiction of the Church authorities or church courts concerned. In this way THE LIVING CHURCH is the guardian and interpreter of the faith once delivered to the saints.

No one pleaded more insistently than Baxter against attempting to enforce uniformity, and his contentions are admitted by all lovers of unity now. He knew the practice of the Primitive Church and the only path to unity in any age—'THE ANCIENT CHRISTIAN SIMPLICITY'.

'You must make me mad, or unacquainted with mankind, before you make me believe that a whole kingdom will ever be so perfect in judgment, or so much of the same temper, education, condition, conversation &c as to be all of one mind in every word, circumstance, ceremony, and mode of worship, and discipline, upon Christian, conscientious terms.' [24]

'We may talk of peace as long as we live, but we shall not obtain it but by returning to the apostolic simplicity.' [25]

'The serpent that beguiled Eve hath long ago tempted almost all the Churches from the ancient Christian simplicity, in doc-

## CAN THERE BE UNITY WITHOUT UNIFORMITY? 309

trine, discipline, and worship, which is THE ONLY WAY OF COMMON CONCORD.'[26]

With Baxter's words we may compare the official policy of the Anglican Church today, as set forth in the *Report of the Commission on Christian Doctrine* (1938):

'The appeal to the Catholic Church or to Catholic tradition appears to us to involve in modern circumstances a refusal to become wholly immersed in the tradition of any one Christian communion.... The term "Catholic" also implies the conviction that according to the Divine Will the true Church on earth was from the beginning, and was meant to continue doctrinally and sacramentally, as well as spiritually, one. The recovery of this unity can only be found in a SYNTHESIS which does full justice to the TRUTH REPRESENTED IN EVERY TRADITION.'[27]

This was summed up by Dr H. P. Van Dusen, when he enunciated the principle of COMPREHENSION:

'There was variety in practice at the outset.
'There has been variety in practice through the Christian centuries.
'There is variety in practice to-day.
'This variety cannot be due wholly to error or sin....
'Christian unity, therefore, should envision the inclusion of persistent variations ... without loss of the essential validities testified to by origin, historic persistence, present fruitfulness.'[28]

Even before the epoch-making World Missionary Conference of 1910 at Edinburgh, which began the great movement of our century towards unity, the Lambeth Conference of 1908 had declared:

'We must fix our eyes on the Church of the future, which is to be adorned with all the precious things, both theirs and ours. We must constantly desire, NOT COMPROMISE BUT COMPREHENSION, NOT UNIFORMITY BUT UNITY.'

To that impressive statement, the Lambeth Conference of 1920 added its own vision of the re-united Church:

'... within whose visible unity all the treasures of faith and order, bequeathed as a heritage by the past to the present, shall be possessed in common, and made serviceable to the whole Body of Christ. Within this unity Christian Communions now separated from one another would retain much that has long been distinctive in their methods of worship and service. It is through a RICH DIVERSITY OF LIFE AND DEVOTION that the unity of the whole fellowship will be fulfilled.'

South India has shown the actual consummation of these hopes in a Church whose Constitution acknowledges that 'for the perfecting of the life of the whole body, the Church of South India needs the heritage of each of the uniting Churches'. The humble boast of this united Church is that 'It is a comprehensive Church, and its members, firmly holding the fundamentals of the faith and order of the Church Universal, are allowed wide freedom of opinion in all other matters, and wide freedom of action in such differences of practice as are consistent with the general framework of the Church as one organized body.' [29]

### 8. *Is there a* WILL *to Unity?*

Carnegie Simpson, a doughty Free Church protagonist for reunion, advocated that we should not negotiate with the idea of conceding, but of CONTRIBUTING.[30] Baxter did not think of a makeshift compromise, of making grudging concessions, but of contributing and sharing the truths and values contained in all sections. This appears from his words:

> 'I have truly told the world near 40 years that I am past doubt that neither the Episcopal, Presbyterian, nor Independent way alone, may well settle the Church; but that each of the three parties (and those called Erastians) have somewhat of the truth in particular and somewhat of faultiness, and if ever the Church be well settled it must be by taking the best and leaving out the worst of every party, and till that can be done, we must bear with what we cannot amend.' [31]

Have all parties today the WILL to contribute to the common treasury of a re-united Church? Do all really desire unity? It is here that the difficulty has always been found. The path to unity has sometimes been blocked by Nonconformist pride, memories of past injuries, and denominational self-sufficiency, by what Bishop Newbigin calls 'group-egotism'. Every setback to union, each failure to respond to a divided world's need in its most tragic hour, indicates how much must still be learnt from those Puritans who suffered in the cause but never lost their vision of the Church Catholic.

Anglicans would probably acknowledge that the same rigidity has been found within their Communion, and that there is not a warm advocacy of re-union on liberal terms from all sections. Fundamentally, we may ask whether the real difficulty lies not in ordination or re-ordination but in a deep doctrinal difference about sacramental grace and the priesthood. An Anglo-Catholic writer has admitted this, with regard to South India :

> 'Quite candidly, but in the friendliest spirit, it does not seem to us that union between the Anglican Church and the Free Churches can have any reality until they desire the PRIESTHOOD. Our impression is that at present they do not.'[32]

The same question, the priesthood, proved the 'hard intractable core' of the disagreement in Anglican–Methodist conferences on re-union in Melbourne in 1947.

The Church of England has sometimes disciplined its Anglo-Catholic extremists but it has belaboured and expelled its Puritans and revivalists, the Nonconformists of the seventeenth century and the Methodists in the following century. It may be wished that the Church of England, which actually proves that it is itself a COMPREHENSIVE Church by including Anglo-Catholics and Low Churchmen, might have a tender regard for the descendants of other Low Churchmen whose forbears were forced by the Church to become Nonconformists in 1662. IF THERE IS A WILL TO UNITY it should not be beyond the wisdom of Churchmen of ALL types to find a basis for re-union.

The Church of England has recognized, and never withdrawn the recognition of, foreign Protestant Churches which are non-episcopal.[33] It welcomes mutual recognition with the Greek Orthodox Church and the Church of Sweden. It should now be willing to follow a similar policy towards English Protestants who have a common origin with the Church of England, who share the essentials of its faith and life, and who have the same language and national cultural heritage. Why not, then, avow our common faith and our historic affinities? Why not admit that we are truly one body of English-speaking Christians?

## CHURCH UNITY WITHOUT UNIFORMITY

This age has witnessed notable achievements in Christian unity. The Church of South India is the most resplendent example; but there have also been the United Church of Canada, the union of the Church of Scotland and the amalgamation of the Methodist Churches in Great Britain and in the United States. The prospects for the union of Presbyterian, Congregational, and Methodist Churches in Australia were never so bright as at present.

Above all, there is the World Council of Churches. Baxter, who styled himself a 'Catholic Christian', would have felt at home at an ecumenical gathering of Christians accepting the one vital belief, that Jesus Christ is God and Saviour. Here Baxter would find the possibility eventually of achieving unity without uniformity. The World Council of Churches would fully agree with Baxter's words:

> 'We own no religion but the Christian religion, nor any church but the Christian Church, nor dream of any Catholic Church but ONE, CONTAINING ALL THE TRUE CHRISTIANS IN THE WORLD, UNITED IN JESUS CHRIST AS THE HEAD.'[34]

The plans we are making for re-union could not have a better summary of their underlying principles than Baxter expressed in one of his earliest and greatest works:

> 'To agree upon a way of union and accommodation—to come as near together as they can possibly in their PRINCIPLES; and where they cannot, yet to unite as far as may be in their PRACTICES, though on different Principles; and, where that cannot be, yet to agree on the most lovable peaceable course in the way of carrying on our different practices; that so . . . we may have UNITY in things necessary, LIBERTY in things unnecessary, and CHARITY in all.'[35]

Baxter's words which follow that oft-quoted phrase are a challenge to Christian leaders in 1962:

> 'THE LORD PERSUADE THOSE WHO HAVE THE POWER TO THIS PACIFICATORY ENTERPRISE WITHOUT DELAY.'

## NOTES TO CHAPTER XIII

1. Matthew Arnold, *Discourses in America*, pp. 70–1.
2. *Towards a United Church, 1913–1947*, p. 56; *Lambeth and Re-union*, by the Bishops of Peterborough, Zanzibar, and Hereford, pp. 78–91, quoted in *Re-union and Christendom* (ed. Marchant).
3. Orme, *Life and Times of Richard Baxter*, vol. 2, p. 207.
4. *Ibid.*, vol. 2, p. 207.
5. Bernard Manning's address to the International Congregational Council, 1930, in *Essays in Orthodox Dissent*, pp. 115–16, 120.
6. 1668, Baxter and Bishop Wilkins, pp. 246–9 of this study; 1673, Baxter and Bishop Morley, pp. 257–9; Baxter and Tillotson, pp. 259–60.
7. *A Second Memorandum on the Status of the existing Free Church Ministry*, 19th June 1925; Bell, *Documents on Christian Unity*, vol. 2, pp. 82–3.
8. Tillotson, 1689, and the Jerusalem Chamber Commission of Anglican divines—see pp. 269–70 of this study.
9. Bell, *Documents on Christian Unity*, vol. 2, p. 83.
10. *Ibid.*, vol. 1, pp. 4–5.
11. *Ibid.*, vol. 1, pp. 158–9.
12. And see *A Second Memorandum on the Status of the existing Free Church Ministry*, 19th June 1925.
13. Bell, *Documents on Christian Unity*, vol. 2, pp. 82–3.
14. *Ibid.*, vol. 1, pp. 264–5.
15. *Ibid.*, vol. 1, p. 166.
16. *Reliquiae Baxterianae*, III, p. 38.
17. *1662 and To-day*, p. 11.
18. *Scheme of Church Union in South India* (1943), pp. 13, 73.
19. *1662 and To-day*, p. 8.
20. Briggs, *Church Unity*, p. 375.
21. *Outline of a Reunion Scheme for the Church of England and the Evangelical Free Churches of England*, p. 9.
22. *Sketch of a United Church*, p. 10.
23. *Ibid.*, p. 14.
24. *Reliquiae Baxterianae*, III, p. 134, in replying to Bishop Morley and the Earl of Orrery.
25. *The Reformed Pastor*, p. 204.
26. *Reliquiae Baxterianae*, III, p. 134.
27. *Report on the Commission on Christian Doctrine*, p. 110.
28. Van Dusen, *World Christianity*, p. 226.
29. *Scheme of Church Union*, pp. 24–5.
30. Simpson in *The Call for Christian Unity*, p. 128.
31. *Reliquiae Baxterianae*, App. IV, p. 69.
32. *Towards a United Church, 1913–1947*, p. 172.
33. Hunkin in *The Call for Christian Unity*, p. 224.
34. 'A Key for Catholicks', preface by Lloyd Thomas in the introduction to the Everyman edition of Baxter's autobiography.
35. 'The Saints' Everlasting Rest', in *Works*, vol. 22, p. 8.

# BIBLIOGRAPHY

(A) Baxter's Writings

*Reliquiae Baxterianae,* Baxter's 'Narrative of his Life and Times', 1696.
*Christian Concord, or the Agreement of the Associated Pastors and Churches of Worcestershire,* 1653.
*The Reformed Pastor,* 1656.
*Five Disputations of Church-government and Worship,* 1659.
*A Treatise on Episcopacy,* 1681.
*Practical Works of Richard Baxter* (including Baxter's 'Reformed Liturgy'), 4 vols. (Henry G. Bohn, London, 1854).
Baxter's *Works,* 23 vols. (James Duncan, London, 1830).

(B) Biographies, etc., of Baxter

BOYLE, G. D.: *Richard Baxter* (Hodder & Stoughton, London, 1883).
EAYRS, G.: *Richard Baxter* (National Council of Evangelical Free Churches, London, 1912).
LADELL, A. R.: *Richard Baxter* (S.P.C.K., London, 1925).
MARTIN, HUGH: *Puritanism and Richard Baxter* (S.C.M. Press, London, 1954).
MORGAN, IRVONWY: *The Nonconformity of Richard Baxter* (Epworth Press, London, 1946).
ORME, W.: *Life and Times of Richard Baxter* (with vol. 1 of Baxter's 23-volume *Works* (James Duncan, London, 1830)).
POWICKE, F. J.: *Richard Baxter, 1615–1691* (Jonathan Cape, London, 1924).
—— *Richard Baxter, under the Cross, 1662–1691* (Jonathan Cape, London, 1927).
THOMAS, J. M. LLOYD: Introduction to *Autobiography of Richard Baxter* (Everyman edition, 1931).
WILKINSON, J. T.: *Richard Baxter and Margaret Charlton* (Allen & Unwin, London, 1928).

(C) General History of the Seventeenth Century

BRETT, S. REED: *John Pym* (John Murray, London, 1940).
BUCHAN, JOHN: *Oliver Cromwell* (Hodder & Stoughton, London, 1943).

# BIBLIOGRAPHY

BURNET, G. : *History of his own Time* (Everyman edition, 1906).
*Cambridge Modern History*, vols. 3, 4, 5 (Cambridge University Press, 1934).
CARLYLE, THOMAS : *Oliver Cromwell's Letters and Speeches* (Chapman and Hall, London, 1888).
CLARENDON, EDWARD HYDE, 1ST EARL OF : *History of the Rebellion and Civil Wars*, also *Life and Continuation of History of the Rebellion* (Oxford University Press, 1843).
CLARK, G. N. : *The Later Stuarts, 1660–1714* (Clarendon Press, Oxford, 1949).
DAVIES, G. : *The Early Stuarts, 1603–1660* (Clarendon Press, Oxford, 1952).
EVELYN, JOHN : *Journal* (Everyman edition, 1906).
FIRTH, C. H. : *Last Days of the Protectorate*, 2 vols. (Longmans Green, London, 1909).
FOX, GEORGE : *Journal* (Everyman edition, 1924).
GARDINER, S. R. : *Constitutional Documents of the Puritan Revolution* (Oxford University Press, 1906).
—— *History of the Commonwealth and the Protectorate*, 3 vols. (Longmans Green, London, 1894).
HUTCHINSON, LUCY : *Memoirs of the Life of Colonel Hutchinson* (Everyman edition, 1908).
HUTCHINSON, F. E. : *Milton and the English Mind* (Hodder & Stoughton, London, 1946).
JONES, DEANE : *The English Revolution, 1603–1714* (Heinemann, London, 1931).
MACAULAY, T. : *History of England*, vol. 1 (Everyman edition, 1906).
MASSON, D. : *Life and Times of Milton*, 6 vols. (Macmillan, London, 1875).
MILTON, JOHN : *Prose Works* (Everyman edition, 1927).
MORLEY, JOHN : *Oliver Cromwell* (Macmillan, London, 1904).
PAUL, R. S. : *The Lord Protector* (Lutterworth Press, London, 1955).
PEPYS, SAMUEL : *Diary* (Everyman edition, 1906).
TANNER, J. R. : *English Constitutional Conflicts of the Seventeenth Century, 1603–1689* (Cambridge University Press, 1928).
TREVELYAN, G. M. : *History of England* (Longmans Green, London, 1937).
—— *England under the Stuarts* (Methuen, London, 1920).
—— *English Social History* (Longmans Green, London, 1944).
WEAVER, F. J. : *English History Illustrated from Original Sources, 1603–1660* (Adam and Charles Black, London, 1908).

(D) Church History of the Seventeenth Century

BARCLAY, R. : *Inner Life of the Religious Societies of the Commonwealth* (Hodder & Stoughton, London, 1876).

BATE, F. : *The Declaration of Indulgence, 1672* (Liverpool University Press, London, 1908).

BEBB, E. D. : *Nonconformity and Social and Economic Life, 1660–1800* (Epworth Press, London, 1935).

*Bicentenary Lectures* (Congregational Union, London, 1889).

BOSHER, R. S. : *The Making of the Restoration Settlement. The Influence of the Laudians, 1649–1662* (Dacre Press, Westminster, 1951).

BOURNE, E. C. E. : *The Anglicanism of William Laud* (S.P.C.K., London, 1947).

BROWN, J. : *Puritan Preaching in England* (Hodder & Stoughton, London, 1900).

CARTER, C. S. : *The Anglican Via Media* (Thynne & Jarvis, London, 1927).

—— *The Reformation and Re-union* (The Church Book-room, London, 1935).

COLLIGAN, J. H. : *The Arian Movement in England* (Manchester University Press, 1913).

COOMER, D. : *English Dissent under the Early Hanoverians* (Epworth Press, London, 1946).

CRAGG, G. R. : *Puritanism in the Period of the Great Persecution, 1660–1688* (Cambridge University Press, 1957).

CURTEIS, G. H. : *Dissent in Relation to the Church of England* (Macmillan, London, 1899).

DAVIES, HORTON : *The Worship of the English Puritans* (Dacre Press, Westminster, 1948).

DEARMER, P. : *The Story of the Prayer Book* (Oxford University Press, London, 1933).

*Documents relating to the Settlement of the Church of England under the Act of Uniformity, 1662* (ed. G. Gould; W. Kent & Co., London, 1862).

DOWDEN, E. : *Puritan and Anglican* (Kegan Paul, Trench, Trubner; London, 1900).

DRURY, T. W. : *How we got our Prayer Book* (Nisbet, London, 8th edition, 1955).

DRYSDALE, A. H. : *History of the Presbyterians in England* (Publication Committee of the Presbyterian Church of England, London, 1889).

## BIBLIOGRAPHY

*Ejectment of 1662 and the Free Churches* (National Council of Evangelical Free Churches, London, 1912).
*Essays Congregational and Catholic* (ed. Albert Peel; Congregational Union, London, 1931).
FLYNN, G. S. : *Influence of Puritanism* (John Murray, London, 1920).
GEE, H., and HARDY, W. J. : *Documents Illustrative of English Church History* (Macmillan, London, 1914).
GORDON, A. : *Freedom after Ejection, 1690–1692* (Manchester University Press, 1917).
HALLER, W. : *The Rise of Puritanism* (Columbia University Press, New York, 1947).
HORTON, R. E. : *John Howe* (Methuen, London, 1895).
HUTTON, W. H. : *William Laud* (Methuen, London, 1896).
—— *History of the English Church, Charles I to Anne* (Macmillan, London, 1913).
LACEY, T. A. : *The Anglo-Catholic Faith* (Methuen, London, 1927).
LUCKOCK, H. M. : *Studies in the History of the Prayer Book* (Longmans Green, London, 1896).
MARLOWE, JOHN : *The Puritan Tradition in English Life* (Cresset Press, London, 1956).
MATTHEWS, A. G. : *Calamy Revised (Edmund Calamy's Account of Ministers Ejected)* (Clarendon Press, Oxford, 1934).
—— *Walker Revised (Sufferings of the Clergy)* (Clarendon Press, Oxford, 1948).
—— *The Savoy Conference of Faith and Order, 1658* (Independent Press, London, 1959).
MOFFATT, J. : *The Presbyterian Churches* (Methuen, London, 1928).
NEAL, D. : *History of the Puritans*, 5 vols. (W. Baynes, London, 1822).
NUTTALL, G. F. : *The Holy Spirit in Puritan Faith and Experience* (Blackwell, Oxford, 1946).
ORR, R. L. : *Alexander Hamilton* (Hodder & Stoughton, London, 1919).
PAYNE, E. A. : *The Free Church Tradition in the Life of England* (S.C.M. Press, London, 1944).
PLUMMER, A. : *English Church History, 1575–1649* (T. & T. Clark, Edinburgh, 1914).
—— *English Church History, 1649–1702* (T. & T. Clark, Edinburgh, 1907).
PROCTOR, F., and FRERE, W. H. : *New History of the Book of Common Prayer* (Macmillan, London, 1920).
RICHARDSON, C. F. : *English Preachers and Preaching, 1640–1670* (Macmillan, New York, 1928).

SELBIE, W. B. : *Congregationalism* (Methuen, London, 1927).
—— *Nonconformity* (Williams & Norgate, London, 1912).
SHAW, W. A. : *History of the English Church, 1640–1660*, 2 vols. (Longmans Green, London, 1900).
SKEATS, H. S., and MIALL, E. : *History of the Free Churches in England, 1688–1891* (James Clarke, London, 1891).
STOUGHTON, J. : *History of Religion in England*, 6 vols. (Hodder & Stoughton, London, 1881).
SYKES, N. : *Old Priest and New Presbyter* (Cambridge University Press, 1956).
TATHAM, G. B. : *Dr Walker and the Sufferings of the Clergy* (Cambridge University Press, 1911).
TAYLER, J. J. : *A Retrospect of the Religious Life of England* (Trubner & Co., London, 1876).
TURNER, LYON : *Original Records of Early Nonconformity under Persecution and Indulgence*, 3 vols. (T. Fisher Unwin, London, 1911).
VAUGHAN, R. : *English Nonconformity* (Jackson, Walford & Hodder, London, 1862).
WAKEFIELD, G. S. : *Puritan Devotion* (Epworth Press, London, 1957).
WAKEMAN, H. O. : *History of the English Church* (Rivingtons, London, 1899).
WALKER, W. : *The Creeds and Platforms of Congregationalism* (Scribner's, New York, 1893).
WHITING, C. E. : *Studies in English Puritanism from the Restoration to the Revolution* (S.P.C.K., London, 1931).
WOODHOUSE, A. S. D. : *Puritanism and Liberty* (Dent, London, 1950).
YULE, G. : *The Independents in the English Civil War* (Melbourne University Press and Cambridge University Press, 1958).

(E) Christian Unity

BELL, G. K. A. : *Documents on Christian Unity*, 1st Series (1924), 2nd Series (1930), 3rd Series (1948), 4th Series (1958) (Oxford University Press).
—— *Christian Unity* (Hodder & Stoughton, London, 1948).
BRIGGS, C. A. : *Church Unity* (Longmans Green, London, 1910).
BROWN, W. A. : *Toward a United Church* (Scribner's, New York, 1946).
*The Call for Christian Unity* (Anglican Evangelical Group Movement) (Hodder & Stoughton, London, 1930).
CAREY, K. M. : *The Historic Episcopate* (Dacre Press, Westminster, 1954).

## BIBLIOGRAPHY

CRAIG, C. T.: *The One Church* (Epworth Press, London, 1952).
DARK, S.: *The Lambeth Conferences* (Eyre & Spottiswoode, London, 1930).
FAIRWEATHER, E. R., and HETTLINGER, R. F.: *Episcopacy and Reunion* (Mowbray, London, 1953).
HEADLAM, A. C.: *Doctrine of the Church and Christian Re-union* (John Murray, London, 1929).
HUNKIN, J. W.: *Episcopal Ordination and Confirmation in relation to Inter-Communion and Re-Union* (Heffer, Cambridge, 1929).
MACGREGOR, G.: *Corpus Christi* (Macmillan, London, 1959).
MACKENZIE, K. D.: *The Case for Episcopacy* (S.P.C.K., London, 1929).
MARTIN, HUGH: *Christian Re-union* (S.C.M. Press, London, 1941).
NEWBIGIN, LESSLIE: *The Re-union of the Church* (S.C.M. Press, London, 1960).
RAWLINSON, A. E. J.: *Problems of Re-union* (Eyre & Spottiswoode, London, 1950).
*The Re-union of Christendom* (ed. J. Marchant) (Cassell, London, 1929).
ROUSE, R., and NEILL, S. C.: *History of the Ecumenical Movement* (S.P.C.K., London, 1954).
SILCOX, C. E.: *Church Union in Canada* (Institute of Social and Religious Research, New York, 1933).
SLOSSER, G. J.: *Christian Unity, its History and Challenge* (Kegan Paul, Trench, Trubner; London, 1929).
STREETER, B. H.: *The Primitive Church* (Macmillan, London, 1929).
SUNDKLER, B.: *Church of South India* (Lutterworth Press, London, 1954).
THOMPSON, E. W.: *The Church, Catholic and Free* (South India) (Epworth Press, London, 1944).
*Towards a United Church, 1913–1947* (Edinburgh House Press, 1947).
*The Union of Christendom* (ed. K. D. Mackenzie; S.P.C.K., London, 1938).
VAN DUSEN, H. P.: *World Christianity* (S.C.M. Press, London, 1948).
Reports of Faith and Order Conferences.
Reports of World Council of Churches, General Assemblies and Conferences.
Plans of Union: South India; Ceylon; North India and Pakistan; Conversations, Church of England–Methodist (England); Relationships, Anglican and Presbyterian (Scotland).
Pamphlets: *Outline of a Re-union Scheme* (S.P.C.K., 1938); *1662*

and *To-day* (S.P.C.K., 1938); *A Sketch of a United Church* (S.P.C.K., 1935); *Practice of Inter-Communion* (S.C.M. Press, 1938); *Melbourne Anglican-Methodist Conferences on Re-union* (1947); *The Faith of the Church* (Presbyterian–Congregational–Methodist, Australia, 1959).

# INDEX

*(As the theme of this book is Baxter's work for Church unity it is superfluous to index events under the heading of his name.)*

Abolition of Episcopacy Bill (1641), 73, 75
Act of 1571 (Subscription Act), 36–7, 55, 157, 159–61
Act of Uniformity (1559), 54
(1662), 225–33
Anglesey, Earl of, 148, 150, 151, 152, 158, 226, 233
Anne, Queen, 280–1, 282
Arminianism, 64
Association of Pastors—*see* Worcestershire Association
Atkins, Sir Robert, 245

Bacon, Francis, 59, 67
Baillie, Robert, 40, 82, 87
Bancroft, Archbishop, 37, 57, 60
Bates, William, 125, 162, 176, 205, 206, 246, 264–5
Bishops' Exclusion Bill, 74, 77
Bishops' War, 70
Bosher, R. S., 143, 158, 164, 192, 199
Bramhall, Bishop, 232
Breda, Declaration of, 122
Bridgman, Sir Orlando, 246, 249
Brownrigg, Bishop, 101, 108
Burnet, Bishop, 174, 178, 282

Calamy, Edmund, 73, 123, 125, 127, 134, 144, 148, 150, 162, 174, 175, 176, 200, 225, 257, 271
Canons, of 1604, 61, 66
of 1640, 70–1
Cartwright, Thomas, 56, 81

Ceremonies, 129–30, 155–6, 164, 165, 185–6, 187, 188, 193–209, 216, 221–2, 247, 248, 270–1, 272
Charles I, 67, 76, 91–2, 94–6
Charles II, 115, 119, 122–7, 133, 142, 148–9, 151, 160, 209, 213, 225, 226, 227, 233–4, 250
*Chorepiscopi*, 29, 129, 139, 217
Chrysostom, 29–30
Clare, Sir Ralph, 42, 115
Clarendon, Earl of, 37, 72, 76, 79, 124, 133, 142–4, 148–9, 150, 160, 161, 163–4, 166–7, 208, 210, 226, 229, 234, 237, 245
Communion, Holy, 20, 21, 25, 55, 63, 78, 102, 145–6, 147, 154, 156, 180–2, 186, 188–9, 214–15, 218, 220, 230, 257–8
Comprehension, 45–6, 89, 108–17, 267–8, 276–80
'Confederate Parish Churches of England', 43–5, 295–7
Confirmation, 138, 153–4, 215
Cosin, Bishop, 35, 36, 148, 170, 172, 205–6, 207, 247
Covenant, National, 70. See also Solemn League and Covenant
Coverdale, Miles, 55
Cromwell, Oliver, 46–7, 71, 90, 97–101, 106, 112–13
Cromwell, Richard, 114
Cyprian, 27, 28, 105–6

Declaration, King's (25th October 1660), 142–4, 151–69, 193, 199, 217–22

## INDEX

Declaration of Indulgence, King's (1672), 252–3
Dering, Sir Edward, 74–5, 77
Digby, Lord, 73
Discipline, 20–7, 102, 127, 129, 139, 145–7, 178, 183, 214–15, 217, 219, 293–4
Downame, Bishop, 37–8

Ejections, of Anglicans, 55, 88, 98–9, 119, 211, 227, 232
of Nonconformists, 226–38
Elizabeth, Queen, 54–7
Episcopacy, 20–2, 27–32, 67. *See also* Laudian episcopacy *and* Modified episcopacy. Abolition of —*see* 'Root and Branch' Petition and Bill
Evelyn, John, 40, 65, 244
Exeter and Salters' Hall dispute, 287–8

Falkland, Viscount, 65, 75
Ferguson, David, 58
Ferne, Dr Henry, 192
Field, Dean, 37

Goodwin, Thomas, 83, 257
Grand Remonstrance (1641), 68, 76–7
Gregory, Thaumaturgus, 29
Grindal, Archbishop, 35, 56
Gunning, Bishop, 101, 149, 172, 205, 206, 207, 231, 238, 264–5

Hacket, Dr John, 192
Hale, Sir Matthew, 122, 167, 246, 249
Hales, John, 187, 201
Hammond, Dr Henry, 31, 115
Hampton Court Conference (1604), 59–60
Henderson, Alexander, 72, 82
Henrietta Maria, Queen, 68, 71
Henson, Bishop Hensley, 232
High Commission Court, 68, 72
Hooker, Richard, 31, 36–7, 38, 43, 66

Howe, John, 38–9, 112–13, 114, 260–1
Hutchinson, Colonel John, 65

Ignatius, 27, 28, 130, 138
Independents, 15, 44–5, 71, 89, 90, 91, 92, 97, 99, 108–14, 134, 148–9, 150, 164, 211, 234–5, 242–3, 258–9
Ireton, Henry, 92
Irish Rebellion, 76

James I, 57–61, 66, 69
Jeffreys, Judge, 40, 46, 263–4
Johnson, Samuel, 17, 184
Juxon, Bishop, 91, 125

Kidderminster, 17, 21, 23, 24, 26, 102, 121

Laud, Archbishop, 25, 45, 48, 63–4, 65–9, 72
Lauderdale, Earl of, 119, 121, 251–2
Laudian episcopacy, 23, 24, 25, 65, 66–8, 71, 194
Liturgy (and Prayer Book), 39–40, 42, 43, 76, 88, 90, 129, 134, 135, 136, 147, 155, 164, 184–91, 192–3, 194, 195–209, 220–1, 247, 249
Baxter's—*see* 'Reformed Liturgy'
Long Parliament, 27, 71 ff.

Manchester, Earl of, 122, 125–6, 150, 208, 246
Manton, Thomas, 121, 125, 134, 162, 176, 246, 250, 251, 257
Melville, Andrew, 58, 60
Millenary Petition (1603), 26, 58–60, 187, 217–22
Milton, John, 40, 73, 87, 98, 121
Modified episcopacy, 14, 43, 71, 74, 77–9, 81, 91, 105–8, 114–15, 126, 127, 128–9, 130–5, 153–4, 172–3, 216, 217–18, 241–2, 293–5
Monk, General (Albemarle), 120, 122–3, 148, 211
Morison, John, 35
Morley, Bishop, 115, 120, 148, 172, 207, 231, 250, 257, 258–9, 265
Morrice, Secretary William, 167

# INDEX 323

Nye, Philip, 83, 109, 113, 114, 150, 234, 257

Occasional conformity, 242, 280–1 and Act (1711), 281
Ordination—*see* Re-ordination
Orrery, Earl of, 257
Owen, John, 97, 120, 242–3, 257

Pepys, Samuel, 123, 171, 209
Powicke, F. J., 11–12, 18, 264, 289
Prayer Book—*see* Liturgy
Presbyterians, orthodox, 14, 15, 44, 55, 56, 69–70, 71, 72–3, 81–2, 91, 92, 93–6, 103–4, 110, 112, 119, 120, 121, 172, 173, 242
  parliamentary, 85–96, 118–19, 120–1
  Scottish, 26–7, 57–8, 60, 69–70, 72–3, 81–6, 134
Pym, John, 63, 74, 76, 83

Rainoldes, John, 59, 60
'Reformed Liturgy' (Baxter's), 27, 42, 43, 178–84, 192
Re-ordination, 34–9, 55–6, 147, 157, 158–61, 166, 216, 229–30, 246–8, 249, 257, 260, 267, 269–70, 297–304
Reynolds, Edward (afterwards Bishop), 120, 125, 144, 162, 172, 176
Roman Catholics, 46, 47, 61, 63–5, 70, 71, 100, 122, 166, 233–4, 264–5
'Root and Branch' Petition and Bill (1641), 73–4, 75, 76–7
Rutherford, Samuel, 65

Sancroft, Archbishop, 170, 265, 266
Savoy Conference (April–July 1661), 170–224
Savoy Declaration (1658), 113
Schism Bill (1714), 281–2
Scottish Presbyterianism—*see* Presbyterians, Scottish
Sheldon, Archbishop, 146, 172, 174, 178, 210, 225, 227, 236–7
'Smectymnuus', 72–3, 172

Solemn League and Covenant, 83, 84–5, 120, 171, 225
Spurstow, William, 73, 125, 150, 176
Stephen, Sir James, 17, 142–3
Sterne, Bishop, 205
Stillingfleet, Bishop, 134–5, 259, 261, 268
Subscription Act—*see* Act of 1571
Sylvester, Matthew, 18, 173, 257

Taylor, Jeremy, 46
Tenison, Archbishop, 268, 271
Tertullian, 28, 210
Test Act (1673), 254
Thorndyke, Robert, 135
Tillotson, Archbishop, 39, 173–4, 206, 259, 268–71
Toleration, religious, 89–90, 122, 148–9, 212–13, 275–6
Travers, Walter, 35
Triers, Committee of, 98, 99, 105

Uniformity, Act of—*see* Act of Uniformity
Usher, Archbishop, 30, 38, 46, 78, 79, 96, 101, 105–8, 139, 201
  'Reduction of Episcopacy', 32, 78, 79, 125, 127–33, 136–7, 139, 144, 145–6, 152, 158, 217–22, 258
Uxbridge, negotiations at, 91

Vane, Henry, 75, 84

Ward, Bishop, 38–9
Wesley, John (and his Puritan ancestors), 83, 232–3, 240
Westminster Assembly, 38–9
Whitgift, Archbishop, 38, 56, 67
Whittingham, William, 35
Wilkins, Bishop, 17, 39, 236, 245, 246–7, 248, 249–50, 251
William III, 266–7, 271–2, 273, 274
Williams, Bishop, 77, 201
Williams, Dr Daniel, 279–80
Worcestershire Association, 21, 23, 24–5, 30–1, 32–3, 101–5, 211, 296
Wren, Bishop, 34, 68, 125